TEMPLES
◆RISING◆

Wilford Woodruff (1807–1898).

TEMPLES RISING

A Heritage of Sacrifice

RICHARD E. BENNETT

SALT LAKE CITY, UTAH

All images are courtesy of the Church History Library of The Church of Jesus Christ of Latter-day Saints, except the following:

Pages 13, 22, and 61: L. Tom Perry Special Collections, Harold B. Lee Library, Brigham Young University, Provo, Utah.

Page 111: C. C. A. Christensen (1831–1912), *Burning of the Temple*, c. 1878, tempera on muslin, 78 x 114 inches. Brigham Young University Museum of Art, gift of the grandchildren of C. C. A. Christensen, 1970.

Page 121: C. C. A. Christensen (1831–1912), *Winter Quarters*, c. 1878, tempera on muslin, 76¾ x 113¾ inches. Brigham Young University Museum of Art, gift of the grandchildren of C. C. A. Christensen, 1970.

© 2019 Richard E. Bennett

All rights reserved. No part of this book may be reproduced in any form or by any means without permission in writing from the publisher, Deseret Book Company, at permissions@deseretbook.com or PO Box 30178, Salt Lake City, Utah 84130. This work is not an official publication of The Church of Jesus Christ of Latter-day Saints. The views expressed herein are the responsibility of the author and do not necessarily represent the position of the Church or of Deseret Book Company.

DESERET BOOK is a registered trademark of Deseret Book Company.

Visit us at deseretbook.com

Library of Congress Cataloging-in-Publication Data
(CIP data on file)
ISBN 978-1-62972-569-7

Printed in the United States of America
Lake Book Manufacturing, Inc., Melrose Park, IL

10 9 8 7 6 5 4 3 2 1

Contents

→ ←

Acknowledgments vii

Introduction 1

1. "It Was a Pentecost and an Endowment Indeed" 11
   Kirtland's House of God, 1831–1836

2. "In the Similitude of a Palace" 47
   The Nauvoo Temple Part One, 1837–1842

3. "The Fulness of Those Blessings" 75
   The Nauvoo Temple Part Two, 1843–1848

4. "We Mean to Conquer or Die Trying" 112
   Temple Work at Winter Quarters, 1846–1848

5. "The Upper Room" 136
   Temple Work in the Wilderness, 1847–1854

6. "A Temple Pro Tem" 165
   Temple Work in Deseret, 1855–1870

7. "What Is Gold or Silver in Comparison to the
   Redemption of Our Dead?" 192
   The St. George Temple, 1870–1877

CONTENTS

8. "They Are Aiming a Blow at the Sealing Ordinances". 231
   Temples, Federal Marshals, and Plural Marriage, 1877–1888

9. "Which Is the Wisest Course?" 262
   The Road to Reconciliation, 1888–1890

10. "Run This Chain Through as Far as You Can Get It" 286
    The Salt Lake Temple and New Advancements in Temple Work, 1890–1898

Epilogue: "The Present Is Only a Beginning" 310

Primary Sources 313

Secondary Sources 319

Index 333

Acknowledgments

This book would not have been possible without the help and encouragement of many wonderful friends and associates. When Leonard J. Arrington was called as Church Historian in 1972, I became one of his research assistants. He introduced me to the world of manuscript and archival research at what was then called the Church Historian's Office and instilled in me an insatiable desire to explore fearlessly and faithfully the history of The Church of Jesus Christ and the many remarkable life stories of the Latter-day Saints. Professor Marvin S. Hill of Brigham Young University taught me the necessary skills to conduct comprehensive, detailed, historical research.

More recently, scholars and administrators, archivists, and colleagues at the Church History Library, the L. Tom Perry Special Collections at the Harold B. Lee Library, and at Brigham Young University and elsewhere, not only encouraged my undertaking of this volume but also offered invaluable suggestions for improving it. In particular, I wish to thank Richard Turley Jr., Steven Harper, Reid Neilson, Keith Erikson, Brandon Metcalf, Kathryn Daynes, and Mark Staker. Others with long experience in temple history and temple administration gave constructive criticism and suggestions for improvement. And to the many staff members at the Church History Library I also give credit, especially reference librarians Anne Berryhill and Elise Reynolds who kindly offered me rich assistance

ACKNOWLEDGMENTS

in choosing the illustrations and images that grace this volume. Several BYU students have been of help along the way, especially Nick Valleta and Lisa Love-Snyder. I also wish to thank my son, Richard S. Bennett, who shares my love of Church history and who was particularly helpful with researching manuscript materials in the Church History Library.

I wish also to thank my employer—Brigham Young University—for the blessed opportunity I have had over the past two decades to teach both undergraduate and graduate classes in Church History and the Doctrine and Covenants to the faithful youth of this rising generation. I owe much of my scholarship to in-depth, in-class gospel discussions with many excellent students. To the staff at Deseret Book, particularly product director Lisa Roper, I also express my appreciation. Lisa showed sincere interest in my research from the beginning and constantly encouraged me to work with Deseret Book to get this manuscript published. And where would this work be without the able assistance of a highly skilled editor, in this case, Leslie Cutler Stitt. No ship can reach harbor without such skilled pilots as Lisa and Leslie. Typographer Rachael Ward and graphic designer Shauna Gibby round out this team of Deseret Book professionals to whom I am indebted.

With a most generous grant provided me from the Frederick W. and Jolene Edmunds Rockwood Family Foundation, I was able to retain the services of some fine research assistants, one of whom in particular has been most faithful and helpful. For six years, Wendy Top, a devoted and lifelong student of Church history, a seasoned temple worker, and a remarkably well-organized, resourceful, and cheerful research assistant was with me almost every step of the way. Her work on the footnotes and with the charts and tables and so much more has been indispensable and is so deeply appreciated. Without her loyal and capable assistance, this work would still be on the drawing boards. Thanks, Wendy!

Above all, I thank my long-suffering wife, Patricia, who also enjoys studying our historical past. From day one of our marriage she has not

ACKNOWLEDGMENTS

only put up with my fascination with Church history—indeed, the other love of my life—but has continually given me all the encouragement, time, and patient support necessary to complete this study. I owe her and all five of our now-grown children my enduring gratitude.

RICHARD E. BENNETT

Introduction

We shall not only build a temple here [Salt Lake City] if we are successful, and are blessed and preserved, but we shall probably commence two or three more, and so on as fast as the work requires, for the express purpose of redeeming our dead. When I get a revelation that some of my progenitors lived and died without the blessings of the Gospel, or even hearing it preached . . . I will go and be baptized, confirmed, washed, and anointed, and go through all the ordinances and endowments for them, that their way may be open to the celestial kingdom.[1] . . . To accomplish this work there will have to be not only one temple but thousands of them, and thousands and tens of thousands of men and women will go into those temples and officiate for people who have lived as far back as the Lord shall reveal.[2]

So prophesied President Brigham Young concerning his vision of the rise of temples in these latter days.

Written primarily to the believing but inquiring member of The Church of Jesus Christ of Latter-day Saints, this study is set to tell the history of latter-day temples and the rise of temple consciousness among members of the Church in the nineteenth century. As we in the twenty-first century are witnessing the construction of temples throughout the

---

1. Brigham Young, in *Journal of Discourses* (Liverpool: F. D. Richards, 1855–1886), 2:138, 3 December 1854.
2. Young, in *Journal of Discourses*, 3:372, 22 June 1856.

world in an ever-hastening manner, this topic takes on greater relevance than ever before. Several studies through the years have examined the architecture, symbolism, and importance of temples. Few, however, have attempted to show the full range and depth of challenges temple work faced throughout the nineteenth century. The common denominator throughout will be the spirit of sacrifice and consecration that characterized the building of each early temple. And since Wilford Woodruff played such an important role, much of this work will follow the footsteps of this fourth President of the Church and will examine the rise of temples through his eyes.

Writing anything about so sacred a topic as temples can be fraught with difficulties. Without trespassing upon the sacred covenants and ordinances themselves, I will nevertheless attempt to assess what they meant to those involved. It is a natural, but often dangerous, inclination of many to interpret the past in the light of present convictions and institutional representations. And when it comes to the sacred topic of temples, the temptation is for many of us to believe that the birthday cake came right out of the oven, steaming hot and finished with icing and lighted candles all ready for the party, a religious *fait accompli*.

The truth is it did not work that way. The history of latter-day temple worship throughout the nineteenth century is, rather, a story of development, of line upon line, a price paid here and an enormous sacrifice made there, a gradual process of revelation, adaptation, and careful implementation, replete with stops and starts, misunderstandings, and varied interpretations. As John Taylor so aptly put it, "We are called upon once in a while to take a new step in this great work. At one time it was polygamy, at another it was baptism for the dead, then it was building Temples, then certain endowments, then the sealing of our children to us, then certain promises made to ourselves, such as God made to Abraham in former days."[3] This gradual process of development is made even more clear when

---

3. John Taylor, in *Journal of Discourses*, 17:177, 9 October 1874.

INTRODUCTION

one considers that two different Restoration faith traditions—The Church of Jesus Christ of Latter-day Saints and Community of Christ (formerly the Reorganized Church of Jesus Christ of Latter Day Saints)—to the present day have radically different views of the nature, place, and meaning of the temple. While others have attempted to document the history of Community of Christ, this book will barely have time and space to tell the Latter-day Saint story.[4] Other "divergent paths of the Restoration"—to borrow Community of Christ historian Steven Shields's phrase—have also laid claim to varied interpretations of temple work, all of which are outside the scope of this work.

The vision of temple work preceded even the organization of the Church. To the believing Latter-day Saint, the visions of the angel Moroni in 1823 to Joseph Smith in which he spoke of turning the hearts of the fathers to the children and vice versa planted some of the first seeds for future redemption for the dead. Since Moroni was also Joseph Smith's mentor in matters of the Restoration, when he appeared annually at the Hill Cumorah, he provided Joseph at each of their interviews with "instruction and intelligence" about "what the Lord was going to do, and how and in what manner his kingdom was to be conducted in the last days" (JS–H 1:54). John the Baptist's vision of 1829 told of the restoration of Aaronic Priesthood keys and of a later "offering . . . in righteousness" by the sons of Levi (D&C 13:1). Once baptized, Oliver Cowdery and Joseph Smith received an outpouring of the Holy Ghost, so much so that Oliver "prophesied many things which should shortly come to pass" and Joseph "prophesied concerning the rise of this Church, and many other

---

4. Two significant histories of the Reorganized Church of Jesus Christ of Latter Day Saints are Mark A. Scherer, *The Journey of a People: The Era of Restoration, 1820 to 1844* (Independence, MO: Community of Christ Seminary Press, 2013); *The Journey of a People: The Era of Reorganization, 1844 to 1946* (2013); *The Journey of a People: The Era of Worldwide Community, 1946 to 2015* (2016); and Roger D. Launius, *Joseph Smith III: Pragmatic Prophet* (Urbana: University of Illinois Press, 1988). Launius argues that Joseph Smith III, founder of the Reorganized Church of Jesus Christ of Latter Day Saints, recognized the doctrine of baptism for the dead "as possibly legitimate, at least in principle." However, over time the doctrine was "shunted into a nether land between belief and practice" (Launius, *Joseph Smith III*, 156–57).

things connected with the Church, and this generation of the children of men" (JS–H 1:73). To what extent the Book of Mormon was a primer on work for the dead and on Joseph Smith's understanding of salvation for the dead is difficult to assess. What he translated and what he understood or taught are two quite different things. However, there are many references to temples in the Book of Mormon, including a dramatic rendering of the resurrected Christ appearing at the temple in the land Bountiful (3 Nephi 11).

With the Book of Mormon now translated and the Church organized on 6 April 1830, Joseph Smith soon turned his attention to the inspired translation or revision of the Holy Bible. Most changes were a word or a phrase long; others were much more extensive, including the Book of Moses with its eight chapters of entirely new scripture. Much of the Book of Moses speaks of Enoch and his glorious "City of Holiness, even Zion" being "taken up into heaven" (Moses 7:19, 21), all of whom are to return prior to the Second Coming of Christ to the New Jerusalem to be built on the American continent.[5] "For there shall be my tabernacle, and it shall be called Zion, a New Jerusalem" (Moses 7:62).

This pre-millennialist command to gather to Zion may well explain why Joseph Smith dispatched Oliver Cowdery, Parley P. Pratt, Ziba Peterson, and Peter Whitmer Jr. on their early mission to the Lamanites in December 1830, and why it was that by 1831 many Saints, from particularly the Colesville, New York, region, were setting up shop in Independence, Jackson County, Missouri. On 2 August 1831, Sidney Rigdon dedicated the land for the gathering of Israel in the last days while Joseph Smith dedicated the temple lot the very next day in Independence, Missouri. He envisioned building not only a great temple there but more precisely a complex or campus of two dozen temples—twelve Aaronic and twelve Melchizedek—to be reared in the expectation of the imminent

---

5. Tenth article of faith.

INTRODUCTION

Second Coming of Christ.[6] And this at a spot "lying westward, upon a lot which is not far from the courthouse" (D&C 57:3). Soon the invitation to gather to this New Jerusalem in western Missouri resulted in 1,200 Saints flocking to Zion and in the process buying up as much as one-third of all available properties in Jackson County. In 1832 Edward Partridge, first presiding bishop, purchased from Jones H. Flournoy a triangular tract of 63.43 acres soon called the "Temple Lot." Although plans were drawn up for such a temple to look very much in size and shape like the Kirtland Temple, it was never built due to religious misunderstandings and persecutions as well as the "conflict of cultures" that inevitably arose between established Missouri settlers, many of whom were from the South and who supported slavery, and Latter-day Saint incomers, most of whom were from northern, free states. Intense persecutions forced the Saints out of Jackson County beginning in the summer of 1833.[7] Eventually they fled northward and across the Missouri River, first into Clay County and eventually further north into Daviess and Caldwell counties before being forced out of Missouri entirely by order of Governor Lilburn W. Boggs in the winter of 1838/39. Today the Temple Lot, owned by Church of Christ (Temple Lot), stands mostly vacant while various "divergent paths of the Restoration" still foster high hopes of "redeeming Zion" and are attempting various "levels of landscape sanctification" in hopes of preparing for Christ's Second Coming.[8]

But if Jackson County was, in the words of religious historian Mario De Pillis, the center of the fledgling Church, Kirtland, Ohio, soon became

---

6. See Joseph Smith, *History of the Church of Jesus Christ of Latter-day Saints*, 2nd ed., rev., 7 vols. (Salt Lake City: Deseret Book Company, 1961), 1:359.
7. Craig S. Campbell, *Images of the New Jerusalem: Latter-day Saint Faction Interpretations of Independence, Missouri* (Knoxville: University of Tennessee Press, 2004); see also Kenneth E. Foote, *Shadowed Ground: America's Landscapes of Violence and Tragedy* (Austin: University of Texas Press, 1997); and Grant Underwood, *The Millenarian World of Early Mormonism* (Urbana: University of Illinois Press, 1993).
8. Campbell, *Images of the New Jerusalem*, 66. These include members of the Remnant Church of Jesus Christ of Latter Day Saints, the Conference of Restoration Elders (or "Restorationists"), and others.

its "epicenter."[9] The 1830 mission to the Lamanites had the collateral effect of converting approximately 130 people in and around Mentor, Ohio. Parley P. Pratt was especially instrumental in converting his former friend, Sidney Rigdon, a Campbellite minister, along with many of his congregation, including Isaac Morley and many of his "Morley Farm" associates, Newel K. and Elizabeth Ann Whitney, Edward Partridge, Lyman Wight, and John and Julia Murdock. When Sidney Rigdon and Edward Partridge travelled to New York to meet the prophet in Waterloo later that fall, Joseph received a revelation that was directed to Partridge, a part of which said: "Wherefore, gird up your loins and I will suddenly come to my temple" (D&C 36:8). Just weeks later the Saints were commanded to "go to the Ohio" where they would be given "my law; and there you shall be endowed with power from on high" (D&C 38:32). By the end of 1831, approximately one thousand Saints were residing in and around Kirtland, Ohio. Thus the Church was gathering simultaneously in two places, 832 miles apart: the center place of Zion in Missouri, and a temporary headquarters in the Western Reserve of Ohio, near Cleveland.[10] The division of time and resources to operate a new church in sites so far removed from each other would prove to be an insurmountable difficulty.

The Latter-day Saints believed that the command to move to the Ohio came with a blessing and a promise, a "blessing such as is not known among the children of men, and it shall be poured forth upon [your] heads. And from thence men shall go forth into all nations" (D&C 39:15). The promised endowment and the restored law of consecration, or "Law of the Church" as it was revealed in 1832, went together: On the one hand, the higher expectation of obedience associated with living a celestial law, and on the other, the endowment of power and sanctification

---

9. Mario Stephen De Pillis, "The Development of Mormon Communitarianism, 1826–1846" (PhD diss., Yale University, 1960), 166, as cited in Campbell, *Images of the New Jerusalem*, 43.
10. James B. Allen and Glen M. Leonard, *The Story of the Latter-day Saints* (Salt Lake City: Deseret Book Company, 1976), ch. 3.

associated with the temple. Thus the temple would mean much more than rites and ordinances; it would call for lives of holiness and purification.

Joseph Smith's inspired translation of the Bible, which he began in June 1830, yielded many other temple-related revelations, including the *Vision*, known today as Section 76. This remarkable revelation, given in February 1832, and which occurred at the John and Elsa Johnson home some forty miles southeast of Kirtland in Hiram, Ohio, spoke not only about degrees of heavenly glory but also about paradise and a redemptive hell of the spirit world where the wicked may repent and be redeemed. It would also appear that what came to be Section 132 with its doctrine of the eternality of the marriage covenant derived from Joseph Smith's translation work of the Bible, particularly the Old Testament.[11]

Parley P. Pratt saw in these revelations a glimpse of temple work for the dead, as he recorded years afterward. "I recollect in 1832 for many long months I had not seen my family or heard the voice of the Prophet that so very few would receive the gospel—and so very few would retain it. And while travelling in the wilderness (with J. Murdock) it came in a [moment?] to both of us there was some day of li[gh]t to come [in] the hereafter for those who had not rece[ived] the gospel—and when we re[turne]d to Kirtland behold the vision of the Cel[estial] Terrestrial and Telestial worlds."[12]

This important work of translation may also have resulted in the late December 1832 revelation called "The Olive Leaf" or "The Lord's message of peace to us" (D&C 88). This revelation not only spoke of the coming Millennium and with it the assurance of an unfolding, universal resurrection and of Michael's eventual conquest over Satan, but also of several

---

11. For more on the impact of the Joseph Smith Translation on the Doctrine and Covenants, see Robert J. Matthews, *A Plainer Translation: Joseph Smith's Translation of the Bible: A History and Commentary* (Provo, Utah: Brigham Young University Press, 1985) and Scott H. Faulring, et al., eds., *Joseph Smith's New Translation of the Bible: Original Manuscripts* (Provo, Utah: Religious Studies Center, Brigham Young University, 2004).
12. General Church Minutes 1839–1877, 6 April 1850, CR 100 318, Church Historian's Office, Church History Library, Salt Lake City (hereafter listed as Church History Library).

other blessings including the Comforter or promise of eternal life to the faithful (D&C 88:4). "Organize yourselves; prepare every needful thing; and establish a house, even a house of prayer, a house of fasting, a house of faith, a house of learning, a house of glory, a house of order, a house of God" (D&C 88:119).

All of these revelations looked forward to the building of a temple, first in Independence and then in Kirtland. But if the first could not be raised due to misunderstandings and bitter persecutions, then perhaps the second would be. Thus this book begins with the Kirtland Temple and a discussion of its origins, construction, and special preliminary ordinances performed therein, the accompanying Pentecostal displays of the Holy Spirit, and how the vision of temple work survived the acute financial crisis that led to the exodus from Kirtland in 1838.

The ensuing two chapters will focus on the Nauvoo Temple and the introduction of additional sacred ordinances performed there, including baptisms for the dead, the sacred endowment, marriage sealings, and other holy ordinances and how such ordinances were received by an ever-growing body of members. Attention will be given to the persecution the Church faced in Illinois, culminating in the martyrdom of Joseph and Hyrum Smith and how the membership clung to the temple in their time of greatest need. Chapter four will discuss how the sense and remembrance of temple devotion survived and gave solace, inspiration, and comfort during the trials of the exodus and early years in the Salt Lake Valley. This chapter will also feature a study of the Salt Lake Council House. Later chapters will discuss the Salt Lake Endowment House, the impact that the coming of the transcontinental railroad had upon the Church and its membership, the decision to construct the St. George, Manti, and Logan temples, and the momentous changes to temple work brought about by the introduction of endowments for the dead beginning on 11 January 1877 in St. George.

Considering President Wilford Woodruff's comments concerning the "wisest course" to follow, it will also be necessary to examine the intense

INTRODUCTION

pressure brought upon the Latter-day Saints by the government of the United States of America over the matter of plural marriage during this era and to appreciate the Saints' commitment to this way of life in the face of such relentless opposition. President Woodruff's decision to sacrifice the "principle" in order to save the temples fundamentally changed the course of Latter-day Saint history. The work will then conclude with a discussion of the long-awaited completion of the Salt Lake Temple in 1893, the creation of the Utah Genealogical Society the following year, and President Woodruff's death four years later at the age of ninety-one.

I make no apology for my beliefs as a committed Latter-day Saint historian; however, I have tremendous respect for the historical record, now more open and available than ever before. My intent is to let the manuscripts speak for themselves. The publication of *The Joseph Smith Papers* has been a tremendous boon to research. The Gospel Topic Essays, now on LDS.org, have also proven helpful. In addition, many scholars have recently been writing and publishing on a wide range of related history topics, some never explored before. Though this work is a more scholarly than a devotional piece, it is faithful to our history.

Why would I assume that I should write a history on so sacred and sensitive a topic? In partial response, I have spent most of my professional life—over fifty years—researching and writing Church history, and I have always wanted to let the early Saints tell the story of the beginning of latter-day temples as much as possible in their own words and from their own rich experiences. I've had a lifetime of exposure to historical records and in the process have gained the trust of Church historians, librarians, and archivists. With their assistance and encouragement, I have been able to access materials essential to the writing of this story, many of which are now available online through the Church History Library catalogue. Several of my professional colleagues also encouraged me to take up the task and have read all or parts of this manuscript, giving me excellent, constructive feedback along the way.

I also have enormous respect for the temple workers and patrons whose dedication to temple work continues to inspire and motivate. I am in constant awe of their examples. This work is dedicated to them and to all those who make temple attendance a meaningful part of their lives. Indeed, the real story and power of temple worship is not to be found in the pages of any one book but in the lives of those who reverence His holy house.

Chapter 1

"It Was a Pentecost and an Endowment Indeed"

KIRTLAND'S HOUSE OF GOD, 1831–1836

We came in sight of the Temple of the Lord before we reached the village and I truly felt to rejoice at the sight as it was the first time that mine eyes ever beheld the house of the Lord built by commandment and revelation. . . . After spending a short time in conversing with my friends a more important scene was now open to my view than Kings ever saw or Princes ever knew in this generation which was to visit the Temple of the Lord and its contents . . . I must confess the scenery is indescribable. When I entered the threshold of the house and passed into the lower room there was great solemnity if not awe immediately overwhelmed me. I felt indeed as if my footsteps were in the Temple of the Lord.[1]

So wrote twenty-nine-year-old Wilford Woodruff upon first seeing the Kirtland Temple in late 1836. For one destined to have so much to do with the rise of Latter-day Saint temples over the next sixty years, his impressions are more than noteworthy—they are foundational. Much of what follows in the pages of this book will be seen through his eyes.

This work begins with a careful study of the first temple built in this modern dispensation, the ordinances performed therein, and the acute

---

1. Wilford Woodruff, *Wilford Woodruff's Journal*, ed. Scott G. Kenney (Midvale, Utah: Signature Books, 1983), 1:106–7, 25 November 1836; also cited in Dean C. Jessee, "The Kirtland Diary of Wilford Woodruff," *BYU Studies* 12, no. 2 (Summer 1972), 4.

financial and related challenges the early Saints faced in Ohio. While in the end they were forced to leave Kirtland, the spirit of temple building would survive this crisis and attend them as they headed west.

"UP TO THE SQUARE"—BUILDING THE HOUSE OF GOD

The building of the Kirtland Temple in less than three years and at a time of extreme poverty, persecution, and distress on every side, will forever stand as a testimony to the faith and sacrifice of the early Saints. Initially, most Saints probably envisioned constructing if not a frame house then at least a large log house. But Joseph Smith had other plans. Speaking on 4 May 1833, he reminded the devoted Saints:

> . . . *They were not making a house for themselves or any other man but a house for God. "And shall we brethren build a house for our God of logs[?] No brethren. I have a better plan than that. I have the plan of the house of the Lord given by himself. [You] will see by this the difference between our calculations and his ideas."*
>
> *He then gave them the plan in full . . . [with] which they were highly delighted and particularly Hyrum who was twice as much animated as though it were for himself.*[2]

Not yet thirty years old, Joseph Smith knew little or nothing about finances or building construction but in the absence of a trained architect, he more or less supervised the temple's overall construction. Few seasoned craftsmen were available, at least at the beginning. Most of the men were away on missions or struggling to support their families. And all the while, local residents resented the continued arrival of these new, highly religious "undesirables" and opposed the temple's construction, to the point that

---

2. Lucy Mack Smith, *Lucy's Book: A Critical Edition of Lucy Mack Smith's Family Memoir*, ed. Lavina Fielding Anderson (Salt Lake City: Signature Books, 2001), 581. The original plan called for two other buildings, a printing establishment and an administrative office, each comparable in size to the temple, to be built on the same lot as the house of the Lord. Straitened finances prevented their construction. Mark Lyman Staker, *Hearken, O Ye People: The Historical Setting of Joseph Smith's Ohio Revelations* (Salt Lake City: Greg Kofford Books, 2009), 424.

"IT WAS A PENTECOST AND AN ENDOWMENT INDEED"

Joseph Smith Jr. (1805–1844).

guards had to be stationed at night to protect the premises. It is miraculous that it was even built at all.

Yet believing that they were commanded to erect such a structure, if not chastised by heaven for not doing so earlier (D&C 95) once it became clear that construction of the Independence Missouri temple would be delayed indefinitely, the Saints commenced building the House of the Lord with all their might. With mortgaged funds and capital raised by John Johnson, the so-called "United Firm" made up of Joseph Smith, Bishop Newel K. Whitney, and other Church leaders, and acting as the financial arm of the Church in Kirtland, first purchased properties owned by Frederick G. Williams on the crest of the south bluffs overlooking the Kirtland Flats, and soon afterward bought the adjacent Peter French and Elijah Smith farms. In June 1833, Joseph Smith appointed a temple-building committee consisting of his older brother, Hyrum, Reynolds Cahoon, and Jared Carter, who were assigned to raise the needed funds and to take the lead in the building's construction. According to a revelation given on 1 June 1833 (D&C 94:4), its dimensions were to be sixty-five feet long by fifty-five feet wide, a comparatively large building for its time and place. Whether or not the temple's design was seen in vision, as Frederick G. Williams affirmed, very few, if any, blueprints or drawings have survived.[3] Determined to be the first at work, an enthusiastic Hyrum Smith and Reynolds Cahoon began removing fences, clearing ground, and digging trenches for the foundations on 5 June 1833. In six weeks' time, they had excavated the foundations, with the cornerstones laid on 23 July, the very day "on which a lawless mob served notice of expulsion on the Saints in Missouri."[4]

The Church was fortunate to gain the services of two remarkable builders: Jacob Bump, a master plasterer and journeyman carpenter from Silver Creek, New York, with years of experience; and Artemus Millet, a seasoned mason from Upper Canada (Ontario) and a recent Brigham Young convert who had built two or three flour mills north of the border. Millet had also served in the British army building the Rideau Canal with its intricate system of stonework and interconnecting locks joining Bytown

---

3. According to Truman O. Angell, later architect of the Salt Lake Temple, at one point Frederick G. Williams, one of President Smith's counselors, came into the temple, when the following dialogue took place in his presence:

"Carpenter Rolph said, 'Doctor, what do you think of the House?' He answered, 'It looks to me like the pattern precisely.' He then related the following: 'Joseph received the word of the Lord for him to take his two counselors Williams and Rigdon and come before the Lord, and He would show them the plan or model of the House to be built. We went upon our knees, called on the Lord, and the Building appeared within viewing distance: I being the first to discover it. Then all of us viewed it together. After we had taken a good look at the exterior, the building seemed to come right over us, and the makeup of this Hall seemed to coincide with what I there saw to a minutia. Joseph was accordingly enabled to dictate to the mechanics, and his counselors stood as witnesses; and this was strictly necessary in order to satisfy the spirit of unbelief in consequence of the weakness of childishness of the Brethren of those days.'" Truman O. Angell, Autobiography, 4, typescript, MSS 937, L. Tom Perry Special Collections, Harold B. Lee Library, Brigham Young University (hereafter listed as Perry Special Collections, HBLL, BYU).

4. James E. Talmage, *The House of the Lord: A Study of Holy Sanctuaries Ancient and Modern* (Salt Lake City: The Church of Jesus Christ of Latter-day Saints, 1912), 104.

(Ottawa) with the St. Lawrence River. Using only local resources, Bump worked the carpentry and interior constructions while Millet oversaw the masonry work and exterior construction, a worthy tandem of commendable expertise. Aware that the foundations were too narrow to support the planned heavy brick construction, Millet recommended instead a rubble stone wall configuration with stucco finish, a style of construction more in common with contemporary Canadian building practices.[5]

Their best intentions notwithstanding, at least four things impeded their progress: the poverty of the people and the strained finances of the Church; the lack of a consistent and well trained workforce; the weather; and the increasing spirit of opposition and persecution from both within and without the Church. Remembered Benjamin F. Johnson: "But such was the poverty of the people at the time of breaking ground for its foundation, that there was not a scraper and hardly a plow that could be obtained among the Saints."[6] Truman Coe, a Presbyterian minister who resided in Kirtland, remembered that most of the Saints lived in a state of "extreme indigence." "They suffer accumulated evils by crowding a multitude of poor people together.... A grotesque assemblage of hovels and shanties and small houses have been thrown up wherever they can find a footing; but very few of all these cabins would be accounted fit for human habitation."[7]

Lacking a working law of tithing, the fledgling Church had not yet established a regular means of income; rather, it relied upon the inconsistent consecrations of its members and on building loans with high rates of interest, obtained from eastern bankers. No support was expected

---

5. "The northern shore of Lake Ontario, where Millet had worked, still has many examples of churches built using rubblework construction techniques during the late eighteenth and early nineteenth centuries." Elwin C. Robison, *The First Mormon Temple: Design, Construction, and Historic Context of the Kirtland Temple* (Provo, Utah: Brigham Young University Press, 1997), 33. For the most recent study of Millet, see Keith A. Erikson and Lloyd D. Newell, "The Conversion of Artemus Millet and His Call to Kirtland," *BYU Studies* 41, no. 2 (2002): 77–115.
6. Benjamin F. Johnson, *My Life's Review—Autobiography of Benjamin Franklin Johnson* (Provo, Utah: Grandin Book Company, 1997), 9.
7. Milton V. Backman Jr., "Truman Coe's 1836 Description of Mormonism," *BYU Studies* 17, no. 3 (Summer 1977): 352.

from their fellow Saints in Missouri, recently driven from their homes in Jackson County and living as refugees in Clay County. Nor did local merchants trade with these "deluded" newcomers, who were often regarded as a blight upon the once quiet community. John Tanner, a recent wealthy convert from upstate New York, and Vienna Jacques, a nurse from Massachusetts and also a recent convert, loaned Joseph Smith $2,000 and $1,400 respectively in January 1835 to keep the original mortgage (no payments had been made in almost two years) from foreclosing. Tanner later provided other loans of up to $13,000 to the Temple Committee.[8] In all, the costs of building the temple amounted to at least $40,000 (approximately $1,000,000 in 2019 dollars), much of it in borrowed money.

The Kirtland economy was based on the ideal of a community of Saints trying to live a law of consecration in which new settlers consecrated their properties and income to the "bishop's storehouse." Each consecrated member received from the bishop a "stewardship" over his own property, often his own original property or portion thereof. In this way, according to historian Leonard Arrington, "the older settlers divided their land and possessions to some extent with the newcomers, and the more prosperous with the poor." Soon a general store, tannery, printing shop, and steam sawmill were established by this method of joint stewardships in what was called the "United Firm" and "Central Board of the United Order." While all of these early efforts eventually proved financially unsuccessful, this concept of a Zion community became the ideal. While the building of the Kirtland Temple provided employment for the needy as workers drew necessities from nearby stores, merchants used consecrations and credit in purchasing supplies. The temple was thus "an essential

---

8. Robison, *The First Mormon Temple*, 152; see also Susan Easton Black, *Who's Who in the Doctrine & Covenants* (Salt Lake City: Bookcraft, 1997), 145.

support to a deficit economy"⁹ and was built in large measure upon the principles of consecration of time, money, property, and means.¹⁰

The second obstacle was the scarcity as well as the ebb and flow of the workforce. When work began in 1833, barely 150 Saints had gathered to Kirtland. Though that number soon rapidly increased, many able-bodied men were sent away on missions during those months of the year that were most conducive to construction. Most workers donated at least one day in seven to the work.¹¹ But they were also facing other demands on their time. With the expulsion of the Saints from Independence in 1833 and Joseph Smith's subsequent call for Zion's Camp, a paramilitary endeavor to reclaim stolen lands in Independence, Missouri, many men were off carrying muskets rather than hauling temple rocks and timbers. As Levi Hancock remembered: "All mechanics were busily engaged in making implements of war all winter [1833/34], to be prepared in the spring to travel to Missouri to replace our brethren upon their land."¹²

A third impediment was the weather. The Connecticut Western Reserve country of northern Ohio, situated just south of Lake Erie, is subject to some of the coldest, snowiest winters in all of America. The northwesterly winds coming across the lake often brought storms of furious intensity that could hold up construction for weeks at a time. Access to the quarries was virtually impossible and the sawmills could not operate because of frozen water. Thus wintertime construction, especially that first year, was highly limited and certainly delayed their progress. It was made even more difficult when Millet returned to Canada in the fall of 1833 to take care of pressing family matters.

The fourth and final challenge was the growing opposition to the

---

9. Leonard J. Arrington, *Great Basin Kingdom: An Economic History of the Latter-day Saints, 1830–1900* (Cambridge, MA: Harvard University Press, 1958), 13.
10. Max Parkin, "Joseph Smith and the United Firm: The Growth and Decline of the Church's First Master Plan of Business and Finance, Ohio and Missouri, 1832–1834," *BYU Studies* 46, no. 3 (Summer 2007): 5–62; see also Matthew C. Godfrey, "Newel K. Whitney and the United Firm," Revelations in Context, https://history.lds.org/section/revelations.
11. Backman, "Truman Coe's 1836 Description of Mormonism," 352–53.
12. Levi Hancock journal, 3, typescript, Perry Special Collections, HBLL, BYU.

Saints that increased in intensity the longer they stayed in Kirtland. Said Joel Hills Johnson: "The building of the temple in Kirtland was a great undertaking considering the poverty and minority of the Church" for it required "the utmost exertion of every member to accomplish so great an undertaking; for we had but very few friends among the world while we had thousands of enemies who were holding their secret meetings to devise a plan to thwart and overthrow all our arrangements."[13] Much of this opposition came from within the Church and had everything to do with the darkening economic prospects about to envelope the nation, indeed the entire world.

Despite these obstacles, the Saints remained intensely committed to the task at hand. After Zion's Camp returned in mid-August of 1834, work went into higher gear, "the spring to all our thoughts" as Joseph's mother, Lucy Mack Smith, described it.[14] For days on end, the Smith family, including Lucy Mack Smith and Emma Smith, gave up their house and beds to exhausted temple workers, choosing to sleep on a single blanket on the hard floor. Needed were 1,500 tons of stones and giant wood girders that required many a strong man and stout heart.[15] Joseph Smith himself, in his tow frock and tow breeches, worked several days with his bare hands as foreman in the Stannard and, to a lesser extent, the Russell quarries. And Brigham Young recalled that although the Church in Kirtland was "few in numbers," when construction began he and Joseph "worked day after day on that building. . . . [We] did not have much fine flour bread to

---

13. Joel Hills Johnson, "A Journal or Sketch of the Life of Joel Hills Johnson," MS 8237, item 67, Church History Library, Salt Lake City. Also at http://boap.org/LDS/Early-Saints/JHJohnson.html.
14. Smith, *Lucy's Book*, 584. Zion's Camp may have failed in its attempt at gaining redress for lost lands in Jackson County, Missouri, but it did succeed in developing a strong cadre of future Church leaders.
15. "Obtaining sufficient wood for the temple was a problem because a vast quantity was needed quickly. Much of the freshly cut wood from neighboring forests had to be dried and seasoned before it could be cut and used." To expedite the drying and seasoning process, the Saints built a board kiln in the flats which, however, was prone to taking fire. Eventually the Saints had to contract with a local businessman to furnish lumber. Karl Ricks Anderson, *Joseph Smith's Kirtland: Eyewitness Accounts* (Salt Lake City: Deseret Book Company, 1989), 160–61.

eat; and they did not always have molasses to eat with their johnny cake; sometimes they had shoes and sometimes they had none; sometimes they would have tolerable pants, and sometimes their clothes would be very ragged."[16] Those who had no teams worked in the quarry preparing the stones for drawing to the house while those with teams assisted in drawing the stone to the temple.

On Saturdays all of the teams were in use hauling roughly cut stones, some weighing as much as a thousand pounds or more, from the quarry two miles away to the temple site for the masons to sculpt, refine, and place during the week to come. And while a few women labored loading wagons and hauling rocks, most were at home or in company one with another sewing, spinning, mending, and knitting clothes for the growing numbers of workers and preparing the veils or curtains as well as carpets for the temple's interior. Recalled Heber C. Kimball: "Our wives were . . . just as busy as any of us."[17]

By February 1835, the walls were "up to the square" and ready for the roof which was completely installed by July. With the 13,983 square-foot, three-story temple now enclosed, the interior finishing work proceeded at a faster pace under the supervision of Jacob Bump and later, Truman O. Angell, after Bump temporarily left the Church. Work progressed at an accelerated pace on the interior in a frenzied rush to complete the temple by the spring of 1836 and in time to receive the much discussed and highly anticipated "endowment of power." The edifice was never designed to be merely a church or meetinghouse but a "House of God," a temple to the Most High. Though taller than the planned Independence Temple, and with a more churchlike appearance, what distinguished it from most other contemporary church buildings were the two main assembly rooms or

---

16. "History of the Church, 1839–ca. 1882," also called "History of Brigham Young," 43:1759–60, 5 November 1871, CR 100 102, Church Historian's Office, Church History Library. "Living on air, and a little hominy and milk, and often salt or no salt when milk could not be had." Young, in *Journal of Discourses*, 2:31, 6 April 1853.
17. Roger D. Launius, *The Kirtland Temple: A Historical Narrative* (Independence, Missouri: Herald Publishing House, 1986), 52, in *Times and Seasons* 6 (15 April 1845): 867.

"courts" located directly one above the other: the lower court for worship meetings, preaching, and administration of the sacrament ("a house of worship"); and the less ornate upper court for sacred ordinances, other forms of worship, and "the school of mine apostles" as well as other educational endeavors ("a house of learning"). The third or attic floor, with its series of five interconnected rooms lit by dormer windows, would serve primarily as office space and for administrative purposes ("a house of order").

Also unique were the four rising pulpits at the east and west end of the assembly room, representing the two Priesthoods, with their various offices inscribed in short form on each pulpit; a system of interchangeable, backless benches set in pew boxes allowing the audience to sit facing either east or west; and an intricate system of pulleys and roll-up curtains that could be lowered from the ceiling "like the sails of a ship" to apportion off the assembly room into much smaller sub-rooms or private compartments.[18] Four separate choir lofts were placed at each corner of the assembly room, providing a stereo sound effect in a very non-circular building. Since there was little provision for heating other than a few stoves in the basement, the expectation was that as worshippers crowded into each compartment, they would provide the necessary body heat.

The exterior design was an eclectic mix of Georgian, Federal, Greek Revival, and Gothic elements—a greatly modified version of a New England meetinghouse—with a well-crafted weathervane atop a polychrome tower, a belfry, large entry doors painted bright olive green, and a vestibule leading

---

18. "Each [row of pulpits] had curtains hanging from the ceiling overhead down to the top of the pulpit, which could be rolled up or dropped down at pleasure, and when dropped down would completely exclude those within the apartment from the sight of all others. The room was also divided into four compartments by means of curtains or veils hanging from the ceiling overhead down to the floor, so that the house could be used for different purposes," Eliza R. Snow, comp., *Biography and Family History of Lorenzo Snow: One of the Twelve Apostles of The Church of Jesus Christ of Latter-day Saints* (Salt Lake City: Deseret News Co., 1884), 12, as cited in Launius, *The Kirtland Temple*, 46. A similar curtainlike design was anticipated for the second floor but was never completed. As for the two sets of twelve pulpits, David Howlett maintains that they served as a "miniaturization of a proposed twenty-four temple compound" planned for the proposed temple complex in Independence, Missouri. David J. Howlett, *Kirtland Temple: The Biography of a Shared Mormon Sacred Space* (Urbana: University of Illinois Press, 2014), 20–21.

into the main sanctuary.¹⁹ A double row of peaked Gothic windows graced each side wall with Venetian windows at the end of each assembly room. The exterior walls featured a bluish-colored, "rough cast" plaster mixture of crockery and glass that Millet used to cover over the rubble stone mix, allowing the building to sparkle like a diamond in the sunshine.²⁰ As a finishing touch, Brigham Young oversaw the painting of the interior using pristine white paint. Placed high above the doors was the inscription "House of the Lord. Built by the Church of Christ A. D. 1834."²¹

Although far from being an architectural wonder and in many cases built of inferior materials and prone to settling and various other design problems, the Kirtland Temple when finished was a garland to the community. Small by modern standards, when completed, it rivaled in size the largest buildings in northern Ohio and beckoned reverence and private meditation. The Saints soon considered it a thing of pride and beauty, their own sacred space of quiet conversion and communion with the heavens. Even before its completion, it hosted a variety of meetings. The first Sunday meeting was held there in the fall of 1835 with congregants seated on workbenches. And the Hebrew School, under the direction of Joshua Seixus, began meeting in the west upper room of the attic on 4 January 1836.

A SEASON OF ENDOWMENTS

Well before the temple's completion, Joseph Smith had begun to prepare his gathered community of believers for the "great blessings [that]

---

19. Robison, *First Mormon Temple*, 9–20. Similar "Georgian Gothic"–style churches by the renowned architect, Asher Benjamin, can be seen on the campus of Dartmouth College in New Hampshire and in New York City. Launius, *Kirtland Temple*, 43–44. A bell was not installed in the belfry until 1892.
20. There is no contemporary evidence that women were asked to crush and donate their finest china to the exterior plaster. However, Lucy Mack Smith, under Artemus Millet's direction, apparently "took her one horse and went around to gather means for glass and nails and also to gather all the broken earthen to put in the outside plaster." https://www.holbrook-family.com/bios/caroline fangell.htm. Robison believes that while some of the material might have come from heirlooms, the "lion's share of the glassware in the stucco came from discard piles and not parlor shelves." Robison, *First Mormon Temple*, 79.
21. For an excellent short primer on the Kirtland Temple, see Barbara Walden and Lachlan Mackay, *House of the Lord: The Story of the Kirtland Temple* (Independence, Missouri: The John Whitmer Historical Association, 2008).

Kirtland Temple, Ohio—circa 1890.

... will soon be poured out upon us. . . . You need an endowment, brethren, in order that you may be prepared and able to overcome all things; and those that reject your testimony will be damned."[22] Thus the spirit of anticipation and excitement rose as did the walls and tower of the temple, a palpable sense of an impending event that would change the lives of many.

Some later observers have tended to regard the Kirtland endowment as merely preliminary to the greater blessings given later in the Nauvoo Temple. Brigham Young, speaking in 1853, said that it was only a "portion of their first endowments or we might say more clearly, some of the first or introductory, or initiatory ordinances, preparatory to an endowment."[23]

---

22. Joseph Smith, *History of the Church* (Salt Lake City: Deseret Book Company, 1961), 2:308–9, 12 November 1835.
23. Brigham Young, *Journal of Discourses*, 2:31, 6 April 1853. Elder Boyd K. Packer said that the ordinances of the Kirtland Temple introduced only in "a limited way" sacred ordinances and ceremonies that would be performed in later temples. Boyd K. Packer, *The Holy Temple* (Salt Lake City:

"IT WAS A PENTECOST AND AN ENDOWMENT INDEED"

However, at the time the Kirtland Saints viewed it as the fulfillment of a divine promise, an empowering benediction to their faith. At the very least, it would be foundational to that which would come later and imprint the importance of temple worship indelibly upon the minds and hearts of faithful members of the Church.

Many have come to refer to the Kirtland endowment as a "season of endowments," with various expressions of the Holy Spirit on at least five different occasions or periods of time: first, the preliminary ordinations, sermons, and related activities in the years leading up to the endowment itself; second, the priesthood ordinances and rituals specifically called the endowment; third, the Pentecostal-like outpourings of the Spirit during the dedicatory services in late March 1836; fourth, the two highly significant temple visions that occurred in 1836; and fifth, as a spiritual afterglow, the lingering endowment season of late 1836 and early 1837. While each one might be said to be an endowment in one form or another, taken together, they constituted a remarkable spiritual outpouring over time and "the beginning of the blessing which shall be poured out upon the heads of my people" (D&C 110:10).

Preliminaries

The ordination of many men from far and near for the first time to priesthood office at an early conference of the Church held 3–5 June 1831 at the Isaac Morley farm near Kirtland might well be considered an early season of endowment. At this special meeting, John Whitmer recorded that "the spirit of the Lord fell upon Joseph in an unusual manner" as he spoke of the gathering of Israel and of particular prophecies pertaining to specific individuals attending the meeting. Wrote John Corrill: "The Melchesideck

---

Bookcraft, 1980), 129. And Richard O. Cowan while observing that although the ordinances as administered "were not as complete as they would be in later times," nevertheless claimed that the building was indeed worthy of the name—a temple of the Lord—in design, function, and inspiration. Richard O. Cowan, "The House of the Lord in Kirtland: A 'Preliminary' Temple," *Regional Studies in Latter-day Saint Church History: Ohio*, ed. Milton R. Backman Jr. (Provo, Utah: Department of Church History and Doctrine, 1990), 106, 119.

Priesthood was then for the first time introduced and conferred on several of the elders. In this chiefly consisted the endowment—it being a new order and bestowed authority."[24] Many received the high priesthood and office of high priest for the first time during this meeting as part of their missionary blessings. As historian Mark Staker has pointed out, this may not have been the conferral of the Melchizedek Priesthood but the ordination to specific offices therein. Whatever the case, "ecstatic religious expression suddenly seemed to break out throughout the congregation" and the gifts of the Spirit were made manifest in a most remarkable manner.[25]

Another example of preliminary endowments came with the formation of the School of the Prophets in 1833. The emphasis on schooling and teaching "one another words of wisdom . . . out of the best books" (D&C 88:118) may have been instrumental in its organization. Reserved primarily for instruction in scripture and doctrine, the School of the Prophets was a springboard for revelation, including that known as the "Word of Wisdom" (D&C 89). They usually met in an upstairs room of the Newel K. Whitney store, and it was during sessions of this spiritual academy that the washing of feet was performed as an initiatory rite (D&C 88:138–41).

An Endowment of Power

The preparation for the endowment may have been as meaningful to the believer as the endowment itself. Many of those hoping to receive their temple blessings had walked hundreds of miles as part of Zion's Camp, had sacrificed much in order now to be in Kirtland, and had been

---

24. John Corrill, *A Brief History of the Church of Jesus Christ of Latter Day Saints, 1839* (St. Louis: self-published, 1839), 24, as cited in Karen Lynn Davidson, et al., eds., *Histories, Vol. 2: Assigned Histories, 1831–1847*, of the Histories series of *The Joseph Smith Papers*, edited by Dean C. Jessee, Ronald K. Esplin, and Richard Lyman Bushman (Salt Lake City: The Church Historian's Press, 2012), 145.
25. Staker, *Hearken, O Ye People*, 157–62. This endowment of power may have included sealing individuals up "unto eternal life" and many outpourings of spiritual blessings. Staker, 164.

"IT WAS A PENTECOST AND AN ENDOWMENT INDEED"

promised that they would receive "power from on high."[26] Others were about to leave on yet another mission. Whoever they were, they were directed to "solemnize their minds, by casting away every evil from them in thought, word, or deed, and let their hearts become sanctified, because they need not expect a blessing from God without being duly prepared for it; for the Holy Ghost would not dwell in unholy temples."[27] They were also to abstain from "strong drink" and conjugal relations, forgive all who had offended them, and to cleanse themselves physically and spiritually "every whit." Said Heber C. Kimball: those coming to the Kirtland Temple "must enter with clean bodies" and be "wash[ed], cleanse[d], purify[ied] for about 30 days" before being admitted into the House of God.[28] Although no temple recommend was required for entrance to the temple, the endowment was no mere recitation of rituals but a blessing predicated upon repentance, a change of heart, and a covenant to improve.[29] "We covenanted with each other in the sight of God and the holy angels and the brethren," said the Prophet Joseph, "to strive henceforward to build each other up in righteousness."[30]

As an "endowment of power," it had been promised to those who held the priesthood and was especially designed to bless and protect the scores of missionaries about to embark upon their proselyting assignments.[31] Consisting of teachings, washings and anointings, blessings that were

---

26. For instance, Edward Partridge was "called and chosen, and is to go to Kirtland and receive his endowment with power from on high; and also, stand in his office as bishop to purchase land in Missouri." "Extract from the Journal of Heber C. Kimball," *Times and Seasons* 2 (1841); 6 (1845).
27. Corrill, *A Brief History of the Church*, as cited in *The Joseph Smith Papers, Histories* 2:154.
28. Heber C. Kimball on the Kirtland Endowment, as recorded by Thomas Bullock, General Church Minutes, 2 July 1854.
29. "No imposition shall be practiced upon any member of the church by depriving them of their [rights] in the house." Brent M. Rogers et al., eds., *Documents, Vol. 5: October 1835–January 1838*, of the Documents series of *The Joseph Smith Papers*, ed. Ronald K Esplin, Matthew J. Grow, and Matthew C. Godfrey (Salt Lake City: Church Historian's Press, 2016): 175, 14 January 1836.
30. Dean C. Jessee et al., eds., *Journals Vol. 1:1832–1839*, of the Journal series of *The Joseph Smith Papers*, ed. Dean C. Jessee, Ronald K. Esplin, and Richard Lyman Bushman (Salt Lake City: The Church Historian's Press, 2008): 141, 17 December 1835 and 1 January 1836.
31. John Corrill stated that the term "endowment" had been used as early as 1831 when some men first received the Melchizedek Priesthood—"it being a new order." Corrill, *A Brief History* as cited in *Joseph Smith Papers, Histories* 2:145.

promised or sealed upon them, and outpourings of the gifts of tongues and healing, this endowment, which Kirtland historian Milton V. Backman Jr. described as "a gift of knowledge derived from revelation, a gift of power emitting from God," was diligently sought after by the Saints.[32]

The Kirtland endowment was an initiatory presentation of three separate and related ordinances performed in the attic rooms and given individually and not collectively, though usually with others of their quorum present and praying in their behalf.[33] According to Oliver Cowdery, the week of January 15–20, 1836, was the first time such ordinances were given of which he wrote: "The glorious scene is too great to be described . . . therefore, I only say, that the heavens were opened to many, and great and marvelous things were shown."[34]

The first ordinance was the washing of the body from head to foot in soap and clear water (sometimes whiskey); the second was the anointing of one's head with perfumed consecrated oil and with it the sealing of promised blessings;[35] and, in the spirit of fasting, prayer, and the partaking of the Sacrament, the third ordinance was that of the washing of feet. In reference to this ordinance, Brigham Young said: "We were instructed to

---

32. Milton V. Backman Jr., *The Heavens Resound: A History of the Latter-day Saints in Ohio 1830–1838* (Salt Lake City: Deseret Book Company, 1983, 2002), 285.
33. "Saturday [February] 6th [I] called the anointed together to receive the seal of all their blessings. The High Priests & Elders in the council room as usual—The Seventy with the Twelve in the second room & the Bishop in the third—I labored with each of these quorums for some time to bring [them] to the order which God had shown to me which is as follows—first part to be spent in solemn prayer before God without any talking or confusion & the conclusion with a sealing prayer by Pres. Sidney Rigdon when all the quorums are to shout with one accord a solemn hosanna to God & the Lamb with an Amen—amen & amen—& then all take seat & lift up their hearts in silent prayer to God & if any obtain a prophecy or visions to rise & speak that all may be edified & rejoice together. I had considerable trouble to get all the quorums united in this order—I went from room to room repeatedly & charged each separately—assuring them that it was according to the mind of God." Lyndon W. Cook and Milton V. Backman Jr., eds., *Kirtland Elders' Quorum Record, 1836–1841* (Provo, Utah: Grandin Book Company, 1985), 7, 6 February 1836.
34. Leonard J. Arrington, "Oliver Cowdery's Kirtland, Ohio, 'Sketch Book,'" *BYU Studies* 12, no. 4 (1972), 4–5.
35. These "promised blessings," as explained by Joseph Smith, were "that they [High Priests] would have power given them to seal up the Saints unto eternal life." Donald Q. Cannon and Lyndon W. Cook, eds., *Far West Record: Minutes of The Church of Jesus Christ of Latter-day Saints, 1830–1844* (Salt Lake City: Deseret Book Company, 1983), 20–21. See also Doctrine and Covenants 68:12. This practice continued until at least 1836 and then was resumed in Nauvoo.

wash each other's feet, as an evidence that we had borne testimony of the truth of the Gospel to the world."[36] Some had received a partial endowment when it was first administered in the attic story of the small adjacent printing office in late January. In an emotional letter to his wife, W. W. Phelps spoke of what happened on 17 January 1836: "The Lord poured out his Spirit in such a manner as you never witnessed. When I was speaking, which was but a few words, the Spirit of the Lord came upon me so that I could not speak, and I cried as little children cry in earnest and the tears from my eyes ran in streams; the audience, which was the largest ever convened in the said room, sobbed and wept aloud. . . . There was speaking and singing in tongues, and prophesying, as on the day of Pentecost."[37] Most others, however, did not receive it until the week of 21 March 1836.[38] Members of the stake presidency, high council, and bishopric in Missouri, including David and John Whitmer, travelled all the way from Missouri to Kirtland in order to receive their blessings.

These ordinances were administered in sequence, at different times throughout the day, and newly endowed recipients often remained in the temple throughout the night in the spirit of prayer and fasting. "The Lord poured out his spirit upon us," said Wilford Woodruff, "and we felt it good to be in the house of God while nature was hushed in silence by the sable shades of night. . . . There was much of the spirit of Prophecy and revelation poured upon the heads of the anointed in the different quorums."[39]

Thereupon "The First Presidency confirmed and sealed upon our heads all the blessings of our ordination, anointing and patriarchal," said Woodruff, "with a seal in the presence of God and the Lamb and holy

---

36. Brigham Young, in *Journal of Discourses*, 2:214. See Clarence L. Fields, "History of the Kirtland Temple," (master's thesis, Brigham Young University, 1963), 59.
37. W. W. Phelps letter to his wife, Sally, Letters of W. W. Phelps, 1835–1841, 17 January 1836, MS 8711, Church History Library; see also http://boap.org/LDS/Early-Saints/Phelps-letters.html.
38. Milton V. Backman Jr., *The Heavens Resound*, 285–300. See also *History of the Church*, 2:379–80, 4–5 April 1837.
39. *Wilford Woodruff's Journal*, 1:13, 4–5 April 1837. The fact that the sisters were not invited to these ordinances did not always sit well. Remembered George A. Smith, "As they were not admitted into the Temple while this washing was being performed . . . some of them were right huffy about it." George A. Smith, in *Journal of Discourses*, 2:215, 18 March 1855.

angels that they should all be fulfilled upon our head . . . and the seal was confirmed upon our heads with a shout of all the anointed with uplifted hand to heaven 'Hosanna, Hosanna, Hosanna, to God and the Lamb. Amen, Amen, and Amen.'. . . This was repeated as it is written and if ever a shout entered the cabinet of heaven that did." Later on, "After the washing of feet, the veils were rolled, which brought the congregation into one assembly." Woodruff further recalled, "President Joseph Smith, Jr. arose and addressed the congregation for the term of three hours clothed with the power, spirit, and image of God he unbosomed his mind and feelings in the house of his friends He presented many things of vast importance to the minds of the Elders of Israel. O that they might be written upon our hearts as with an iron pen to remain forever."[40] On many occasions, the gifts of tongues, the interpretation of tongues, healing, and prophecy were likewise poured out upon the participants. Some pronounced blessings; others, like Chapman Duncan, laid a few curses upon Lieutenant Governor Lilburn W. Boggs for not doing more to help the Saints reclaim their properties in Jackson County, Missouri.[41] Although not part of the endowment ordinances, many received their patriarchal blessings at the same time under the hands of Joseph Smith Sr., the first patriarch of the Church.[42]

Wrote Parley P. Pratt:

> *The ordinances of the priesthood were revealed to a greater extent than had been known among men since the prophets and Apostles of old fell asleep; and many were anointed to their holy calling, and were instructed in principles which were great and glorious in themselves, and calculated to enlarge the mind and prepare the chosen servants of God for the great work before them. Many great and marvelous things were prophesied, which I am not at liberty to record, and many of which have since been fulfilled to the very letter. Many*

---

40. *Wilford Woodruff's Journal*, 1:132, 6 April 1837.
41. Autobiography of Chapman Duncan, 6, typescript, Perry Special Collections, HBLL, BYU.
42. Journal of Truman O. Angell, 3, Perry Special Collections, HBLL, BYU.

persons were carried away in the visions of the Spirit, and saw and heard unspeakable things; and many enjoyed the ministering of angels, and the gift of healing and of speaking in tongues.[43]

These endowments were repeated three more times in 1836, at least twice between March and June of 1837, and at least once again in 1839 when Brigham Young pronounced them upon John Taylor while his fellow apostles were on their way to serve missions in Great Britain.[44]

The origin of the Kirtland Temple endowment has not yet been determined. If a revelation, it was never recorded or printed in the Book of Commandments or, later, the Doctrine and Covenants, perhaps because of its sacred nature. Joseph Smith's work of revising the Holy Bible, beginning in June 1830, had already resulted in several previous revelations and visions, as for example, his *Vision* of God and the three degrees of glory (D&C 76) given to him and to Sidney Rigdon in the John Johnson home in 1832.[45] Certainly one can find references in the book of Exodus

---

43. Parley P. Pratt, *Autobiography of Parley P. Pratt* (Salt Lake City: Deseret Book Company, 1980), 129–30. Benjamin Brown, in a contemporary account, spoke of "many marvelous things" occurring "even greater than at the day Pentecost." "Many visions are given and also revelations by night and by day . . . there appeared a light over the House of the Lord and extended from west to East." Steven C. Harper, "Pentecost Continued: A Contemporaneous Account of the Kirtland Temple Dedication," *BYU Studies* 42, no. 2 (2003), 13.
44. Many years later, Orson Pratt spoke of the Kirtland endowment, which he himself had received, as developmental and incremental in nature.
    "When the Temple was built, the Lord did not see proper to reveal all the ordinances of the Endowments, such as we now understand. He revealed little by little. No rooms were prepared for washing; no special place prepared for the anointings, . . . Neither did we know the necessity of the washings. . . . It is true, our hands were washed, our faces and our feet. The Prophet Joseph was commanded to gird himself with a towel, doing this in the Temple. What for? That the first Elder might witness to our Father and God, that we were clean from the blood of that wicked generation, that then lived. . . . The holy anointing was placed upon the heads of his servants, but not the full development of the Endowments in the anointing. These administrations in the Kirtland Temple were revealed, little by little . . . according to His own will and pleasure." Orson Pratt, in *Journal of Discourses*, 19:16, 20 May 1877.
45. In his pioneering study of the Joseph Smith Translation, Robert J. Matthews gives compelling evidence that several sections of the Doctrine and Covenants trace their origins to Joseph Smith's translation of the Holy Bible. These include Sections 74, 76, 77, 86, 88, 91, 93, 132, and very likely 84. Robert J. Matthews, *A Plainer Translation*, 34–38. Thus the Holy Bible not only gave rise to the First Vision and Joseph's motivation from his reading James 1:5 but it was also the text for much of Moroni's instruction and scriptural commentaries in 1823. It was also the platform for some of what became unique Church doctrines and practices including, perhaps, part of the Kirtland endowment.

(chapter 29:4, 7) to the ancient Israelites receiving washings with water and anointings of oil and related blessings in the "tabernacle of the congregation" at the hand of the Levite priests of Israel, although the Prophet makes no corrections or emendations of this particular text. The JST-inspired revelation of the Book of Moses, with its many references to Enoch and to the building of "my tabernacle" in the New Jerusalem, may have been another reference point.

It may also be highly significant that by January 1836 Joseph Smith was already familiar with the writings found on the papyrus scrolls which he had obtained from Michael Chandler in July 1835.[46] Specifically, he had done a good deal of translating from the Book of Abraham in October and November 1835. As previously noted, in December he was preparing a room for translation near the place he intended to store and display the papyri. Evidence would therefore suggest that by the end of the year he

---

46. The Prophet spent much of the summer and fall of 1835 preparing an alphabet of the Egyptian characters (similar to what he had done with the Book of Mormon characters back in 1828) and translating the writings from the scrolls. See *History of the Church*, 2:238, 16 December 1835. On 20 November 1835, he was "making rapid progress." *History of the Church*, 2:318. By the end of the year he had set up a "translating room" in the west room in the upper part of the temple where the Hebrew School was held for several months in 1836. W. W. Phelps recorded in his journal for 20 July 1835 that in reference to the two papyrus scrolls taken from the four Egyptian mummies that made up the purchase, Joseph Smith already knew what they were and said that the scrolls of papyrus contained a sacred record kept by Joseph in Pharaoh's court in Egypt and the teachings of Father Abraham. See Bruce A. Van Orden, ed., "Writing to Zion: The William W. Phelps Kirtland Letters (1835–1836)," *BYU Studies* 33, no. 3 (Fall 1993): 9. For the most recent study on the Book of Abraham, see John Gee, *An Introduction to the Book of Abraham* (Provo, Utah: Religious Studies Center, Brigham Young University, 2017).

A good deal of recent scholarship has centered on the so-called Kirtland Egyptian Papers housed in the Church History Library. These papers are a collection of documents related to the Book of Abraham written during (and after) the Kirtland period, a few by Joseph Smith but most in the hands of his various scribes and assistants. While scholars continue to question their significance, their existence points to the fact that the Prophet was well aware of the Book of Abraham and was certainly translating part of it before the end of 1835. For the most recent scholarship on the Kirtland Egyptian Papers, see Robin Scott Jensen and Brian M. Hauglid, eds., *Revelations and Translations Vol. 4: Book of Abraham and Related Manuscripts,* in the Revelations and Translations series of *The Joseph Smith Papers*, ed. Dean C. Jesse, Ronald K. Esplin, and Richard Lyman Bushman (Salt Lake City: Church Historian's Press, 2018); Hugh Nibley, "The Meaning of the Kirtland Egyptian Papers," *BYU Studies* 11, no. 4 (Summer 1971): 350–99; Brian M. Hauglid, *A Textual History of the Book of Abraham: Manuscripts and Editions, Studies in the Book of Abraham,* 5 (Provo, Utah: Neal A. Maxwell Institute, 2010); and H. Michael Marquardt, *Joseph Smith's Egyptian Papers: A History* (Cullman, Ala: Printing Service, 1981).

had translated at least through Abraham 2:18 and possibly to the end of Abraham 3 and Facsimile No. 2 with its references to temple worship.[47]

As previously discussed, the Prophet's emphasis on schooling and "teaching one another words of wisdom . . . out of the best books" had been instrumental in the prior organization of the School of the Prophets and may have influenced the Prophet's thinking at this time. The School of the Prophets ended in April 1833 only to be later succeeded by the more broadly attended School of the Elders which first convened in Missouri in the summer of 1833 and later in Kirtland intermittently from 1834 to 1836. Its course of instruction was somewhat more secular in nature than its predecessor school, although it was during a session of the School of the Elders in Kirtland that Joseph Smith and Sidney Rigdon delivered their well-known Lectures on Faith.[48] These later schools did not observe the earlier initiation rites and formalized salutations of the School of the Prophets.

In early January 1836 Joseph Smith organized the Hebrew School with Joshua Seixas as instructor, and classes were held in the upper rooms of the not-yet completed temple. Joseph came to view the acquisition of languages as "a vital part of Mormon spirituality, a necessary contribution to the Zion project, and an educational ideal among the Latter-day Saints."[49] He almost certainly viewed a knowledge of Hebrew as an asset to

---

47. Kerry Muhlestein and Megan Hansen, "'The Work of Translating': The Book of Abraham's Translation Chronology," in *Let Us Reason Together: Essays in Honor of the Life's Work of Robert L. Millet*, ed. J. Spencer Fluhman and Brent L. Top (Provo, Utah: Religious Studies Center, Brigham Young University; Salt Lake City: Deseret Book Company, 2016), 142–44, 154–55. If this is so, Joseph Smith was well aware of the system of astronomy found in Abraham's writings, the doctrines of premortal intelligences and their various degrees of valiancy, and the doctrines of ancient patriarchal priesthood authority. Muhlestein also infers that Joseph was probably aware of Facsimile no. 2 by this time and its references to "writings that cannot be revealed unto the world; but is to be had in the Holy Temple of God." See "Explanation," Figure no. 8 of Facsimile no. 2, Book of Abraham.
48. Steven R. Sorensen, "Schools of the Prophets," in *Encyclopedia of Mormonism: The History, Scripture, Doctrine, and Procedure of The Church of Jesus Christ of Latter-day Saints*, ed. Daniel H. Ludlow (New York: Macmillan Publishing Company, 1992), 3:1269.
49. Matthew J. Grey, "'The Word of the Lord in the Original.' Joseph Smith's Study of Hebrew in Kirtland," in *Approaching Antiquity: Joseph Smith and the Ancient World*, ed. Lincoln H. Blumell,

translate the papyri.[50] Over 115 members attended the school's seven-week course (often interrupted by temple construction duties).[51] Referring back to the Book of Abraham, chapter 3 is "full of Hebrew transliterations that match perfectly with the Hebrew grammar, lexicon, and lessons that Joseph began after he stopped translating Egyptian at the end of 1835."[52] Joseph clearly believed the Hebrew School would prepare the Church for the "glorious endowment."[53]

Whatever its derivation, the Kirtland endowment did not come out of a spiritual vacuum and likely owes as much to the Old Testament as it does to the New Testament or to any other book of scripture.[54] It was more Levitical or Aaronic in flavor than later temple ordinance renditions, and more preparatory in nature than crowning or culminating. Nevertheless, it was a remarkably rich blessing that left a powerful religious imprint upon the memory of the early Saints, one that prepared and inoculated them spiritually for very difficult times to come. Perhaps no better description of the power of the Kirtland Temple endowment can be given than that provided in the dedicatory prayer itself: "And we ask thee, Holy Father, that thy servants may go forth from this house armed with thy power, and that thy name may be upon them, and thy glory round about them, and thine angels have charge over them" (D&C 109:22).

This much is certain: the Kirtland Temple endowment was strictly for the living and not for the dead. Nor did it include marriages, sealings of spouses, or baptisms for the dead. It was reserved for the most faithful of

---

Matthew J. Grey, and Andrew H. Hedges (Provo, Utah: Religious Studies Center, Brigham Young University; Salt Lake City: Deseret Book Company, 2015), 257.
50. Grey, "The Word of the Lord," 282.
51. D. Kelly Ogden, "The Kirtland Hebrew School (1835–36)," in *Regional Studies in Latter-day Saint Church History: Ohio*, ed. Milton R. Backman Jr. (Provo, Utah: Department of Church History and Doctrine, Brigham Young University, 1990), 63–88. The class translated a considerable number of Old Testament verses.
52. For example, transliterations such as "Kokob" and "Kokaubeam" are clearly influenced by the Hebrew grammars which Joseph was then studying. Muhlestein and Hansen, "The Work of Translating," 150.
53. *Joseph Smith Papers, Journals* 1:84, as cited in Grey, "The Word of the Lord," 260.
54. One cannot, however, dismiss the possible influence of Luke 24, Acts 1:8, and Acts 2 (a day of Pentecost) in this regard.

men, those who had served in Zion's Camp, or on missions or other challenging assignments, and for those who had labored diligently in building the temple itself. Joseph said that "[they] were to be remembered. That those who build it should own it, and have the control of it."[55] And it was especially enjoined upon those who were about to leave on missions. "Remember you are not to go to other nations, till you receive your endowment," said Oliver Cowdery in his charge to the Twelve. "Tarry at Kirtland until you are endowed with power from on high. You need a fountain of wisdom, knowledge, and intelligence such as you never had. Relative to the endowment . . . The world cannot receive the things of God. He can endow you without worldly pomp or great parade. He can give you that wisdom, that intelligence and that power which characterized the ancient Saints and now characterizes the inhabitants of the upper world."[56]

A Season of Dedication

The period of time from 27 March to 3 April 1836 has gone down in Latter-day Saint history as one series after another of heavenly manifestations. Open to both men and women, these solemn assemblies, attended by upwards of 1,000 people at a time, were filled with sermons, songs, sustainings, stirring testimonies, and the offering of dedicatory prayers. Some spoke of seeing angels. Others claimed they saw the apostles Peter and John.[57] William Draper recalled that it was "such a time of the outpouring of the spirit of the Lord that my pen is inadequate to write it in full or my tongue to express it. But I will here say that the spirit was poured out and came like a mighty rushing wind and filled the house, that many that were present spoke in tongues and had visions and saw angels and prophesied;

---

55. Kirtland High Council Minutes, December 1832–November 1837, 7 March 1835, MS 3432.
56. Kirtland High Council Minutes, December 1832–November 1837, 21 February 1835.
57. Autobiography of Truman O. Angell (1810–1856), "His Journal," in Kate Carter, comp., *Our Pioneer Heritage* (Salt Lake City: Daughters of Utah Pioneers, 1967), 10: 194–98; see also Heber C. Kimball, "Journal Excerpts, 1833–1837," as referenced in Orson F. Whitney, *Life of Heber C. Kimball* (Salt Lake City: Stevens and Wallace, Inc., 1945), 86. Zebedee Coltrin said that he even saw the Savior "crowned with glory upon his head above the brightness of the sun." *History of the Church*, 2:386–87.

and had a general time of rejoicing such as had not been known in their generation."[58] Several others told of cloven tongues of fire appearing inside the building while others told of external manifestations. As Joseph more succinctly phrased it: "It was a Pentecost and an endowment indeed, long to be remembered for the sound shall go forth from this place into all the world."[59]

The initial dedicatory services held on 27 March were particularly a time to be remembered. Five hundred believers lined up at the doors before 7 a.m. and were ushered into the pew box benches by 8 a.m., all crowded tightly together. Hundreds of others soon filled the aisles. They then spilled out into the vestibule and gathered around open windows. Many others, disappointed at not getting in, milled about in the temple yards. Recognizing the press of people, Joseph Smith promised to repeat the service during the week. At 9 a.m., the service commenced with singing and prayer after which Sidney Rigdon sermonized for two hours on Matthew 8 in which Christ spoke of the foxes having holes and the birds having nests but the "Son of man hath not where to lay his head" (v. 20). He praised the congregation for their work in building the temple and promised them rich blessings for their heroic efforts.

The climax of the meeting came with Joseph Smith offering the dedicatory prayer that lasted twenty minutes, the first such temple dedication prayer ever given in Church history. He prayed for the Lord "to accept of this house" given "out of our poverty," "that the Son of Man might have a place to manifest himself to his people." He further prayed that "no unclean thing" should ever be permitted to enter the temple, that "no weapon formed against" the Church should prosper, that their enemies near and far might be confounded and that the Saints might be delivered, that their recent priesthood anointings "be sealed upon them with power from on

---

58. William Draper, "Biographical Sketch of the Life and Travels and Birth and Parentage of William Draper who was the son of William Draper and Lydia Lathrop Draper," 2–3, typescript, Perry Special Collections, HBLL, BYU.
59. *Joseph Smith Papers, Journals* 1:261, 30 March 1836.

high," and that missionary work might go forward as never before. He went on to pray for the Constitution of the United States, for kings and rulers elsewhere, for the rapid gathering of Israel, and for the return of Judah to their ancient appointed lands and ended by praying for the Church, that it may come forth out of the wilderness "fair as the moon, clear as the sun, and terrible as an army with banners" (D&C 109). One observer recalled the moment: "I saw there Joseph the prophet standing with his hands raised toward heaven, his face ashy pale, the tears running down his cheeks as he spoke on that memorable day."[60]

After the service ended with the singing of W. W. Phelps's stirring new temple anthem, "The Spirit of God Like a Fire Is Burning," some spoke of hearing heavenly singing, of seeing angelic visitors, and of participating in additional Pentecostal-like experiences. For instance, Prescindia Lathrop Huntington remembered, "The whole of the congregation were on their knees, praying vocally, for such was the custom at the close of these meetings when Father Smith presided. . . . While the congregation was thus praying, we both heard from one corner of the room above our heads, a choir of angels singing most beautifully . . . their sweet harmony filled the temple of God."[61] Eliza R. Snow remembered angels appearing to some, "while a sense of divine presence was realized by all present, and each heart was filled with joy inexpressible and full of glory."[62]

After Hyrum Smith and Sidney Rigdon made a few concluding remarks at about 4 p.m., the congregation ended the meeting shouting, "Hosanna! Hosanna! Hosanna! To God and the Lamb," repeated three times.

Although infants and very little children were not usually allowed

---

60. *History of the Church* 2:416–26; *Messenger and Advocate* 2 (March 1836): 276–77, as cited in Launius, *The Kirtland Temple*, 67–68.
61. Edward W. Tullidge, *The Women of Mormondom* (New York: Tullidge and Crandall, 1877), 207–10, 213.
62. Truman O. Angell autobiography, as cited in Launius, *The Kirtland Temple*, 68. Some reported angels clothed in white covering the roof. Many others sung and spoke in tongues. Tullidge, *The Women of Mormondom*, 207–10, 213.

Interior of Kirtland Temple.

to attend these services, some exceptions were made. During the Sunday 27 March services one woman brought her child, about two months old.

> *She stood out of the door for a long time, manifested an anxious desire to enter. At length one of the Elders said Brethren we do not exercise faith my faith is this child will not cry a word in the house today. On this the woman and child entered and the child did not cry a word from 8 till 4 in the afternoon. But when the saints all shouted Hosanna the child was nursing but let go and shouted also when the saints paused it paused when they shouted it shouted for three times when they shouted amen it shouted also for three times then it resumed its nursing without any alarm.*[63]

But if most children were not allowed inside the temple during these sacred convocations, some of them thought they saw an assembly of quite another kind. Prescindia Huntington recalled years later:

---

63. Benjamin Brown letter as cited in Harper, "Pentecost Continued," 19.

"IT WAS A PENTECOST AND AN ENDOWMENT INDEED"

> *A little girl came to my door in wonder, exclaiming, "The meeting is on the top of the meeting house!" I went to the door, and there I saw on the temple angels clothed in white covering the roof from end to end. They seemed to be walking to and fro; they appeared and disappeared. The third time they appeared and disappeared before I realized that they were not mortal men. Each time in a moment they vanished, and their reappearance was the same. This was in broad daylight, in the afternoon. A number of the children in Kirtland saw the same.*[64]

While most were thrilled with these heady visions and blessings, others held mixed feelings, not quite certain what to make of it all. Some local residents criticized the Saints for getting too high on whiskey and wine. And while some were more prepared for this new form of worship, others were decidedly not so. Such things had never before been seen in a Church that was so quickly changing and which some believed was still fundamentally Protestant in nature. As George A. Smith remembered, "All this was plain and simple, yet some apostatized because there was not more of it, and others because there was too much."[65]

A Season of Visions

Climaxing this season of endowments were two remarkable visions that have come to define much of modern temple doctrines and practices. Ironically, although the Kirtland Temple did not have a baptismal font, these two visions said much about the doctrine of redemption for the dead. The first came on 21 March 1836 during the initial ordinance of anointing with oil, in the west end of the third or attic floor of the temple in Joseph Smith's office. This revelation, now found in section 137 of the Doctrine and Covenants, spoke of "the celestial kingdom of God, and the glory thereof" and of Joseph seeing Adam and Abraham, as well as his own father and mother and his brother, Alvin, "that has long since slept." The vision of his deceased brother already in the celestial kingdom

---

64. Tullidge, *Women of Mormondom*, 207.
65. George A. Smith, in *Journal of Discourses*, 2:215, 18 March 1855.

was somewhat surprising since Alvin had died thirteen years before without receiving the required ordinance of baptism and whom the officiating minister at Alvin's funeral had virtually condemned to hell. It guaranteed the immortality of the soul and clarified the doctrine that all those who have died without a knowledge of the gospel but "who would have received it" had they lived "shall be heirs of that kingdom. For I, the Lord, will judge all men according to their works, according to the desires of their hearts." Furthermore, the vision gave assurance that all children who die before reaching the age of accountability will likewise be "saved in the celestial kingdom of heaven." This new understanding greatly expanded the scope of salvation and exaltation for both the living and the dead, like Alvin, who had righteous desires but who had died before the Restoration of the gospel.[66]

The ensuing vision, recorded by Warren Cowdery, Oliver's older brother, and now known as Section 110, came by way of a vision to Joseph and Oliver two weeks later on Easter Sunday, 3 April 1836. W. W. Phelps, in describing the events of the day to his wife, Sally, wrote: "On Sunday, April 3, the twelve held meeting and a[d]ministered the sacrament. It was a glorious time. The curtains were dropt in the afternoon. And there was a manifestation of the Lord to Br Joseph and Oliver, [by] which they [learned] thus the great and terrible day of the Lord as mentioned by Malichi [sic] was near, even at the doors."[67] It tells of the Savior appearing and accepting "this house" and pronouncing the endowment of forgiveness of sins—"your sins are forgiven you." He was followed by the appearance of Moses, Elias, and Elijah, all in fulfillment of, and in compliance

---

66. Joseph Smith Sr. was performing the ordinance of anointing with oil when his son, Joseph Smith Jr., received this vision. Whether this vision of his father and mother was set in future time is not clear. The vision does not negate the need for Alvin to receive temple ordinances for the dead, but it does indicate that he would not be kept back from receiving his blessings even though he had died without being baptized. The key point is that the fulness of salvation can come to all, living and dead, including little children.
67. W. W. Phelps to Sally Phelps, April 1836, as cited in Howlett, *Kirtland Temple*, 25.

with, the apostolic keys that Joseph and Oliver had already received from Peter, James, and John.

Moses restored the "keys of the gathering of Israel from the four parts of the earth," a reference to missionary work in the expanded sense of taking the gospel to all the nations of the earth. It may be significant to note that the highly successful mission of the Twelve Apostles to Great Britain (1838–1841) did not occur until after this vision had taken place.

Who, precisely, Elias was has been a matter of speculation; however, what he restored clearly refers to the gospel and promises given to Abraham. In the Book of Abraham, the Lord promised Abraham that in his posterity, "that is to say, the literal seed, . . . shall all the families of the earth be blessed" (Abraham 2:11) and that his posterity would be in number comparable to the sands upon the seashore and the stars in the heavens—"I will multiply thee, and thy seed after thee, like unto these; and if thou canst count the number of sands, so shall be the number of thy seeds" (Abraham 3:14). Thus the gospel of Abraham pertains to the blessings of futurity "in us and our seed."[68]

The third messenger, Elijah, revealed sealing powers pertaining to the past through the work of redemption for the dead. He spoke of revealing the keys to turn the hearts of the fathers to the children, and the children to the fathers, "lest the whole earth be smitten with a curse"—which

---

68. As to the coming of Elias, Elder Bruce R. McConkie gave this perspective:

"Now what was the gospel of Abraham: Obviously it was the commission, the mission, the endowment and power, the message of salvation, given to Abraham. And what was this? It was a divine promise that both in the world and out of the world his seed should continue 'as innumerable as the stars; or, if ye were to count the sand upon the seashore ye could not number them' (D&C 132:30; Genesis 17; Abraham 2:1–12). Thus the gospel of Abraham was one of celestial marriage. . . . This power and commission is what Elias restored, and as a consequence, the righteous among all future generations were assured of the blessings of a continuation of the seeds forever, even as it was with Abraham of old." Bruce R. McConkie, *Mormon Doctrine*, 2nd ed. (Salt Lake City: Bookcraft, 1979), 219–20.

Milton V. Backman and Robert L. Millet added the following: "Elias thus returned and delivered that directing power through which eternal family units may be organized and perpetuated through the new and everlasting covenant of marriage." Milton V. Backman Jr. and Robert L. Millet, "Heavenly Manifestations in the Kirtland Temple," 109, 110, 137, in *Studies in Scripture Volume One: The Doctrine and Covenants*, ed. Robert L. Millet and Kent P. Jackson (Salt Lake City: Deseret Book Company, 1989), 426.

pertained to the work of redemption for the dead.[69] Elijah's blessings, as many Church leaders have since commented upon, embraced the work of sealing past generations one to another and implied saving ordinances for the dead. Still, no baptisms for the dead were ever performed in the Kirtland Temple, nor eternal marriages for either the living or the dead.[70] And it would be decades before temple work included the sealing of one generation to another.

A Season of Residual Splendor

The final season of endowment came intermittently afterward throughout 1836 and into 1837. According to John Corrill, an early Church historian, soon after the dedication many experienced an afterglow of spiritual manifestations, "a marvelous spirit of prophecy." "Every man's mouth was full of prophesying, and for a number of days or weeks their time was spent in visiting from house to house, making feasts, prophesying, and pronouncing blessings on each other, to that degree, that from the external appearance, one would have supposed that the last days had truly come."[71] Many who had been away on missions, or for one reason or another were not in Kirtland in the spring of 1836, or if they had been in Kirtland, had been unable to attend, sought for and received similar blessings.[72] Though there were no dedications the following year, several spoke

---

69. Sections 109 and 110 were not added to the Doctrine and Covenants until 1876. Section 137 would not be added for another century.
70. Alexander L. Baugh, "'For Their Salvation is Necessary and Essential to our Salvation': Joseph Smith and the Practice of Baptism and Confirmation for the Dead," 71, in *An Eye of Faith: Essays Written in Honor of Richard O. Cowan*. ed. Kenneth L. Alford and Richard E. Bennett (Provo, Utah: Religious Studies Center, Brigham Young University; Salt Lake City: Deseret Book Company, 2015), 120–21.
71. John Corrill, *A Brief History of the Church*, in *Joseph Smith Papers, Histories*, 2:154.
72. George Burket, a missionary who arrived in Kirtland 10 April 1836, wrote on 12 April: "On this day at candle light I received the washing the first time with soap and water, and the 13th received the washing with salt water and whiskey and with perfume and on the 14th I attended a feast of bread and wine and at candlelight I received the anointing with oil in the name of the Lord. . . . On the 15th we made preparations to hold a Pentecostal feast in the house of the Lord to be held on the 16th and administered in like manner as the first, and on the 16th we attended to the washing of feet in the forenoon and the balance of the day we spent in fasting and prayer. And at night we held a feast and watched all night until near the sunrise in the morning." George Burket Journal, 12–13, 1835 September to 1836 May, transcript, MS 10340, Church History Library.

"IT WAS A PENTECOST AND AN ENDOWMENT INDEED"

Kirtland Temple in the early 1900s.

of manifestations similar to those of the year prior. In a letter to her sister, Mercy, Mary Fielding spoke of yet another round of temple meetings and spiritual displays. She wrote:

> *The hearts of the people were melted and the Spirit and power of God rested down upon us in a remarkable manner. Many spake in tongues and others prophesied and interpreted. . . . Some of the Sisters while engaged in conversing in tongues their countenances beaming with joy, clasped each others hands and kissed in the most affectionate manner. They were describing in this way the love and felicities of the Celestial World. . . . Some of the prophecies delivered in tongues and interpreted were so great that I cannot begin to describe them. . . . I believe as do many others that angels were present with us. A bright light shone across the House and rested upon some of the congregation. What I felt that day seemed to outweigh all the affliction and distress of mind I have suffered since I came here.*[73]

---

73. Letter of Mary Fielding to her sister, Mercy Fielding Thompson, 8 July 1837, as cited in Kenneth W. and Audrey M. Godfrey and Jill Mulvay Derr, *Women's Voices: An Untold History of*

Some of the sermons given in the winter of 1836 also seemed designed to prepare the people for what was to come. Parley P. Pratt, writing to his Canadian converts and friends, waxed eloquent about one such sermon given in mid-November by the Prophet Joseph Smith:

> One of the most interesting meetings I ever attended was held in the Lord's house Sunday before last. One week before [it] was publicly given that Br. J. Smith, Jr. would give a relation of the coming forth of the records and also of the rise of the Church and of his experience. Accordingly a vast concourse assembled at an early hour. Every seat was crowded and 4 or 5 hundred people stood up in the aisles. Br. S[mith] gave the history of these things relating many particulars of the manner of his first visions and the Spirit and power of God was upon him in bearing testimony insomuch that many if not most of the congregation were in tears—as for myself I can say that all the reasonings in uncertainty and all the conclusions drawn from the writings of others . . . however great in themselves dwindle into insignificance when compared with living testimony when your eyes see and your ears hear from the Living Oracles of God.[74]

A Season of Despair

Yet within two years, Joseph Smith was barred from entering the temple. Many lives were threatened and most of the faithful were forced to leave Kirtland for Missouri. A full rehearsal of such an ugly turn of events, what Benjamin F. Johnson referred to as "the first great apostasy," is beyond the scope of this work.[75] Suffice it to say that there was some lingering disaffection over aspects of Zion's Camp. More to the point, the Prophet had become entangled in a series of business activities,

---

the *Latter-Day Saints 1830–1900* (Salt Lake City: Deseret Book Company, 1982), 61.
74. Letter of Parley P. Pratt "to the Elders and Brethren of the Church of Latter Day Saints in Canada," John Taylor Collection, 27 November 1836, MS 1346, Church History Library. This is one of the very few accounts recorded in Church history where the Prophet spoke in a public meeting of his "first visions."
75. Anderson, *Joseph Smith's Kirtland*, 213.

most notably as cashier of the Kirtland Safety Society Bank, with Sidney Rigdon, president. Rich in land but poor in specie (gold and silver reserves), the Church needed a bank to pay debts, keep money in the town, and make credit available to the mercantile establishments in the community.

Formed in November 1836 but never chartered by the state of Ohio, the Kirtland Safety Society was forced to close its doors within a year in large measure because of a rampant spirit of greed and speculation then affecting so many in Kirtland, one greatly exacerbated by the worldwide Panic or economic collapse of 1837/38, in severity not unlike the Great Depression a century later. Hundreds of other banks across the country, many much larger than Kirtland's, failed or were at least temporarily forced to close. With the ensuing devaluation, the more than $150,000 in loans that the Church had taken out with merchants, banks, and eastern capitalists, left it in an exposed and precarious financial situation. Individuals holding large sums of irredeemable and virtually worthless banknotes, or who had lost their savings, complained bitterly of their losses. Soon Joseph was "wracked" with lawsuits. Whatever the various complicated reasons for the bank's failure, many believed that Joseph Smith, as revelator, should have seen it coming and done more to preserve their earnings and savings.[76] Though there was no intention on his or Sidney Rigdon's part to defraud any of their creditors, circumstances soon spiraled out of their control. As Eliza Ann Carter wrote at the time: "With regard to Joseph and Sidney's confessions they acknowledge they were men subjected to [like] passions as other men and they had [er]red in some things as well as others."[77]

As a consequence, many previously devoted members, including

---

76. Arrington, *Great Basin Kingdom*, 14. For much more recent primary research on the Kirtland Safety Society, see www.josephsmithpapers.org/the-papers/legal-business-and-financial-records/legal-business/jspplb1 (online only).
77. Eliza Ann Carter to James C. Snow, 22 July 1837, unpublished letter, in Reid N. Moon, "Jane Austen Meets the Wild West: Letter from a Young Woman in Kirtland," in *Meridian Magazine* (25 April 2017), http://ldsmag.com/jane-austen-meets-the-wild-west-letter-from-a-young-woman-in-kirtland/ (accessed 3 October 2018).

several of the John Johnson family, once so supportive, turned their backs on the Church in what was surely a disappointing, even devastating, night of apostasy. Other stalwarts such as Oliver Cowdery, Frederick G. Williams, and Orson and Parley P. Pratt also found themselves wavering in the faith. Caught up in the maelstrom of criticism, doubt, acrimony, and backbiting, dissenters disrupted temple meetings, mocked the faithful, and carried on disturbances of every kind. Things so deteriorated that Joseph and his wife, Emma, were locked out of the temple and, fearing mob violence, fled for their lives in the dead of night on 12 January 1838, never to return. The financial reversals at Kirtland and the lingering indebtedness may account for why the Church never built a temple in Far West or Adam-ondi-Ahman.

The collapse of the bank was a stinging reminder to Joseph Smith that he was a prophet, not a bishop, and certainly not a businessman, let alone a banker, and that he had a clearly defined spiritual mission but that "in temporal labors thou shalt not have strength, for this is not thy calling" (D&C 24:9). He could not afford to let his robust spiritual convictions and ambitions get too far ahead of the financial means to support them. It was a weakness that others would exploit and one that he would have to be reminded of over and over again.[78]

For many months the temple was left virtually vacant. But starting in 1840, some Latter-day Saints again began to gather to Kirtland. Under the direction of Almon W. Babbitt, the Church regrew in Kirtland reaching as many as 500 members, many arriving from Great Britain. Joseph Smith, however, called for them to leave Kirtland and gather in Nauvoo, where the Church had begun to settle in 1839. After Joseph Smith's death in 1844, various dissident groups tried to claim ownership of the temple but could not do so, since temple ownership was tied up in the complex legal

---

78. Marvin S. Hill, C. Keith Rooker, and Larry T. Wimmer, *The Kirtland Economy Revisited: A Market Critique of Sectarian Economics* (Provo, Utah: Brigham Young University Press, 1977), 40–42. Elder Dallin H. Oaks said of Joseph: "He was mortal and therefore subject to sin and error, pain and affliction." Dallin H. Oaks, "Joseph, the Man and the Prophet," *Ensign* (May 1996), 71.

"IT WAS A PENTECOST AND AN ENDOWMENT INDEED"

wrangling over the estate of Joseph Smith. Later Brigham Young tried hard to sell church properties, including both temples (Nauvoo and Kirtland) for much needed funds to finance the exodus west (see chapter 4).

In 1847 William E. McLellin, one of the original Twelve Apostles, established his short-lived Church of Christ in Kirtland and convinced Martin Harris, one of the Three Witnesses to the Book of Mormon, to become a member and caretaker of the temple, an assignment he followed assiduously for several years. McLellin's church failed, however, only to be followed by James Colin Brewster in 1849 and his efforts at establishing a church. Eventually Zadoc Brooks, Jason W. Briggs, and Zenos Gurley Sr. prevailed upon Joseph Smith's son, Joseph Smith III, to accept the leadership of the "New Organization" or Reorganized Church of Jesus Christ of Latter Day Saints organized in Amboy, Illinois, in 1860. Under Smith's steady direction the Reorganized Church gradually strengthened its claims to the temple. Finally gaining legal ownership of the temple in 1880 after protracted legal proceedings, the RLDS Church (today the Community of Christ) has ever since performed an admirable service in continuing to maintain and safeguard the Kirtland Temple and to welcome visitors to this shared sacred space.[79]

CONCLUSION

Kirtland was a crucible of faith for the Latter-day Saints, a place of glory as well as agony. While several deserted the Church, many more retained their allegiance. But there was little future for them in what had become a bedrock of internal dissension and persecution, a tragic end to a once glorious enterprise. "All our friends design leaving this place as soon as possible," wrote Hepzibah Richards in January 1838. "The feeling seems

---

79. Kim Loving, "Ownership of the Kirtland Temple: Legends, Lies and Misunderstandings," *Journal of Mormon History* 30, issue 2 (2004); see also Howlett, *Kirtland Temple*. Over the past 140 years, members of both The Church of Jesus Christ of Latter-day Saints and Community of Christ have sometimes sparred over the meaning and significance of the Kirtland Temple. Both would agree, however, that it is indeed shared "sacred space," a place for religious pilgrimage, and a remarkable legacy of revelation and community, hope and faith.

to be that Kirtland must be trodden down by the wicked for a season. Probably several hundred families will leave within a few weeks."[80] In what is remembered as the "Kirtland Camp" or "Camp of the Saints," 515 faithful Saints left Kirtland for good on a forlorn day in July 1838 bound for somewhere in Missouri to join with the rest of the faithful. Besides ninety-seven horses, seventy cows, twenty-two oxen, and one bull, along with a host of smaller animals, they took with them a caravan of memories, some good and some cruel.[81] Helen Mar Kimball Whitney, daughter of Newel K. and Elizabeth Ann Whitney, remembered the moment with sadness: "For years after we left Kirtland, I used to look back and pine for the old scenes and school companions; those happy days were lived over again and again in bright dreams and when I would awaken . . . the thought that I could never see or enjoy them again would make me sad, and sometimes I would cry bitterly."[82]

They may have left their temple on a hill still sparkling in the afternoon sun, but not the memory of its endowment of hope and promise, a pillar of their faith. The fact is, as historian Richard Bushman argues, by the time Kirtland was vacated, temples "had become an obsession" to Joseph Smith and others.[83] Temples, not chapels, were the critical thing and they would be worth every sacrifice and every expenditure, no matter what the cost or the controversy. And if they had their way, the Kirtland Temple would not be their last.

---

80. Hepzibah Richards, "Letter to Willard Richards," 18 January and 29 January 1838, as cited in Max H. Parkin, "Conflict at Kirtland: A Study of the Nature and Causes of Internal and External Conflict of the Mormons in Ohio Between 1830 and 1838" (master's thesis, Brigham Young University, 1966), 326.
81. Staker, *Hearken, O Ye People*, xxxiv.
82. Helen Mar Whitney, "Life Incidents," *Woman's Exponent* 9 (August 15, 1880): 42, as cited in Staker, *Hearken, O Ye People*, 555.
83. Richard Lyman Bushman, *Joseph Smith: Rough Stone Rolling* (New York: Alfred A. Knopf, 2005), 218.

Chapter 2
"In the Similitude of a Palace"
THE NAUVOO TEMPLE PART ONE, 1837–1842

As we approached it we lifted up our eyes and beheld the greatness grandeur and glory that presented itself to our view in a conspicuous manner. While she was covered with the silver rays of the Queen of the night who was pouring the whole strength of the brightness of her glory upon her it presented an imposing, grand, and sublime scenery to the beholder. . . . I prayed that the Saints might have power to finish the Temple according to the pattern given, and accepted at their hands, that the Saints might receive their endowment, and be prepared to plant the work of God in all the world.[1]

So wrote Wilford Woodruff in August 1844—two months after the martyrdom of Joseph and Hyrum Smith—of a Nauvoo Temple still awaiting completion. A member of the Council of the Twelve Apostles since 1838, Woodruff was drawn to temple work in early Latter-day Saint history more than almost any other person. Like iron filings to a magnet, he was captivated by a relentless desire to work for the redemption of his deceased family. It became for him a righteous obsession. The next two chapters, therefore, will place the history of the original Nauvoo Temple and its budding sacred ordinances as revealed by the Prophet Joseph Smith

---
1. *Wilford Woodruff's Journal*, 2:456–57, 27 August 1844.

within the context of the rapidly developing doctrine of redemption of the dead in Latter-day Saint history.

While Kirtland was rapidly growing, many Saints had been striving to build up the Church in Missouri since 1830. Mention has already been made of the failed attempt to build the Independence Temple, prohibited in large measure by persistent persecution that drove the Saints first across the Missouri River into Clay County in 1832/33. Three years later the Saints began to congregate northward in Daviess and Caldwell counties, which the Missouri state legislature carved out of a western wilderness as a stopgap effort to solve the "Mormon problem." In Caldwell County, in April 1837, under the inspired direction primarily of John Whitmer, one of the Eight Witnesses to the Book of Mormon, the Saints established their aptly named community of Far West (originally called Shoal Creek) some sixty miles north of present-day Kansas City, Missouri. Laid out in blocks twenty-four rods square with four principal avenues, the city soon grew to some 5,000 inhabitants. Joseph Smith and his family, along with most faithful Kirtland Saints, moved there in early 1838 to escape the deepening Ohio persecutions.

Far West is fondly remembered for many highly significant reasons. While there, Joseph Smith received eight revelations in the current edition of the Doctrine and Covenants (Sections 113–120) concerning the law of tithing, the official name of the Church, Adam-ondi-Ahman and the Ancient of Days, and the calling of Wilford Woodruff and others to replace original apostles who had fallen away. Far West was also the beginning place of the amazingly "effectual" mission of the Twelve to Great Britain (1839–1841) and the organization of a stake in Zion. Likewise it was there that Joseph Smith began his dictation of his well-known account of the First Vision "owing to the many reports which [had] been put in circulation by evil-disposed and designing persons" (Joseph Smith–History 1:1).

"IN THE SIMILITUDE OF A PALACE"

Far West Temple Site, Missouri.

Many also contemplated building another temple there. At eight-thirty on the morning of 3 July 1837, after prayer, singing, and exhortation, the Saints broke ground and excavated a 120-foot by 80-foot area for the proposed new temple. Within hours more than 500 men using mattocks, spades, and wheelbarrows had dug a cellar to the depth of five feet. They soon hauled in stone from a nearby quarry and put three cornerstones in place with a fourth one added by members of the Council of the Twelve early in the morning of 26 April 1839 when they returned at the risk of their lives to be set apart for their mission to Great Britain.[2] Had it not been for the financially strained condition of the Church and further rounds of persecution that ended in the massacre at Haun's Mill and the infamous extermination order of Governor Lilburn W. Boggs in October of 1838, perhaps a temple might now stand in Far West. But by April 1839, after Joseph Smith's guard-assisted escape from Liberty Jail, he and most of the Saints had already fled east to Quincy, Illinois, in search of a

---

2. From an account by W. W. Phelps in "History of Joseph Smith," *Millennial Star* 16:13, as quoted in Ronald E. Romig, *Eighth Witness: The Biography of John Whitmer* (Independence, Missouri: John Whitmer Books, 2014), 315–16, also 543–44.

friendlier environment. Today, Far West is but a windswept memory with little remaining of a thriving city that once boasted hundreds of homes, workshops, stores, hotels, schoolhouses, and much more.

The Latter-day Saints also considered building a temple at Adam-ondi-Ahman, a two-square-mile settlement of 1838 in Daviess County, Missouri. The Prophet indicated this was the site where Adam, after having been driven out of the Garden of Eden (Jackson County), gathered his righteous posterity and bestowed upon them his final blessing. He also prophesied that it will be "the place where Adam shall come to visit his people, or the Ancient of days shall sit as spoken of by Daniel the Prophet."[3] Lyman Wight was among the very first of some 400 people who settled there. Adam-ondi-Ahman was soon abandoned, however, and fell into the hands of other settlers beginning in the summer of 1839, but not before the Saints had laid out a four-acre lot on a two-mile public square upon which they envisioned building yet another temple. Brigham Young dedicated a site for such a temple somewhere on this public square site.[4] Had the Independence, Far West, and Adam-ondi-Ahman temples been built, they likely would have performed much the same role as the Kirtland Temple, i.e., a point of departure for mission service, a place for living ordinances for men only, and possibly further spiritual outpourings as witnessed in Ohio.

In retrospect, the Saints could not have chosen a more difficult place at a more difficult time and among a more difficult people to establish their dream of a new Zion than Missouri. One can try to explain these intense Missouri persecutions on cultural, economic, and religious grounds. For example, no doubt the issue of slavery was a critical cultural incompatibility. Most of the Latter-day Saints were from New England and New York. Some, like William W. Phelps, the editor of the *Evening and Morning Star*, the Church's first newspaper, were abolitionists trying to set up shop

---

3. *JSP, Journals* 1:271, 19 May 1838; see also D&C 116.
4. Alexander L. Baugh, "The History and Doctrine of the Adam-ondi-Ahman Revelation (D&C 116)" in *Foundations of the Restoration: Fulfillment of the Covenant Purposes*, ed. Craig Ostler, Michael MacKay, and Barbara Morgan Gardner (Provo, Utah: Religious Studies Center, Brigham Young University; Salt Lake City: Deseret Book Company, 2016), 176–77.

in a state that had paid dearly to enter the Union in 1820 as a slave state. Jackson County, nicknamed "Little Dixie" well before the Saints arrived, saw more slave-holding, Southern immigrants settle there than in any other county in the state. The Nat Turner Rebellion in Virginia of August 1831 had placed the South on a war footing, with mobs and lynchings widely proliferating in its wake. William Ellery Channing, theologian and social critic, remembered 1834 as a time when American "society was shaken to its foundations." And John Quincy Adams despairingly wrote in that same year, "My hopes of the long continuance of this Union are extinct."[5] Indeed, 1834 is still remembered as the most violent year in American history for its recurring scene of riots all across the land and was, in the words of historian Carl Prince, "politics-out-of-doors."[6]

According to their own revelations, however, the primary reason for their failure to establish Zion in Missouri was one of their own making—a matter of failing to live a higher law of righteousness. "I, the Lord, have suffered the affliction to come upon them, wherewith they have been afflicted, in consequence of their own transgressions. . . . There were jarrings, and contentions, and envyings, and strifes, and lustful and covetous desires among them; therefore by these things they polluted their inheritances" (D&C 101:2, 6).

Their situation only deteriorated in Caldwell and Daviess counties later that decade. Internal contentions led to the defection and excommunication of such renowned leaders as Oliver Cowdery, David and John Whitmer, Frederick G. Williams, W. W. Phelps, Thomas B. Marsh, and many others.[7] All these difficulties led to the "Mormon Missouri War" of 1838 with atrocities committed on both sides.

The forced confinement of Joseph Smith and his colleagues in Liberty Jail from December 1838 until their escape in April 1839 will forever rank

---

5. Carl E. Prince, "The Great 'Riot Year': Jacksonian Democracy and Patterns of Violence in 1834," *Journal of the Early Republic* 5 (1985): 3–4.
6. Prince, "The Great 'Riot Year,'" 4.
7. Many of these same men came back to the Church in later times. These included Cowdery, Williams, Phelps, and a great many others.

as a most poignant interlude in history. Suffering through five months of cold, winter darkness, filth, rotten food, sickness, and solitude, Joseph described it as a place of "grates and screeking iron doors," "dirty straw couches," and "nauseous" smells, a perfect "hell surrounded with demons."[8] Innocent of any crime and waiting for a trial to prove it, the Prophet had ample time to reflect not only on his own sufferings but also on the even worse sacrifices of the members in Kirtland and Missouri, particularly those who were giving their lives for joining the Church—as seventeen men and boys had recently done at Haun's Mill. As former Church historian Leonard Arrington once noted, while in jail Joseph was free from the press of daily business and "had uninterrupted time to think out the wider implication of the Latter-day movement. The Liberty Jail experience brought him to communicate in an unhurried manner with the Lord."[9] And as H. Dean Garrett has written, "Liberty Jail was a spiritual watershed for Joseph Smith. He left jail a different man than when he entered it. His own spiritual depths were plumbed, and a deeper understanding gained."[10] As dark and miserable as it surely was, Liberty Jail was nevertheless temple-like in that it was a time of reflection, soul-searching, and revelation.

Near the end of his incarceration, Joseph penned a most revealing letter to Prescindia Buell, one of his later plural wives, in which he hinted at some of the great truths he was about to reveal.

> *I want the blessing once more to lift my voice in the midst of the Saints[.] I would pour out my soul to God for their instruction it has been the plan of the Devil to hamper me and distress me from*

---

8. Dean C. Jessee, "'Walls, Grates and Screeking Iron Doors': The Prison Experience of Mormon Leaders in Missouri, 1838–1839" in *New Views of Mormon History: Essays in Honor of Leonard J. Arrington*, ed. Maurine Ursenbach Beecher and Davis Bitton (Salt Lake City: University of Utah Press, 1987), 25.
9. Leonard J. Arrington, "Church Leaders in Liberty Jail" in *BYU Studies* 13, no. 1 (Winter 1973): 23.
10. H. Dean Garrett, "Seven Letters from Liberty" in *Regional Studies in Latter-day Saint History: Missouri*, ed. Arnold K. Garr and C. V. Johnson (Provo, Utah: Department of Church History and Doctrine, Brigham Young University, 1994), 198; see also Jeffrey R. Holland, "Lessons from Liberty Jail," 17 September 2008, CES Fireside, BYU Speeches of the Year.

"IN THE SIMILITUDE OF A PALACE"

Liberty Jail, Missouri.

the beginning to keep me from explaining myself to them and I never have had opportunity to give them the plan that God has revealed to me for many have run without being sent crying tidings my Lord and have done much injury to the Church giving the Devil more power over those that walk by sight and not by faith. [But troubles] will only give us that knowledge to understand the minds of the Ancients[.] [F]or my part I think I never could have felt as I now do if I had not suffered the wrongs that I have suffered all things shall work together for good to them that love God.[11]

More than anything else, the Prophet longed for additional time and opportunity to explain to the Saints "the plan that God has revealed to me . . . the minds of the Ancients." Whatever that "plan" was in detail, it

---

11. Mark Ashurt-McGee, et al., eds., *Documents, Volume 6: February 1838–August 1839* in Documents series of *The Joseph Smith Papers*, ed. Ronald K. Esplin, Matthew J. Grow, and Matthew C. Godfrey (Salt Lake City: The Church Historian's Press, 2017), 355. See also Dean C. Jessee, *The Personal Writings of Joseph Smith* (Salt Lake City: Deseret Book Company, 1984), 386–87, 15 March 1839.

would require the building of a temple in which to reveal it. "Verily I say unto you, let this house be built unto my name, that I may reveal mine ordinances therein unto my people," declared a revelation to him in 1841. "For I deign to reveal unto my church things which have been kept hid from before the foundation of the world, things that pertain to the dispensation of the fulness of times. And I will show unto my servant Joseph all things pertaining to this house, and the priesthood thereof, and the place whereon it shall be built" (D&C 124:40–42).[12] Joseph Smith did live to escape to Illinois and had another five years to explain to the Saints those things he had learned from experience, deep sorrow, and revelation.

The exodus east from Far West, Missouri, to Quincy, Illinois, that mournful winter of 1838/39 was a harrowing, horrible experience that resulted in the death and suffering of many souls. Little wonder that Joseph, on his escape to Quincy in April, praised the citizens there as "good Samaritans" for taking in so many thousands of his people. While some believed it best for the Saints not to become an assembled target and to remain in scattered settlements in Adams County, Joseph announced in the May conference held in Quincy that it was best to congregate in one place, if for no other reason than to have the assembled manpower to build a "palace" to the Lord. His vision of a new temple in large part led to the decision to leave Quincy in 1839 for Commerce, Illinois, some fifty miles north, where they had procured sufficient property to build their "City Beautiful"—Nauvoo.[13]

"GLAD TIDINGS FROM CUMORAH"
—BAPTISMS FOR THE DEAD

The legacy of the Nauvoo Temple is far more than brick and mortar, as important as the building's architecture may be. It is the remarkable account of a developing doctrine of salvation for all men and women,

---

12. See also D&C 128:16 where Joseph Smith references Paul's statement on baptism for the dead.
13. See Susan Easton Black and Richard E. Bennett, eds., *A City of Refuge: Quincy, Illinois* (Salt Lake City: Millennial Press, 2000).

living and dead. There were three key additions to the temple work in Nauvoo that were not in evidence in Kirtland: 1) the application of saving ordinances for the dead; 2) the inclusion of women in all the saving/exalting ordinances that would soon be revealed; and 3) an emphasis on the Melchizedek Priesthood and its keys. And if such were part of the "plan of the Ancients," then one must think of the Book of Mormon, the Book of Moses, and perhaps even the Book of Abraham, as ever-increasing influences on the Prophet's thought.

To simplify a sacred complexity, temple work as revealed and taught by the Prophet Joseph Smith in Nauvoo might best be understood doctrinally from four complementary perspectives: priesthood and priesthood keys; the universality of the Resurrection; marriage, gender, and family as prerequisite to eternal progression; and finally, personal covenant-making, validated by the Holy Spirit. Paradoxically, all these ordinances associated with temple work in Nauvoo, including baptisms for the dead, anointings, the endowment, and eternal or celestial marriage were first given outside of the temple while Joseph Smith was still alive, as if he never expected to live to see the temple completed. What he needed to reveal to his people had to be done in a relatively hurried and distracted way, some things here and other things there, and often in the face of increasing persecutions from without and criticisms from within. He did not have the luxury of presenting all these new truths in a careful, measured way. What he was able to do was to teach and prepare the Quorum of the Twelve, led by Brigham Young, in all these matters and to prepare them sufficiently to become the "sympathetic stewards" of these ordinances in case of his absence.[14]

The origins of Joseph Smith's revelation on the ordinance of baptisms for the dead remain unclear. Obviously it owed much to the doctrine of baptism for the living for the remission of sins which John the Baptist had proclaimed in his earthly ministry and again on the banks of the

---

14. Andrew F. Ehat, "Joseph Smith's Introduction of Temple Ordinances and the 1844 Mormon Succession Question" (master's thesis, Brigham Young University, 1982), 9.

Susquehanna River when, as a resurrected being, he had supervised and directed the baptisms of Joseph Smith and Oliver Cowdery. "Except a man be born of water and of the Spirit, he cannot enter into the kingdom of God" (John 3:5). "Glad tidings from Cumorah" is how Joseph referred to this new ordinance in an 1841 revelation. Moroni's 1823 instructions on turning the hearts of the fathers to the children and vice versa found fruition in Joseph's teachings on the banks of the Mississippi eighteen years later.[15]

There were at least four causal factors for his Nauvoo pronouncement of the ordinance of baptism for the dead. Though not listed in any particular order, the first may have been the developing understanding of the priesthood, the place and purpose of the spirit world—that state of existence between death and the Resurrection—and the role of Jesus Christ in its redemptive purposes. From the Book of Moses as revealed in 1830, Joseph had learned that the spirits of evil men and women consigned to the prison of the spirit world would suffer there in torment *until* Christ completes His work (Moses 7:39). This same doctrine was reiterated in 1832 in the Vision (D&C 76:85, 106) in which Joseph and Sidney Rigdon learned not only about the three degrees of glory in the eternities hereafter but also much concerning the interim state of men and women in the spirit world. The wicked who are consigned to the nether realms of the spirit world, in some cases for thousands of years (since "the days of Noah" as the apostle Peter declared, 1 Peter 3:20), will suffer there but only "*until* the last resurrection" and "*until* the fulness of times, when

---

15. The standard doctrinal study of temples in Latter-day Saint theology remains James E. Talmage, *The House of the Lord*. For his treatment of baptisms for the dead, see pages 79–82. See also Boyd K. Packer, *The Holy Temple* (Salt Lake City: Bookcraft, 1982). Two recent introductory academic studies of baptisms for the dead in ancient times are David L. Paulsen, Roger D. Cook, and Brock M. Mason, "Theological Underpinnings of Baptism for the Dead," *Brigham Young University Studies Quarterly*, 55, no. 3 (2016): 101–16, which is more a theological essay. For a more historical study, see Ryan G. Tobler, "'Saviors on Mount Zion': Mormon Sacramentalism, Mortality, and the Baptism for the Dead," *Journal of Mormon History* 39, no. 4 (2013): 181–238; John A. Tvedtnes, "Baptism for the Dead in Early Christianity," *The Temple in Time and Eternity*, ed. Donald W. Parry and Stephen D. Ricks (Provo, Utah: The Foundation for Ancient Research and Mormon Studies, Brigham Young University, 1999), 43–54; and Jeffrey A. Trumbower, *Rescue for the Dead: The Posthumous Salvation of Non-Christians in Early Christianity* (New York: Oxford University Press, 2001).

Christ shall have subdued all enemies under his feet, and shall have perfected his work" (D&C 76:85, 106, italics added). Eventually, after a period of gospel instruction, personal repentance, and the miracle of Christ's redemption, even they will come forth to some degree of heavenly reward. In other words, God's punishment is not eternal in the sense that it is endless, but "eternal" in that it is named after Him and will mercifully have an end (D&C 19:6–12).[16] The prison or hell of the spirit world is, therefore, a temporary and redemptive one, not an eternal and everlasting vengeful consignment. The work of redemption will eventually lead almost all men who repent to some degree of heavenly glory. Again from James E. Talmage: "Some degree of salvation will come to all who have not forfeited their right to it."[17] Though not a Universalist doctrine that taught the same heavenly reward eventually for everyone, the doctrine of spirit world redemption is nonetheless a doctrine of minimizing hell and maximizing heaven, yet without either robbing justice or restricting mercy. As the Prophet taught in a July 1838 sermon in Far West: "All those who have not had an opportunity of hearing the gospel, and being administered to by an inspired man in the flesh, must have it hereafter before they can be finally judged."[18] A year later he further added: "The hearts of the children of men will have to be turned to the fathers & the fathers to the children, living or dead, to prepare them for the coming of the Son of Man. If Elijah did not come the whole earth would be Smitten."[19]

In a pivotal sermon given in October 1841, Joseph Smith returned

---

16. Rodney Turner put it this way: "The quality of God's punishment is transcendently superior to that of men, being truly redemptive in nature. Its purpose is not only to meet the demands of injured justice but to allow mercy, on conditions of repentance, to claim its own. Salvation through reformation is the grand goal of eternal punishment." Rodney Turner, "Jesus Christ and the Command to Repent (D&C 18 and 19)," in *Studies in Scripture: Volume One, The Doctrine and Covenants*, ed. Robert L. Millet and Kent P. Jackson (Salt Lake City: Deseret Book Company, 1989), 104.
17. James E. Talmage, *House of the Lord*, 84.
18. *Elders' Journal of The Church of Jesus Christ of Latter-day Saints* 1:43, July 1838, as cited in Alexander L. Baugh, "'For This Ordinance Belongeth to My House': The Practice of Baptism for the Dead Outside the Nauvoo Temple," *Mormon Historical Studies* 3, no. 1 (Spring 2002): 47.
19. "Discourse, between circa 26 June and circa 4 August 1839–A, as reported by Willard Richards," in *JSP, Documents* 6:546.

to the doctrine of the living being saviors on Mt. Zion. He said of this new ordinance of baptism for the dead that by actively engaging in rites of salvation "substitutionally," men and women become "instrumental in bringing multitudes of their kin into the kingdom of God." He continued: "There is a way to release the spirit of the dead; that is by the power and authority of the Priesthood—by binding and loosing on earth. This doctrine appears glorious, inasmuch as it exhibits the greatness of divine compassion and benevolence in the extent of the plan of human salvation. . . . Those saints who neglect it in behalf of their deceased relatives, do it at the peril of their own salvation."[20]

A second contributing factor was of long-standing consideration and extended back to the untimely death of his beloved older brother, Alvin, in 1823, a remarkable stroke of misfortune. As Samuel Brown has commented, "The Mormon prophet never fully recovered from Alvin's death" and it cast "a long shadow" over the rest of his life.[21] Joseph Smith's vision of Alvin in the Kirtland Temple thirteen years after his brother's death proved remarkably therapeutic and redemptive. "I saw Father Adam, Abraham; and my father and my mother; [and] my brother Alvin, that has long since slept; [I] marveled how it was that he had obtained an inheritance in that kingdom, seeing that he had departed this life before the Lord had set his hand to gather Israel . . . and had not been baptized for the remission of sins" (D&C 137:5–6). As historian Guy Bishop and others have noted, the vision may well have contributed to the restoration of the doctrine and practice of baptism for the dead.[22] The further

---

20. Sermon delivered by Joseph Smith at the general conference of the Church in Nauvoo 3 October 1841, as found in *Times and Seasons* 2 (15 October 1841): 577–78; see also *History of the Church*, 4:425–26.
21. Samuel Morris Brown, *In Heaven as It Is on Earth: Joseph Smith and the Early Mormon Conquest of Death* (Oxford and New York: Oxford University Press, 2012), 35.
22. M. Guy Bishop, "'What Has Become of Our Fathers?' Baptism for the Dead at Nauvoo," *Dialogue: A Journal of Mormon Thought* 23, no. 2 (Summer 1990): 86.

fact that Alvin's proxy baptism was one of the very first performed in the Mississippi River lends credence to this point of view.[23]

A third and most immediate prompt for declaring baptism for the dead might likely have been the specter of death and dying that surrounded its pronouncement. Certainly the doctrine came out of a context of death that hovered over them as a gloomy cloud as they valiantly drained the malaria-infested swamps near the Mississippi River. Scores were dying from exposure brought on from their forced exodus from Missouri, their lack of proper medical treatment, and diseases such as malaria and others. Over fifty Saints had died during the Missouri persecutions, at least sixty-one perished in 1839, and another sixty-three in 1840, for an alarmingly high mortality rate of approximately 30/1,000.[24] Although he called their city "Nauvoo the Beautiful," Joseph once described it as "a deathly sickly hole" and admitted that "although we have been keeping up appearances, and holding out inducements to encourage immigration, that we scarcely think justifiable in consequence of the mortality that almost invariably awaits those who come from far distant parts."[25]

Although Joseph and others administered healing blessings upon many, the doctrine of baptism for the dead gave comfort to the dying and their survivors alike. Joseph's own father took sick early in 1839 and suffered in ill health until his death on 14 September 1840. Don Carlos, Joseph's brother, died less than a year later at age twenty-five of pneumonia. Before his death, the Smith patriarch called his children to his bedside, gave each one a final blessing, and assured his son, Joseph, that he would live to finish his work. In his final moments, he saw Alvin, his

---

23. The precise date of Alvin's proxy baptism in 1840 is not given. The ordinance was performed for Alvin a second time by Hyrum in 1841, and was probably repeated in the temple after the font was completed and dedicated. Baugh, "'For This Ordinance Belongeth to My House,'" 49. Many of the baptisms performed in the river were repeated later in the temple.
24. Evan Ivie and Douglas C. Heiner, "Deaths in Early Nauvoo, Illinois, 1839–1846, and in Winter Quarters, Nebraska, 1846–1848," in *Religious Educator* 10, no. 3 (2009): 163–74. For the numbers who died in Missouri, see remarks by B. H. Roberts, Conference Reports (October 1907), 118–19.
25. Joseph Smith letter to Horace R. Hotchkiss, *History of the Church*, 4:407, 25 August 1841. Joseph and Emma's fourteen-month-old son, Don Carlos, died less than a month later.

oldest, who had died seventeen years before.[26] With death striking down men, women, and children all around, it was probably not coincidental that the Prophet proclaimed the practice of baptism for the dead on 15 August 1840 at a funeral—specifically, that of forty-one-year-old Seymour Brunson, a devoted friend of the Prophet's and a member of the Nauvoo High Council, a man who died "in the triumph of faith, and in his dying moments bore testimony to the Gospel that he had embraced."[27]

A fourth factor may well have been Joseph's translation or rather inspired revision of the Holy Bible, particularly the writings of Paul the Apostle. "I cannot in this letter give you all the information you desire on the subject," he wrote to the Traveling High Council in October 1840, "but . . . I would say that it was certainly practiced by the ancient churches; and St. Paul endeavors to prove the doctrine of the resurrection from the same, and says, 'Else what shall they do which are baptized for the dead, if the dead rise not at all? Why are they then baptized for the dead?'"[28]

At first, baptisms for the dead were no more associated with temple work than were living baptisms. The first documented baptism for the dead occurred less than a month after Brunson's funeral when on 12 September 1840 Jane Neyman requested that Harvey Olmstead baptize her in behalf of her deceased son, Cyrus Livingston Neyman. Vienna Jacques, a nurse and convert from Massachusetts, splashed into the river on horseback to witness the performance of the ordinance. Many other such baptisms soon followed with men and women being baptized indiscriminately for

---

26. Gary A. Anderson, "Joseph Smith Sr.," in *Encyclopedia of Mormonism*, 3:1349. According to Lucy Mack Smith, Joseph's mother, Joseph informed his dying father "that it was then the privilege of the Saints to be baptized for the dead, and Mr. Smith requested that Joseph be baptized for Alvin immediately." Scot Facer Proctor and Maurine Jensen Proctor, eds., *The Revised and Enhanced History of Joseph Smith by His Mother* (Salt Lake City: Deseret Book Company, 1996), 433. Joseph himself did not perform any proxy baptisms, but his brother, Hyrum, did. "Nauvoo Baptisms for the Dead, Book A" as cited in Larry C. Porter, "Alvin Smith: Reminder of the Fairness of God," *Ensign* (September 1978): 65–67.
27. *Joseph Smith Papers, History* 1838–1856, volume C–1 [2 November 1838–31 July 1842], 1089, http://www.josephsmithpapers.org/paper-summary/history-1838-1856-volume-c-1-2-november-1838-31-july-1842/261 (online only). Entry for Seymour Brunson who caught cold one night while seeking after stray cattle and died.
28. *History of the Church*, 4:231, and 1 Corinthians 15:29.

"IN THE SIMILITUDE OF A PALACE"

The Mississippi River at Nauvoo, Illinois.

deceased friends and ancestors, regardless of gender. Wrote Vilate Kimball: "Since this order has been preached here, the waters have been continually troubled."²⁹

Word soon spread as the appeal of this unique ordinance stirred the souls of the Saints even beyond Nauvoo. For instance, in November 1840 members in Quincy, Illinois, were performing baptisms for the dead in the Mississippi. The same occurred back in Kirtland where in May 1841, Almon W. Babbitt, stake president there, supervised twenty-five proxy baptisms in the Chagrin River in the shadow of the Kirtland Temple, before receiving instructions to suspend the practice until further notice.³⁰

---

29. Vilate Kimball to Heber C. Kimball on 11 October 1840 as cited in Tobler, "Saviors on Mount Zion," 203.
30. A few baptisms for the dead were performed in the Chagrin River in Kirtland in the early 1840s under the direction of Almon W. Babbitt, but these were soon discontinued. Alexander L. Baugh, "'For Their Salvation Is Necessary and Essential to Our Salvation': Joseph Smith and the Practice of Baptism and Confirmation for the Dead," in *An Eye of Faith: Essays Written in Honor of Richard O. Cowan,* ed. Kenneth L. Alford and Richard E. Bennett (Provo, Utah: Religious Studies Center, Brigham Young University; Salt Lake City: Deseret Book Company, 2015), 120–21. A lawyer by profession and known for his headstrong, often contrary personality, Babbitt led independent efforts to revive Kirtland as a gathering place, which brought him rebuke and chastisement from Church leaders in Nauvoo and likely contributed to Joseph Smith's determination to

Like children on Christmas morning, and with a budding sense of victory over death, the Saints' enthusiasm was unbounded. "Brother Joseph has opened a new and glorious subject of late," wrote Vilate Kimball to her husband, Heber C. Kimball, "which has caused quite a revival in the Church . . . that is baptism of the dead."[31] Where and when the ordinance was performed, who the witnesses were, and what the gender was were far less important than the ordinance itself.[32] This informality gradually systemized, however, beginning in early January 1841 when the Prophet revealed that it was to be performed in "a baptismal font" and that "it belongeth to my house, and cannot be acceptable to me, only in the days of your poverty . . . I command you, all ye my saints, to build a house unto me" (D&C 124:29–31). Further instructions followed in September 1842 which called for the keeping of careful records and the appointment of "a recorder" to be an "eye-witness of your baptisms . . . that in all your recordings it may be recorded in heaven; whatsoever you bind on earth, may be bound in heaven" (D&C 127:6–7). Such instructions were very much in accordance with the tradition of the Church since its formation of keeping careful records of all ordinances performed since it was well established even then that an ordinance without a proper record was invalid.[33]

Still, there was a grace period given for "I grant unto you a sufficient time to build a house unto me; and during this time your baptisms shall be

---

restrict baptisms for the dead to the Nauvoo Temple only. See also Baugh, "'For This Ordinance Belongeth to My House,'" 52.

31. Tobler, "Saviors on Mount Zion," 203.
32. Years later, Brigham Young commented on the experimental nature of these initial baptisms for the dead:

"You recollect that when this doctrine was first revealed and in hurrying in the administration of baptisms for the dead, that sisters were baptized for their male friends, were baptized for their fathers, their grandfathers, their mothers and their grandmothers, etc. I just mention this so that you will come to understanding, that as we knew nothing about this matter at first, the old Saints recollect, there was little by little given, and the subject was made plain, but little was given at once. Consequently, in the first place people were baptized for their friends and no record was kept. Joseph afterwards kept a record, etc. Then women were baptized for men and men for women." Young, in *Journal of Discourses* 16:165, as cited in Baugh, "For This Ordinance Belongeth to My House," 49–50.

33. *History of the Church*, 5:141.

acceptable unto me" (D&C 124:31). River baptisms therefore continued throughout much of 1841. At least 6,818 baptisms for the dead were performed in the river with most being done for deceased aunts, uncles, and parents, followed closely by grandparents and great-grandparents. While 55 percent were for males and 45 percent for deceased females, 43.9 percent of those baptisms were done by women for men or men for women, many of which were redone in future years in Utah.[34] Several people took it upon themselves to baptize for the dead such leading political figures as Benjamin Franklin, James Madison, Thomas Jefferson, and George Washington. Emma Smith was baptized in behalf of her father, Isaac Hale, who had died just two years before and who had so vehemently opposed her marriage to Joseph Smith. Lucy Mack Smith performed the ordinance for her parents, Solomon and Lydia Mack, and for her sister, Louisa Tuttle. Hyrum Smith acted as proxy for his brother Alvin. Although Joseph Smith himself is never listed as a proxy, he personally performed at least 105 baptisms in the Mississippi River.[35]

Then on 8 November 1841 in the basement and underneath the main hall of the temple, Brigham Young dedicated a temporary, oval-shaped covered wooden font made of pine timber. The font rested on the backs of twelve beautifully carved oxen, four on each side, representing the twelve tribes of Israel.[36] There, less than two weeks later on 21 November, Brigham Young, Heber C. Kimball, and John Taylor performed the first baptisms for the dead in the temple for approximately forty persons with Willard Richards, George A. Smith, and Wilford Woodruff performing the confirmations.[37] Observed Wilford Woodruff: "It was the first

---

34. Bishop, "What Has Become of Our Fathers?," 88.
35. Bishop, "What Has Become of Our Fathers?," 92.
36. Put together with tongue-and-groove staves, the font was sixteen feet long east and west, twelve feet wide and seven feet high. The basin was four feet deep with water supplied from a well thirty feet deep in the east end of the basement. The oxen, carved and designed by Elijah Fordham, were made of pine plank, glued together, and copied after "the most beautiful 5-year old steer that could be found in the country." *History of the Church*, 4:446. A flight of stairs in the north and south sides led up and down into the basin, guarded by side railings.
37. *Times and Seasons* 6 (20 January 1846): 1096; see Baugh, "For This Ordinance Belongeth to My House," 53.

font erected for this glorious purpose in this last dispensation."[38] On 28 December Joseph baptized Sidney Rigdon "for and in behalf of his father, William Rigdon, who had died in 1810, and his mother, Nancy Gallagher Rigdon, who had died just two years before."[39] Wilford Woodruff reported going "to the pool" on 15 May 1842 and baptizing "in company with Charles C. Rich about 100 persons," including his great-grandfather and many of the progenitors of his wife, Phoebe.[40] Not until early 1846 did a stone font replace the temporary wooden structure. Gradually it became standard procedure to allow only those who were paying their tithing to have access to the baptismal font, establishing a precedent for the current practice of requiring temple recommends for entrance to the temple. Said John Taylor, "A man who has not paid his tithing is unfit to be baptized for his dead."[41]

There are no available data for the number of baptisms for the dead performed in 1842, but in 1843 at least 1,329 proxy baptisms were performed and another 3,359 the following year. For no clear reason, only twenty-four were counted in all of 1845, perhaps because of rising persecutions and intensifying preparations to leave for the West.[42] By February 1846, with the Saints beginning to leave Nauvoo for a new home in the West, over 15,000 proxy baptisms had been performed in Nauvoo. The impact upon the membership is hard to overstate. Concluded scholar

---

38. *Wilford Woodruff's Journal*, 2:138, 21 November 1841. A most devoted disciple of this new work for the dead, Woodruff performed at least 130 proxy baptisms in the year 1842. See *Wilford Woodruff's Journal*, 2:204–5.
39. Andrew H. Hedges, Alex D. Smith, and Richard Lloyd Anderson, eds., *Journals Vol. 2: December 1841–April 1843*, in Journal series of *The Joseph Smith Papers*, ed. Dean C. Jesse, Ronald K. Esplin, and Richard Lyman Bushman (Salt Lake City: The Church Historian's Press, 2011), 19.
40. *Wilford Woodruff's Journal*, 2:176, 15 May 1842.
41. Journal History of The Church of Jesus Christ of Latter-day Saints, 6 October 1844, CR 100 137, Church Historian's Office, Church History Library, Salt Lake City; as cited in Bishop, "What Has Become of Our Fathers?," 93. The Journal History is a massive collection of news clippings and other news items covering daily events in Mormon history. Compiled by the late Andrew Jensen and covering the years from 1830 to 2008, the collection is open to all.
42. Nauvoo Baptisms for the Dead, Book A, microfilm 183379, Family History Library; see also Bishop, "What Has Become of Our Fathers?" 91, 95. In 1844, Brigham Young hinted at a coming slowdown in baptisms for the dead when he "thought it best to attend to other matters." *History of the Church*, 7:254.

Ryan G. Tobler: "Because their lives were difficult and death was fearsome, Latter-day Saints hailed proxy baptism and Nauvoo's doctrines for the dead as a form of deliverance, both for their families and themselves . . . they were not helpless. As agents for the race, they could take an active part in achieving God's grand design."[43]

"SINGING THE SONGS OF ZION"
—CONSTRUCTION OF THE TEMPLE

The ordinance of baptisms for the dead became a key reason for building the temple and to do so as quickly as possible; otherwise, their blessing would become their burden. They believed there was, in effect, a time limit. "But I command you, all ye my saints, to build a house unto me; and I grant unto you a sufficient time to build a house unto me; and during this time your baptisms shall be acceptable unto me. But behold, at the end of this appointment your baptisms for your dead shall not be acceptable unto me; and if you do not these things . . . ye shall be rejected as a church, with your dead, saith the Lord your God" (D&C 124:31–32). Woodruff summed it up quite succinctly: "If that house is not built, then in vain is all our cares, faith, and works."[44] Add to this the prevailing and ever increasing likelihood that Joseph Smith might not survive the rising tide of persecution and one senses a shortened window of time.

On 3 October 1840 during the fall general conference, the Prophet first publicly announced plans to build the temple on Block 20 on the western edge of the Daniel H. Wells farm in the city's upper bluff overlooking the Mississippi River.[45] At that same time he also appointed a three-member building committee consisting of Elias Higbee, Reynolds Cahoon, and Alpheus Cutler. Joseph, who some believed had seen the

---

43. Tobler, "Saviors on Mt. Zion," 238.
44. *Wilford Woodruff's Journal*, 2:298, 9 September 1843.
45. The Church purchased the four-acre temple block from Daniel H. Wells, a local farmer/businessman, not then a member of the Church. Bounded by Wells Street on the west, Knight Street on the north, Woodruff Street on the east, and Mulholland Street on the south, the temple block sold for a modest $1,100. Quentin Thomas Wells, *Defender: The Life of Daniel H. Wells* (Logan: Utah State University Press, 2016), 35.

temple in vision, appointed William Weeks, a twenty-seven-year-old New Englander who had converted while in the Southern states, as chief builder (*architect* may be too grand a term), with Wandle Mace in charge of interior framing and millwork, and William N. Play as master stonemason. Although the architecture of the temple showed a "familiarity with the traditions of New England," Weeks's final plans "[did] not depend on a specific source and are novel in their adaptation of architectural motifs."[46]

From the outset, the Nauvoo Temple was to be "after the similitude of a palace" (D&C 124:2), as if to compensate for the unbuilt Independence, Far West, and Adam-ondi-Ahman temples all in one. Furthermore, it was to be so constructed "as to enable all the functions of the Priesthood to be duly exercised, and where instructions from the Most High will be received, and from this place go forth to distant lands."[47] Weeks followed the basic Benjamin outline for a Federalist church, with a classical, pilastered front and a tiered, segmented bell tower ornamented with classical orders. Designed to be 128 feet long, 88 feet wide, and 65 feet high, with a massive clock and bell tower reaching to a height of 165 feet, at over 50,000 square feet, the Nauvoo Temple would be three times the size of its Kirtland counterpart. "It is expected to be considerably larger than the one in Kirtland," the Prophet enthused in a letter to the Twelve then serving missions in Great Britain, "and on a more magnificent scale, and which will undoubtedly attract the attention of the great men of the earth."[48]

Within a week of Joseph's call for the temple, stonemasons were busy at work in a nearby quarry.[49] Shortly after the groundbreaking of the temple on 18 February 1841, workers began digging the basement with foundation

---

46. Laurel B. Andrew, *The Early Temples of the Mormons: The Architecture of the Millennial Kingdom in the American West* (Albany: State University of New York Press, 1978), 62.
47. "A Proclamation of the First Presidency of the Church to the Saints Scattered Abroad," *History of the Church*, 4:269, 8 January 1841.
48. "An Epistle of the Prophet to the Twelve," *History of the Church*, 4:229, 19 October 1840.
49. Modern ground-penetrating radar work and aerial studies of the changing course of the Mississippi River indicate that the long-assumed Nauvoo temple quarry was then under water and therefore could not have been the site of the original temple quarry, leaving the precise location of the original quarry somewhat of a mystery. "We can see from aerial photos that there was no quarry on that site until the 1960s." Email from Steve Nelson, professor of geochemistry, Department

The Nauvoo Temple.

stones laid in March. During the April 1841 general conference, Joseph laid the chief cornerstones, beginning with the southeast corner. The expectations of divine acceptance and instruction were as real and as motivating in the building of the Nauvoo Temple as they had been in Kirtland. And with workers donating one in ten days as a tithe of free labor, and a growing number of skilled artisans arriving almost every week, work accelerated. Women made dinners, sewed clothing, and carried water for the masons, sometimes assisted by older children. They also donated carpets, bedspreads, quilts, clothing, and hosiery as their tithing. Even some non-Latter-day Saints in the community were asked to contribute.

Workers sometimes found the time and energy to record their experiences. Many of them, as Luman Shurtliff recalled, were paid for their labors but often in kind, not cash. "Many times we got nothing," he recalled. Other times we "got a half pound of butter, or three pounds of fish, beef, and nothing to cook it with. . . . I have seen those that cut stone by the year eat nothing but parched or browned corn for breakfast and take some in their pockets for their dinner and go to work singing the songs

---

of Geological Sciences, Brigham Young University, to Richard E. Bennett, 21 November 2018.

of Zion."[50] Joseph Hovey thanked God for the opportunity just to play a small part: "I do work hard on the Temple of the Lord cutting and sawing stone and I do get so fatigued when I leave my labors that I have not much courage to write my life." He nevertheless recorded, "I am a poor man in the things of this world. But thanks be unto [the] God of Israel that I am here in Nauvoo and have the privilege with the Saints of the Most High for the light and the intelligence is worth more [than] the riches of the Gentiles."[51]

Compared to Kirtland, Nauvoo enjoyed several advantages and inducements to temple construction. These included enhanced security, a larger, more experienced and skilled workforce, greater economic stability, and access to higher quality resources. The securing of the Nauvoo Charter in December 1840 by act of the Illinois state legislature, and in large measure due to the lobbying efforts of John C. Bennett, assured Nauvoo not only a municipal court and a public university but also religious freedom as well as military protection in the form of the Nauvoo Legion. Unlike the infamous Danites, a band made up largely of Latter-day Saint vigilantes back in Missouri that caused no end of trouble, the Legion was a legally chartered militia of the state of Illinois operating under the local command of Joseph Smith as lieutenant general but ultimately answerable to the governor of the state. As an American construct, it helped the state fulfill its obligations to the Militia Act of 1792, which statute called for the enlistment of all able-bodied men between the ages of eighteen and forty-five to serve in a unit of the state militia. Thus the Legion afforded "the protection of law, the security of life, liberty, and the peaceable pursuit of happiness"[52] and an extended period of relative peace during which construction could proceed apace without conflict or interruption. As the

---

50. Biographical Sketch of the Life of Luman Andros Shurtliff, 1807–1864, 251, typescript, MSS SC 88, Harold B. Lee Library, Brigham Young University.
51. Joseph G. Hovey Papers, 1845–1856, 32, MS 1576, circa 1933, Church History Library.
52. *History of the Church*, 4:268. For a definitive study of the Legion, see Richard E. Bennett, Susan Easton Black, and Donald Q. Cannon, *The Nauvoo Legion in Illinois: A History of the Mormon Militia, 1841–1846* (Norman, Oklahoma: Arthur H. Clark Company, 2010).

First Presidency reported in a spring 1841 communiqué: "We hope that those scenes of blood [in Missouri] will never more occur . . . and that in the Temple, the foundation of which has been so happily laid, will the Saints of the Most High continue to congregate from year to year in peace and safety."[53]

While calling for the "speedy erection" of the temple, leaders were also encouraging the Saints everywhere, but especially the rich harvests of new British converts, to gather to the Mississippi not only to build the temple but also to escape the "overflowing scourge" that was soon to engulf the nations of the earth. Such gathering "is agreeable to the order of heaven," Joseph Smith said.[54] One newly arrived British convert, in encouraging his fellow countrymen to migrate, said that a key reason to do so was that "they may build a sanctuary to the name of the Most High, that there they may behold the glorious going forth of the Holy one, and learn of his judgments and attend to such ordinances and receive such blessings as they could not while scattered upon the face of the whole earth."[55]

And come they did! The mission of the Twelve to Great Britain from 1838 to 1841 with its conversion of almost 6,000 souls, was already paying rich dividends.[56] Thousands more converted soon afterward and came to Nauvoo, including seasoned carpenters, stonecutters, glaziers, and craftsmen of every kind providing a work force of skilled laborers unknown in Kirtland. Thus the temple became a beacon for the gathering.[57] Between 1840 and 1846, Nauvoo grew in size from 2,450 to over 11,000.[58]

---

53. The Church was experiencing such growth in the British Isles that the First Presidency reported: "The time has gone by when it [the Church] is looked upon as a transient matter, or a bubble on the wave. . . . The truth, like the sturdy oak, has stood unhurt." *History of the Church*, 4:337.
54. *History of the Church*, 4:269.
55. Francis Moon, editorial dated 4 November 1840, *Millennial Star* 1, no.10 (February 1841): 252.
56. *History of the Church*, 4:332.
57. The 1840 Hancock County census recorded 2,450 people as residents of Nauvoo Precinct. Two years later, a Church-sponsored census counted 4,000 people living in 800–900 households.
58. The 1845 Illinois state census counted 11,000 people living within the Nauvoo city limits. Susan Easton Black, "How Large Was the Population of Nauvoo?" *BYU Studies* 35, no. 2 (Spring 1995): 91–94; see also George W. Givens, *In Old Nauvoo: Everyday Life in the City of Joseph* (Salt Lake

Temple construction also led to the "concentration" of local Saints from outlying areas into Nauvoo itself, a policy that led to the disbanding of the Zarahemla Stake across the river in Iowa and the removal of others from Adams County and elsewhere. "Here the Temple must be raised," wrote Joseph Smith in March 1841, "the University built, and other edifices erected which are necessary for the great work of the last days, and which can only be done by a concentration of energy and enterprise."[59] Nauvoo never witnessed the construction of a chapel or a tabernacle. The site for the temple and the temple itself, even in its infancy and various later stages of unfinished construction, were always the centers of worship among the growing Latter-day Saint beehive.

A third advantage to the building of the Nauvoo Temple was the strong and growing local economy, the gradually improving financial condition of the Church, increased tithing receipts due to a steadily growing membership base, and the various safeguards established to protect Church leaders from financial setbacks. Although the harmful effects of the Panic of 1837 which had so devastated the Kirtland economy were only gradually receding, there was more than enough land available in Nauvoo to accommodate the influx of new arrivals without the same kind of rapid escalation in land values that had marred the Ohio experience. While the numbers of Nauvoo merchants grew, the Nauvoo economy was fundamentally a barter economy based on the honest exchange of goods and services. Furthermore, learning from past mistakes, the Church decided against establishing a bank like the one in Kirtland, opting instead for other means of securing needed cash, especially through business partnerships. To this end, the Nauvoo Agricultural and Manufacturing Association—a modern chamber of commerce—was incorporated in February 1841. Twenty trustees managed its affairs, aimed at funding

---

City: Deseret Book Company, 1990), 3–8, and Richard L. Jensen, "Transplanted to Zion: The Impact of British and Latter-day Saint Immigration upon Nauvoo," *BYU Studies* 31 (Winter 1991): 76–87.

59. *History of the Church*, 4:362.

and promoting all branches of agriculture, husbandry, and manufacturing in an effort to encourage flour mills and a lumber industry and to make Nauvoo, a river city, as self-reliant as possible by depending on more than a farming economy. To paraphrase Napoleon, Nauvoo was a "nation of shopkeepers" with over 200 in operation by 1844, and included skilled artisans and independent entrepreneurs. Although Nauvoo never became a boomtown, Glen Leonard noted, "Nauvoo's Saints made the best of their situation and rejoiced in their lives as common working people."[60]

The prime source of funding came from the tithing of the membership and "all they find in their hearts" to contribute. The failed United Order of Kirtland times had been replaced by the consecrated living of the law of tithing—a heritage of Far West (D&C 119). The Saints were required to give one-tenth of all they possessed at the commencement of construction and one-tenth of their increase after that. Workers who gave of their time, means, and talents had their names taken and written in "the Book of the Law of the Lord," a record which doubled as Joseph Smith's journal and record of temple donations. According to this record, 5,742 members made contributions.[61] The Council of the Twelve and various other individuals embarked on "tithing missions" to branches of the Church everywhere seeking tithing funds and other types of donations.[62] Meanwhile Joseph Smith became trustee-in-trust or sole trustee of the Church on 30 January 1841 and was "vested with plenary powers . . . to receive, acquire, manage or convey property, real, personal, or mixed, for the sole use and benefit of said Church."[63] Such was done in part to shield

---

60. Glen M. Leonard, *Nauvoo: A Place of Peace, A People of Promise* (Salt Lake City: Deseret Book Company; Provo, Utah: Brigham Young University Press, 2002), 171.
61. Kenneth Godfrey, "The Importance of the Temple in Understanding the Latter-day Saint Nauvoo Experience Then and Now," paper presented at the Leonard J. Arrington Mormon History Lecture Series no. 6, paper 5, 25 October 2000, Utah State University Digital Commons at USU.
62. For instance, John Snider took a mission to Great Britain in 1841 and returned with 201 pounds, the equivalent of $976.25. *JSP, Journals* 2:17.
63. *History of the Church,* 4:286–87. The term "trustee-in-trust," which seems to have currency only among the Saints, may have been a corruption of the legal phrase, "trustee-in-trust, in trust for . . ." Arrington, *Great Basin Kingdom,* 431.

himself and others from the kinds of vexing lawsuits they had experienced in Ohio.

Yet another advantage to Nauvoo was the availability of better building materials, including wood and stone. Well known is the mission to the "Pineries" of Wisconsin under the direction of George Miller and Lyman Wight that resulted in the floating down to Nauvoo of hundreds of thousands of feet of quality lumber cut from the Wisconsin forests. And limestone cut from nearby quarries was significant in improving the overall quality of the temple.[64]

As if the building of a massive four-story temple was not enough work to do, Joseph's 1841 revelation also called for the erection of a hotel—the so-called Nauvoo House—as "a resting-place for the weary traveler." So unlike their failed attempts at outreach and positive public affairs in both Ohio and Missouri, Nauvoo was to be a place of welcoming strangers and critics "that he may contemplate the glory of Zion, and the glory of this, the cornerstone thereof" (D&C 124:60). Made largely from the same cut limestone used in the temple, the Nauvoo House, though never completed, also provided employment for the swelling number of new emigrants and represented a friendlier, more inviting face of the Church for members and nonmembers alike.

Construction on the temple progressed well enough that on 23 October 1842 workers laid down a temporary floor in the basement allowing the Saints to meet there the following week for the first time. In November the recorder's office moved from the Red Brick Store to a newly built small brick building near the temple called the "Committee House" where properties, tithes, consecrations, and "means" for the construction of the temple were "recorded in due form."[65] By 6 April 1843 the walls were between four and twelve feet high.

Nevertheless, in Joseph Smith's mind, the work lagged behind. The

---

64. Dennis Rowley, "The Mormon Experience in the Wisconsin Pineries, 1841–1845," *BYU Studies* 32 (Winter/Spring 1992): 122–25, 140.
65. *Times and Seasons*, 15 October 1842, and *JSP, Journals* 2:166.

"IN THE SIMILITUDE OF A PALACE"

The Nauvoo House, circa 1890.

Nauvoo House proved a diversion of talent and resources until work thereon finally ceased in March 1844. The death of temple committee member Elias Higbee in June 1843, by which time the walls had reached the first tier of windows, complicated matters. And Joseph Smith pronounced "a curse" on "the merchant and the rich" for not sufficiently helping out.[66] Many of the earliest British emigrants were of the poorer classes, "there not being one in ten persons that could set themselves to work, to earn those indispensable things for the comfort of their families."[67] Only later and more slowly did the richer, more skilled artisans and craftsmen arrive in the city. The work in the Pineries proved frustratingly slow. These, however, were minor details in comparison to the bigger picture.

---

66. *History of the Church,* 4:601, 24 April 1842. William Jones claimed that he heard Joseph Smith say: "The Lord has commanded us to build that Temple. We want to build it, but we have not the means. There are people in this city who have the means, but they will not let us have them. What shall we do with such people? I say damn them." *Juvenile Instructor* 27, no. 2 (15 January 1892): 66.
67. *JSP, Journals* 2:66.

CONCLUSION

Nauvoo represented a major step forward in the history of temple work. For a variety of reasons, the first great temple ordinance in the "plan" that Joseph Smith had envisioned since at least Liberty Jail was that of baptisms for the dead. Enthusiastically received and then performed in the Mississippi River and later in a wooden font, this remarkably faith-building ordinance gave life and hope to a people surrounded by death. It also infused within the rapidly growing number of Nauvoo residents an unquenchable zeal to sacrifice as much as they could to build their "palace" in time to receive not only this ordinance of salvation but also to prepare themselves for whatever other ordinances might soon be revealed.

Chapter 3
"The Fulness of Those Blessings"
The Nauvoo Temple Part Two, 1843–1848

The Saints had labored faithfully and finished the temple and were now received as a church with our dead. This is glory enough for building the temple and thousands of saints have received their endowment in it. And the light will not go out.[1]

The construction of the Nauvoo Temple and Joseph Smith's introduction of other important temple ordinances in addition to baptisms for the dead occurred against a backdrop of rapidly developing events that proved increasingly distracting and troubling and, in the end, fatal for its prophet leader. These included several disruptive extradition attempts by the state of Missouri aimed at bringing Joseph Smith back to trial in Missouri for alleged wrongdoings; the attempted assassination of former Missouri governor, Lilburn W. Boggs, with Missouri officials censuring Joseph as an accomplice to the crime; various and sundry trials and difficulties associated with the introduction of plural marriage; the defection of John C. Bennett and his treacherous activities against his former leader; the apostasies of William and Wilson Law and others once friendly to the Church and their publication of the *Nauvoo Expositor* newspaper in June 1844; and finally the murder of Joseph and Hyrum Smith while under the "protection" of Governor Thomas Ford in Carthage Jail on 27 June 1844.

---

1. *Wilford Woodruff's Journal*, 3:46–47, 3 May 1846.

It was during these highly turbulent times that Joseph Smith introduced the temple endowment, eternal marriage, and an ordinance of hope and salvation that proved extraordinarily comforting to the Saints as they prepared to move west. After Brigham Young's and the vanguard companies' departure for the West in early 1846, those left behind worked overtime to complete the temple, which they did, and to see it dedicated, which it was, in May 1846. Efforts to sell it eventually failed for a variety of reasons. By 1849, the temple lay in ruins, the victim of an arsonist's torch and an angel's tornado.

"THE FULNESS OF THOSE BLESSINGS"— THE NAUVOO ENDOWMENT

The endowment of power given back in Kirtland consisted primarily of washings and anointings and was reserved for men only, mainly in preparation for mission service—what Brigham Young called "a faint similitude" of future temple work.[2] The Nauvoo Temple endowment, on the other hand, was something far greater. As its name implies, it was viewed as a divine gift, a provisional promise of eternal life, and a harbinger of eternal marriage. It therefore proved to be of enormous hope, comfort, and assurance to its recipients.

The Nauvoo endowment went well beyond its Kirtland predecessor and, as religious educator Alma Burton once succinctly explained, consisted of at least four elements. To begin with, it was a preparatory ordinance, a ceremonial washing and anointing, similar to that given at Kirtland but ending with the donning of sacred underclothing in remembrance of the covenants entered into during the ceremony. Second, it was a course of instruction presented through lectures, personal participation, and dramatic representations leading to a knowledge of sacred, spiritual truths. Third, it included the making of essential, scripture-based, Christ-centered covenants of obedience designed to help one live a life of personal

---

2. *Journal of Discourses*, 2:29–33.

worthiness and "holiness to the Lord." Fourth, the endowment provided a sacred sense of one's eternal progression and ultimate exaltation after passing through various estates before finally and figuratively entering into the presence of God.[3] Brigham Young described it this way: "Your endowment is, to receive all those ordinances in the House of the Lord, which are necessary for you, after you have departed from this life, to enable you to walk back to the presence of the Father, passing the angels who stand as sentinels, being enabled to give them the key words, the signs and tokens, pertaining to the Holy Priesthood, and gain your exaltation in spite of heaven and hell."[4] Although no endowments for the dead were ever administered in Nauvoo, like the ordinances of baptism and baptism for the dead, the endowment was seen as a saving or salvific ordinance. As such, the Prophet taught that it would be incumbent upon all of humanity, living and dead, to receive this ordinance eventually.

The first endowments were given outside of the temple in Joseph Smith's Red Brick Store on Water Street, which he had opened for business in early January 1842. As with baptisms for the dead, little is known about the origin of this sacred ordinance but it seems also to have developed over time and may have been sparked by his translation of the Book of Abraham. On 1 March 1842, after spending most of the day preparing for publication in the *Times and Seasons* newspaper the "commencement of the Book of Abraham," including the circular Facsimile no. 2 with its rather oblique reference to temples, Joseph invited the Twelve and their wives to his Red Brick Store office. That evening he explained to them "many important principles in relation to progressive improvement in the scale of intelligent existence."[5] A fortnight later on 17 March he organized

---

3. Alma Burton, "Endowment," in *Encyclopedia of Mormonism*, 2:454–55.
4. Brigham Young, in *Journal of Discourses*, 2:31, 6 April 1853, as cited in Dennis Largey, ed., *Doctrine and Covenants Reference Companion* (Salt Lake City: Deseret Book Company, 2012), 187–88.
5. *JSP, Journals* 2:39. Facsimile no. 2 contains, among many other things, "writings that cannot be revealed unto the world; but is to be had in the Holy Temple of God." See Figure no. 8. Much of the wording of parts of the endowment mirrors that found in the book of Abraham.

The Nauvoo Red Brick Store, circa 1890.

the "Female Relief Society of Nauvoo" in the same building. Then on Sunday 1 May 1842 he preached an open sermon in the shadow of the temple (then but one story high) on the keys of the kingdom during which he said that such keys were "certain signs and words by which false spirits and personages may be detected from true," that "the rich can only get them in the Temple" and the poor "on the mountain top as did Moses." He continued: "There are signs in heaven earth and hell" and "the elders must know them all to be endued with power to finish their work and prevent imposition."[6]

Three days later, at a special council held in the upper floor of the same Red Brick Store, Joseph "instituted the Ancient order of things for the first time in these last days."[7] In preparation for this event and with the help of some handpicked associates, he brought in some potted plants, small trees, and an altar. Using canvas curtains, he then partitioned the room into several subsections. He then administered the endowment to several carefully

---

6. *JSP, Journals* 2:53.
7. *JSP, Journals:* 2:54.

selected men, including Bishops Newel K. Whitney and George Miller, Brigham Young, Heber C. Kimball, Willard Richards, Temple Recorder James Adams, William Law, and William Marks. He there instructed them "in the principles and order of the . . . Aaronic Priesthood, and so on to the highest order of the Melchizedek Priesthood, setting forth the order pertaining to the Ancient of Days, and all those plans and principles by which any one is enabled to secure the fulness of those blessings which have been prepared for the Church of the First Born, and come up and abide in the presence of the Eloheim in the eternal worlds."[8] The following day, 5 May, these same brethren, led by Brigham Young, in return gave Joseph and Hyrum their endowments.[9] Prayer circles or prayer meetings associated with these ordinances began as early as 27 June 1842. Even after Joseph Smith's death, Church leaders continued to hold such meetings twice a week "for the salvation and peace of the Saints."[10]

---

8. *JSP, Journals* 2:54–55; see also *History of the Church*, 5:2, 4 May 1842. According to Willard Richards, Joseph's instructions "were of things spiritual, and to be received only by the spiritual minded: and there was nothing made known to these men but what will be made known to all saints, of the last days, so soon as they are prepared to receive, and a proper place is prepared to communicate them, even to the weakest of the saints; therefore let the saints be diligent in building the Temple and all houses which they have been or shall hereafter be commanded of God to build, and wait their time with patience, in all meekness and perseverance unto the end, knowing assuredly that all these things referred to in this council are always governed by the principles of Revelation." Joseph Smith draft notes, 4 May 1842, as cited in *JSP, Journals* 2:54. Willard Richards's notes for this meeting indicate that Joseph and Hyrum Smith, having officiated in the ordinance the previous day for others, were endowed the next day, 5 May 1842. *JSP, Journals* 2:54, fn 199.
9. Franklin D. Richards, Journal of Franklin D. Richards, 29 September 1886, in Richards Family Collection, 1837–1961, MS 1215, Church History Library, Salt Lake City. Many years later, during preparations for introducing the endowment in the St. George Temple, John L. Nuttall recorded the following conversation he had with Brigham Young about the Nauvoo endowment.
   "When we got our washings and anointings under the hands of the Prophet Joseph at Nauvoo we had only one room to work in with the exception of a little side room or office where we were washed and anointed had our garments placed upon us. . . .Then after we went into the large room over the store in Nauvoo. Joseph divided up the room the best he could [,] hung up the veil, marked it and gave us our instructions as we passed along from one department to another giving us . . . [instructions] . . . and after we had got through, Bro. Joseph turned to me and said Bro. Brigham Young this is not arranged right but we have done the best we could under the circumstances in which we are placed." John Nuttall, Diary of John L. Nuttall, 7 February 1877, in L. John Nuttall Papers, 1854–1903, MS 1269, Church History Library, Salt Lake City; also in *New Mormon Studies CD-ROM, 2009 edition*.
10. Brigham Young to Wilford Woodruff, 27 June 1845, typescript, Brigham Young Office Files, Church History Library, as cited in Matthew J. Grow et al., eds. *The Joseph Smith Papers:*

The circle of those endowed slowly expanded from the original nine to include several others in September 1843 in what became known as the "quorum," "the temple quorum," or "quorum of the anointed" and which also included women. Emma Smith received her endowment 28 September 1843, the first Latter-day Saint woman to do so.[11]

The positive impact the endowment had on several recipients may well be measured by the following reflections of Heber C. Kimball in a letter to fellow apostle Parley P. Pratt, then still on assignment in England.

> *Brother Joseph feels as well as I [have] ever see[n] him. One reason is he has got a small company that he feels safe in thare ha[n]ds. And that he can open his bosom to and feel himself safe. . . . I wish you was here so as to feel and hear fore your self. We have received some pressious things through the Prophet on the preasthood that would cause your soul to rejoice.*[12]

Meanwhile Joseph Smith's establishment of the Female Relief Society of Nauvoo on 17 March 1842 with his wife, Emma Smith, the "elect lady," as founding president was an organizational development far in advance of Kirtland. A charitable organization designed to meet the needs of the poor, the sick, and the needy among Nauvoo's growing immigrant population, and to protect and upgrade the moral standing of both women and men, the Nauvoo Relief Society also played a pivotal role in the history of

---

Administrative Records, Vol. 1: Council of Fifty Minutes, March 1844–January 1846 of the Administrative Records series of *The Joseph Smith Papers,* ed. Ronald K. Esplin, Matthew J. Grow, Matthew C. Godfrey (Salt Lake City: The Church Historian's Press, 2016), 448.

11. Jill Mulvay Derr et al., eds., *The First Fifty Years of Relief Society—Key Documents in Latter-day Saint Women's History* (Salt Lake City: The Church Historian's Press, 2016), 75. Approximately thirty-six men and twenty-nine women received this blessing before Joseph Smith's death in 1844. Sidney Rigdon apparently never received this blessing, evidence of his gradual retreat from Church leadership and eventual removal from the Church. About fifteen more received their endowments at the hands of the Twelve Apostles before the temple opened. Lisle G. Brown, "Nauvoo Sealings, Adoptions, and Anointings: A Comprehensive Register of Persons Receiving LDS Temple Ordinances, 1841–1846" (Salt Lake City: Smith-Pettit Foundation, 2006); see also Lisle G. Brown, "The Sacred Departments for Temple Work in Nauvoo: The Assembly Room and the Council Chamber," *BYU Studies* 19, no. 3 (Fall 1979): 365.

12. Heber C. Kimball to Parley P. Pratt, 17 June 1842, Church History Library, as cited in Ehat, "Temple Ordinances," 41, spelling retained.

the Nauvoo Temple. It prepared many through acts of charity and kindness to become worthy of temple attendance; exposed sinners, scalawags, and opponents of the Church and its leadership; contributed money, clothing, supplies, and many other kinds of assistance to the building of the temple; and fostered a higher code of conduct and standard of living. By May 1842 the total number of women enrolled in the Nauvoo Relief Society reached 1,341. Their final meeting in Nauvoo was held on 16 March 1844.

The establishment of the Relief Society seems to have been almost prerequisite to the presentation of the endowment and certainly was instrumental in the unfolding development of temple work. The place of woman, eternal marriage, and the family were becoming ever more central to Joseph Smith's doctrines of salvation and of his temple-centered teachings. Speaking at a meeting of the Society on 30 March 1842, he told the sisters "that the Society should move according to the ancient Priesthood, hence there should be a select Society separate from all the evils of the world, choice, virtuous and holy." He further remarked that "he was going to make of this Society a kingdom of priests as in Enoch's day."[13] Reynolds Cahoon, a member of the Nauvoo Temple building committee, explicitly tied the new women's organization to the temple when he said: "This Society is raised by the Lord to prepare us for the great blessings which are for us in the House of the Lord in the Temple."[14] Bishop Newel K. Whitney, presiding bishop, added: "In the beginning God created man male and female and bestowed upon man certain blessings peculiar to a man of God, of which woman partook, so that without the female all things cannot be restored to the earth. It takes all to restore the Priesthood."[15] The unfolding doctrines and ordinances associated with

---

13. Minutes of the proceedings of the Third Meeting of the Society, Lodge Room, 30 March 1842, in *The First Fifty Years of Relief Society,* 43. See also *History of the Church,* 4:570.
14. Minutes of the proceedings of the Seventh Meeting of Society, Second Ward, 13 August 1843, in *The First Fifty Years of Relief Society,* 43, 116.
15. Minutes of the proceedings of the Tenth Meeting of the Society, 27 May 1842, in *The First Fifty Years of Relief Society,* 75–76.

temple work thus raised the women of the Church to a place of greater vision and equality, well in advance of their sisters in most other contemporary Christian religions in terms of expectations, participations, and responsibilities.

Meanwhile the first Masonic lodge in Nauvoo was established in December 1841. In short order, the Nauvoo Lodge became the largest in the state of Illinois. The Nauvoo Masonic Hall, begun in 1842, was dedicated in 1844. Joseph Smith, who "rose to the sublime degree" of Masonry in March 1842, an honor more ceremonial than deserved, attended only a handful of their meetings. Masonry was then a highly popular institution in most American cities at the time and claimed the allegiance of many leading citizens including George Washington, Benjamin Franklin, Andrew Jackson, and a host of other popular figures. Like many other elected civic officials of his day, Joseph Smith understood that belonging to the Masons was almost an expectation and certainly a way to gain a network of friends and allies. However, unlike his brother, Hyrum, he stood aloof from most things Masonic. While it is true that there are some shared similarities between the symbols and trappings of Masonic induction rites and the endowment, and while they may have served as another "catalyst" for revelation, the endowment presented by Joseph Smith fundamentally differed from Masonic rituals in many important ways.[16] First,

---

16. See "Masonry," in Gospel Topics, lds.org. A well-known and then highly popular benevolent fraternity with roots extending back to late Middle Ages Scotland, the Masonic order began as an elite guild or brotherhood of master stonemasons responsible for building many of the great medieval castles and cathedrals, complete with their exquisite geometrical ceiling designs and magnificent Gothic architecture. Admission eventually was restricted to fellow craftsmen through an elaborate system of secret signs and tokens by which one proved membership and admittance. While many through the years have tried to connect Masonry to ancient Solomon temple rituals and rites, the assertion has never been proven. Most Masons were content to be members of a benevolent brotherhood that promised to take care of one another, provide for the widow and her family, and extend short and long-term assistance to those in need. John C. Bennett tried hard to accuse Joseph Smith of borrowing the endowment from Masonic ceremonies; however, Bennett never received his Priesthood endowment. Nonetheless, some Masons believed Joseph stole parts of their ceremonies from them and accused him of breaking the oath of secrecy he had taken, a charge never proven. For the most recent study on the relationship of Masonry to Mormonism, see Michael W. Homer, *Joseph's Temples: The Dynamic Relationship between Freemasonry and Mormonism* (Salt Lake City: The University of Utah Press, 2014) and

it was a scripture-based, Christ-centered, deeply religious ordinance and revelation of salvation, full of sacred covenants and promises. Second, it provided for full female participation, something almost unheard of in the fraternal order of contemporary Masonry. Third, the concept of progression from kingdom to kingdom, if somewhat similar to the Masonic rituals of advancement, preceded Nauvoo by several years and likely owed much to Joseph's 1832 vision of the three degrees of glory. Of the thousands of Saints who eventually received their endowment in the Nauvoo Temple, many of whom were Masons, few ever criticized it as a plagiarism or something having been borrowed from the Masonic fraternity. James Adams, for instance, a patriarch and president of the branch of the Church at Springfield, Illinois, and Deputy Grand Master Mason of Illinois, never condemned Joseph for creating a sham or counterfeit.[17]

"THE NEW AND EVERLASTING COVENANT" —ETERNAL MARRIAGE

The endowment was in many ways a precursor to the eternal union of man and woman—celestial marriage. The doctrine of marriage and the family was enshrined in Latter-day Saint thought and practice well before Nauvoo. The account of Adam and Eve becoming "one flesh" as equal marriage partners is an essential teaching of both the Book of Moses and the Book of Abraham, let alone Genesis in the Holy Bible. The Book of

---

Matthew B. Brown, *Exploring the Connection between Mormons and Masons* (American Fork, Utah: Covenant Communications, 2009). See also Steven C. Harper, "Freemasonry and the Latter-day Saint Temple Endowment Ceremony," in Laura Harris Hales, ed., *A Reason for Faith: Navigating Latter-day Saint Doctrine and Church History* (Provo, Utah: Religious Studies Center, Brigham Young University, 2016). Three recent reputable studies of Freemasonry generally are Margaret Jacob, *The Origins of Freemasonry: Facts and Fictions* (Philadelphia: University of Pennsylvania Press, 2006); W. Kirk McNulty, *Freemasonry: Symbols, Secrets, Significance* (London: Thames and Hudson, Ltd., 2006); and Mark Stavish, *Freemasonry: Rituals, Symbols and History of the Secret Society* (Woodbury, MN: Llewellyn Publications, 2007).

17. A prevailing sentiment among many in Nauvoo was that Masonry was a "vestige of ancient truths" as Benjamin Johnson put it, or in the words of Joseph Fielding, a "stepping stone or preparation for something else." See Benjamin F. Johnson, *My Life's Review* (Independence, Mo.: Zion's Printing and Publishing Company, 1947), 93; and Andrew F. Ehat, ed., "They Might Have Known That He Was Not a Fallen Prophet: The Nauvoo Journal of Joseph Fielding," *BYU Studies* 19, no. 2 (Winter 1979), 145.

Mormon account of the 200 years of paradisiacal peace following Christ's coming to the America's speaks of the righteous Nephites living after the manner of happiness. "They were married, and given in marriage, and were blessed according to the multitude of the promises which the Lord had made unto them" (4 Nephi 1:11). And in 1831, while examining the doctrine of Shaker celibacy, Joseph Smith received another revelation: "Whoso forbiddeth to marry is not ordained of God, for marriage is ordained of God . . . that the earth might answer the end of its creation; and that it might be filled with the measure of man" (D&C 49:15–17).

The Latter-day Saint doctrine of marriage, however, soon far transcended the realms of traditional matrimony. The central tenet of this new article of faith was that marriage, when performed by one holding the proper priesthood authority and if and when sealed by the Holy Spirit of Promise or in other words, the Holy Ghost, may endure beyond the grave. In fact, such a marriage was a prerequisite for attaining the highest degree of glory in the hereafter. While instructing a group of Saints in Ramus, Illinois, in May 1843, Joseph taught that "in the celestial glory there are three heavens or degrees; and in order to obtain the highest, a man must enter into this order of the priesthood [meaning the new and everlasting covenant of marriage]" (D&C 131:1–2). As B. H. Roberts later observed, "The primary principle of the marriage system of the church, I repeat, is *the eternity of the marriage covenant*; but owing to the fact that this system also included the doctrine of the rightfulness—under given specific conditions—of a plurality of wives, the importance and grandeur of the doctrine of the eternity of the marriage covenant, to a very great extent, has been obscured."[18]

Like a three-legged stool, this doctrine of eternal marriage rested upon a triple foundation: first, the necessity of restored priesthood authority; second, the universality of the Resurrection and the eternality of the soul;

---

18. B. H. Roberts, *A Comprehensive History of the Church of Jesus Christ of Latter-day Saints* (Provo, Utah: Brigham Young University Press, 1965), 2:95, italics in the original.

and third, the doctrine of exaltation individually granted but mutually enjoyed. As to priesthood authority, a comparison to the doctrine of baptism might well be illustrative. In a revelation given to the Church in April 1830, baptism was enjoined upon everyone, whether or not they were baptized in any other church before, for the distinct reason that those previous baptisms were unauthorized "dead works," lacking lasting force or recognition beyond this life.

> *Behold, I say unto you that all old covenants have I caused to be done away in this thing; and this is a new and an everlasting covenant, even that which was from the beginning.*
>
> *Wherefore, although a man should be baptized an hundred times it availeth him nothing, for you cannot enter in at the strait gate by the law of Moses, neither by your dead works.*
>
> *For it is because of your dead works that I have caused this last covenant and this church to be built up unto me, even as in days of old (D&C 22:1–3).*

In 1830s America most, if not all, civil marriages fell within religious jurisdiction and were usually performed by clergy. Although the Church recognized such unions, it did not regard them as divinely authorized ordinances, certainly not ones that would extend beyond the grave. Like baptism, such marriages would need to be redone, eventually, by one holding proper keys and authority so that what was done on earth would be "bound in heaven."

Many of Joseph Smith's sermons in Nauvoo pertained to the doctrine of death and resurrection. All of his teachings on the temple, including baptisms for the dead, the endowment, and marriage, were contingent upon the doctrine of immortality or a universal, unconditional resurrection; a resurrection that guaranteed that both bond and free, male and female, white and black, would be eventually resurrected to "the same body which was a natural body; even ye shall receive your bodies" (D&C 88:28). The doctrine of eternal marriage was, therefore, based upon the doctrine of a literal resurrection of gender, individual personality, and a perfectible identity.

As early as 1831, while working on his revision of the Holy Bible, Joseph taught that for any resurrected being to attain unto exaltation, the highest heaven in the celestial kingdom, "a man must enter into . . . [the new and everlasting covenant of marriage]; and if he does not, he cannot obtain it. He may enter into the other, but that is the end of his kingdom; he cannot have an increase" (D&C 131:1–4). Thus marriage was more than an earthly ceremony but a priesthood ordinance of lasting duration and eternal consequence. Joseph and his wife, Emma, set the example by being sealed for eternity on 28 May 1843.

Further, in comparison to baptisms for the dead, the Prophet revealed that baptism for the dead represented a "welding link of some kind or other" between dispensations, and keys and powers and glories as well, perhaps, of generations, past, present, and future. It was as though this revelation on baptism foreshadowed later revelations on endowments and marriage sealings. Baptism for the dead represented, therefore, more than a remission of sins but also foreshadowed a sealed interrelationship of genders and generations, an eventual reconstruction of the entire earthly family and biological relationships. Little wonder it was revealed first, before the endowment, and in anticipation of celestial or eternal marriage.

And again like baptism and the subsequent bestowal of the Holy Ghost which seals one's baptism, a marriage became eternal not merely because of priesthood authority or the surety of a resurrection but upon it being "sealed . . . by the Holy Spirit of Promise" (D&C 132:19), i.e., "the earnest of our inheritance" (Ephesians 1:13–14). As the Prophet declared: "We believe in the gift of the Holy Ghost being enjoyed now, as much as it was in the Apostles' days; we believe that it is necessary to make and to organize the Priesthood, that no man can be called to fill any office in the ministry without it; . . . . we believe that no man can know that Jesus is the Christ, but by the Holy Ghost. We believe in it in all its fulness, and power, and greatness, and glory."[19] To paraphrase the Prophet, a man might as well be baptized a hundred times, or endowed or sealed or married a hundred times, but until ratified by the Holy Ghost, such ordinances mean little and will have no lasting validity in the eternities.

The response to this doctrine of the potential eternal union of the sexes was cautiously enthusiastic. Confided Parley P. Pratt: "It was from him [Joseph] that I learned the true dignity and destiny of a son of God, clothed with an eternal priesthood, as the patriarch and sovereign of his countless offspring. It was from him that I learned that the highest dignity of womanhood was, to stand as a queen and priestess to her husband, and to reign for ever and ever as the queen mother of her numerous and still increasing offspring."[20]

On 26 May 1843 Joseph Smith sealed several couples in his Red Brick Store in the new and everlasting covenant of celestial or eternal marriage, most of whom were of the aforesaid anointed quorum. Four more couples were sealed two days later. After Joseph's death, Brigham Young performed dozens of other such sealings in his office adjacent to the celestial room in the temple. During the three-month period between December 1845 and February 1846 when so many living endowments were being performed, approximately 2,682 sealings of all different kinds—spousal marriages, children sealed to parents, and adoptions—were performed in the Nauvoo Temple, of which over 80 percent (2,000) were marriage sealings. Almost all of these were done by members of the Quorum of the Twelve. Additionally, a limited number of marriage sealings had been performed in private homes, including those of Presiding Bishop Newel K. Whitney and Patriarch John Smith, since 1843. Most, if not all, cases of children being sealed to their parents were of living children being sealed to living parents. Such was the case, for example, of Newel and Elizabeth Whitney whose eight grown, living children were sealed to them at noon on 12 January

---

19. *History of the Church*, 5:27.
20. Parley P. Pratt, *Autobiography of Parley P. Pratt*, 259–60.

1846 by Brigham Young.[21] Less common were adoption sealings or, in other words, the spiritual adoption of children to nonbiological parents, usually Church leaders.[22] There were few, if any, sealings of deceased children to parents recorded in Nauvoo, likely because of the blizzard of temple activity for the living in preparation for their pending exodus. Nor did such ordinances occur during the next nine years. Richard Cowan, a career scholar of temple work, estimates that by the time the Saints began leaving Nauvoo, they had performed at least 369 proxy and 2,420 living eternal marriages.[23]

Meanwhile, what of marriages for the dead or "proxy marriages"? While it is true that most, if not all, eternal marriages performed by Joseph Smith in Nauvoo were of living spouses, Brigham Young and other members of the Twelve later sealed some living spouses to deceased partners in the Nauvoo Temple.[24] And after Joseph Smith's death, at least seventy-one living children were sealed to their deceased parents.[25] There is strong circumstantial evidence to show that such proxy marriages began in early 1842. Thus was the precedent established for the reconstruction of family units in the Resurrection, that righteous mothers would have the joy of raising their deceased infants in the Millennium, that the destiny of

---

21. Nauvoo Temple Sealings and Adoptions of the Living and Index, book A, microfilm, 561, Family History Library; see also Lisle G. Brown, "Nauvoo Sealings, Adoptions, and Anointings."
22. An example was the sealings and adoptions of George Miller to his three wives and fifteen "natural" and "adopted" children. Nauvoo Temple Sealings and Adoptions, microfilm, 415–16. On 31 January 1846, Brigham Young sealed to Alpheus Cutler and Lois Cutler their three sons and five daughters. Nauvoo Temple Sealings and Adoptions, 227. A total of 211 males and females were adopted to seventeen couples in the Nauvoo Temple. Jonathan Stapley, "Adoptive Sealing Ritual in Mormonism," *Journal of Mormon History* 37, no. 2 (Summer 2011): 66, and Brian Hales, *Joseph Smith's Polygamy*, vol. 3 (Salt Lake City: Greg Kofford Books, 2013).
23. Richard O. Cowan, *Temple Building Ancient and Modern* (Provo, Utah: Brigham Young University Press, 1971), 29. Proxy sealings for spouses both of whom were dead did not begin until later.
24. Daniel D. McArthur recalled the following: "On the first of February 1846, I and my wife went into the temple. . . . We went to the sealing room, and I had Matilda Caroline Fuller sealed to me for time and all eternity by President Willard Richards over the altar prepared for that purpose. I also had Cordelia Clark, my first wife who was dead, sealed to me." Daniel D. McArthur, Autobiography of Daniel D. McArthur, typescript, Perry Special Collections, HBLL, BYU.
25. Joseph Earl Arrington, "Construction of the Nauvoo Temple," Perry Special Collections, HBLL, BYU; as cited in Kenneth W. Godfrey, "The Importance of the Temple," 435.

woman is to become a divine partner with her husband, and that family bonds may extend beyond the grave.[26]

In his famous King Follet discourse given in April 1844 at yet another funeral, Joseph Smith elaborated on a good many other unique doctrines. These included the eternal nature of God, the Resurrection, and the potential for both men and women, when bound together in an eternal union, to retain their personality and identity, their shared power of eternal increase, and the ability to continue onward toward eternal progression. Through the promised blessings of the temple, the Saints could be "one with relatives, with other righteous people, and with God."[27] "When a seal is put upon the father and mother, it secures their posterity," said Joseph Smith, "so that they cannot be lost, but will be saved by virtue of the covenant of their father and mother."[28]

In that same King Follet discourse, Joseph taught that seeking after the salvation of the dead would ever be an imperative responsibility of the Saints. He said:

> *The greatest responsibility lade upon us in this life is in relation to our dead . . . the seals are in our hands to seal our children and our dead for the fullness of the dispensation of times . . . the spirits of our friends should be searched out and saved. Any man that has a friend in eternity can save him if he has not committed the unpardonable sin. . . . What have we to console us in relation to our dead? We have the greatest hope in relation to our dead of any people on earth.*[29]

In the same revelation (D&C 132) given in 1831 after inquiring into the matter of the plural marriages of Abraham, Isaac, and Jacob, Joseph Smith was instructed to enter into the practice of plural marriage "for all who have this law revealed must do the same." Joseph Smith's plural marriages predated Nauvoo, perhaps by as much as a decade. Fearing

---

26. Joseph F. Smith, *Gospel Doctrine*, 454–55.
27. Leonard, *Nauvoo, A Place of Peace*, 241.
28. *History of the Church*, 5:530.
29. *Wilford Woodruff's Journal*, 2:386–87, 7 April 1844.

resistance and a harmful backlash if publicly announced, he had begun the practice quietly.[30] Evidence suggests that he married his first plural wife, Fanny Alger, in 1835. And well before he informed his wife, Emma, he also had married Louisa Beaman, his first plural wife in Nauvoo, in April 1841.[31] By May 1843 when Joseph married nineteen-year-old Emily and her twenty-two-year-old sister Eliza Partridge, he had already married as many as eighteen other women. In all, he likely married as many as thirty women, some for time and others for time and eternity.[32]

Hyrum Smith eventually accepted plural marriage, but Emma was at best ambivalent toward it and at worst highly scornful of it. Wanting to support her husband but unwilling to share his affections with other wives, for Emma polygamy was "an excruciating ordeal" and she "vacillated" in her support of it. When Hyrum tried to convince her of its divine authenticity during a meeting with her on 12 July 1843, he reported that "she did not believe a word of it and appeared very rebellious."[33] Emma's growing opposition to, and eventual denial of, the practice, along with a protracted legal debate over the ownership of several Nauvoo properties after her husband's death, led to her rejection of leadership by the Twelve and her refusal to go west with the Saints. Her later marriage to Lewis Bidamon in 1847 was clear evidence of her commitment to stay back.[34] William Marks, William and Wilson Law, Sidney Rigdon and his family,

---

30. Address of Brigham Young, Brigham Young Papers, Church History Library, 8 October 1866.
31. "Plural Marriage in Kirtland and Nauvoo," Gospel Topics, https://www.lds.org/topics/plural-marriage-in-kirtland-and-nauvoo?lang=eng.
32. Todd Compton, *In Sacred Loneliness: The Plural Wives of Joseph Smith* (Salt Lake City: Signature Press, 1997). To date, no solid evidence has been located to indicate that he had any children from any of his plural wives. See Ugo A. Perego, Natalie M. Myers, and Scott R. Woodward, "Reconstructing the Y-Chromosome of Joseph Smith: Genealogical Application," *Journal of Mormon History* 31 (Summer 2005): 70–88; see also *Journal of Mormon History* 31 (Fall 2005): 42–60.
33. Journal of William Clayton, 12 July 1843, as cited in James B. Allen, "One Man's Nauvoo: William Clayton's Experience in Mormon Illinois," *Journal of Mormon History* 6 (1979): 52.
34. "Emma's union with Lewis Bidamon ended speculation that she might someday accept the Twelve's offer of assistance to go west, and although her name was never removed from the membership records, in their eyes it affirmed her separation from the church." Linda King Newell and Valeen Tippetts Avery, *Mormon Enigma: Emma Hale Smith: Prophet's Wife, 'Elect Lady,' Polygamy's Foe* (Garden City, New York: Doubleday and Company, Inc., 1984), 248.

and several others, some even of the anointed quorum, quit the Church in large measure because of their opposition to the practice and how it was introduced. The Prophet also instructed several others to follow his lead with most plural marriages performed in private homes. William Clayton married his first plural wife in April 1843. At least twenty-nine other men and fifty women married plurally before Smith's death.[35] For these couples, "celestial marriage" meant not only eternal marriage but plural marriage as well. Some observers have estimated that as many as 523 plural marriages were performed in Nauvoo.[36]

A seriously complicating element in the introduction of plural marriage in Nauvoo was John C. Bennett. Relieved of his duties as mayor and released from his callings in Church leadership because of immoral activity, when the excommunicated Bennett learned of plural marriage he fastened upon it as a system of "spiritual wifery" and a way to frame and disgrace his former prophet-leader if not to defend his own perfidies.[37] It was trial enough for most, including Hyrum Smith, to accept the practice when taught in the best of circumstances; it proved almost impossible for some others such as William Law and William Marks, who may have first heard of it from such a miscreant as Bennett. Most members at that time came from strong Protestant backgrounds with a religious mindset inherently opposed to anything but monogamy. As Brigham Young once said, "The brethren were not prepared to receive it."[38] We will return to our discussion of plural marriage among the Utah Saints in a later chapter but

---

35. "Plural Marriage in Kirtland and Nauvoo," Gospel Topics.
36. George D. Smith, *Nauvoo Polygamy: "But We Called It Celestial Marriage"* (Salt Lake City: Signature Books, 2008), 285.
37. The most complete biography of John C. Bennett is Andrew F. Smith, *The Saintly Scoundrel: The Life and Times of Dr. John Cook Bennett* (Urbana: University of Illinois Press, 1997). Governor Thomas Ford once said of Bennett: "[He] was probably the greatest scamp in the western country . . . and was everywhere accounted the same debauched, unprincipled and profligate character." *Saintly Scoundrel*, 135.
38. Ehat, "Joseph Smith's Introduction," 55, fn 156. Even Brigham Young, as loyal as he ever was to Joseph, admitted that plural marriage was a fearful trial. As he phrased it when first hearing of the practice, "It was the first time I desired the grave." Young, in *Journal of Discourses*, 3:266.

suffice it here to say that it was a characteristic of Nauvoo life and temple work that would not be publicly proclaimed until 1852.

A fourth and final temple ordinance administered in Nauvoo—"the crowning ordinance of the fullness of the Melchizedek Priesthood" as some then preferred to call it—was a highly prized "second anointing" and sealing wherein one's "calling and election" was made sure—with the expectation of one's continued worthiness. Joseph introduced this blessing to a very select audience of believers, including his wife and nine members of the Quorum of the Twelve who had already received their endowment, many of whom had also embraced eternal marriage. They began in late September 1843 in Joseph Smith's home and were intermittently given in the Red Brick Store, the Mansion House, the Brigham Young home, and of course later in the temple.[39] It was essentially an external confirmation of an internal spiritual witness borne of the Holy Spirit of Promise.

This "Second Comforter" ordinance was particularly sought after in light of the imminent challenges and formidable difficulties many foresaw coming in the months ahead. Those who were sick and dying sensed that they might not live to see the Rocky Mountains or that their spouse would never survive the ordeal. This priesthood ordinance was therefore often given for comfort and hope. While Joseph Smith initiated this ordinance, Brigham Young multiplied the numbers who received it as spiritual preparation for the physical demands of the pending exodus. Thus the temple, because of all its saving ordinances, became their great comforter and preparer, fortifier and guarantor in light of the pending exodus. As Truman O. Angell put it: "I received my endowments in the . . . attic [of the temple], together with Polly, my wife, and afterward our sealing and second anointings, which far excelled any previous enjoyments of my life up to that time."[40] In light of this ordinance, William Clayton's well-known anthem

---

39. Andrew H. Hedges, et al., eds., *Journals Volume 3: May 1843–June 1844* of the Journals series of *The Joseph Smith Papers*, ed. Ronald K. Esplin and Matthew Grow (Salt Lake City: Church Historian's Press, 2015), xxi. See also *JSP, Documents*, 6:524–26.
40. Truman O. Angell autobiography, "His Journal."

of the exodus, "Come, Come, Ye Saints," may take on added meaning: "And should we die before our journey's through, happy day, all is well; We then are free from toil and sorrow too, with the just we shall dwell."[41]

It must be acknowledged, however, that not everyone accepted these new temple ordinances, any more than the membership had accepted the Vision of the three degrees of glory given back in 1832 (D&C 76).[42] The doctrines and practices of the Church were admittedly in a state of constant flux, especially with a prophet-leader who sensed his time was short and with a people who were about to flee to the West. And some of these changes were almost revolutionary in substance. Just six months before his death Joseph expressed his frustrations:

> *The question is frequently asked can we not be saved without going through with all these ordinances. I would answer No not the fullness of salvation. . . . But there has been a great difficulty in getting anything into the heads of this generation. It has been like splitting hemlock knots with a corn do[d]ger for a wedge and a pumpkin for a beetle; even the Saints are slow to understand. I have tried for a number of years to get the minds of the Saints prepared to receive the things of God, but we frequently see some of them after suffering all they have for the work of God will fly to pieces like glass as soon as anything comes that is contrary to their traditions. They cannot stand the fire at all . . . many are called but few are chosen.*[43]

"THE LIGHT WILL NOT GO OUT"—THE COMPLETION AND DEDICATION OF THE NAUVOO TEMPLE

The deaths of Joseph and Hyrum Smith in Carthage Jail sounded a note of foreboding to those still working on the temple, as if they sensed

---

41. William Clayton, "Come, Come Ye Saints" *Hymns* no. 30 (Salt Lake City: The Church of Jesus Christ of Latter-day Saints, 1985).
42. Ronald K. Esplin, "The Emergence of Brigham Young and the Twelve to Mormon Leadership, 1830–1841" (PhD diss., Brigham Young University, 1981).
43. *Wilford Woodruff's Journal*, 2:342, 21 January 1844. A beetle is a heavy wooden mallet for crushing or smoothing. A corn dodger is a cake of corn bread or a boiled dumpling.

they were now working against time. After a sustaining vote by the assembled Nauvoo membership, Brigham Young, as president of the Council of the Twelve, rose to leadership over the Church, discrediting in the process the contending claims to succession and guardianship of Sidney Rigdon and James Strang. Aware that they alone held the sealing keys delegated to them by the Prophet himself, the Twelve became the accepted guardians of temple worship. They knew that they had received not merely a stewardship over temple affairs but also the keys to administer in such matters. And the majority of the Saints supported them in that claim.[44] Remembered Brigham Young: "By the aid of sword in one hand, and trowel and hammer in the other, with fire arms in hand, and watchings, and prayings, [we] completed the temple despite the devices of the mob."[45]

On Saturday 24 May 1845 at precisely 6:00 a.m., the thronged assembly sang W. W. Phelps's new anthem composed specifically for the occasion entitled "Cap Stone." And as the band played and as many shouted "Hosanna! Hosanna! Hosanna! to God and the Lamb," Brigham Young gently moved the final capstone into place. "The last stone is laid upon the Temple," he declared, "and I pray the Almighty in the name of Jesus to defend us in this place and sustain us until the Temple is finished."[46] Three months later the dome was completed and installed and on 30 November they dedicated the attic. The building was by this time a most imposing structure with its thirty pilasters, moonstones ringed around the walls at ground level with rising sunstones each bearing trumpets near the top. And above the sunstones was a ring of five-pointed stars encircling the building, in symbolism perhaps of the various degrees of glory and of Christ, the

---

44. Esplin, "The Emergence of Brigham Young and the Twelve"; see also D. Michael Quinn, "The Mormon Succession Crisis of 1844," *BYU Studies* 16, no. 2 (1976): 187–233. Not all, however, accepted Quorum leadership. William Marks, Nauvoo stake president, and others believed that the Lord rejected the Saints and their religion for not completing the temple in a timely fashion. Many of those who did not go west, sometimes called the "stay backs," who later galvanized into the Reorganized Church of Jesus Christ of Latter Day Saints, were strong in their belief that these temple ordinances, most particularly eternal and plural marriage, did not come by revelation and therefore were unnecessary, if not foreign, to the plan of salvation.
45. Brigham Young, in *Journal of Discourses*, 2:32, 6 April 1853.
46. Journal of William Clayton, 24 May 1845, as cited in *JSP, Council of Fifty Minutes*, 459.

bright morning star. Rectangular windows graced the top of the temple and round windows filled the spaces between the floors. A weather vane, featuring the angel Moroni, capped the bell tower. Four large lanterns, placed at the corners of the temple at night, served to detect intruders and to thwart assassination attempts on the life of Brigham Young.

The attic consisted of two subsections: a large, boxlike council room called the "half-story" on the west end of the building; and on the east end, a long rectangular hall beneath a gabled roof. The half-story was, in turn, divided into several small rooms.

When painted and carpeted, the large council room, which was over twice the size of the upper floor of the Red Brick Store, was divided by canvas partitions. "Six rooms were separated off for the convenience of the holy priesthood, two large ones and four smaller ones and a hall passing through between the small ones."[47] The temple was surely a most imposing structure, one that the contemporary artists John Banvard and John R. Smith declared to be "the finest building in the west, and if paid for would have cost over half a million dollars."[48]

Endowments—all for the living—were first administered in the attic of the Nauvoo Temple on 10 December when twenty-eight men and women, including most members of the Quorum of the Twelve and their wives, "went through" the temple.[49] Following an established order, the next group to come were temple construction workers and their wives, followed by the various priesthood quorum members and wives in numbered sequence. Most of those who had been previously endowed were

---

47. Heber C. Kimball, *On the Potter's Wheel, The Diaries of Heber C. Kimball*, ed. Stanley B. Kimball (Urbana: The University of Illinois), 157. One room, the garden room, was furnished with pots of evergreens. For more on the layout, see Lisle G. Brown, "The Sacred Departments for Temple Work," 369.

48. John Francis McDermott, *The Lost Panoramas of the Mississippi* (Chicago: The University of Chicago Press, 1958), 59–60.

49. Prior to the temple's completion, Brigham Young said that the first floor mezzanine rooms with their large circular windows would be used for the endowment; however, he later changed his mind and adopted the Kirtland Temple model of using canvas partitions to subdivide a small meeting hall in the temple's attic. Lisle G. Brown, "'Temple Pro Tempore': The Salt Lake City Endowment House," *Journal of Mormon History* 34, no. 4 (Fall 2008): 3.

The Nauvoo Temple completed, 1846.

here re-endowed, as "it is now given in a more perfect manner because of better convenience."[50] Some days were devoted solely to the women. And all such work proceeded under the careful direction of Brigham Young, Heber C. Kimball, and other members of the Twelve in the attic or third floor of that sanctuary so many had worked so long and hard to build. In all, over 5,600 people received their endowments between 10 December 1845 and 8 February 1846.[51]

---

50. Joseph Fielding Journals, 1843–1859, MS 1567, Church History Library; see also "'They Might Have Known That He Was Not a Fallen Prophet': The Nauvoo Journal of Joseph Fielding," ed. Andrew F. Ehat, *BYU Studies* 19 (Winter 1979): 137.
51. "Nauvoo Temple Endowment Register," 3 vols., microfilm, Family History Library, Salt Lake City.

And the response was gratifying. Norton Jacob, who received his endowments with his wife on 12 December, forever praised the day. "At about 5 o'clock p.m. we were washed and anointed in the House of the Lord. It was the most interesting scene of all my life and one that afforded the most peace and joy that we had ever experienced since we were married, which has been over fifteen years."[52] Besides giving and receiving the ordinances, several of the Saints also met in the grand assembly room of the temple to teach and exhort, partake of the sacrament, dance, sing, pray, speak in tongues and testify, and otherwise "make a joyful noise unto the Lord." Their dancing was in the form of cotillions or the "french four"[53] and was designed "to drive away the enemy and melancholy and sadness of our persecutions, sicknesses and death."[54]

Temple workers, especially members of the Twelve, worked virtually around the clock, even sleeping in the temple, to accommodate the press of those wanting to receive their blessings before leaving for the West. At one point, the Twelve decided to devote one day, 20 December 1845, to cleaning and washing and to suspend temple operations; however, "on account of the anxiety of the Saints to receive their ordinances, the brethren and sisters volunteered to wash clothes every night."[55]

Women also played a key role in temple work. Approximately sixty females became ordinance workers.[56] Others performed in different ways,

---

52. The Life of Norton Jacob, typescript, Perry Special Collections, HBLL, BYU.
53. The "french four" is a form of country dance, almost a square dance, of four partners arranged in a square format. Cotillions was a more courtly version of the same, a forerunner of the quadrille.
54. Journal of Franklin D. Richards, 27 February 1895. Remembered Brigham Young: "After the dancing had continued about an hour, several excellent songs were sung, in which several of the brethren and sisters joined. The Upper California was sung by Erastus Snow, after which I called upon Sister [Elizabeth Anne] Whitney who stood up and invoking the gift of tongues, sang a beautiful song of Zion in tongues. The interpretation was given by her husband, Bishop [Newel K.] Whitney and me, it related to our efforts to build this house, to the privilege we now have of meeting in it, our departure shortly to the country of the Lamanites, their rejoicing when they hear the Gospel and of the ingathering of Israel." "History of the Church 1839–ca. 1882," 14:319–20, 30 December 1845, Church Historian's Office, Church History Library.
55. "History of the Church," 14:308, 20 December 1845.
56. The first women to assist in the washing and anointing of the sisters were Mary Ann Young, Vilate Kimball, and Elizabeth Ann Whitney. William Clayton, *An Intimate Chronicle: The Journals of William Clayton*, ed. George D. Smith (Salt Lake City: Signature Books, 1991), 203.

sometimes even bringing their young children with them, since babysitters were at a premium. Mercy R. Thompson, Mary Fielding Smith's sister who joined the Church in Toronto, Upper Canada (Ontario), went to work in the Nauvoo Temple the very first day it opened. She worked there constantly until the temple closed. She had one child, a daughter, and was "obliged to take her with her. She lived in the temple, the baby sometimes being in there for days without ever seeing outside the temple." Mercy worked in all the temple departments, including the washing and ironing of clothes for the workers, the cooking department, the clerk's office, and other places.[57]

As the time of exodus approached, the clamor to attend the temple became ever more insistent. As Brigham Young wrote on 3 February 1846:

> *Notwithstanding that I had announced that we would not attend to the administration of the ordinances, the house of the Lord was thronged all day, the anxiety being so great to receive, as if the brethren would have us stay here and continue the endowments until our way would be hedged up, and our enemies would intercept us. But I informed the brethren that this was not wise, and that we should build more temples, and have further opportunities to receive*

Among the many other sisters who worked as ordinance workers ("hands") in the temple were the following: Sarah Smith, Nancy Cahoon, Hormelia Dayton, Julia P. Martin, Sylvia Lance, Elvira Teeples, Susan A. Chapman, Margaret M. Raney, Caroline Crosby, Zeruah Goddard, Lucina Sessions, Myrza Alexander, Kermelia Dayton, Rahamah Derby, Catherine Mulliner, Chelmicia Hamilton, Louisa Clark, Susan Townsend, Mary E. Frost, Zilpha Jacobs, Sarah B. Barney, Margaret Ann Merrill, Cyntha Ann Eldridge, Lovina Mitchel, Altemira Shirtliff, Mariah E. Edwards, Almira Tufts, Lydia Granger, Mary H. Richards, R. M. Carrington, Deborah Ann Clements, Mary H. Parker, Eunice Holbrook, Martha L. Haven, Hester A. E. Brown, Constantia Hutchinson, Eda Rodgers, Electa Whitesides, Anna Harman, Eliza Anne Felt, Mary Jane Farnham, Caroline Huntington, Mary Smith, Nancy Rockwood, Mary Isabella Horne, Jane Ann Green, Rusina Sessions, Caroline Bird, Phebe Chase, Lucinda Harris, Elizabeth Colledge, Agness Taylor, Elizabeth Durphy, Sophronia Barmans, and Mary E. Frost.

57. *The Young Woman's Journal 1889–1929*, 4, no. 6 (April 1893). Joseph Smith never wrote down the endowment ceremony. However, Brigham Young and others mastered its contents. Young performed the ordinances several times under Joseph Smith's personal direction "and each time I got something more so that when we went through the Temple at Nauvoo I understood and knew how to place them there. We had our ceremonies pretty correct." L. John Nuttall Diary, 7 February 1877, as cited in Ehat, 255. Just months before his death, Young instructed Wilford Woodruff, the first temple president of the St. George Temple, to write down the full ordinance to ensure consistency and regularity in all future temples.

the blessings of the Lord, as soon as the Saints were prepared to receive them. In this Temple we have been abundantly rewarded, if we receive no more. I also informed the brethren that I was going to get my wagons started and be off. I walked some distance from the Temple supposing the crowd would disperse, but on returning I found the house filled to overflowing. Looking upon the multitude and knowing their anxiety, as they were thirsting and hungering for the word, we continued at work diligently in the House of the Lord.[58]

The last Nauvoo Temple endowments were given very early in the morning of Sunday, 8 February 1846, starting at 1:40 a.m. and lasting till past 7:40 a.m. at which time the temple doors finally and forever closed to such sacred activity. Later that morning, the Twelve met in the southeast corner, room 1, in the upper story where they knelt down around the altar and dedicated the so-far constructed temple, seeking heaven's blessings upon their pending departure. They also asked God "to enable them someday to finish the lower part of the building and dedicated it to Him and to preserve the temple as a monument to Joseph Smith."[59]

As various companies were preparing to head west in the footsteps of the vanguard company, preparations were also being made to formally dedicate the now fully completed Nauvoo Temple. Actually, parts of the temple had been dedicated on several past occasions, as different portions were finished. The altar was dedicated on 7 January 1846 and the attic prior to that time. On the evening of 30 April 1846, Orson Hyde and Wilford Woodruff, dressed in "Priestly robes" conducted a private dedication for a handful of Church leaders. Joseph Young offered the temple to the Lord "as an evidence of the willingness of His people, to fulfil His commandments, and build His holy house, even at the risk of their lives, and the sacrifice of their labor and earthly goods."[60] Wrote Wilford Woodruff:

---

58. Brigham Young Journal, 15:31, 3 February 1846.
59. Autobiography of Henry William Bigler, 8 February 1846, typescript, Perry Special Collections, HBLL, BYU.
60. "History of the Church," 15:32, 30 April 1846.

"At the close of the dedication we raised our voices in the united shout of Hosanna to God and the Lamb which entered the heavens to the joy and consolation of our hearts."[61]

During the following three days, in what must have been a forlorn celebration, Orson Hyde and Wilford Woodruff presided over the public dedication of the temple from 1 to 3 May. Admission was one dollar, to be used to meet building expenses. Franklin D. Richards, who attended the meetings along with some 5,000 others, recorded his feelings of satisfaction that the temple was finally completed. "Today seemed to me to be the consummation of what the Saints have anticipated for more than five years," he happily recorded in his journal, "and the spirit seems to testify that the offering is an acceptable one to him who commanded it to be built, and the satisfaction of feeling that we and our dead are not rejected, is a consolation to the faithful of the Priesthood that is almost unspeakable."[62] What Richards and other leaders were trying to impress was not the fact that they were about to abandon the temple, as if evidence of a failed promise, but rather as a somber celebration that they had accomplished the command of the Lord to complete it. Orson Hyde, who presided, echoed that sentiment: "We have only been saved as it were by the skin of our teeth."[63] Wilford Woodruff then added: "The Saints had labored faithfully and finished the Temple, and were now received as a church with our dead. This is glory enough for building the temple, and thousands of the Saints have received their endowment in it. And the light will not go out."[64]

As the Saints moved across the Mississippi and into Iowa Territory on the first leg of their exodus to the West, many stopped to turn around one

---

61. *Wilford Woodruff's Journal*, 3:41, 30 April 1846.
62. Franklin D. Richards Journal, 30, MS 1215. Richards is referencing the belief many held that if the temple were never finished, the Lord would reject the Saints and their kindred dead.
63. *Wilford Woodruff's Journal*, 3:43, 1 or 2 May 1846.
64. Wilford Woodruff, as cited in Leonard, *Nauvoo*, 590–91. There were some, like Lyman Wight and William Meeks, who felt that God had rejected the Church and its leadership for not finishing the temple in a timely manner as required by Joseph Smith's revelation of 1841. This, however, was a distinct minority point of view but one that Church leaders were anxious to refute in a very public way. See *JSP, Council of Fifty Minutes,* 263, 438.

last time to gaze upon this imposing structure and symbol of their faith. "While crossing over a ridge seven miles from Nauvoo," Priddy Meeks later recalled, "we looked back and took a last sight of the Temple. . . . We were sad and sorrowful. The emotions of our mind at that time I cannot describe. The thoughts of it almost disqualify me for writing, although so many years have passed away since that time."[65]

"HAS THE LORD TURNED BANKRUPT?"—EFFORTS TO SELL THE NAUVOO AND KIRTLAND TEMPLES

What may come as news to some is that while the Saints were toiling to complete the temple, the Twelve were making quiet but determined efforts to sell it. Despite every good intention and promise of those better off to help the poor and the widowed get out of Nauvoo, the immediate question remained: Where would the money come from to transport thousands of people, many penniless and utterly destitute, into the wilderness? So much of the tithing funds had gone into building the temple and the Nauvoo House that little, if any, was available for the exodus. Furthermore, Emma Smith and Brigham Young clashed over whether properties other than the temple held in the name of her husband belonged to her or to the Church, effectively placing a legal bar on any other land sales in Joseph's name. And Nauvoo economics, based fundamentally on a bartering system, were anything but robust. While many clung to the hope that they would be able to sell off their properties and improvements at reasonable prices, potential buyers, aware that the Latter-day Saints were abandoning their city, would bide their time until the city, wasted and deserted, would be sold off at bargain prices.

To ensure the best possible sale price of Church lands and properties, as well as private homes now abandoned by the Saints, the Twelve appointed Almon W. Babbitt, Esq., Joseph L. Heywood, and John S. Fullmer trustees to remain in Nauvoo with power of attorney for the Church to negotiate

---

65. Priddy Meeks, https://www.boap.ord/LDS/Early-Saints/PMeeks.html.

the best possible terms. "For myself," confided Fullmer, "I am chosen together with two of the Brethren as 'Trustee-in-Trust' to dispose of all Church property and to use it in assisting the poor to go to the West. We shall about finish the temple by the first of May, when it will be dedicated to the Most High God, after which we think we will sell it. We expect to get $200,000 for it [about one quarter of its cost]."[66] Babbitt had been earlier entrusted to sell off properties in Kirtland. These three were the only members of the Church allowed by enemies of the Church to stay in Nauvoo.

Those private properties they were able to dispose of went for mere cents on the dollar. Nevertheless, the Church leaders clung to the hope that because of its size, imposing appearance, and quality workmanship, the temple would sell for at least $200,000. In fact, Brigham Young's directive was not only to sell the Nauvoo Temple but also to divest the Church of the Kirtland Temple in Ohio as well as other properties. The proceeds from such sales would serve the following purposes: 1) fund the costs of exodus, including wagons and provisions which many could not afford; 2) charter steamboats in the spring "to convey a freight of the [sick] and poor to the highest navigable point on the Missouri River if it can be, to Council Bluffs"; 3) pay off debts owed to hundreds of unpaid temple laborers; 4) pay off various legal expenses incurred by Joseph Smith over the past several years; and 5) pay off legitimate land and mortgage debts owed to Nauvoo landowners.[67]

As for the Kirtland Temple, the trustees placed an advertisement in the *Hancock Eagle* seeking to sell it "on advantageous terms."[68] Babbitt boasted in early 1847 that he had found a buyer for $10,000. The truth

---

66. John S. Fullmer to H. H. Blackhead, John S. Fullmer Letter book, 1836–1881, 24 April 1846, Church History Library.
67. For much more on the highly complicated story of the attempted sale of the Nauvoo and Kirtland temples, see Richard E. Bennett, "'Has the Lord Turned Bankrupt?' The Attempted Sale of the Nauvoo Temple, 1846–1850" *Journal of the Illinois State Historical Society* 95, no. 3 (Autumn 2002): 235–63.
68. Leonard, *Nauvoo: A Place of Peace*, 592–94.

is, however, that Babbitt, ever inclined to exaggeration, if not deception, never did sell it and for a long time no one purchased it.[69]

Their best chance of selling the Nauvoo Temple was to the Roman Catholic Church, which might have been able to use so large a building with so many rooms as a college or gathering place for Catholics emigrating from overseas. At the invitation of Almon Babbitt, Bishop John Purcell of Cincinnati appointed Rev. Hilary Tucker and Rev. George Hamilton to go to Nauvoo, which they did in December 1845. Given a private tour of the temple by Brigham Young himself, both gentlemen seemed "highly pleased with the temple and the City and appear to feel sanguine that the Catholics should get this temple and vicinity."[70] They reported back to Bishop Purcell their favorable inclinations and promised "a decided answer" by Christmas. To their great disappointment, however, Church leadership heard back from Rev. Tucker in early January 1846 that the bishop could not raise enough money to purchase the properties.

The decision to sell the temple was not publicly made known until it was finally completed and dedicated on 1 May 1846. Prudence seemed to

---

69. J. Tyler wrote to William E. McLellin in February 1847 from Batavia, New York: "A. Babbitt preaches here tonight, but I shall oppose him. He says he sold the Temple at Kirtland when he was there for $10,000, but I believe him to be a right Rev. liar." McLellin replied: "Babbitt's sale of the Temple here was a mere sham, as events since have proved." *The Ensign of Liberty of the Church of Jesus Christ*, 1847–1849, 1, no. 4 (January 1848): 60; see also Loving, "Ownership of the Kirtland Temple." John Taylor once roundly excoriated Christopher Dixon for seeking to lease the Kirtland Temple in perpetuity for much less than what Taylor thought it was worth. "You speak of disposing of the temple with as much coolness as you would that of disposing of an old broken down horse," he began his 1855 letter. "Perhaps it cost you nothing; but it cost the martyr'd Prophet Joseph and his brother Hyrum and their revered and honored father and hundreds of dead and living saints, many, many, days of toil, labor and anxiety, who labored on its walls in the midst of poverty reproach and almost the lack of everything. . . . Stalwart men labor'd in that Temple with nothing but musk and milk to live upon and in many instances, barely bread and water until their knees trembled with weakness. And would you part with it in perpetuity, if you had the power? And for what? Is it so small a matter that it is not worth mentioning? Take care what you are doing lest peradventure in attempting to dispose of the Lords House, the Lord may dispose of you with as much coolness." John Taylor to Christopher Dixon, Miscellaneous Letters, John Taylor Collection 1829–1894, 27 April 1855, MS 1346, Church History Library.
70. Journal of Heber C. Kimball, Autobiography and Journals, 1837–1845, 10 December 1845, typescript, MS 2737, box 7, Church History Library; see also Heber C. Kimball Journals, MSS 6142, Perry Special Collections, HBLL, BYU.

dictate such a course.[71] Not known was how the Saints, who had sacrificed so much to build the structure, would respond to overtures to sell it. However, such reservations evaporated when, during the dedication services, a vote was taken to gain sustaining support for the Twelve's decision to do so. Lorenzo Young, Brigham's younger brother, reported the motion was "carried with one dissenting voice."[72]

There were, however, other considerations in selling the temples besides strictly financial. John Taylor wrote in September 1845:

> *[We] considered that we had a perfect right so to do, that we had been driven from and despoiled of our property long enough and that we should be justified in taking a course of that kind, that the City and temple would be more likely to be preserved in safety by wealthy and influential men purchasing property and settling here, than by apostates and half-hearted Mormons having charge of affairs during our absence, and that if we should return we should again inherit our places, and if we do not inherit them in Time, we and our children will inherit them in hereafter.*[73]

Among those Taylor was referring to was the colorful and charismatic James J. Strang who had converted just a few months before Joseph Smith's

---

71. *JSP, Council of Fifty Minutes,* 506; see also Richard E. Bennett, *Mormons at the Missouri: Winter Quarters, 1846–1852* (Norman: University of Oklahoma, 1987, 2004), 40. The Quorum of the Twelve were never very enthusiastic about selling the Nauvoo Temple. "We have felt much anxiety on that subject," admitted George A. Smith in a letter to Brigham Young. "But if you in your wisdom should think it best to sell the same to help the poor in the present emergency we frankly concur, notwithstanding we feel opposed to a Methodist congregation ever listening to a mob [preach] in that holy Place, but are willing to sacrifice our feelings at all times for the good of the saints." George A. Smith to Brigham Young and Council, Brigham Young Papers, 26 April 1846. Consideration was also given to selling the Seventies Hall to the Catholics, if only for $1500. William Quarter, the Catholic Bishop of Chicago, did purchase the Hall from James E. Furness, interim owner, in 1847 for $700. *JSP, Council of Fifty Minutes,* 520.
72. Journal of James Allen Scott, 1 May 1846, MS 1398, Church History Library. The decision to sell the Kirtland Temple, along with the Nauvoo Temple, was reiterated by the Twelve in their deliberations on 29 April 1846 while crossing Iowa. "A vote was taken whether the Temple at Nauvoo and Kirtland with public lands should be sold—reasons w[ere] advanced—the poverty of the Church, the probability of our enemies getting it, or destroying it, if not sold—vote unanimous in favor of selling." Diary of William C. Staines, 29 April 1846, MS 2453, Church History Library.
73. *John Taylor's Nauvoo Journal,* ed. Dean C. Jessee (Provo, Utah: Grandin Book Company, 1996), 109, 14 September 1845.

death. He wasted little time proclaiming a secret letter of his prophetic appointment, allegedly signed by Joseph Smith himself. Dubbed the "Voree Prophet," Strang was by late 1845 well into his newly chosen career of persuading many Latter-day Saints that he was Joseph Smith's legitimate successor. Expert with pen and press, Strang busied himself publishing revelations, finding and translating ancient buried plates, and laying claim to Church leadership from his home base in Spring Prairie, Wisconsin, which he renamed "Voree." Strang sensed not merely a vacuum of leadership but also an intense longing among many for a new prophet-leader. As one of his followers put it: "A Church without a Prophet, is not the Church for me; If it has no head to lead it, in it I would not be."[74]

Far more successful than Sidney Rigdon's claim for guardianship over the Church ever was, Strang acted quickly to fill the void as the lead companies of Saints headed west. Flashing like a meteorite across the sky, Strang soon appointed himself president of the Church, and claimed total authority by excommunicating Brigham Young, criticizing his plan of exodus as one doomed to failure, and initiating a very ambitious, far-reaching missionary campaign among scattered congregations of Saints along the East Coast and in Great Britain. He even persuaded Martin Harris, one of the Three Witnesses, to join his British proselyting crusade—at least for a time. As another of Strang's followers wrote: "Now I ask who could obtain a revelation or commandment of the Church to abandon the temple, the Nauvoo House, and the Holy City which God had appointed for a place of refuge and for the deliverance of his people? Was not the Lord able to protect them from the mob and to fulfill his part of the covenant?"[75] If not "worth the skin of a flea," as Young derisively once said of him, Strang, at least for a short time, was proving a formidable contender. And nothing

---

74. Samuel M. Reese to James J. Strang, James Jesse Strang Collection, Yale collection of Western Americana, Beinecke Library, Yale University, 12 July 1846.
75. Samuel Moore Reeve to James J. Strang, James Strang Collection, 12 July 1846.

James Jesse Strang (1813–1856). *Sidney Rigdon (1793–1876).*

would have validated his claim to succession more than possessing, if not owning, the Nauvoo Temple.[76]

Thus all the way west, the Twelve kept a wary eye on Strang's maneuverings. In a carefully crafted letter to Emma Smith, Strang wrote in February 1846:

> *Should it please God to forgive the iniquity of the people and save Nauvoo from impending ruin, . . . possibly I might make it my residence at some future day. In such an event I should be greatly pleased to have you for a neighbor and think you would not have reason to complain of quite such a state of things as has existed there since the death of your husband. . . . Now sister . . . if you intend to remain in Nauvoo, you cannot well imagine how much I should rejoice in your full and hearty cooperation in my efforts of the regulation and*

---

76. Strang had convinced himself and others that he rightly owned both the Kirtland and Nauvoo temples as the only claimant to the presidency of the Church. "As James Strang is the successor in the Presidency and nobody else holds that office or pretends to hold it, there can be no difficulty as to the title [of the Nauvoo Temple], whatever there may be as to the possession," *Voree Herald* 1, no. 9 (September 1846): 2.

salvation of the city. . . . I am led to believe that from your influence and inclination you would be able to accomplish much.[77]

By courting Emma's favor and by commandeering the temple, Strang hoped to claim legitimacy and influence. The record shows, however, that Emma was quite cool toward the Wisconsin charismatic and remained suspicious of his teachings and intentions, even though she met with him on different occasions.[78] Strang did break ground near Burlington, Wisconsin, for a temple and dug out a foundation but it was never constructed. Strang's tragic murder in 1856 on Beaver Island in Lake Michigan virtually ended the Strangite movement. Eventually most of his followers drifted into the "New Organization" or Reorganized movement.

Strang was not the only defector to consider the importance of temple work. Apostle Lyman Wight, the "Wild Ram of the Mountains" and a member of the Council of Fifty, believed the commission he had received from Joseph Smith to explore southern Texas as a possible Zion location brought with it authority to perform various temple ordinances in the Texas wilderness. Resolute in his convictions that he was equal to Brigham Young in apostolic authority and opposed to moving west, Wight was eventually excommunicated.[79] Likewise Alpheus Cutler, a high councilor in Nauvoo and a fellow Council of Fifty member, eventually broke with the Church at Winter Quarters over the timing of the redemption of Zion in Missouri and moved with his followers to Manti, Iowa. He and his followers also continued forms of temple worship in Iowa and later in northern Minnesota. A remnant of his disciples still survives in Independence, Missouri, and performs a form of temple ritual and ceremony.[80] And while

---

77. James J. Strang to Emma Smith, Brigham Young Papers, Mormon Manuscript Collection, Perry Special Collections, HBLL, BYU, 22 February 1846.
78. Trustees to Brigham Young, Brigham Young Papers, 19 February 1847.
79. Melvin C. Johnson, *Polygamy on the Pedernales: Lyman Wight's Mormon Villages in Antebellum Texas, 1845 to 1858* (Logan, Utah: Utah State University Press, 2006), 112–13, 122.
80. Danny L. Jorgensen and Andrew Leary, "Anointed Queens and Priestesses: Alpheus Cutler's Plural Wives," *The John Whitmer Historical Association Journal*, 38, no. 1 (Spring/Summer 2018): 55–79; Christopher James Blythe, "The Upper-Room Work: Esotericism in the Church of Jesus Christ (Cutlerite), 1853–1912," *Journal of Mormon History* 40, no. 3 (Summer 2014): 43–92; see also

the Reorganized Church of Jesus Christ of Latter Day Saints considered very early on in its history the doctrinal validity of baptisms for the dead, its conviction that the Nauvoo Temple was never fully completed and that plural marriage was a wrong and misdirected practice, meant a divine rejection of the "Mormon Saints" and of the need for any kind of temple ordinances.[81]

"NOW THE MORMONS ARE DRIVEN"

The scepter of hate and persecution did not wane with the departure of the Latter-day Saints beginning in February 1846. For the most destitute who could not afford to leave and despite every best effort of the trustees to sell off properties and to stay the day of pending execution, September 1846 spelled disaster. One struggling, faithful widow, Elizabeth Gilbert, who, like many others, sensed rightly the coming storm, begged for help from Brigham Young who then was leading the Saints some 300 miles west at the Missouri River.

> *It [Nauvoo] is truly a lonesome and dismal place. . . . I want to know what I shall do[.] Is it best for me to remain among the gentiles? . . . My body is almost worn out a struggling to get a shelter for my head. . . . Tell all my friends that I yet live and my faith in the gospel is as firm as the everlasting hills and strangism [the teachings of James Strang] has no effect on my mind. . . . If you think it wisdom for me to come out this fall how shall I gather[?] Council me as though I was your child or Sister and whatever you say that I will do.*[82]

Richard Bennett, "Lamanism, Lymanism and Cornfields," *Journal of Mormon History* 13, no. 1 (1987): 45–60.

81. Community of Christ (RLDS) still very much believes in temples, as it owns and operates the original temple in Kirtland, Ohio, and another temple (1994) in Independence, Missouri—both majestic reminders of its commitment to faith, peace, and community. It does not, however, believe, in practicing baptisms for the dead, endowments, and marriage sealings of any kind. Mark A. Scherer, *The Journey of a People: The Era of Restoration, 1820 to 1844*; *The Journey of a People: The Era of Reorganization, 1844 to 1946*; *The Journey of a People: The Era of Worldwide Community, 1946 to 2015* (Independence, Mo.; Community of Christ Seminary Press, 2013-2016).

82. Elizabeth Gilbert to Brigham Young, Brigham Young Papers, 13 August 1846.

Led by Thomas C. Sharp, editor of the *Warsaw Signal* and a key operative in the martyrdom of Joseph and Hyrum Smith, some 1,200 restive mob militiamen stormed the city of Nauvoo beginning 11 September. In the ensuing "battle of Nauvoo," four men were killed, three on the Nauvoo side and at least one among the advancing force. After three days of stalled conflict, the remaining defenders were overwhelmed and fled across the river. Some 900 straggling remnants were forced out of the city at the point of gun, cannon, and bayonet. Many were "rebaptized" in the river by the mobs, their homes desecrated, their meager crops and gardens destroyed, their belongings stolen or discarded. Most of these so-called "Poor Camps" somehow managed to cross the river to find refuge in Montrose, Iowa, where the "Miracle of the Quail" resulted in their temporary deliverance. When Brigham Young heard of their desperate plea for help, rescue parties dashed back across eastern Iowa in a bold effort to save their fellow believers in what will ever be remembered as one of the most telling rescue efforts in all of Latter-day Saint history. Thanks to what many perceived as divine intervention and the unselfish and courageous efforts of the rescuers, only a few in the Poor Camps perished that hurtful fall. Many spent the winter at Garden Grove, Mt. Pisgah, or Council Bluffs.

But in Nauvoo, with the Saints all but completely gone, the possessing vigilante army wreaked havoc with the temple, breaking off the horns of the oxen in the baptismal font, urinating everywhere, smearing feces from one place to another, and desecrating whatever stood in their path. A mob preacher wasted little time in ascending to the top of the tower from where he triumphantly shouted, "Peace, Peace, Peace to all the inhabitants of the earth, now the Mormons are driven."[83] Soon the conquered city lay desolate and deserted, a forlorn memory of once happier days.

On 2 October 1848, the Home Missionary Society of New York, a

---

83. Thomas Bullock to Franklin D. Richards, *Millennial Star*, 10 (January 15, 1848), as cited in Leonard, *Nauvoo, A People of Faith*, 614.

historic Protestant missionary society founded in 1826, made overtures to rent the temple for up to fifteen years.[84] Before final arrangements were made, however, on the night of 9 October 1848, a fire broke out, starting in the spire of the temple, likely the work of an arsonist. Flames soon engulfed the entire structure and the sound of falling timbers and stones cracking from the intense heat could be heard clear across the river. "It was a sight of mournful sublimity," the *Hancock Patriot* reported. "Who," the editor asked, "would destroy such an elegant and celebrated work of art?"[85]

In early 1849 a group of some 300 Icarians, a communitarian/utopian religious society from France under the direction of Etienne Cabet, moved to Nauvoo to take advantage of the depressed land prices. They purchased abandoned houses for back taxes, rented 800 acres of farmland, and made plans to buy the temple site and its charred remains in March of that year from the trustees for $2,000.[86] But before they could restore the structure as a meeting hall and school, a vicious storm roared through town on 27 June 1850 leaving barely one stone upon another. To save what they could of their investment, the Icarians salvaged the temple stones for use in a communal dining hall, a boarding school, and other local buildings. By 1855, most of them had abandoned Nauvoo in hopes of better settlements elsewhere.

CONCLUSION

The Nauvoo Temple will forever hold a place of reverent remembrance to the Latter-day Saints. Building upon the foundation first laid in the Kirtland Temple, the legacy of Nauvoo must include not only baptisms for the dead but also endowments for the living, priesthood blessings of comfort and strength, and the introduction of eternal marriage. Furthermore, it became the symbol of their faith, the pledge of great expectations and

---

84. Journal History, 2 October 1848, as cited in Don F. Colvin, "The Fate of the Temple," in *Nauvoo Temple: A Story of Faith* (Provo, Utah: Religious Studies Center, Brigham Young University, 2002), 261.
85. Leonard, *Nauvoo: A Place of Peace*, 629.
86. Leonard, *Nauvoo: A Place of Peace*, 629.

"THE FULNESS OF THOSE BLESSINGS"

The burning of the Nauvoo Temple.

the promise of blessings yet to come, and the hope of their future in an untamed wilderness. Though abandoned at the point of its dedication, the Nauvoo Temple gave the Saints a visible anchor to their faith and a literal expression of their devotion and sacrifice. And to repeat Wilford Woodruff: that "light" would not go out.

As the Saints moved across the Mississippi and into Iowa Territory on the first leg of their exodus to the West, some stopped to turn around one last time to gaze upon this symbol of their faith. Lewis Barney never forgot that poignant moment:

> *On reaching the summit between the Mississippi and Des Moines Rivers the company made a halt for the purpose of taking a last piercing look at the Nauvoo temple, the spire of which was then glittering in the bright shining sun. The last view of the temple was witnessed in the midst of sighs and lamentations, all faces in gloom and sorrow bathed in tears, [from] being forced from our homes and temple that had cost so much toil and suffering to complete its erection.*[87]

---

87. Life Sketch of Lewis Barney, Nauvoo Lands and Records Office, Nauvoo, Illinois, as cited in Ronald O. Barney, *One Side By Himself: The Life and Times of Lewis Barney, 1808–1894* (Logan, Utah: Utah State University Press, 2001), 85.

Chapter 4

"We Mean to Conquer or Die Trying"
TEMPLE WORK AT WINTER QUARTERS, 1846–1848

I feel as though Nauvoo will be filled with all manner of abominations. It is no place for the Saints; and the Spirit whispers to me that the brethren had better get away as fast as they can. . . . I hope the brethren will not have trouble there, but the dark clouds of sorrow are gathering fast over that place.[1]

This chapter will attempt to show the continuity, vitality, creative adaptability, and robust flexibility that contributed to the maintaining of a lively temple consciousness among the Latter-day Saints in their trying flight into the wilderness and more especially at their Winter Quarters. They may have left their temples far behind but they brought their covenants and faith in temple work very much with them. Brigham Young, who was finally ordained President of the Church at the Kanesville Tabernacle in December 1847, showed that he was considerate of the needs of his people, even if it meant making adjustments to his own policies and practices. It was, after all, a church in flux and on the road west, adopting and adapting as circumstances demanded, and was very much in transition and development. This was most especially so in regard to temple worship and blessings.

---

1. Brigham Young to Joseph Young, Journal History, 9 March 1846.

"IN THE MIDST OF SIGHS AND LAMENTATIONS"

In the minds of its enemies, The Church of Jesus Christ of Latter-day Saints, with a powerful, charismatic leader who was both mayor and prophet-leader, a religious doctrine that did not adhere to traditional Protestant teachings, and new marriage practices, was perceived as anti-American, anti-Christian, and anti-family. And Brigham Young, as virtual leader of the Saints in his capacity as president of the Quorum of the Twelve, could read the writing on the wall better than any other. For the survival of the Church, he had rightly reasoned, they would have to leave Illinois sooner rather than later.

The revocation of the Nauvoo Charter in early 1845 by an Illinois legislature once friendly to the Saints was, if not a Governor Boggs-like extermination order, a legislative decree that Nauvoo could no longer exist as a municipality under Illinois statute. Despite objections from a few legislators, "the tide of popular passion and frenzy was too strong to be resisted."[2] The act to disincorporate Nauvoo stripped the city of its legal identity, abolished the right to its own civic government, police force, municipal court, university, and Nauvoo Legion. It likewise reduced its corporate status from a city to a town merely one square mile in size (to include the temple) and in other ways terminated Nauvoo's right to exist. Everything Joseph Smith and others had worked so long and hard for was repealed by an overwhelming vote of the state legislature. In its place, the Saints unofficially renamed Nauvoo the "City of Joseph" but, in law, it was only the town of Nauvoo with limited rights and protections under state law. Nevertheless, converts continued to arrive from Great Britain, Canada, and other parts of the United States. New homes were built throughout the city, missionaries continued to sally forth, and life continued much the same as before.

However, an ever-widening, ever-deepening and suspicious local

---
2. Josiah Lamborn to Brigham Young, *History of the Church*, 7:370, 28 January 1845, as cited in Leonard, *Nauvoo: A Place of Peace*, 467.

opposition seriously began to galvanize in the fall of 1845. Enemies began setting fires in small settlements outside Nauvoo, burning down farms and farmhouses. By October, Hancock County residents were spelling out in one public resolution after another that either the Saints leave the following spring or they would take the law into their own hands. Even the once friendly city of Quincy (fifty miles south) passed a series of resolutions demanding a complete withdrawal of the Saints by the following 1 May—if only for their own good! Soon afterward the city of Carthage held a convention of its own made up of angry citizens from several surrounding counties calling for the establishment of an organized area-wide militia to drive the Saints out of Hancock County, by force if necessary. In late October, Governor Ford, fearful of an imminent outbreak of hostilities, ordered a peacekeeping army to the Nauvoo area to postpone what he foresaw as inevitable wide-scale violence, perhaps even civil war.

Meanwhile Brigham Young, in consultation with his fellow members of the Quorum of the Twelve and the Council of Fifty acting in its political and economic advisory role to the Twelve, had already made up his mind. At least as early as 28 August 1845 he had decided to send out 3,000 abled-bodied men to take their families with them and find a new home the next spring in "Upper California."[3] "The prejudice[s] of the people are such," he confided in a letter to Wilford Woodruff, "that the state cannot possibly protect us and that it is therefore advisable for us to remove as the only conditions of peace. We have determined to do so in the Spring."[4] Irene Hascall, a young woman living in Nauvoo, sensed their determination and desire to let their enemies know of some of their plans when she wrote the following: "The Twelve have issued a proclamation that if they will let them alone this winter . . . and do what they can to prepare us for journeying, all that follow the Twelve will go where they will not trouble [the] United States with Mormon religion. . . . I think probably [we] will

---

3. Brigham Young, "History of the Church, 1839–ca. 1882," 14:16, 28 August 1845.
4. Brigham Young to Wilford Woodruff, Brigham Young Office Files, 16 October 1845, CR 1234 1.

cross the Rocky Mountains to a healthier climate."⁵

As he had done before, when leading so many Saints eastward from Far West, Missouri, to Quincy, Illinois, in the winter of 1838/39 while Joseph Smith languished in Liberty Jail, Brigham Young once more called for a covenant of exodus. Abiding by the wishes of Church leaders, many heads of households promised to consecrate their properties, possessions, and energies to assist in every way the pending exodus of the many widowed, infirm, and destitute among them. This temple-inspired "Nauvoo Covenant"—that "we would never cease our exertions, by all the means and influence within our reach, till all the Saints who were obliged to leave Nauvoo should be located at some gathering place of the Saints"—was prerequisite to the successful completion of their departure plans. And Brother Brigham, in his characteristic care for the poor and the needy, would hold them to it.⁶

Brigham Young (1801–1877).

---

5. Irene Hascall to Ursula B. Hascall, Brigham Young Office Files, 26 September 1845, CR 1234 1.
6. "Second General Epistle of the Presidency of the Church of Jesus Christ of Latter-day Saints scattered throughout the earth," in *Settling the Valley, Proclaiming the Gospel: The General Epistles of the Mormon First Presidency*, ed. Reid L. Neilson and Nathan N. Waite (New York City: Oxford University Press, 2017), 87.
   Another covenant that some members made while still in Nauvoo was the so-called "Oath of Vengeance" for the murders of Joseph and Hyrum Smith. Not part of any salvific temple ordinance, this was a promise that some made in the Nauvoo Temple to pray that God would somehow avenge the deaths of Joseph and Hyrum and that "earth must atone for the blood of that man" or men. *Smoot Hearing, Proceedings before the Committee on Privileges and Elections of*

Through the fall of 1845, Nauvoo was alive with busy preparations of every kind. The sisters prepared winter clothing, sewed, and whether resolutely or reluctantly organized for departing. And "nearly every man was some kind of a mechanic to build wagons," as one woman remembered, "and the whole mind of the people was engaged in the great work of emigrating west in the Spring."[7] Even an unfinished portion of the temple was used in making, repairing, and finishing wagons and other articles for the pending departure. By the end of the year, almost 2,000 wagons were completed or in late stages of construction. And by January, in an attempt to buy more time, the Nauvoo High Council stated that at least Church leaders would begin leaving sometime in March, with the rest to leave in April or May, in time to meet the Quincy Convention deadline.

At an 18 January 1846 meeting in the attic story of the temple, it was ascertained what number of the Saints were "ready and willing to start should necessity compel our instant removal, being aware that evil is intended towards us, and that our safety alone will depend upon our departure from this place."[8] Why the Saints began leaving Nauvoo on 4 February 1846 in the teeth of a winter's callous cold, had everything to do with rumors of being intercepted by the United States Army intent on stopping them in their westward course. Also circulating were intensifying threats of arrest and assassination of Brigham Young and other leaders. But above all, by beginning to leave in February, they hoped to show clear evidence of their intention to quit the state, buy time of their enemies, and in so doing protect the remaining membership as they planned for a more orderly departure in the spring. They hoped it would also ensure time to

---

the United States Senate in the Matter of the Protests Against the Right of Hon. Reed Smoot, A Senator from the State of Utah, to Hold His Seat, 4 vols. (1906, Washington: Government Printing Office) 4:6–7; see also 1:741–43, 791–92; 2:77–79, 148–49, 151–53, 160–62, 181–83, 189–90, 759, 762–764, 779; 4:68–69, and 495–97.

7. Letter of Irene Hascall, Hascall Family Letters, 29 October 1845, MS 22096, Church History Library.

8. Brigham Young, "History of the Church," 18 January 1846, CR 100 102.

complete and dedicate the temple and time and opportunity to sell off Church and private properties to finance the staggering costs of exodus.

ZION IN THE WILDERNESS

It had all started off well enough, the Iowa crossing that is, despite their unexpectedly early wintry departure and noticeable lack of provisions among the many in the vanguard company of the Twelve. They hoped to reach the Missouri River no later than the end of April, regroup at Council Bluffs, and then head west and reach the Rockies later that same season.[9]

The cruel fact was, however, that they would never make the Missouri on schedule for a wagon full of reasons. Too many of the early vanguard companies left Nauvoo ill-provided, unprepared, and under-provisioned for the taxing journey ahead of them. To support their struggling families, many ended up subcontracting themselves out for spring work among Iowa and Missouri farmers all along the way.[10] Meanwhile, camp organizations and chains of command had to be continually reshuffled and streamlined as plans changed almost from day to day. And changing routes on at least two or three occasions cost them precious time. Such delays drove Brigham Young to exasperation:

> *The Saints have crowded on us all the while, and have completely tied our hands by importuning and saying: Do not leave us behind. Wherever you go, we want to go, be with you, and thus our hands and feet have been bound which has caused our delay to the present time, and now hundreds at Nauvoo are continually praying . . . that they may overtake us and be with us . . . They are afraid to let us go on and leave them behind, forgetting that they have covenanted to help the poor away at the sacrifice of all their property.*[11]

---

9. For a full rendition of the crossing of Iowa see Bennett, *Mormons at the Missouri*; see also Susan Easton Black and William G. Hartley, eds., *The Iowa Mormon Trail: Legacy of Faith and Courage* (Orem, Utah: Helix Publishing, 1997).
10. Journal History, 21 May 1846.
11. Journal History, 3 May 1846.

But by far their most aggravating problem was the weather. Spring was so late that season that prairie pasture did not appear until mid-April, much later than anticipated. "We were traveling in the season significantly termed 'between hay and grass'," wrote Eliza R. Snow, "and the teams . . . wasted in flesh had but little strength."[12] "All that could were obliged to walk to favor the poor animals," Helen Mar Whitney recalled. "Our feet would sink into the deep mud at every step, and some of us came near being minus of shoes; as for umbrellas, they were rare articles."[13] One cannot exaggerate the havoc wrought upon these struggling pioneers as they suffered, slid, and sloshed across Iowa Territory, what they called "a great mud hole" from Nauvoo to Grand River.

The net result was that it took them 130 days to cross the 327 miles between the Mississippi and the Missouri rivers. By the time the advanced company of the Twelve finally reached the Omaha hills in mid-June they were already two months behind schedule, in need of immediate rest, and facing the troubling reality that going on to the Rockies that year was sheer madness. After toying briefly with the idea of camping at Grand Island (Nebraska) or Fort Laramie (Wyoming), the Twelve decided to winter on the banks of the Missouri River for reasons compelling and obvious. Their cattle herds could graze on either side of the river on the pea vines and rush bottoms that provided excellent feed even during the winter; they were relatively close to the Missouri settlements where they could trade for food and supplies; the area was well-watered; the river could provide means of steamboat transportation for those too sick to travel overland; and finally, they could get right to work preparing for the coming winter. In retrospect, one wonders where else they could have gone given their many delays, broken plans, and frustrated timetables. It was not the Rockies, but for a season "Zion" would rest in the borders of the wilderness.

---

12. Tullidge, *Women of Mormondom*, 312.
13. Helen Mar Kimball Whitney, "Our Travels beyond the Mississippi," *Woman's Exponent* 12 (1 January 1884), 15.

"WE MEAN TO CONQUER OR DIE TRYING"

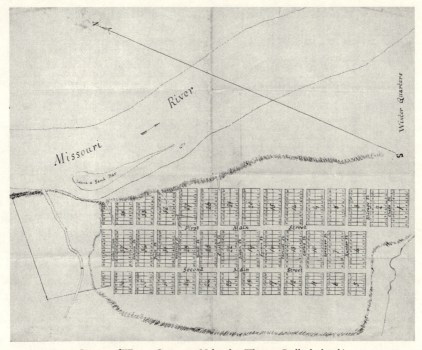

Layout of Winter Quarters, Nebraska (Thomas Bullock sketch).

After two false starts at settling at Cold Springs and Cutler's Park, Church leaders selected a permanent site in September nearer the river with higher bluffs for protection from the prairie winds and better natural fortifications. They quickly surveyed their new city into five-acre blocks measuring twenty by forty rods (380 feet by 660 feet) each with twenty lots per block. The city plat initially called for forty-one blocks, sixteen named streets, and 594 lots. All cabins were to be built on the outside of each block near the streets with yards running inward up against those of the homes behind them so as to form a well-ventilated, protected garden area. By the end of December 1846 their town of Winter Quarters, consisting of 538 log cabins, 83 sod houses and caves, and a bustling population of 4,000 had all the makings of a great prairie city.[14]

---

14. Journal History, 1 April 1848.

"WE MEAN TO CONQUER OR DIE TRYING"

However, the toils of leaving Nauvoo, the exhausting trek across Iowa, the endless spring storms, their insufficient provisions and scanty diet, inadequate winter shelter, and unhealthy riverbank encampments were anything but conducive to good health. Whereas the majority of deaths before the year's end were arguably exposure-related, those in the winter and spring of 1847 resulted from vitamin, protein, and other dietary insufficiencies. Most fatal of all was the outbreak of scurvy, or as they often called it, the "black-leg" or "black-canker." Contemporary accounts brim with references to this wrenching scourge and Parley P. Pratt, upon returning to the settlement in the spring of 1847 after a mission to England, admitted to great numbers "being borne away by the disease."[15] Without vegetables, fresh fruits, and other ready sources of vitamins and protein, and lacking modern refrigeration and transportation, little wonder they began to perish. In fact, before that first year was over, at least 723 would die in Winter Quarters and across the river in Kanesville and in many of the smaller Iowa settlements, an epidemic rate of one in twelve! At least 300–400 would die the next year, pushing the mortality rate far above normal levels.[16]

The tragic occurrences of sickness and death at Winter Quarters tested the faith of the Saints and greatly taxed their loyalty, but like any other deeply believing people, most did not easily surrender. It was part of the price they knew they must pay for the role they had carved out for themselves and, regardless of the suffering or its causes, they were determined to turn it to their advantage. Sounded Young in characteristically unflinching terms:

> *We are willing to take our full share of trouble, trials, losses and crosses, hardships and fatigues, warning and watching, for the kingdom of heaven's sake: and we feel to say: Come, calm or strife, turmoil*

---

15. Pratt, *Autobiography of Parley Parker Pratt*, 357.
16. Extrapolated from Cutler's Park and Winter Quarters cemetery records, the Journal History, Mt. Pisgah Historical Record, and various private journals in the Church History Library. For a more elaborate discussion of deaths at Winter Quarters, see Bennett, *Mormons at the Missouri*, 134–39.

"WE MEAN TO CONQUER OR DIE TRYING"

Winter Quarters, Nebraska.

or peace, life or death, in the name of Israel's God we mean to conquer or die trying.[17]

During this "Valley Forge," many turned to temple covenants for strength and renewal. It will forever be to his credit that Brother Brigham listened to heaven with one ear and to the sufferings and requests of his people with the other. Early in the fall of 1846 while beginning to settle at the Missouri, he had indicated that "the use of the Lord's house is to attend to the ordinances of the Kingdom therein; and if it were lawful and right to administer these ordinances out of doors where would be the necessity of building a house? We would recommend to the brethren to let those things you refer to, dwell in the Temple, until another house is built in which they may be transferred or continued."[18] And even as late as January 1847, he was reminding the Saints that until the construction

---
17. Journal History, 16 April 1847.
18. Brigham Young to George Miller, Brigham Young Office Files, 20 September 1846, CR 1234 1.

of another temple, "let such administrations, and covenants belonging thereto, not be named among you."[19]

However, events soon occurred that made Brigham Young reevaluate his decision not to perform saving ordinances outside of a temple. With the call for a 500-man Mormon Battalion to march off to California to fight in the Mexican-American War, with many beginning to sicken and die in unparalleled numbers (some of whom never received their temple blessings in Nauvoo, or who had only received the preparatory ordinances in Kirtland) and with many wanting to marry and start a new life in an unforgiving wilderness, Brigham prayed for guidance to make exceptions for a people willing to sacrifice their all for the cause of Zion.[20] Hesitant to practice in private what he had been preaching against in public, and unwilling to undermine a primary argument for their moving west, he was nonetheless mindful of their travel delays and the painful circumstances surrounding them. Compassionate to the cries and beliefs of his people, and anxious to continue what he fervently claimed Joseph Smith had taught, he began sanctioning exceptions to his own rule. He would learn by trial and error, implementing and retracting practices as new to him as any other. Experimentation and adaptation would dictate his cautious course.

One other factor is prerequisite to a discussion of temple blessings at Winter Quarters. On 14 January 1847 Brigham Young proclaimed his one and only canonized revelation—the "Word and Will of the Lord"—which may not have indicated anything about their ultimate destination but said in effect that they would find their place if they would follow their God. Furthermore, this revelation declared that Joseph Smith's death was "needful" in order to seal his testimony with his blood, that the Church was still accepted of God and was "under the direction of the Twelve Apostles," and

---

19. Journal History, 6 and 29 January 1847.
20. Brigham Young counselled those men serving in the Battalion who had received their endowment in the Nauvoo Temple, not to go "without his under garment" of protection. "History of the Church," 16:86–87, 18 July 1846.

that "you have received my kingdom," that is, that the keys of priesthood authority and temple blessings remained with the Church (D&C 136:1, 3, 39, 41). While George Miller, James Emmett, Alpheus Cutler, and a few others broke from the Church over what they saw as Brigham Young's imperiousness and preemption of authority, most others rejoiced at the news of this revelation. Well received by the vast majority of the Saints in all their varied settlements on both sides of the river, the Word and Will of the Lord gave sanction and support to the idea of temple blessings in their wilderness home.[21]

Records show that on 9 January 1847 Brigham Young privately performed what may have been his first temple-based marriage sealing in Winter Quarters: specifically, Elizabeth Hendricks to Isaac Grundy.[22] Two weeks later he sealed Elijah Sheets to his twenty-seven-year-old critically ill wife, Margaret Hutchinson, who would die only eight days later from complications due to childbirth.[23] Having served a faithful mission to England, Elijah had returned to Nauvoo with his wife but not in time to be sealed together in Nauvoo. Her affliction, combined with their faithfulness, were surely factors in Brigham Young's decision to bless his people. Wrote a grieving but determined Elijah, "Her happy spirit has gone to the mansions of bliss where she will rest till the morn of the Resurrection of the righteous, when I shall have the unspeakable joy of seeing and having her again, where death will never separate us again."[24]

Many other such missionaries and emigrant converts arrived in Nauvoo after the Saints had evacuated the city and likewise never shared in the blessings of the temple there. Before the advanced company of the Twelve left Winter Quarters for the Rocky Mountains in April 1847,

---

21. For the most recent study of Section 136, see Chad M. Orton, "'This Shall Be Our Covenant': Brigham Young and D&C 136," *Religious Educator* 19 no. 2 (2018): 119–51.
22. "History of the Church," 17:17, 9 January 1847.
23. Journals of Elijah F. Sheets and Margaret Hutchinson, August 1845–July 1904, 24 January 1847, MS 1314, Church History Library. The next sealings occurred on 29 January, 4 February, and 9 February. Starting in early March they were performed more regularly.
24. Richard Hyatt Davis, "Biography of Elijah Funk Sheets," photocopy of typescript, MS 9874 (1987), Church History Library.

twenty-nine more such sealings were performed, some by "candle light," and all but one by Brigham Young. All but two were, like the Sheets, for time and eternity. Some were monogamous while others were polygamous in nature.[25] It was a practice he at first carefully guarded, hardly delegating the right or responsibility to others. While many of these sealings were performed in his own log cabin, others were performed quietly at the Council House or at the recorder's office in Willard Richards's "Octagon," which also served as a hospital and post office. Some were performed in John Vance's cabin, others at Alexander Hill's house, Heber C. Kimball's house, and more than one at Elias Gardner's log home. None occurred during the summer months when most of the Twelve were in the West but another eighteen took place after their return from their newly discovered Salt Lake Valley home in the fall. There were no sealings of deceased couples one to another but seven were of one living spouse to a deceased spouse.[26] Thus at least forty-eight marriage sealings were performed in Winter Quarters in 1847.

In the early months of 1848, before Brigham Young set out the second time to the Salt Lake Valley, and in his new capacity as President of the Church (the reorganization of the First Presidency had occurred on 26 December 1847 in the Kanesville Log Tabernacle), he authorized 106 more sealings that were performed in the Winter Quarters Council House, the recorder's office, and in various houses on both sides of the Missouri River (some in Iowa), the majority of which he himself performed. A handful were also done by his new first counselor, Heber C. Kimball, and three by George A. Smith.[27] Thus there were a minimum of 154 sealings

---

25. For example, Brigham Young sealed three women from Tennessee to John D. Lee all at once "for time and all eternity." *Journals of John D. Lee, 1846–47 and 1859*, edited by Charles Kelly (Salt Lake City: Western Printing Company, privately printed for Rolla Bishop Watt, 1938), 27 February 1847, in Church History Library.
26. Pre-Endowment House Ordinances 1847–1854, Endowment House, microfilm, Family History Library, Salt Lake City.
27. After returning from the Valley in the fall of 1847, George A. Smith stayed back at the Missouri for two years. He may have performed other marriage sealings in the fall of 1848 and spring of 1849.

performed at Winter Quarters/Council Bluffs throughout 1847 and 1848, bringing hope and redemption to a suffering people waiting to go further west.[28]

A very few baptisms for the dead were performed at Winter Quarters by Wilford Woodruff. Records show that he baptized a mere handful of Saints for their deceased family members in the Missouri River. But these were very few and far between. Baptisms for the dead was an ordinance largely put on hold until a better time and place.

"THE PRIESTHOOD MUST BE CONNECTED" —THE LAW OF ADOPTION

Members today are well accustomed to performing vicarious ordinances for their deceased ancestors, including baptisms, sealings, and endowments for the dead. Before 11 January 1877, however, no endowments for the dead had ever been performed anywhere in the Church. In the absence of such, members, both living and dead, were occasionally sealed not to their ancestors but to a prominent Church authority, usually prophets and apostles, men who held restored priesthood keys of salvation in what was called "spiritual adoptions" or more simply stated, "the law of adoption." Later discontinued by President Wilford Woodruff in favor of family sealings, the law of adoption was evident more at Winter Quarters than ever before. To quote Brigham Young, it served as a "schoolmaster," a pointer, or a steppingstone to tying or linking ancestral families together in one perfect chain of family salvation from modern-day times back to Father Adam and Mother Eve.[29]

---

28. On 22 April 2001 President Gordon B. Hinckley dedicated the 16,000-square-foot Winter Quarters Nebraska Temple of the Church. Adjacent to the Mormon Pioneer Cemetery and immediately west of the Mormon Trail Center, this impressive structure, with its two ordinance rooms, two sealing rooms, and beautiful history-themed stained-glass art is a testimony to the faith of the early pioneers and a lasting tribute to their commitment to temple work during those trying years of suffering and death at Winter Quarters.
29. For an excellent overview into the history of the law of adoption, see Gordon Irving, "The Law of Adoption: One Phase of the Development of the Mormon Concept of Salvation, 1830–1980," *BYU Studies* 14, no. 3 (Spring 1974): 291–314; Bennett, *Mormons at the Missouri,* 191–94; and Bennett, "'Line upon Line, Precept upon Precept:' Reflections on the 1877 Commencement of

Joseph Smith's Nauvoo-based doctrine of baptism for the dead implied a linkage of some kind bridging multi-generations back through time. Said he: "Again, the doctrine or sealing power of Elijah is as follows: If you have power to seal on earth and in heaven then we should be wise, the first thing you do, go and seal on earth your sons and daughters unto yourself: and yourself unto your fathers in eternal glory and go ahead, and not go back, but use a little wisdom, and seal all you can. . . . I will walk through the gate of heaven and claim what I seal, and those that follow me and my Council."[30] Unfortunately, he never fully elaborated on how this chain was to be forged. After his death and in preparation for the pending exodus, the twelve apostles initiated a temple ceremony wherein a faithful male member (and in rare cases, an unmarried, widowed, or divorced female) was sealed to one of the Twelve, men who held such priesthood keys of salvation. At least 211 such adoptions occurred in Nauvoo before the Saints headed west, with some others performed in Winter Quarters and in early Salt Lake City.[31] Seventy-four percent of all Nauvoo adoptions were to Church apostles. For example, Thomas Bullock, chief clerk of the Twelve and the Council of Fifty, was sealed as an "adopted son of Willard Richards" in the Nauvoo Temple just ten days before the exodus began and quietly changed his name to Thomas Bullock [Richards].[32] So likewise did John D. Lee become part of Brigham Young's very large spiritual family while still in Nauvoo and became John D. Lee [Young]. In turn, others were sealed to Lee. "I had application made to me to receive a man

---

the Performance of Endowments and Sealings for the Dead," *BYU Studies* 44, no. 3 (2005): 38–77. For the most recent study of the law of adoption see Jonathan A. Stapley, "Adoptive Sealing Ritual in Mormonism," *Journal of Mormon History* 37, no. 355 (Summer 2011) and Stapley, *The Power of Godliness: Mormon Liturgy and Cosmology* (New York: Oxford University Press, 2018).

30. *The Joseph Smith Papers*, 10 March 1844, History, 1838 to 1856, E–1 (1 July 1843 to 30 April 1844), 1922, https://www.josephsmithpapers.org/paper-summary/history-1838-1856-volume-e-1-1-july-1843-30-april-1844/294 (accessed 14 February 2018, online only).
31. Joseph F. Smith, comp., "Sealings and Adoptions, 1846–1857," microfilm, 183374, Special Collections, Family History Library, Salt Lake City; as cited in Devery S. Anderson and Gary James Bergera, eds., *The Nauvoo Endowment Companies, 1845–1846: A Documentary History* (Salt Lake City: Signature Books, 2005), 585–86.
32. Church Historian's Office Journal, 25 January 1846, Church History Library.

and his wife into my family," he recorded in January 1846. "After speaking freely upon the Law of Adoption I accepted James Wools[e]y and Sevina his wife into my family by the Law of adoption—he choosing to retain his [sur]name for the present and to have mine named upon him—this however was a prerogative that I gave to him."[33]

Scores, if not hundreds, of others did the same while still in Nauvoo, choosing to be "grafted" into Joseph Smith's, Brigham Young's, or some other leader's family and thus becoming "legal heirs" to the covenant blessings. Other Church authorities practicing the law of adoption included Heber C. Kimball, Orson Hyde, Amasa Lyman, Wilford Woodruff, John Taylor, John Smith, Samuel Bent, Albert P. Rockwood, and Newel K. Whitney. A total of 320 men and women (a small number of whom were deceased), many with their children, were adopted into Brigham Young's family alone between 1847 and 1854.[34] This practice continued at Winter Quarters.[35]

Being sealed to the "priesthood" on earth also implied a measure of spiritual security hereafter. The common belief was that being sealed to one's own ancestry was filled with risk since it was not at all certain that such progenitors would accept the gospel in the hereafter. By being sealed to or "grafted" into families of covenant believers and those faithfully exercising the priesthood, and from them back through Joseph Smith to the ancient patriarchs, salvation was, if not assured, much more likely.

During the cold days and long nights at Winter Quarters while the "Camp of Israel" waited for the coming spring, many a family gathered by their cabin fireplaces to talk about such sacred things. In a series of memorable February 1847 meetings, Brigham Young, Heber C. Kimball, and Willard Richards talked long into the night about this true order of family linkages and eventual redemption of the entire human race. "There

---

33. *Journals of John D. Lee*, 11 January 1846.
34. Hosea Stout, *On the Mormon Frontier: The Diary of Hosea Stout*, ed. Juanita Brooks (Salt Lake City: University of Utah Press, 1964), 1:242, 23 March 1847.
35. Brigham Young Papers, 21 November 1847.

must be a connection from Adam to the last man born of woman the same as in the Priesthood in Eternity," Brigham Young said. "If men are not saved together, they cannot be saved at all. . . . The Priesthood must be connected."[36] He was only teaching what he believed Joseph Smith had taught: that in the pre-earth councils in heaven, God had established a "pattern" or an order for all the families of the earth, a sequence of familial belonging starting with Adam and Eve, with each generation to be sealed one to another in an unbroken line of priesthood lineage, as with the Biblical patriarchs of old.

Brigham Young also taught that because of disbelief and transgression, the apostasy that had occurred after the death of the original apostles had "disgraced the priesthood" and thrown into disarray and "great confusion" the original template of human existence.[37] He further explained: "Had the keys of the Priesthood been retained and handed down from father to son throughout all generations . . . there would have been no necessity of the law of adoption, for we would all have been included in the covenant without it."[38] However, in much the same way Christ redeemed the fall of Adam, God likewise prepared a way to reconstruct, legitimize, and redeem the families of the children of God. And such a reconstruction was essential to the exaltation of all families upon the earth.

Another reason the law of adoption was utilized was because so many converts had abandoned home and country to join the cause of Zion. As first-generation members, they sought spiritual parenting and shepherding and a sense of belonging. The law of adoption was, therefore, a principle under construction, more of an experimental ordinance that would later be discarded in favor of intergenerational family sealings as the doctrine of post-mortal spirit world salvation became ever more clear.

It would be erroneous, however, to conclude that Brigham Young and

---

36. Journal of Willard Richards, Willard Richards Papers, 1821–1854, 16 February 1847, MS 1490, Church History Library.
37. General Church Minutes, 12 March 1848, CR 100 318.
38. *Journals of John D. Lee*, 16 February 1847.

his peers among the Twelve did not understand that the saving mission of the Church and its membership would eventually have to perform all the needed temple ordinances for deceased ancestors. The question was not what or why but rather *when* and *how*. Speaking in Winter Quarters in March of 1848, now as President of the Church, he taught as follows: "We have now the privilege of acting for our dead. We have grandparents and ancestors with whom we have to act for. It can't be done in five or ten years. We can get our own ordinances and as many of our ancestors as we can. This will have to be done in the millennium by Saviors who will be in Mount Zion."[39] In other words, there wasn't time then to perform such an immense task before Christ's imminent Second Coming, nor were the records available for such research-intensive work. The sentiment appeared to be that it was better to postpone such reconstruction until the Millennium when Joseph Smith, who will ever hold the keys of this dispensation, along with other chosen souls, would direct the work of sealing past generations with knowledge, power, and unimaginable resources unavailable at that present time. Said Heber C. Kimball after listening to comments from his adopted son, Presiding Bishop Newel K. Whitney:

> *I have been much edified by the conversation of Brother Whitney— and we always had the same feelings in common—and our views always met, and our thoughts flow in the same channel. . . . I am your head, your lawgiver, and king, and will be, to all eternity, and I am responsible to my head and President—and you are responsible to me, your file leader. I believe that some of my old progenitors, of whom I have no knowledge, will appear and tell me when the time shall come for me to rise up and administer in the ordinances for them, and I shall receive a great deal of knowledge from them. . . . I want to have power, when I see my brother and sister, to tell Death to depart.*[40]

---

39. General Church Minutes, 12 March 1848.
40. Horace K. Whitney Journals, 14 February 1847, as cited in *The Journey West: The Mormon Pioneer Journals of Horace K. Whitney with Insights by Helen Mar Kimball Whitney*, ed. Richard E. Bennett

Heber Chase Kimball (1801–1868).   *Vilate Murray Kimball (1806–1867).*

Until that time, and for the foreseeable future, they would practice the law of adoption, a kind of shortcut remedy, and be sealed first to favored Church leaders and after them to Joseph Smith as head of this dispensation. And as with marriage sealings, such priesthood-conducted adoption ceremonies were performed quietly on demand and on invitation outside of the temple when deemed necessary and helpful.[41]

Not only did the law of adoption connect families in this chain of salvation but many Saints interpreted it as a means to kingdom-building on this earth and a heightened glory in the eternities to come. Some felt that the larger and more extensive family of sons and their wives and children

---

(Provo, Utah: Religious Studies Center, Brigham Young University; Salt Lake City: Deseret Book Company, 2018), 172–73.

41. Years later, Brigham Young returned to this theme of temple work in the Millennium:

"In the Millennium, when the Kingdom of God is established on the earth in power, glory, and perfection . . . the Saints of God will have the privilege of building their temples, of entering into them, becoming, as it were, pillars in the temples of God, and they will officiate for their dead. . . . And we will have revelations to know our forefathers back to Father Adam and Mother Eve. . . . Then man will be sealed to man until the chain is made perfect." *Journal of Discourses*, 15:138–39, 24 August 1872.

a worthy priesthood holder may have in this life, the greater his kingdom hereafter—a family network of salvation.[42]

The law of adoption was never, however, clearly understood. Even Brigham Young confessed in a meeting of 16 February 1847 that he understood "only a smattering of these things" although he fully expected to learn more. The very next day, 17 February, he spoke of a dream vision the night before of Joseph Smith who showed him the "pattern" of the families of God on earth, "how they were in the beginning and . . . how it must be joined together." To Brigham Young's questions about spiritual adoption and whether it was the right way to go, Joseph Smith simply told him to "tell the people to be humble and faithful, and be sure to keep the Spirit of the Lord, and it will lead them right."[43]

If the doctrinal intricacies of this order were never fully developed or defined, its social implications were even less understood. For a people struggling to be one in heart and mind and with hopes of establishing a Zion of unity in the Rocky Mountains, the law of adoption posed some social complications. Nowhere was one's family tribal order more clearly evident than in Winter Quarters. It often dictated social spheres of influence and one's circle of friends and associates, even the locale of their tents or cabins. Winter Quarters was, in fact, laid out, apportioned, and settled by this system of family connections. The scores of families adopted into Brigham Young's family, for instance, occupied the center of the city; those belonging to Heber C. Kimball, including the Whitneys, settled the southern blocks; Willard Richards's families were on the east side; and so on. Summer farms, including Summer Quarters located several miles north of the Winter Quarters site, consisted of some of Brigham Young's expanded family.

For some, the expectation was that in return for spiritual blessings and

---

42. Willard Richards remembered hearing Brigham Young say once, "When I have a 100, I will soon have a 1,000. My sons each have their 10 sons each one is a king and I am king of kings, etc." Journal of Willard Richards, 1846–1847, 16 February 1847.
43. Journal History, 23 February 1847.

eternal inheritances due their spiritual fathers, adopted sons and families owed them physical support. Said Brigham Young:

> *Those that are adopted into my family . . . I will preside over them, throughout all eternity and will stand at their head. Joseph [Smith] will stand at the head of this Church and will be their president, prophet and god to the people in this dispensation. When we locate [in the mountains] I will settle my family down in the order and teach them their duties. They will then have to provide temporal blessings for me instead of my boarding from forty to fifty persons as I do now, and will administer spiritual blessings for them.*[44]

The original plan of their travels west was supposed to have followed after this adoptive-family pattern. In their wintertime deliberations in mid-January at the newly constructed Council House, the Twelve drew up plans to have the first company or "division" of 100 be drawn from Brigham Young's adopted/spiritual family, the second hundred from Heber C. Kimball's, and so forth, with a liberal sprinkling of Mormon Battalion family members apportioned throughout.[45] Though this plan was largely discarded in favor of a handpicked crew of well-skilled teamsters, farmers, fishermen, surveyors, explorers, and other pioneers, several of those in the vanguard company identified themselves as belonging to one family clan or another. Likewise, so did many others in the Emigration or Big Camp that left for the West later in the spring of 1847.

Meant in part to break down social, cultural, and ethnic differences among peoples, the system unfortunately bred more disagreements and divisions than it solved as various families stumbled over each other for social rank and priority within the new larger family order. Rival family dynasties, jealousies, and kingdom-building (even among some of the Twelve) were unintended consequences. In return for assured spiritual blessings in the present and the hereafter, some leaders taught that those so

---

44. Journal of John D. Lee, 16 February 1847, as cited in *Mormons at the Missouri*, 192.
45. *The Mormon Pioneer Journals of Horace K. Whitney*, 156–158, 18–22 January 1847.

grafted in were to commit all of their physical and natural energies to the welfare of the expanded family. Thus at Winter Quarters, along the trail, and in early Salt Lake City, the larger one's family with numerous healthy adopted sons, the easier it was to build cabins and fenced in pastures, plant crops, and oversee flocks and herds. The need for clarification and equality may have been one reason why Brigham Young established a system of pastoral bishops in Winter Quarters, to ensure the physical well-being and social equality of all families, especially those who had sacrificed sons, husbands, and fathers to serve in the Mormon Battalion. By the time the Latter-day Saints reached the Great Basin, Brigham Young tried to put the whole matter of adoption on the backburner. However, spiritual adoptions continued while the Saints waited for future inspiration and revelation.

"BY THEIR UNITED FAITH AND WORKS"

Women, meanwhile, exercised their faith in Winter Quarters in remarkable ways. Seldom called upon to preach or speak in any of their Church meetings, the sisters found other forms of faithful expression. With the Nauvoo Relief Society discontinued, women were less likely to gather together for support from each other. Many of them, as plural wives and mothers in Zion, felt a divinely appointed commission to bear and raise children in righteousness. However, with so many men away serving in the Battalion, working in the Missouri settlements for needed money and provisions, or away on various missions and expeditions, women had to become involved in a variety of activities, from cattle feeding, milking, and other farm chores to cabin building. But they were most obviously involved in the nursing and comforting of the sick. Vilate Kimball, first wife of Heber C. Kimball, and one of the most beloved of all the sisters in Winter Quarters, often made the rounds seeking after, comforting, and blessing the sick and infirm. She went "from door to door ministering food and consolation to the sick, and pouring out blessings upon them, during which time she scarcely touched food herself." Remembered her daughter, "By their united faith and works, with fasting and prayer, the sick were healed."[46]

Vilate Kimball and other women who had received their endowments and other promised blessings in the Nauvoo Temple were also in great demand for spiritual blessings. They felt empowered to lay their hands upon the sick and afflicted, to pronounce blessings according to need and affliction. One man told of how he called in "all the men and women who had their endowment" to lay their hands on his infant son's head and "according to the Holy order and with the signs of the Priesthood" anoint and bless him.[47] With so many men away and at a time of rising sickness and death, the occasions in which women blessed and administered to the sick and dying by faith and by the assurance of their temple covenants multiplied. Some claimed to have received angelic visitations while others spoke of rebuking evil spirits "by the power of the priesthood which had been conferred upon us in the house of God in connection with our husbands."[48] There seems little question that those women who had received their temple blessings in Nauvoo felt a special empowerment not to exercise priesthood authority per se—which they never claimed to hold—but to exercise faith in that priesthood for the benefit of all. Such ministrations attest to how the Nauvoo Temple continued to bless the Saints in their westward journeys.

CONCLUSION

The faith of the Latter-day Saints was tested to the core during their challenging ordeal crossing Iowa and their subsequent dreary stay at the Missouri. Many suffered from every kind of sickness and ailment while hundreds of others gave their lives in sacrifice to the cause of Zion. Although it is true that some quit the faith, the overwhelming majority remained committed and ready to follow the Twelve into an unknown

---

46. Helen Mar Whitney, "Scenes and Incidents at Winter Quarters," *Women's Exponent* 14:98.
47. *Diary of Hosea Stout,* 1:170, 25 June 1846.
48. Whitney, "Scenes and Incidents at Winter Quarters," 14:106.

wilderness. And Brigham Young listened to the pleas of his people. A pragmatic as well as a spiritual leader, he clearly understood the importance of temple ordinances in developing and retaining the faith of the members of the Church. Thus it was that those ordinances performed at Winter Quarters, including the law of adoption, played a major role in fortifying and developing the discipleship of the Saints and would continue to do so as they prepared to leave once more for their new Zion in the West.

Chapter 5

"The Upper Room"

Temple Work in the Wilderness, 1847–1854

My mind is full of reflection on the scenes through which we have passed and being brought through the deserts of sage to this distant region. God's ways are not as our ways. . . . This movement is one of the greatest that has taken place among this people. . . . Isaiah says (Chapter 62) speaking of the City of Zion, "it shall be sought out, a city not forsaken, etc." Many in this congregation know what is meant by the garments of salvation and the robe of righteousness. . . . We have gathered out the stones out of the road and thousands will yet fulfil this prophecy. . . . If ever there was a place sought out it is this. We have inquired diligently and have found it. . . . "It shall come to pass in the last days, that the mountain of the Lord's house shall be established in the tops of the mountains . . . and all nations shall flow unto it. And many people shall go and say, Come ye, and let us go up to the mountain of the Lord, to the house of the God of Jacob, . . . for out of Zion shall go forth the law and the word of the Lord out of Jerusalem."¹

Thus said Orson Pratt on 1 August 1847, in a Sabbath day meeting held in a hastily built bowery on what is now Temple Square.

Stirring words, these, given under a blazing desert sun that could easily have dented the resolve of almost everyone in attendance.

One might almost conclude that during the difficult years of finding

---

1. Journal History, 1 August 1847.

and establishing a new home in the valleys of the West that devotion to temple work would have gone into decline. Such was not quite the case. While it is true that baptisms for the dead retreated into remission during these times, temple work for the living in the form of sealings and endowments continued under new surroundings and in much altered circumstances. And much was said during these years about the "gather[ing] together in holy places," the derivation of authority for temple work and blessings, laying the groundwork for future developments. This chapter will show how significant a role the new Council House in Salt Lake City played in the ongoing development of temple work in early Utah Territory and how temple blessings entered into the very homes of the Saints.

"WE HAVE FOUND A SWEET LITTLE VALLEY"

So much attention has been devoted to the physical challenges the Saints encountered during the exodus and their first few years in the western valleys that one might overlook the many spiritual aspects involved. There was as much trial as there was trail in the Mormon exodus. As with Zion's Camp years before, and as clearly implied in Brigham Young's January 1847 Word and Will of the Lord, they would find their place if they followed their God and remained true to the covenants they had made in the Nauvoo Temple. The lives of thousands of Saints depended on it.

After a most trying winter of darkness, death, and much despair at Winter Quarters, the spring of 1847 finally dawned and with it the hope and expectation of better times. Recalibrating their original plan to cross the plains in 1846 with a vanguard company of the finest pioneers, Brigham Young, still acting as president of the Quorum of the Twelve, carefully selected 148 (including three women and two children) of the most experienced, best prepared farmers and fishermen, hunters and builders, surveyors and mechanics to make their dash to the Rocky Mountains. Their plan was to find some good valley in the "Upper California" in time to plant late crops and found a settlement. From all they had studied and heard about, the Valley of the Salt Lake looked especially promising; if not, there remained other possibilities. It likewise called for a large "Emigration Camp" or "Big Camp" of over 1,400 men, women, and children, including many of the Mormon Battalion families, to leave Winter Quarters by late May 1847 and to arrive at wherever their new home might be before winter set in. If the advanced company were to fail in its designs, the specter of starvation and ruin would cripple their entire enterprise, leaving their future gravely in doubt. The Donner-Reed Party would learn that lesson the hard way. Relying only on Fremont's maps, trappers' tales, and the hope of divine guidance, they knew they were risking life and limb as well as faith and hope.

Leaving the Elkhorn River rendezvous site in early April, Brigham Young's pioneer company headed west, not along the Oregon/California trails south of the Platte River, but north of it so as to escape interference and take advantage of the best grazing and camping facilities. Choosing to drive right through the heart of Pawnee country rather than to skirt it, they made good time reaching Chimney Rock, the approximate halfway point, by late May. Averaging some fifteen miles a day in ox-drawn wagons, they followed up the North Platte to Fort Laramie and eventually along the Sweetwater River past Devil's Gate and over South Pass to Fort Bridger and Green River. Traveling down Echo Canyon and eventually over Big and Little Mountain, Orson Pratt's advanced company finally reached the Great Salt Lake Valley on 22 July 1847.

Along the way, members of the Twelve and other selected brethren often donned their temple robes and excused themselves from the camp to find secluded places to have prayer circles to ask the Lord's blessings on their journey.[2] Never was such a prayer circle more earnestly convened than when Brigham Young became desperately ill with Rocky Mountain spotted fever. It looked for a time as if he would succumb to this

---

2. Just north of Ash Creek near Scottsbluff, after the camp had partaken of the sacrament, the Twelve and nine others "with their clothing repaired to a basin in the hills and stationed O. P. Rockwell and A. Carrington on the lookout, while the rest clothed, and went through the usual (rites) and prayed, the President being mouth. Soon after they dressed, it began to sprinkle." Journal of Amasa Lyman, 30 May 1847, MS 2737, Church History Library.

"THE UPPER ROOM"

Chimney Rock, Nebraska.

tick-borne illness. Fortunately, he recovered well enough to raise himself in Woodruff's more comfortable carriage and, while gazing out upon the Valley of the Great Salt Lake, whisper his approval. While some cheered at the sight of their new Zion, others, like William Clayton, seeing nothing but an arid desert with a scarcity of vegetation, admitted that he was "happily disappointed."[3] Still, the nearby mountains with their copious streams, abundant timber, and mineral prospects all looked promising. And in due time, after exploring other nearby smaller valleys to the north and south, a now fully recovered Brigham Young declared more robustly on 8 August, "This is the spot that I had anticipated!"[4]

Once in the Valley, these hardy pioneers lost little time planting late

---

3. William Clayton, *William Clayton's Journal: A Daily Record of the Journey of the Original Company of "Mormon" Pioneers from Nauvoo, Illinois, to the Valley of the Great Salt Lake,* published by the Clayton Family Association (Salt Lake City: The Deseret News, 1921), 309.
4. *Horace K. Whitney Journals,* 324, 8 August 1847. Forty years later, Wilford Woodruff, who was with Brigham Young as they entered the Valley, recorded the following: "I brought Pres. Young into the valley of the Great Salt Lake in my carriage. He was sick but he began to mend from the hour he came into the Valley. He had seen the valley before by vision and when he looked upon it he said it was the right place." *Wilford Woodruff's Journal,* 8:447, 24 July 1887.

summer crops, building a fort for protection from the nearby Ute and Shoshone Indian tribes, irrigating the soil, surveying their new city which they called "the Great Salt Lake City" and in countless other ways improving their new Zion home. A determined Brigham Young soon identified the spot on which to build a new temple. At five in the evening on 28 July 1847, while still recovering from mountain fever, he identified a center spot between creeks and declared to his fellow apostles, as he waved his hands in the air, "Here is the forty acres of temple lot." He went on to give instructions on how to build the basement and the baptismal font of the new temple.[5] Two weeks later he indicated that work on the temple would commence as soon as possible. As important as the physical temple was in administering sacred ordinances, he would not delay certain temple blessings unnecessarily while the temple was being built. He also wanted to teach the people about the temple, not just build it, and to give himself and his people, now preoccupied with making a living from the wilderness, ample time to understand and implement temple work in its fullness. "As soon as we get up some adobe houses for our families," he said, "we shall go to work to build another Temple and as soon as a place is prepared we shall commence the Endowments long before the Temple is built. And we shall take time and each step the Saints take, let them take time enough about it to understand it."[6] Although the site was identified in 1847, the groundbreaking for the Salt Lake Temple would not take place for another six years. The demands of building a city in the wilderness and bringing the rest of the Saints out west could not be delayed.

To add to his emphasis on covenant-making, in the absence of a desert temple and with only a hastily built bowery for their outdoor meetings, Brigham Young instituted the practice of rebaptizing the living for the

---

5. Thomas Bullock Journal, 28 July 1847, Church History Library. Brigham Young did not act arbitrarily in choosing a site for the temple. Heber C. Kimball, Willard Richards, Orson Pratt, Wilford Wodruff, and Thomas Bullock accompanied President Young as he designated the site for the temple block. Then "on motion of Orson Pratt, it was unanimously voted that the Temple be built on the site designated." Journal History, 28 July 1847.
6. *Wilford Woodruff's Journal*, 3:259–60, 15 August 1847.

remission of their sins and the restoration of health starting on 6 August 1847 at City Creek.[7] On that day, he "recovenanted" his fellow members of the Twelve, while in return Heber C. Kimball rebaptized Brigham Young. Of the slightly more than 4,000 total baptisms for the living performed in the Salt Lake Valley between 1847 and 1852, approximately 75 percent were rebaptisms.[8] Not only were those present of the Twelve Apostles rebaptized (Parley P. Pratt, Orson Hyde, and John Taylor were away at the time) but Wilford Woodruff stated that Brigham Young at the same time also "confirmed us and sealed upon us our Apostleship and all the keys, powers and blessings belonging to that office."[9]

Meanwhile, back along the trail, the Big Camp soldiered on under the direction of apostles Parley P. Pratt and John Taylor. There are records of sealings being performed near Chimney Rock, at the Sweetwater River, and again at South Pass before the Big Camp reached the Salt Lake Valley in late September and early October 1847.[10] With the return of various detachments of the Mormon Battalion from Colorado and California, by the end of 1847 the combined numbers of new settlers was 1,681. Soon they had laid out the "Great Salt Lake City" in a grid-pattern fashion of 135 ten-acre blocks stemming north, east, south, and west of the original temple block, and with wide enough avenues to allow the turning around of a full wagon team. In February of that year, the Salt Lake Stake was organized with nineteen wards. Encouraged by their bounteous crops in 1850, Church leadership felt more confident than ever in inviting and

---

7. Journal History, 1 August 1847; see also Jonathan A. Stapley and Kristine L. Wright, "'They Shall be Made Whole': A History of Baptism for Health," *Journal of Mormon History* 34, no. 4 (Fall 2008): 83–88.
8. "Rebaptisms," Salt Lake Stake Record Book, Church History Library. For a good study on this topic see D. Michael Quinn, "The Practice of Rebaptism at Nauvoo," *BYU Studies* 18, no. 2 (Spring 1978): 226–32. There were, of course, some convert baptisms in the Valley in these early years. Sabino Hierro was the "first Mexican" to be baptized (25 June 1852), and Francis Burr, "a black man," was baptized by Tarleton Lewis on 8 August 1852.
9. Journal History, 6 August 1847.
10. General Church Minutes, 7 September 1847, box 1, folder 7; see also Brigham Young to John Smith, Brigham Young Papers, 1 September 1847.

imploring the many thousands of Saints lingering at the Missouri or waiting patiently in Great Britain to gather to Zion.

Even during these trying years, missionary work continued to move forward with thirty-two missionaries called in 1846 and another forty in 1847. Two years later President Young announced a grand plan for expanding global missionary work, assigning members of the Twelve to particular regions of the world, with a special focus on Europe. Thus 1849 saw the opening of missions in Italy, France, and Scandinavia and by 1850 missionaries were also proselyting in Switzerland, South America, and Hawaii. Another 106 were called in 1852, some to go to China, Gibraltar, India, and Prussia. As one scholar described it, "Never before had missionaries been spread across the globe to such an extent."[11]

With Brigham Young's implementation of the highly successful Perpetual Emigration Fund in 1849, the gathering renewed in full force, so that by 1851, approximately 15,000 people were calling Deseret home, with many more thousands in transit or biding their time.[12] While most crossed the plains in wagon trains, many walked the entire way. Ten companies travelled with handcarts between 1850 and 1860, most quite successfully. The notable exceptions were the Martin and Willie companies of 1856, which, due to a late start and early snows on the high Wyoming plains, suffered a tragic loss of life. By the mid-1850s, this unique commonwealth consisted of some ninety-six communities stretching over 250 miles north and south. And by 1870, 51,000 Saints had immigrated to Utah Territory—including 35,000 from Great Britain and another 13,000 from Scandinavia and elsewhere in Europe.

"THE UPPER ROOM"

Recognizing that it would take years to build the Salt Lake Temple, Brigham Young determined to build, in the meantime, another Council

---

11. William E. Hughes, "A Profile of the Missionaries of The Church of Jesus Christ of Latter-day Saints, 1849–1900," (master's thesis, Brigham Young University, 1986), 13.
12. Allen and Leonard, *The Story of the Latter-day Saints,* 258.

House somewhat similar to the one in Winter Quarters.[13] Such a structure would double as a "state house" or seat of government, with chambers for both the general assembly and senate of the proposed state of Deseret, and as a place for temple work. Designed by Truman O. Angell and built in two stages, the Council House was a rather simple forty-five-foot-square, two-story building with walls of stone and adobe. Built at a cost of $45,833 and located on the southwest corner of East Temple (Main) and South Temple streets, it was financed through a poll tax of one dollar and by the tithing of one day's labor per week donated by craftsmen and laborers from the nineteen Salt Lake City wards who were working under the direction of building superintendent Daniel H. Wells. Brigham Young himself worked several days as a "common laborer."[14]

Work began on the foundation 7 November 1848 and the structure was above ground by March 1849 after a very intense winter. That same spring, many of the pioneer settlers abandoned their apartments in the city forts in favor of houses on city lots.[15] While construction lagged due to such problems as recurring cricket infestations, the Council House remained a pioneer priority. As John Taylor reminded everyone in October 1848, "The first thing to build up Zion is to build a Council House."[16]

The Council House had a dual secular and religious purpose. The first floor was given over to meetings of the original territorial legislature, classes of the University of Deseret, and sittings of territorial and

---

13. Other Council Houses were included as part of original forts in outlying areas, including one in Iron County. See letter of George A. Smith to Brigham Young, 28 January 1851, George A. Smith Papers, Church History Library. It is likely that some temple sealings occurred in such places, although in Iron County George A. Smith conducted temple sealings in the "upper room" of his own dwelling house. Letter from George A. Smith, 25 December 1852, "History of the Church," 22:102.
14. Thomas Bullock Journals, 2 April 1849, microfilm, MS 2737, box 65, Church History Library; see also Gilbert Bradshaw, "The Council House as a House for Sacred Ordinances in the Early Church" (unpublished undergraduate research paper in possession of the author), 3–4.
15. Thomas Bullock Journals, 9 March 1849. By April, 450 houses had been erected in "Great Salt Lake City" with another 47 in North Mill Creek (Farmington) and 53 in South Cottonwood. Bullock Journals, 2 April 1849.
16. Salt Lake Stake General Minutes 1869–1977, 41, 29 October 1848, LR 604 11, Church History Library.

TEMPLES RISING

Council House, Salt Lake City.

city courts. It also included the territorial library. In addition it hosted meetings of the Salt Lake Stake bishops and high council.[17] Though not yet completed, the Council House opened for its first social gatherings early in June 1849.[18] If not a hotel in the envisioned sense of the Nauvoo House, the Council House was nonetheless *the* gathering place in early Salt Lake City, the place for banquets and balls, court trials and disputes, and socializing for guests and travelers.[19]

On the other hand, the second floor, designated the "upper room," was dedicated, reserved, and divided into rooms separated by partitions for the performance of endowments, prayer circles, sealings, and other temple-related ordinances, although it had no baptismal font. "Our Council House was so far completed during the fall," the First Presidency wrote in 1851, "that the several apartments have been occupied through

---

17. *Wilford Woodruff's Journal*, 4:114, 2 and 3 March 1852.
18. Bradshaw, "The Council House as a House for Sacred Ordinances in the Early Church," as cited in Brown, "Temple Pro Tempore," 5n16.
19. Arrington, *Great Basin Kingdom*, 54, 111.

the winter, to the great joy of this people."[20] William Carter Staines referred to "Endowment rooms" being specially set aside in the Council House, complete with an "inner room."[21] Once these endowment rooms were properly carpeted, furnished, and partitioned complete with stoves, washing tubs, and an office for Brigham Young similar somewhat to Nauvoo's Red Brick Store, ordinance work in this "House of the Lord" (as it was called) could begin "about 11:00 a.m" on 16 April 1851. Work continued throughout the summer with Brigham Young "superintending all the transactions in the upper room."[22] Those wishing to attend had to be full tithe payers and in good moral standing. Prior to receiving their endowments, candidates "bathed in the bathhouse" nearby and were then washed and anointed.[23] Clearly the line between church and state was a thin one indeed in early Utah Territory!

"TO STIR UP THE DEVIL, THAT'S ALL": ENDOWMENTS IN THE WILDERNESS

But what of other ordinances? In sharp contrast to the approximately 5,600 living endowments performed in the Nauvoo Temple during the span of just two months, the total number of living endowments performed in the five years between 1849 and 1854 amounted to only 2,222, all but one of which were performed in the Salt Lake Council House.[24]

---

20. *Messages of the First Presidency of The Church of Jesus Christ of Latter-day Saints, 1833–1964*, comp. James R. Clark, (Salt Lake City: Bookcraft, 1965), 2:65.
21. William Carter Staines Diary, Church Historian's Office Journal, 16:254, 3 February 1854. The largest number of patrons ever to "pass thro" the Council House was forty-one, which occurred on 1 April 1854. Church Historian's Office Journal, 16:302, 1 April 1854.
22. "Endowment House Records (Council House) 1851–1855," microfilm, Family History Library, Harold B. Lee Library, Brigham Young University. For Brigham Young's role in superintending activities, see Church Historian's Office Journal, 14:146, 18 February 1851. Brigham Young and some members of the Twelve received their washings and anointings on 20 February 1851. See "Endowment House Records 1851–1855." According to yet another source, William C. Staines began giving endowments the following week. See William C. Staines, "Reminiscences of William C. Staines," *Contributor* 12, no. 4 (February 1891): 123. For furnishings, see Church Historian's Office Journal 14:144–49, 15–22 February 1851.
23. Bradshaw, "Council House," 6.
24. Endowment and Sealings, 1851–1855, microfilm, Family History Library, Salt Lake City. See also Anderson, *The Development of Latter-day Saint Temple Worship*, xxvii.

Such endowments were administered in a far more selective, measured, and intermittent manner than they had been in Nauvoo, less on demand and far more often by invitation. Save for Addison Pratt, who received his endowment atop Ensign Peak on 21 July 1849, all the other endowments were administered in the Salt Lake City Council House.[25]

The first endowments performed in the Council House occurred on 21 February 1851 when twenty-nine-year-old Francis A. Hammond and his twenty-year-old wife, Mary Jane Dilworth Hammond, received this ordinance prior to embarking just days later on their mission to the Sandwich Islands.[26] Of the next fifteen persons endowed on February 25 and 26, at least three of them were about to depart on faraway missions. This pattern indicates that a primary reason for Council House endowments was to prepare recipients for mission service, including that of fifteen-year-old Taylor Crosby who received his endowment on 26 February 1851.

The pending missionary service of Parley P. Pratt to the Pacific Mission may also explain why two of his plural wives—Phoebe Eldred Soper Pratt (married February 1846) and Ann Agatha Walker Pratt (married April 1847)—were also endowed. Such was also the case with Sarah Zufelt Murdock (married March 1846) when her husband, John Murdock, was called to serve in the Pacific Mission, with the specific assignment of Australia. Thomas E. Broderick, having been called on his mission to England, was endowed on 24 April 1852.

These early Council House endowments were also administered to

---

25. Church Historian's Office Journal, 19:107, 21 July 1849. Addison Pratt received his endowments on Ensign Hill at 6 a.m. on the morning of 21 July, "the place being consecrated for the purpose. Ten others participated." These included six members of the Twelve, three presidents of the Seventy and "Father Morley." According to Franklin D. Richards, Pratt's endowment was "immediately bestowed" indicating that this may have been a shortened, highly abbreviated form of this sacred ordinance. Franklin D. Richards Journals, 20 July 1849, MSS 1215, box 6, Church History Library. Further to the endowment, there are occasional references to both the Aaronic Priesthood endowment and the Melchizedek Priesthood endowment, as if one could be given at one time and place and the other at another. Church Historian's Office Journal, 8 April 1849, CR 100 318, box 2, folder 10.
26. Endowment and Sealings, Book A, 1.

those long-faithful and worthy members who, for one reason or another, had never received this blessing in the Nauvoo Temple and who were now getting on in years. They were given almost as a reward for their many years of faithful service. Said Brigham Young: "I wish to say to the old brethren who were in Missouri, and in Nauvoo, we choose to give you your blessings first, and when any such [others] present themselves, we give you the preference; you have borne the heat and burden of the day and are entitled to these blessings first."[27] Among these were Daniel H. Wells, leader in the Battle of Nauvoo; Aphek Woodruff, Wilford Woodruff's father; Eleazer Miller, who had baptized Brigham Young; and at least three members of the 1834 Zion's Camp, including Reuben McBride and Solomon Angell, older brother to Truman O. Angell.

Those being called to colonize far-distant places in the new and expanding territories were also high on the priority list.[28] For instance, Harriet Sargent Rich, sixth wife of Apostle Charles C. Rich, whom she married at Winter Quarters in March 1847, was also among the first endowed prior to their moving to San Bernardino, California, with Amasa Lyman to establish a settlement there. As in the Nauvoo Temple, some particularly busy days ended in a season of rejoicing as the following account of 1 April 1852 indicates: "Afterwards all met in the celestial room . . . Sister [Elizabeth Ann] Whitney sung in tongues. Bro. [Samuel S.] Sprague danced while singing in tongues and received the blessing of President Young when we all separated greatly rejoicing in the presentation of the Lord."[29]

During its four years of service, 966 men and 1,256 women were endowed in the Council House.[30] Put in perspective, more than twice this number had been endowed in the Nauvoo Temple in the three months between December 1845 and February 1846. For Council House

---

27. Journal History, 8 April 1852, 5–6.
28. General Church Minutes, 7 October 1852, CR 100 318, box 2, folder 41.
29. Endowment and Sealings Book A, 1 April 1852.
30. This number likely included Addison Pratt's endowment on Ensign Peak.

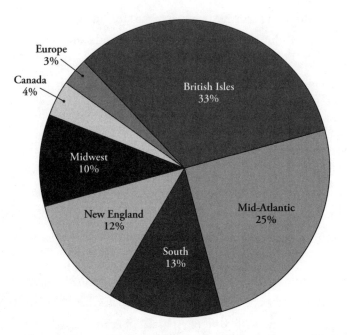

Figure 1: Percent of Early Utah Territory Immigrants by Country of Origin

endowments, the busiest months of the year were March, April, and July, with most sessions beginning at 10:00 a.m. Reflecting the rapidly changing emigration patterns of those newly arriving in the Valley, many of whom had never known Nauvoo, 39 percent of those endowed were from the British Isles, 4 percent from Canada, 2 percent from Europe, less than one percent (one each) from Jamaica and West Indies, one not designated, and the remaining 55 percent from New England, the Atlantic seaboard, and Southern states[31] (see Figure 1). Among those officiating in these ordinances were W. W. Phelps, W. C. Staines, S. S. Sprague, Albert P. Rockwood, and Wilford Woodruff. Among female officiators, the busiest

---

31. In 1851, 30 percent of those endowed were from the British Isles. In 1852 the percentage grew to 37 and by 1854, it was 53 percent. Endowment and Sealings Book A, 1851–1855. See also Bennett, "The Upper Room," 19.

three were Elizabeth Ann Whitney, Prescinda Huntington Buel Kimball, and Eliza R. Snow.

A look at the numbers of endowments per year shows that more than twice as many were performed in 1852 than in 1851. According to Council House records, Brigham Young ceased the performance of all such ordinances in November 1852 and did not resume them until February 3, 1854—a period of over fourteen months—apparently on account of "inferior oil brought by merchants," but which the original records say "for some reason now unknown."[32] Other factors, however, were likely at play, such as flooring problems, the issue of needed privacy in what was a very crowded, oft-times noisy building, and a somewhat troubling sentiment that such endowments would likely have to be repeated later anyway, once a temple was built. Brigham Young said as much at the October 1852 conference: "There are many in this congregation who are aware that we do not give all the endowments, neither can we, legally, until we build a temple. Again, those parts that are already given, and will be given, in the place we at present use, will be given over again in the temple, when it is finished. The endowments we now give, are given merely by permission, as we have not a house in which to officiate in these ordinances of salvation, that is legal, though we have got a comfortable place, which we have dedicated to the Lord."[33]

Counterbalancing repeated statements about the importance of the endowment was a somewhat contrasting sentiment that all would work out

---

32. Church Historian's Office Journal, 15:335, 31 October 1852, and Endowment and Sealings Book A, handwritten title page. The downturn in tithing contributions may have been another factor. As early as August 1851, Brigham Young was prohibiting persons from receiving their endowments "until they can show a certificate of settlement from the Tithing Office." William Clayton to Bishop Elias Blackburn, Brigham Young Letterpress Copybook, 1844–1879, 106, 14 October 1851, CR 1234 1. See also Brigham Young, in *Journal of Discourses*, 2:144, 3 December 1854. In 1851 "President Young gave orders for no man to receive his endowments . . . unless he first presents his receipts from the tithing office showing that he has paid his tithing up." Endowments and Sealings Book A, 11 August 1851.

33. Journal History, 6 October 1852. See also General Church Minutes, 6 October 1852. It was later made clear, however, that such ordinances would be "valid" if recipients died before a future temple was constructed. General Church Minutes, 5 November 1852.

well regardless, even for those who wanted them but who could not, for one reason or another, obtain them. Speaking in 1857 President Young said:

> We work one day in a week [giving endowments] in order to stir up the devil, that's all. The brethren that are going out, if they have not had their endowments, if they will keep the commandments of God, and do as well as [they] know, they shall live and be protected just the same as those that have had them. Bless your souls. . . . If you do right you shall have your endowments, and God shall bless you just the same; and men and women that do not honor and magnify their callings, their endowments will do them no good, but only add sorrow to them.[34]

The last endowments administered in the Council House came on a very rainy Monday, 29 April 1854, when thirty-one people crowded their way through a building that had served its purposes. Included in that company was fifteen-year-old Joseph F. Smith who was about to serve his mission to the Sandwich Islands and whose 1918 "Vision of the Redemption of the Dead" would later have such a profound impact on temple work.[35]

To summarize, temple endowments in early Salt Lake City were performed in a Council House that proved not entirely adequate to the task. Such endowments were done "by permission" and were strictly for the living. They were also administered to those about to serve missions or colonize far-distant places, as a reward for lifelong service to the Church, and for immigrant converts arriving in ever-increasing numbers. The operative word was be patient, remain faithful, and all will work out. Thus Brigham Young tried to remove the urgency of receiving the endowment without sacrificing the need for it, thereby buying time in the hearts and minds of the Saints to build a more suitable temple or temple-like place. As he put it years later: "I want to see the temple finished as soon as it is reasonable and practicable. Whether we go in there to work or not makes

---

34. General Church Minutes, 16 August 1857, CR 100 318, box 3, folder 17.
35. Endowments and Sealings, Book A, 78.

"THE UPPER ROOM"

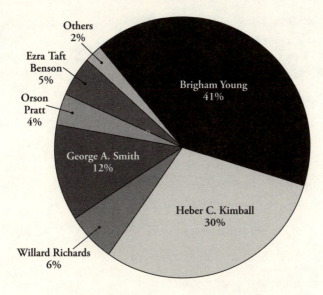

Figure 2: Sealers by Percentage of Sealings 1847 to 1855

no difference; I am perfectly willing to finish it to the last leaf of gold that shall be laid upon it, and to the last lock that should be put on the doors, and then lock every door, and there let it stand until the earth can rest before the Saints commence their labors there. They receive more in the House of the Lord now than is their due."[36]

"FOR TIME AND ETERNITY": SEALINGS

In contrast to the virtual absence of baptisms for the dead and the limited number of endowments, the most prevalent of temple-related ordinances during these early years in the Salt Lake Valley was that of sealings. These included marriage sealings of living partners for "time and eternity" as well as for "time" only; proxy sealings in which one of the marriage partners was deceased at the time of the sealing ceremony; and the sealing adoptions of men and women to prominent priesthood leaders. There is no record of children being sealed to their parents.

---

36. Brigham Young, in *Journal of Discourses*, 11:372, 8 April 1867.

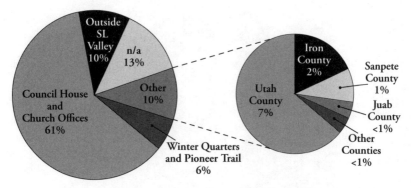

Figure 3: Location of Sealings 1847 to 1855

While there was at least one sealing performed in the "old Salt Lake Fort" on 2 January 1848, the largest number occurred once the Council House was in full operation, beginning in 1851. Of the 2,201 marriage sealings recorded by Thomas Bullock between 9 February 1847 and 24 April 1855, 881 (41 percent) were performed personally by Brigham Young, with Heber C. Kimball and Willard Richards, his counselors, performing 780 (36 percent) more. As Figure 2 shows, Brigham Young and his counselors performed a total of 76 percent of all sealings. The only unnamed "others" to do sealings were Isaac Morley and John Smith (three between them).

While the majority were performed in the Council House—in Brigham Young's office, the East Room, or elsewhere in that edifice—well over four hundred were performed in private homes, not only in Salt Lake City, such as Brigham Young's "log house" and the homes of W. W. Phelps, Heber C. Kimball, Benjamin Rolfe, and Rhonda Richards, but also in several other cities and towns all over Utah Territory (see Figure 3). Care was taken to perform such sacred ceremonies privately and not under the gaze of "too many people." In a situation where he once again listened to the cries of his people, most of whom he had sent out on one kind of mission or another, President

Young authorized taking this temple-based ordinance to his people—a case of the temple going to the people and not the other way around.[37]

In several cases, sealings were performed for those suffering with consumption or who were otherwise so ill they were confined to their deathbeds within their own homes.[38] For example, E. T. Benson sealed John Wood of Salt Lake City at 9:00 p.m. on 7 September 1851 to his ailing thirty-year-old wife, Ann Leigh, who died the next day.[39] Erastus Snow conducted one marriage sealing in Danish in 1854, the first occasion of a temple-related ordinance being given in a language other than English.[40] Apostle George A. Smith was particularly busy performing sealings in southern Utah. On 30 May 1854 he "crossed Provo River on horseback, found water deep and rapid but got over safely by assistance of President Higbee and came to Dry Creek. Attended to sealing several couples."[41] Between 1851 and 1855, this intrepid traveling sealer conducted 255 such ceremonies, as many as all his fellow apostles (excluding the First Presidency) combined, and in other Utah towns such as Payson, Lehi, Springville, Parowan, and Fillmore, though always "by permission of President Young."[42] Records show that in Iron County where he built

---

37. John Taylor justified the giving of certain temple ordinances outside of a temple as follows: "Although it is very important that temples should be built, the Priesthood is not for the Temple but the Temples are for the priesthood, and while the Saints are doing all in their power to build temples, the Lord will accept of ordinances performed, under the conditions named, in a place, if it [is] not a regular Temple, that has been especially set apart for those purposes." John Taylor, Salt Lake Stake General Minutes, 125, 15 November 1877, LR 604 11.
38. Brigham Young likewise authorized the cancellations of some previous sealings in cases of abuse, lack of financial support, disharmonies of a serious nature, or severe incompatibility.
39. Endowments and Sealings Book A, 7 September 1851. See also Familysearch.org, Person Identifier KWJT-DWM.
40. Church Historian's Office Journal, 17:88, 2 July 1854.
41. Church Historian's Office Journal, 17:55, 30 May 1854.
42. Church Historian's Office Journal, 22 February 1856. A large number of such sealings were done without the person receiving his or her own personal endowments. The prevailing sentiment was that such a blessing would come at some future time. Years later, David H. Cannon, counselor in the St. George Temple presidency, spoke of this as follows: "Many people have been sealed by authorities outside of the Temple and some have been sealed without first having their endowments, and though they were thus sealed they came here to have their endowments, and are sealed over the altar and have their children sealed to them." St. George Temple Meeting Minutes, 7:215, 1 December 1896, CR 343 44, Church History Library.

a home, George A. Smith "dedicated in it an upper room and organized a prayer circle."[43]

In what is a reflection of the changing demographics of the Latter-day Saints in Salt Lake City in particular, the origins of those sealed from 1851 to 1854 shows that 12 percent were from New England, 25 percent from the Atlantic states (mostly New York), 10 percent from the Midwest, 13 percent from the southern United States, 33 percent from Great Britain, 4 percent from Canada, and 3 percent from Europe. Many of these were recent immigrants who had never set foot in Nauvoo. Likely a large number of the British couples had been converted by the Twelve during their 1839–42 missions there. This decision to restrict the performance of sealings to the Twelve Apostles bonded the Saints to their apostolic leaders in a way not otherwise attainable. This carefully guarded control of sealings ensured order, inspiration, loyalty, and allegiance to Church priesthood authority and direction.

In the matter of personal worthiness, whether for sealings or more particularly for endowments, Church authorities also found a way to bind their people to the teachings and expectations of membership, particularly tithing. As already noted, on 11 August 1851 President Young gave orders "for no man to have his endowment after that date unless he first presents his receipts from the tithing office showing that he has paid his tithing up."[44] Though formal temple recommends were not yet in use, the demand for sealings carried with it the expectation of improved personal behavior. That Church officials accepted repentance, however, is evident from an 1853 entry for a couple about to be sealed: "The girl has a child in her arms which he is the father of and they have not been previously married."[45]

This effort to perform sealings where the people were, in their own language, in their less than perfect behaviors, and in times of severe illness and incapacitation manifests a surprising flexibility and adaptability to

---

43. Church Historian's Office Journal, 22:102, December 1852.
44. Endowments and Sealings Record, Book A, 11August 1851.
45. Endowments and Sealings Record, Book A, 16 April 1853.

"THE UPPER ROOM"

meet pressing needs and special circumstances. These exceptions to the rule of sacred space were endearing to the people and, while not surrendering the importance of restricting ordinances to a temple or templelike place, signaled understanding and compassion, thus bringing Church authorities into the hearts and homes of the members in a most memorable way.

The vast majority of marriage sealings were for "time and eternity," meaning the hope and promise that a marriage would endure beyond the grave and into the Resurrection. While there are instances of divorces and of unions being broken or "dismissed," most were for "time and eternity," with far fewer for "time in eternity only," as they so used the phrase. During these years, 95 percent of all marriages were for "time and eternity" and only the remaining 5 percent were for "time." There is one instance in April 1853 of a woman being sealed to her second husband "for time" with this notation: "Her former husband . . . was not baptized, to whom she wishes to be sealed for eternity, when the temple is built."[46]

Nevertheless, not a few were for a living spouse to a deceased partner, even on at least one occasion to a nonmember such as Henry Howland, who began his trek to Zion but died of cholera after crossing the Missouri River before he could be baptized.[47] On very rare occasions, a deceased couple were sealed as a married unit, as long as both were well remembered and their marriage certified by living posterity. No records have yet been found for ancestral marriages more than one generation past, likely due to the scarcity of records.

The majority of marriage sealings appeared to be monogamous, from as low as 52 percent in 1849 to as high as almost 90 percent in 1855, with 88 percent being between one man and one woman. Obviously plural marriages occurred when one man and two or more women were present together during the ceremony. However, simply because a husband and one wife were sealed together does not necessarily mean that the husband

---

46. Endowments and Sealings, Book A, 9 April 1853.
47. Endowments and Sealings, Book A, 31 December 1852.

TEMPLES RISING

Breaking ground for the Salt Lake Temple, 14 February 1853.

was marrying for the first time or that he did not have one or more other spouses. Identifying what percentage of marriages were truly monogamous and what were of multiple or later wives is difficult. What is clear is that the ceremony itself was attended to "by a form of words most sublime" as one woman described the giving of her husband in marriage to another woman. When done she said, "My destiny has taken its bent and I am satisfied in the man the Lord has given me for a husband."[48]

"A LOVELY, VERNAL MORN"—LAYING THE CORNERSTONES TO THE SALT LAKE TEMPLE

In addition to many other priorities, temple consciousness among the Saints transcended place and personality and played an integral role in building and deepening the faith and devotion of the Latter-day Saints in early Utah Territory. Soon after Brigham Young had identified a place

---
48. Joyce Kinkead, "A Schoolmarm All My Life: Personal Narratives from Frontier Utah, Martha Spence Haywood 1811–73," 23, in *New Mormon Studies CD-ROM*.

for the temple in the summer of 1847, he began work building a wall around the temple block, which soon was reduced in size to ten acres. This temporary wall was completed in 1852 with a more permanent stone wall constructed beginning in 1852 and being completed in 1855.[49]

Groundbreaking for the Salt Lake Temple occurred on 14 February 1853, at which time President Young said: "We want a temple more than we want dwelling houses."[50] Two months later during conference proceedings on the "lovely, vernal morn" of 6 April 1853, the cornerstones to the Salt Lake Temple were laid with promises and prophecies galore. In ceremonies lasting several hours, the First Presidency laid the southeast cornerstone, the Presiding Bishop and Council, with the Presidents of the lesser Priesthood and Council then followed laying the southwest cornerstone. Then the President and Council of the High Priests Quorum, with the President of the Salt Lake Stake and High Council laid the northwest cornerstone. And last of all, the Quorum of the Twelve Apostles, with the First Presidency of the Seventies, and the President and Council of the Elders Quorum laid the northeast cornerstone.[51] "The work for the redemption, and salvation of Israel has commenced, as were anew, on the earth," wrote the First Presidency in celebratory tones, "which makes Satan mad, and causes devils to howl; but their doleful moans are not heeded by the Saints in the mountains, their hearts are cheered to press forward with all their energies, to complete the Lord's House, as speedily as possible."[52]

On this special day, the choir sang a six-verse temple anthem especially written for the occasion entitled "The Temple" by Zion's poetess, Eliza R. Snow. The first verse and chorus went as follows:

---

49. Not to be confused with the so-called City Wall built around the entire city and made out of mud, straw, and gravel and begun in 1853, the stone wall around the temple block, begun in 1852, replaced an earlier temporary wall begun in 1847. It was a much more permanent structure built out of the tithing contributions of the Saints. Eleventh General Epistle of the First Presidency, *Settling the Valley,* 204.
50. *Wilford Woodruff's Journal,* 4:196, 14 February 1853.
51. Ninth General Epistle of the First Presidency, April 1853, *Settling the Valley,* 185.
52. Ninth General Epistle of the First Presidency, April 1853, *Settling the Valley,* 186.

> *Our Era this day numbers three years and twenty,*
> *And lo! A great people inhabit the West;*
> *The Lord God of Abra'm, the great God of battles,*
> *Who leads forth to vict'ry, appointed our rest.*
>
> *(Chorus)*
>
> *The Temple, The Temple, We'll build up The Temple,*
> *A court of salvation, iniquity's rod—*
> *A glorious beacon—a light on the mountains—*
> *A portal for angels—a threshold for God.*[53]

Leaders also took time to look backward to what had happened to both the Kirtland and Nauvoo temples as well as ahead to the building of the Salt Lake Temple. In reference to the first temple built in this dispensation, President Young said the following:

> *Before these endowments could be given at Kirtland, the Saints had to flee before mobocracy, and by toil, and daily labor they found places in Missouri where they laid the cornerstones of the temples in Zion, and her stakes, and then had to retreat to Illinois to save the lives of those who could get away from Missouri alive; where fell the apostle David W. Patten, with many like associates, and where were imprisoned in loathsome dungeons, and fed on human flesh, Joseph and Hyrum and many others; but before all this had transpired, the Temple at Kirtland, had fallen into the hands of wicked men, and by them polluted like the Temple at Jerusalem, and consequently was disowned by the Father and the Son.*

And as for the Nauvoo Temple, it too had "passed into the hands of the enemy who polluted it to that extent the Lord not only ceased to occupy it, but he loathed to have it called by his name and permitted the wrath of its possessors to purify it by fire, as a token of what will speedily

---

53. Eliza R. Snow, "The Temple, the Temple," Journal History, 3, 6 April 1853. A song sung during the cornerstone laying ceremonies for the Salt Lake Temple.

fall on them and their habitations, unless they repent."[54] And looking to the future, he made the following prediction during the cornerstone laying of the Salt Lake Temple:

> *Brethren, shall the Son of Man be satisfied with our proceedings this day? Shall he have a house on the Earth which he can call his own? Shall he have place where he can lay his head, and rest over night, and tarry as long as he pleases, and be satisfied and pleased with his accommodations?*
>
> *These are questions for you to answer. If you say yes, you have got to do the work, or it will not be done. We don't want any whiners about this Temple. If you cannot commence cheerfully and go through the labor of the whole building cheerfully, start for California, the quicker the better. Make you a golden calf and worship it. If your care for the ordinances of salvation, for yourselves, your living, and dead, are not first, and foremost in your hearts, in your actions, and in every thing you possess, . . . Go in peace do your duty. . . . But if you are what you profess to be . . . Stay with the Saints; pay your Tithing . . . and the Temple will arise in beauty and grandeur in a manner and time which you have not hitherto known or contemplated.*[55]

"THE KEYS OF THE ETERNAL PRIESTHOOD"

The General Epistles of the First Presidency from the Valley, and the cornerstone laying ceremony for the Salt Lake Temple construction, afford the careful observer a glimpse into how Church leaders were then interpreting temple doctrines. The key vision most often referenced was not Joseph Smith's First Vision as modern missionaries are prone to do, but rather Moroni's appearances to Joseph Smith in September 1823. Moroni spoke not only about the Book of Mormon but he also cited several Biblical scriptures from both the Old and New Testaments, including quoting Malachi's prophecy of the hearts of the fathers being turned to

---

54. Brigham Young, General Conference Minutes, Journal History, 2, 6 April 1853.
55. Journal History, 2, 6 April 1853.

the children and vice versa (D&C 2). Such "glad tidings from Cumorah" clearly pointed to temple work.

Similarly, President Brigham Young said relatively little about Elijah's return, as modern dialogue dictates, but looked more to "the Angels"—usually in reference to the return of Peter, James, and John—as one of Joseph Smith's greatest visions. And that "with the introduction of the Priesthood upon the earth was also introduced the sealing ordinance, that the chain of Priesthood from Adam to the latest generation might be united in one unbroken continuance . . . the same power and the same keys that Elijah held, and was to exercise in the last days."[56] President Young later developed this thought further:

> *The first light of the morning, in this age and the time referred to by the Saviour, was the angel who had the everlasting gospel, which was to be preached to all people, preaching and ministering to Joseph Smith Jr., and commanding Joseph to preach and administer to others, even as he had received of the angel; and the light continued to shine and spread, as others believed on the testimony of Joseph, for they repented of their sins, and were baptized by him; and he, having received the holy Priesthood from the Angels, conferred the same Priesthood on the believers, and they, in turn went forth proclaiming the same gospel, administering the same ordinances, calling on all the faithful to gather themselves together to the upbuilding of Zion . . . and the faithful saints must be gathered together in holy places, and build temples, and do all necessary works to open up the way of life and salvation to the dead as well as the living, before they can complete the work which is given them to do in this dispensation and probation.*[57]

---

56. Brigham Young, in, *Journal of Discourses*, 9:269, 6 April 1862.
57. Sixth General Epistle of the First Presidency, September 1851, *Settling the Valley*, 137. A study of the Journal History of the Church will show that between 1845 and 1856, Elijah in his capacity as conferring the "sealing power" is rarely mentioned. One exception, however, is 25 August 1845, in the *New York Messenger*.

"THE UPPER ROOM"

Surprisingly, throughout most of Joseph Smith's time in Nauvoo and Brigham Young's tenure as President of the Church—that is throughout the late 1840s, 1850s, and 1860s— relatively little was recorded concerning the return of Elijah, Elias, and Moses—at least not by name. While more will be said of this later (see chapter 7), during the 1850s and 1860s the doctrinal and historical justification for temple work centered on the return of the Angel Moroni and the restoration of apostolic priesthood keys performed by Peter, James, and John, under whom almost all visions and revelations stemmed.[58]

These apostolic keys even extended to temple work, as Brigham Young once again so well illustrated during the cornerstone-laying ceremonies of the Salt Lake Temple of April 1853:

> *I speak thus to show you the order of the Priesthood. We will now commence with the Apostleship—where Joseph commenced. Joseph was ordained an Apostle, that you can read and understand. After he was ordained to this office, then he had the right to organize, [and] build up the kingdom of God, for he had committed unto him the keys of the Priesthood, which is after the order of Melchizedek, the High priesthood, which is after the order of the Son of God. And this, remember, by being ordained an Apostle. Could he have built up the kingdom of God without first being an Apostle? No, he never could. The keys of the Eternal Priesthood, which is after the order of the Son of God, is comprehended by being an Apostle. All the Priesthood, all the keys, all the gifts, all the endowments, and everything preparatory to entering back into the presence of the Father and the Son, is in, composed of, circumscribed by, or I might say incorporated within the circumference of the Apostleship. . . . I know that Joseph received*

---

58. These apostolic keys given to the Prophet Joseph Smith in 1829 also allowed for him to become President of the Church less than a year later, establishing a precedent for apostolic succession to the presidency and which provided for Brigham Young's own ascendency to the presidency of the Church in 1847 after a three-and-a-half-year "apostolic interregnum." Such was his argument, at least, that eventually carried the day with his colleagues of the Quorum of the Twelve in Kanesville in December 1847.

his Apostleship from Peter, James and John, before a revelation on the subject was printed, and he never had a right to organize the Church before he was an Apostle.[59]

Parley P. Pratt pursued this line of reasoning further. "Who ordained . . . our first founders to the apostleship, to hold the keys of the kingdom of God, in these the times of restoration?" he asked. "Peter, James, and John, from the eternal world. Who instructed him in the mysteries of the kingdom, and in all things pertaining to priesthood, law, philosophy, sacred architecture, ordinances, sealings, anointings, baptisms for the dead; and in the mysteries of the first, second, and third heavens, many of which are unlawful to utter? Angels, and spirits from the eternal world."[60]

Endowed with such apostolic keys, which constitute "the spiritual blessings of the church," Joseph and Oliver, Brigham Young taught, now enjoyed the *right* to receive further heavenly revelations and manifestations. Even John the Baptist, who had preceded them, came "under the direction" of Peter, James, and John, who held the apostolic keys. And what are these keys? "To have the privilege of receiving the mysteries of the kingdom of heaven, to have the heavens opened unto them, to commune with the general assembly and church of the Firstborn, and to enjoy the communion and presence of God the Father, and Jesus the mediator of the

---

59. Brigham Young, Journal History, 6–8, 6 April 1853. President Joseph F. Smith once declared that Peter and James had a great work to perform after their own martyrdoms. "I have always believed, and still do believe with all my soul, that such men as Peter and James and the twelve disciples chosen by the Savior in his time, have been engaged all the centuries that have passed since their martyrdom for the testimony of Jesus Christ, in proclaiming liberty to the captives in the spirit world and in opening their prison doors. I do not believe that they could be employed in any greater work. Their special calling and anointing of the Lord himself was to save the world, to proclaim liberty to the captives, and the opening of the prison doors to those who were bound in chains of darkness, superstition, and ignorance." Joseph F. Smith, *Gospel Doctrine*, 460.
60. Parley P. Pratt, General Conference Minutes, Journal History, 5–6, 6 April 1853. Commenting further, George Q. Cannon said that through the restoration of the apostleship, God has "restored the authority by which the ordinances shall be performed on the earth that will bind man to woman, woman to man, children to parents and parents to children. So that these relationships which are so acceptable in the sight of God may not only exist for time, but may be perpetuated throughout the endless ages of eternity." George Q. Cannon, in *Journal of Discourses*, 14:1127, 8 April 1871. Upon reflection, the presentation of the endowment in large measure depends upon Peter, James, and John, that none receive this blessing from any other source.

new covenant" (D&C 107:18–19). Thus the right to future revelations, visions, and directives from divine messengers, including Moses, Elias, and Elijah, was an essential part or fulfilment of the restoration by Peter, James, and John of the Melchizedek Priesthood and its apostolic keys, claiming even earlier visions within its permitting scope and jurisdiction.

CONCLUSION

Such positive sentiments notwithstanding, almost everyone recognized that the Salt Lake Temple was but a distant dream. Whereas the Kirtland Temple had taken three years to build and the Nauvoo Temple five, the Salt Lake Temple, for a whole battery of reasons, would take forty years to complete, outlasting the lives of most speakers at its groundbreaking.

The history of temple work from 1847 to 1855, as understood by the Latter-day Saints while journeying to the West and once in the Valley, stayed in line with leadership policy, interpretations, and expectations on the one hand, while keeping pace with the needs of the people on the other. In building the Council House, Church leaders showed surprising flexibility and adaptability with an emphasis clearly on the living rather than on the dead. The various temple ordinances bestowed in Winter Quarters, across the plains, and in early Salt Lake City focused on the needs of the living—spiritual, emotional, and physical. Endowments for the dead would have to wait for another twenty years while baptisms for the dead were virtually nonexistent, as were intergenerational sealings. The exigencies of both time and place, and the promises of later revelations and prophecies of a future Millennium, all pushed their temple efforts toward the living and not yet to the dead.

Still, one of Brigham Young's central contributions to Latter-day Saint history in early Utah Territory, in addition to being a remarkable pioneer, colonizer, and frontiersman, was to retain within the members a consciousness of the abiding place for temple ordinances. He did so by selectively administering temple blessings in Salt Lake City and throughout the settlements of the Saints as need demanded and as inspiration directed. He also taught much about priesthood keys and how they applied to temple work, even though a temple was far from being completed. And he gave indications to the need to build another temporary sacred house on what is now Temple Square—an exciting initiative that now begs our attention.

Chapter 6

"A Temple Pro Tem"

Temple Work in Deseret, 1855–1870

In the days of our poverty, and while we had no Temple in which to administer ordinances for the dead . . . the Lord permitted us to erect an Endowment House.[1]

In the years from 1855 to 1870, the Church continued to grow under the direction of President Brigham Young. Missionary work expanded, the gathering of the Saints continued, and colonization efforts forged ahead. Although there were serious delays in the building of the Salt Lake Temple, these years also witnessed a multiplication of temple ordinances with the construction of a new temporary facility (pro tem) in the form of the Endowment House in 1855, successor to the outgrown Council House. Nevertheless, these advances came at a time of severe challenges in many forms, near and far. The invasion of Utah Territory by the U.S. Army in 1857 intent on putting down the so-called "Mormon Rebellion" resulted in the entire evacuation of Salt Lake City, the plowing over of the foundation to the temple, and the temporary closing of the Endowment House. And although the Saints remained relatively neutral during the tragedy of the Civil War, that conflict claimed the attention of almost everyone in Utah Territory. President Abraham Lincoln's postwar assassination sent a

---

1. First Presidency to the Church, 25 October 1876, as cited in Kirk M. Curtis, "History of the St. George Temple" (master's thesis, Brigham Young University, 1964), 106–7.

chill all across the nation and foreshadowed a time of vindictiveness and recrimination with the rise of a new political party intent on punishing both the vanquished South and the stubborn Latter-day Saint presence in the West. And with the completion of the transcontinental railroad in 1869, Utah Territory's era of "splendid isolation" came to an end. Yet paradoxically it also heralded a bright new day in temple consciousness.

"A TEMPLE PRO TEM"—THE ENDOWMENT HOUSE

The Council House discussed in the previous chapter was but a temporary stepping-stone to something greater. It had functioned almost exclusively for temple ordinances for the living, not the dead. Brigham Young said as much in 1852: "It is absolutely necessary that we should have a Temple to worship the Most High God in. A tabernacle is to assemble the multitude for meetings but a Temple is to gather the priesthood in that they may do the work of the Lord. . . . Is there a place prepared to go and redeem our dead? No there is not. We give Endowments here [Council House], but it is like trying to step on the top round first. . . . We do these things until we have time to build a Temple."[2]

Perhaps it was the press of secular and political business in the Council House, or the building was too small, or the Salt Lake Temple was taking too long to construct—whatever the reasons, in the spring of 1854 it was decided to erect a new, separate structure on Temple Square to be used solely for temple ordinances. Needed was another larger sacred space dedicated and set apart solely for living endowments and baptisms, baptisms for the dead, and marriage sealings. Consequently, on 4 August 1854 work began on the foundation of a "Temple pro tem," or temporary temple, which came to be later known as the Endowment House.[3] Likely designed

---

2. *Wilford Woodruff's Journal* 4:123, 9 April 1852.
3. Alonzo Raleigh Journal, 1853 September–1861 February, 4 August 1854, MS 13912, Church History Library, Salt Lake City; see also Lamar C. Berrett, "Endowment Houses," in *Encyclopedia of Mormonism*, 2:456. Very little else has been written on the Endowment House. James Dwight Tingen, "The Endowment House, 1855–1889" (an unpublished research paper, 1974), Perry Special Collections, HBLL, BYU. See also Lisle G. Brown, "'Temple Pro Tempore': The Salt Lake City Endowment House," *Journal of Mormon History* 34, no. 4 (Fall 2008):1–68.

by Church architect Truman O. Angell, this small, rectangular-shaped, thirty-four-foot by forty-four-foot, two-story building, running north and south on the present northwest corner of Temple Square, was completed in less than one year's time on 27 April 1855 at a reported cost of $10,000.[4] In his dedicatory remarks of 5 May 1855, Brigham Young distinguished this facility from a temple, calling each by a different name: "The President remarked the house was clean and named it 'The House of the Lord.' Said the spirit of the Lord would be in it for no one would be permitted to go into it to pollute it. Also said, 'when the temple is built, we will call that The Temple of our God.'"[5] Nevertheless, as one early worker carefully recorded, "President Young stated that all Sealings and Endowments would be valued as though they were in a Temple."[6]

An unimposing, two-story, gabled, adobe structure, the Endowment House looked very much like an ordinary dwelling house until the completion of two additions to the building late in the fall of 1856 and the addition of a baptistry that same year.[7] Water was pumped into the building

---

4. Tingen, "Endowment House," 5, 7, 9.
5. Journal History, 5 May 1855. It was not until early 1855 that the phrase "the Endowment House" was used in reference to this building. See Tingen, "Endowment House," 7. The first endowments were performed on 10 August 1855. Church Historian's Office Journal, 18:99, 10 August 1855.
6. William C. Staines Diary, 15 August 1855. The first floor consisted of the washing and anointing room, the garden room, the world room, and the terrestrial room. The celestial rtoom and sealing rooms were located on the second floor. Tingen, "Endowment House," 9–10. Although President Young said in 1852 that "those endowments which are now given will all have to be done over again, when the temple is completed," this was not ever made an official policy. General Church Minutes, 6 October 1852, CR 100 318, box 2, folder 41. Temporary as it may have been, all ordinances performed in the Endowment House were fully recognized as valid and binding upon the Church and its membership. As Wilford Woodruff once made clear: "The work for the dead that has been done in the endowment house, I consider has been done by the priesthood and legal authority, which is acceptable and the work is not necessary to be done over again." Wilford Woodruff to Edward Faulkner, Wilford Woodruff Letterpress Copybook, 57, 13 November 1882, MS 23181, Church History Library.
7. Similar to what had happened shortly after the vanguard company entered the Salt Lake Valley nine years before, during the dedication services of the baptismal font on the east side of the building on 1 and 2 October 1856, the First Presidency, Presiding Bishopric and many members of the Twelve were rebaptized and reconfirmed members of the Church with their unique special priesthood callings, responsibilities, keys, and blessings likewise reconfirmed at the same time. *Wilford Woodruff's Journal*, 4:459–62, 2 October 1856. This was very much in accordance to the spirit of the Mormon Reformation, then very much in full swing. This stone font was to be used for baptizing both the living and the dead. Defects in the workmanship of the font led

TEMPLES RISING

The Endowment House within the walls of early Temple Square, Salt Lake City, circa 1863.

from nearby City Creek. The baptistry, with its font made of hewn stone, occupied the lowest of all the rooms in the building. The structure was so unremarkable in appearance that one visitor dismissed it as "not much of a building to look at."[8] However, the interior featured something not seen before in either the Kirtland or Nauvoo Temple or even the Council House. Occupying the first floor were the garden and world rooms with specially designed murals, and on the second floor were the instruction, celestial, and sealing rooms.[9] The Endowment House set a pattern for most future temple construction to follow, with its separate lecture rooms for the endowment presentation and "progressively ascending ordinance rooms, using stairs to emphasize the upward ascent."[10] Thus patrons

---

to extensive repairs and a later rededication on 4 June 1864. *Wilford Woodruff's Journal*, 6:173, 4 June 1864.

8. W. G. Marshall, *Through America: Or Nine Months in the United States* (London: Sampson, Low, Marston, Searle & Irvington, 1881), 169, as cited in Brown, "Temple Pro Tempore," 28.

9. The Endowment House was the final building to have a garden room with potted living plants. It was also the first to have murals, perhaps at the suggestion of William War, the artist who was then serving as Church architect. Brown, "Temple Pro Tempore," 63.

10. Brown, "Temple Pro Tempore," 55.

The Endowment House, Salt Lake City, circa 1880.

physically participated in the endowment in an "ascending circular pattern." It also contained, for the first time, multiple veil segments and the first sealing room specifically designed for marriages.[11]

First supervised directly by Heber C. Kimball and later by Daniel H. Wells, and with Wilford Woodruff taking a prominent role, the Endowment House, more popularly referred to as simply the "endowment rooms," provided a place for baptisms and confirmations for both the living and the dead, endowments for the living (including washings and anointings), and marriage sealings for both the living and the dead.[12] The first endowments administered in the Endowment House occurred on 5 May 1855, the same day it was dedicated. "I having been notified by Pres. Kimball, I took Elizabeth up to the endowment house a new building just erected, to get her endowments," wrote George Q. Cannon in his journal. "After the house had been dedicated by the brethren, they

---

11. Brown, "Temple Pro Tempore," 65, 67.
12. *Wilford Woodruff's Journal*, 7:231, 16 June 1875. Some deceased spouses were sealed to living partners. *Wilford Woodruff's Journal*, 7:280, 26 July 1876; see also Leonard J. Arrington, *Brigham Young: American Moses* (New York: Alfred A. Knopf, 1985), 193.

proceeded to give them, five men and three women, their endowment."[13] Various wards and stakes were asked to send a certain number of their members to the Endowment House at specific dates and times and specific members were invited to come "to receive their Endowments."[14] Those attending were required to be tithe payers, "who pray in their families," who neither "steal, nor lie, nor interfere with their neighbors things" and "who attend strictly to meetings and prayer meetings . . . and who do not swear."[15] Such were to have an informal endorsement from their local leaders.[16] Charles Walker traveled all the way from St. George just to attend. "D. H. Wells . . . cordially invited [me] to the Endowment House to witness the baptisms for the dead," for friends and family members, he recorded in the summer of 1872. "I went with him to the font and acted as a witness, after which Br J F Smith very courteously asked me to assist in confirming. I spent the day there and assisted in baptizing and confirming over 500. Never felt better in my life . . . and though I had to travel 350 miles to attend to it, and 350 back again, I do not think it too much."[17]

Although closed in 1876, just before the new St. George Temple opened, the Endowment House reopened for special prayer circle ceremonies in behalf of President Young who was then terminally ill.[18] After Brigham's death the following year, John Taylor temporarily reopened it on a very limited basis to serve the needs of the youth who wanted to marry and the aged, infirm, and seriously ill who could not make the arduous

---

13. Journal of George Q. Cannon, 5 May 1855, https://www.churchhistorianspress.org/george-q-cannon?lang=eng (accessed 21 June 2017, online only).
14. "President H. C. Kimball and Elder W. Woodruff attend at the Endowment House, two days in the week, administering the ordinances thereof, on an average, to fifty persons each day. Prest. Kimball has, recently, invited the young people from the Northern settlements, to come and receive their Endowments; and, also to Tooele, for two weeks to come. He devotes several hours each day in giving instruction, which he does in his emphatic style. He did so today, with a new set of teeth, which bothered him some." Manuscript History of Brigham Young, 35:147, March 1865, CR 100 102.
15. Church Historian's Office Journal, 26:280–81, 19 May 1856.
16. Provo Utah Central Stake General Minutes, Priesthood Meeting, 5 November 1881, LR 9629 11, Church History Library.
17. Walker, *The Diary of Charles Lowell Walker*, 1:346, 19 June 1872.
18. See Alonzo Raleigh Journal, 29 August 1877. The Endowment House was also closed temporarily from March 1858 to August 1859 because of the Utah War.

trip south to St. George. By late 1879 and after the completion of the St. George Temple, the Endowment House had returned to its regular schedule but it never enjoyed the patronage of earlier days. It was finally torn down in November 1889 on order of President Wilford Woodruff. During its thirty-four-year lifespan, the unofficial count of ordinances performed in the Endowment House was 134,053 baptisms and confirmations for the dead, 31,052 marriage sealings for the living, 37,715 proxy marriage sealings for the dead, and 54,170 endowments for the living.[19] However, few, if any, children, either living or dead, were sealed to their parents, and no endowments for the dead were performed there.[20]

As useful as the Endowment House proved itself to be, it was always understood that, like the Council House, it was but another substitute for a temple, a temporary precursor to something far greater. "There are some of the sealing ordinances that cannot be administered in the house that we are now using," Brigham Young remarked in October 1863. "We can only administer in it some of the first ordinances of the Priesthood pertaining to the endowment. There are more advanced ordinances that cannot be administered there; we would, therefore, like a Temple, but I am willing to wait a few years for it. I want to see [it] built in a manner that it will endure through the Millennium. This is not the only Temple we shall build; there will be hundreds of them."[21] Speaking in conference the year following, George Q. Cannon addressed the same theme. "The Lord has not yet revealed to us all that is to be revealed. There are many great and

---

19. Tingen, "Endowment House," 15.
20. Said Brigham Young on this matter of children: "Children born unto parents before the latter enter into the fullness of the covenants [endowment], have to be sealed to them in a Temple to become legal heirs of the Priesthood. It is true they can receive the ordinances, they can receive their endowments and be blessed in common with their parents; but still the parents cannot claim them legally and lawfully in eternity unless they are sealed to them." Young, in *Journal of Discourses*, 16:186–87, 4 September 1873.
21. Brigham Young, *Journal of Discourses*, 10:254, 6 October 1863. See also Journal History, 9 October 1863. On another occasion when referring to the building of the Salt Lake Temple, he said that it "was for the use of the Priesthood for them to receive instructions in." He said, "We were but babes and sucklings in the things of God. Said he wished to build a Temple to the Holiness of the Lord." Walker, *Diary*, 142, 8 October 1860; see also Irving, "The Law of Adoption," 291–314, particularly 308.

glorious principles and truths pertaining to exaltation in the kingdom of God which we are not yet prepared to receive."[22]

Nor was the Endowment House the only place in which marriage sealings were performed. General Authorities continued to perform such in areas far removed from Salt Lake City. These included George A. Smith, Erastus Snow, and Amasa Lyman and probably many others of the Twelve.[23]

On another occasion, Brigham Young differentiated even more clearly between what could and what could not be done outside the temple, although the precise reasons were rarely spelled out. "We can, at the present time," he said, "receive our washings and anointing, etc. . . . We also have the privilege of sealing women to men, without a Temple . . . but when we come to other sealing ordinances . . . they cannot be done without a Temple. . . . We can seal women to men, but not men to men."[24] It would appear that intergenerational linkages, at least further back than one generation, was the critical element of proxy work not available without a temple.

"In the days of our poverty, and while we had no Temple in which to administer ordinances for the dead . . . the Lord permitted us to erect an Endowment House," the First Presidency wrote in 1877 on the eve of the dedication of the St. George Temple. "This we have used for many years, and many ordinances have been administered therein; but there are other important ordinances which have not been, and cannot be, administered, except in a Temple built and dedicated to the Most High for that purpose."[25]

The fact is that temple work had not become a staple in the worship practices of most Latter-day Saints in Deseret, primarily because no temples were completed in Utah Territory between 1847 and 1877. And

---

22. Journal History, 23 October 1864.
23. "History of the Church," 29:70, January 1859.
24. Brigham Young, in *Journal of Discourses*, 16:186, 4 September 1873. This is likely in reference to the law of adoption.
25. First Presidency to the Church, 25 October 1876, "First Presidency and the Twelve, To the Bishops and Members of The Church of Jesus Christ of Latter-day Saints Residing in the Various Settlements throughout these Mountains," Journal History, 3, 25 October 1876.

of those who received their endowments in either the Council House or the Endowment House, most did so only when invited or permitted. Even during the zeal of the "Mormon Reformation" of 1856, the symbol of recommitment among the Saints was not increased temple worship but rather rebaptism and a renewed commitment to plural marriage. The emphasis was not on the law of consecration but on the payment of tithes.[26] Had there ever been a better time to introduce endowments for the dead, a practice which clearly would have demanded more temple attendance, it would have been during these Reformation years. However, such was not the case. Joseph Young, President of the Quorum of Seventy and older brother to President Brigham Young, speaking in conference in April 1857, called for a recommitment to build the Salt Lake Temple so "that we may have a renewal of our endowments." He continued: "The endowments are going on. That is true, a portion of the endowments are going on, but there are other things that never will until the Temple is built; of which are . . . our endowments proxy for our dead friends. Are they going on? No. Will they before that house is built? No, not that I know of."[27]

We leave the final postscript to the work of the Endowment House to Daniel H. Wells, its longtime supervisor and later member of the First Presidency, in this tender 1888 letter to Joseph F. Smith: "You and I spent so many happy hours and days in laboring in the Endowment House, hours and days never to be forgotten. Bless that old Temple, though not aspiring to the dignity of a Temple, yet within its humble walls and lowly and spireless roof, many a soul was made happy and made to rejoice in the

---

26. As one careful student of the Mormon Reformation has observed, "Consecration was never a major consideration during the Reformation of 1856–57, the stress being placed instead on payment of tithes. This lack of emphasis on consecration was deliberate as Reformation missionaries were instructed . . . to be cautious and circumspect when discussing it with Church members." Paul H. Peterson, "The Mormon Reformation" (PhD diss., Joseph Fielding Smith Institute for Latter-day Saint History, Brigham Young University, 2002), 15. As for the practice of rebaptism, it flowered during the Reformation and became a "binding directive." Brigham Young set the pattern himself by being once again rebaptized on 2 October 1856, as was Heber C. Kimball. Peterson, "Mormon Reformation," 26.
27. Joseph Young, Journal History, 8 April 1857.

deliverances wrought out for them through the Ordinances of the House of God."[28]

IMPEDIMENTS TO TEMPLE WORK

The coming of a 2,500-strong United States Army to Utah Territory in 1857 put a temporary end to all aspects of temple work, and set the entire region on a war footing. "The Utah War of 1857–58," in the words of William MacKinnon, a leading scholar of that unfortunate episode, "was the armed conflict over power and authority in Utah Territory between Mormon leaders and US President James Buchanan."[29] Sometimes referred to as "Buchanan's Blunder," the war was the result of years of misunderstanding and increasingly harsh feelings between the Latter-day Saints and Washington over such matters as mail contractors, relations with Native American tribes, land ownership, the administration of Utah Territorial courts, the (in)competency of federal officeholders in the uneven treatment of emigrants passing through the Territory, and perhaps most importantly the public's negative reaction to plural marriage as publicly announced in 1852.[30]

Perceiving a so-called "Mormon Rebellion," Buchanan moved to replace Brigham Young as governor of the Territory and to provide his successor, Alfred Cumming, with a large expeditionary escort that eventually involved nearly one-third of the U.S. Army. The large and well-trained Territorial Militia or Nauvoo Legion, under the command of Daniel H. Wells, resisted "this massive military intervention" with a series of guerilla warfare tactics that stalled the army's advance through the mountain passes east of Salt Lake City.[31] The threat of a full-scale military attack prompted Governor Young to declare martial law, which announcement created a

---

28. Daniel H. Wells to Joseph F. Smith, Manti Temple Letterpress Copybook, 2:26, 25 June 1888, CR 348 5.
29. William P. MacKinnon, "Epilogue to the Utah War: Impact and Legacy," *Journal of Mormon History* 29, no. 2 (Fall 2003): 186–87.
30. William P. MacKinnon, "Into the Fray: Sam Houston's War," *Journal of Mormon History* 39, no. 3 (Summer 2013): 200.
31. MacKinnon, "Epilogue to the Utah War," 189.

warlike atmosphere, bordering on panic. Such turmoil in part led to the horrors of the Mountain Meadows Massacre where, on 11 September 1857, near Cedar City, several Latter-day Saint militiamen, in company with Piute Indians, massacred some 120 people of the ill-fated Baker-Fancher emigrant camps from Arkansas.[32]

Thanks in large measure to the intercession and wise counsel of Colonel Thomas L. Kane, the U.S. government and the territorial government negotiated a settlement that resulted in a compromise that allowed for a change of governors, the establishment of Camp Floyd with its army garrisons forty miles southwest of Salt Lake City, and the signing of a pardon for the Saints and a negotiated peace, but not before some 30,000 Latter-day Saints had evacuated Salt Lake City for destinations further south. And not before Brigham Young ordered the tearing down of what little had been built of the temple and the plowing over of a now vacant and deserted temple lot. Meanwhile, all ordinance work in the Endowment House temporarily ground to a halt.

The conflicting feelings that the Latter-day Saints held toward the United States at the time, coupled with the sounds and fury of America's Civil War and the very real possibility of a national rupture, rekindled a desire on Brigham Young's part to reconsider returning the Church to Independence, Jackson County, Missouri, where revelations to Joseph Smith years before had identified the region as the final gathering place prior to Christ's Second Coming.[33] Barely three months into the Civil War, President Young saw it as a possible signal for the Saints to return.

---

32. Ronald W. Walker, Richard E. Turley Jr., and Glen M. Leonard, *Massacre at Mountain Meadows: An American Tragedy* (Oxford: Oxford University Press, 2008); Juanita Brooks, *The Mountain Meadows Massacre* (Norman, Oklahoma: University of Oklahoma Press, 1950); Will Bagley, *Blood of the Prophets: Brigham Young and the Massacre at Mountain Meadows* (Norman, Oklahoma: University of Oklahoma Press, 2002).

33. In the fall of 1860, Brigham Young delivered a talk concerning the possible return to Missouri: "Bro. Brigham showed how we should return to Jackson Co. Mo. The Lord would open the way before us. Said that he asked no odds of our enemies or their riches and expected to see the time when we should ride in our carriages while they were naked and barefoot. . . . Said also that the time would come when there would not be as much as a dog to wag his tongue in all the mountains of Ephraim." Walker, *Diary*, 1:143, 21 October 1860.

"Just as soon as the Latter-day Saints are ready and prepared to return to Independence, Jackson County, in the state of Missouri, just as soon will the voice of the Lord be heard, 'arise now, Israel, and make your way to the center stake of Zion.'" He continued: "Do you believe that we, as Latter-day Saints, are preparing our own hearts—our own lives—to return to take possession of the center stake of Zion, as fast as the Lord is preparing [it]? . . . We must be pure to be prepared to build up Zion. To all appearance the Lord is preparing that end of the route faster than we are preparing ourselves to go."[34]

A year later he picked up where he left off. "If we do not hurry with this," he said in August 1862, referring to the recurring problems encountered with building the Salt Lake Temple, "I am afraid we shall not get it up until we have to go back to Jackson County which I expect will be in seven years. I do not want to quite finish this temple for there will not be any temple finished until the one is finished in Jackson County, Missouri, pointed out by Joseph Smith."[35] And all throughout the Civil War, the Salt Lake City press paid particular attention to the scenes of havoc and destruction in Jackson County, as evident in the following October 1863 clip found in the *Deseret News*:

> *The interest of the people of Utah in Jackson County, Missouri, prompts the publication of the following extracts: "Devastation in Jackson Co., Missouri." The depopulation of the counties in Jackson, Cass, Bates, and Vernon is thorough and complete. One may ride for hours without seeing a single inhabitant and deserted houses and farms are everywhere to be seen. The whole is a grand picture of desolation.*[36]

---

34. Journal History, 28 July 1861.
35. *Wilford Woodruff's Journal*, 6:71, 23 August 1862. Heber C. Kimball, Young's first counselor, predicted in 1857 much the same. "If you will live your religion and do right you shall none of you fall by the hand of our enemy, but you shall eat peaches and apples in this valley until you go to Jackson County, Missouri and your enemies shall not conquer you." Church Historian's Office Journal, 27: 200, 20 October 1857.
36. From the *St. Joseph (Mo.) Herald*, as reprinted in the *Deseret News*, 18 October 1863. For more on the Latter-day Saints and the Civil War, see *Civil War Saints*, ed. Kenneth L. Alford (Provo, Utah:

"A TEMPLE PRO TEM"

With the recent Battle of Gettysburg fresh in the public's memory and the Civil War raging at fever pitch at the end of 1863, even Wilford Woodruff concluded that this might be the long-awaited time of return. "The Lord is watching over the interests of Zion and sustains his Kingdom upon the earth and [is] preparing the way for the return of his saints to Jackson County, Missouri, to build up the waste places of Zion. Jackson County has been entirely cleared of its inhabitants during the year 1863 which is one of the greatest miracles manifested in our day and those who have driven the Saints out and spoiled them are in their turn now driven out and spoiled."[37]

Some saw all this as a fulfillment of prophecy and a necessary precursor to the Saints' returning to Missouri. One can only guess at what disruptions would have happened had the Church actually pulled up stakes and reconfigured even a portion of itself in Missouri. The challenges would have been immense and the costs enormous. The Civil War, however, finally ended in April 1865 and with it most talk about a return to Jackson County.

Meanwhile Temple Square took on a new look with the completion of a tabernacle spacious enough to hold "some 15,000 people" to replace the much smaller, rectangular adobe tabernacle that had been in use since 1851.[38] The dedication of the Salt Lake City Tabernacle, with its famed oval roof and superb acoustic capabilities, occurred in 1867 and the first conference to assemble there took place on 6 October. Celebrating the moment, Wilford Woodruff recorded: "For the first time in this generation some 8 or 10,000 Latter-day Saints met in the Great Tabernacle in Great Salt Lake City to hold a General Conference. The Tabernacle was crowded full. President Brigham Young soon called the meeting to order

---

Religious Studies Center, Brigham Young University; Salt Lake City: Deseret Book Company, 2012).
37. *Wilford Woodruff's Journal*, 6:147, 1 January 1864.
38. *Wilford Woodruff's Journal*, 6:71, 23 August 1862.

Salt Lake Tabernacle with Endowment House in back on the right, circa 1870.

and offered up the first prayer in a public capacity that was ever offered up in that Tabernacle. The new organ was only partly finished."[39]

The ending of the Civil War, along with the coming of the transcontinental railroad, jolted Church leadership into a renewal of temple building commitment. Work on the Salt Lake Temple resumed after the war in a slow, measured way. Work on the new foundation walls began in July 1863. The building of the transcontinental railroad triggered a vigorous response to what Brigham Young and others saw as the inevitable end to their period of "splendid isolation." While choosing not to foster a siege mentality, the Saints nevertheless prepared for a cautious welcome to the inexorably advancing technology of the Industrial Revolution. They would brace themselves for the coming onslaught of "Gentile" customs, religions, and thought as well as new economic priorities in mining and industry. As

---

39. *Wilford Woodruff's Journal*, 6:367, 6 October 1867.

Leonard Arrington has so well argued, much of modern Latter-day Saint thought and practice developed in answer to the approaching iron horse.[40]

Before the joining of the Central and Union Pacific rails at Promontory Point in Utah Territory on 10 May 1869, the Saints—now numbering 80,000 in the West—had already joined themselves together in an all-out, carefully orchestrated effort to accept the best the new technology had to offer, while protecting themselves from its worst effects. For example, the revitalized School of the Prophets, first organized back in Kirtland, Ohio, and reconstituted in December 1867, consisted of approximately 5,000 lay priesthood holders who underbid outside contractors and laid virtually every mile of new track in Utah Territory.

The Women's Relief Society organization, moribund since its formation in Nauvoo in 1842, was also revitalized in 1867. Placed under the general direction of Eliza R. Snow, a plural wife of Joseph Smith and of Brigham Young, the Relief Society was soon marshaled into a female force at the local ward and stake levels to ensure a strong and united voice for women, to provide an organized charitable service to assist the poor, and to preserve feminine virtues.[41] In November 1869, Brigham Young organized the Young Women's Retrenchment Society, designed to cut back excesses in dress, eating, and speech while combatting the degrading influences and counterclaims of the outside world. A similar society was organized for the young men in 1875 under Junius F. Wells. Three years later in 1878, following the inspiration of Aurelia Spencer Rogers, the Primary auxiliary was organized for the benefit of little children throughout the Church territory. Even the establishment of the Church-sponsored system of high schools or "academies" beginning with Brigham Young Academy in 1875 in Provo, Utah, (later Brigham Young University) owed much of its *raison d'etre* to encroaching secular thought and outside educational influences. As Arrington has concluded, "The School of the Prophets

---

40. Arrington, *Great Basin Kingdom*, 236–40.
41. Jill Mulvay Derr, *Women of Covenant: The Story of Relief Society* (Salt Lake City: Deseret Book Company, 1992), 86–87; see also Arrington, *Great Basin Kingdom*, 252.

and Relief Society managed to prevent, for good or for ill, the immediate and complete assimilation of Mormon institutions, in the years immediately after 1869, by the dominant laissez-faire institutions of postbellum America. At least two decades were to pass before the Great Basin Kingdom was to make substantial accommodation to the more powerful institutions characteristic of America at the turn of the century."[42]

However, nothing would preserve their way of religious life and distinctive beliefs more effectively than the revival of temple devotions. It may not be coincidental, facing the coming of the railroad as well as ongoing and frustrating delays in building the Salt Lake Temple, that an anxious Brigham Young revealed in 1870, less than a year after Promontory Point, his plans for the building of the St. George Temple in the arid desert landscape of "Utah's Dixie."

"WE ARE NOW BAPTIZING FOR THE DEAD"

When it comes to temple work during these years, perhaps nothing is more perplexing, at least to the modern reader, than the absence of baptisms for the dead. This ordinance had lain moribund for twenty-one years for reasons yet to be fully determined. As case in point, conspicuously missing in the Council House was a baptismal font. Save for Wilford Woodruff's performing this ordinance for a handful of people at Winter Quarters, another in City Creek in Salt Lake in August 1853, and a scattered few in 1865 and 1866, this ordinance did not reappear until 1867. It was as if the practice had gone into a long desert hibernation.[43]

The ordinance of baptisms for the dead was never performed in the Council House and did not recommence in a serious way until 1867, well after the Civil War, when expectations of a return to a Missouri Zion were on the wane. As early as 1851 Brigham Young had planned on erecting a font in Temple Square. "The President directed Truman O. Angell to get

---

42. Arrington, *Great Basin Kingdom*, 256.
43. "Endowment House Baptism for the Dead Record Books, Book A," microfilm, 1–12, Family History Library, Salt Lake City.

up a font for the baptisms for the dead on the temple block and another font to be baptized in for sickness."[44] When the Salt Lake Endowment House was completed in 1855, it featured an outdoor stone font and later an indoor font dedicated on 1 October 1856. It appears, however, that both of these fonts were used primarily, if not exclusively, for baptisms for the living and rebaptisms until 1867.[45]

Why was this the case? Possible answers might include the lack of a proper place, insufficient faith among the Saints as evidenced by declining tithing contributions, and the press of so many other things to do. Surely the challenges of missionary work, the gathering, colonization, and the Utah War were all-consuming in their demands upon the membership.

More to the point, however, was the lack of a sufficient number of trustworthy family genealogies and other reliable ancestral records. Said Parley P. Pratt in conference in April 1853: "Our fathers have forgotten to hand down to us their genealogy. They have not felt sufficient interest to transmit us their names, and the time and place of birth, and in many instances they have not taught us when and where ourselves were born, or who were our grandparents, and their ancestry." Blaming it all on that "veil of blindness" cast over the earth by the apostasy, Pratt lamented the lack of "sacred archives of antiquity" with the resultant lack of knowledge of "the eternal kindred ties, relationship or mutual interests of eternity." He pointed out that the "spirit and power of Elijah" had only begun "to kindle in our bosoms that glow of eternal affection which lay dormant" for so many centuries. "Suppose our temple was ready?" he asked. "We could only act for those whose names are known to us. And these are few with most of us Americans. And why is this? We have never had time to look to the heavens, or to the past, or to the future, so busy have we been with the things of the earth. We have hardly had time to think of ourselves, to

---

44. Church Historian's Office Journal, 7 December 1851.
45. Church Historian's Office Journal, 19:127, 2 October 1856, and 19:216, 30 December 1856; *Wilford Woodruff's Journal*, 6:173, 4 June 1864; see also Brigham Young Letter to Cyrus Smith, Brigham Young Letterpress Copybooks, 4 October 1856.

say nothing of our fathers."[46] Thus they did as much as their immediate memories and available records allowed.[47]

Twenty-three years later, Wilford Woodruff, later founder of the Utah Genealogical Society, spoke of this same impediment to temple work for the dead, although by then in more encouraging terms:

> *If there is anything I desire to live for on the earth, or that I have desired, it has been to get a record of the genealogy of my fathers, that I might do something for them before I go hence into the spirit world. Until within a few years past it has seemed as if every avenue has been closed to obtaining such records; but the Lord has moved upon the inhabitants of this nation and thousands of them are now laboring to trace their genealogical descent. . . . Their lineages are coming to light, and we are gradually obtaining access to them, and by this means we shall be enabled to do something towards the salvation of our dead.*[48]

The eventual solution to the problem of the scarcity and incorrectness of human records would be revelations of a most unusual kind. As Brigham Young said in 1852:

> *About the time that the temples of the Lord will be built and Zion is established, there will be strangers in your midst, walking with you, talking with you; they will enter your houses and eat and drink with you, go to meeting with you, and begin to open your minds, as the Savior did the two disciples who walked out in the country in days of old. . . .*

---

46. Parley P. Pratt, in *Journal of Discourses*, 1:13, 7 April 1853.
47. A related concern was that of accurate recordkeeping to meet the requirements of Doctrine and Covenants 128. Glen Leonard, in his bountiful study of Nauvoo, writes that when Joseph Smith discovered in the fall of 1842 an "inconsistent pattern" in the records of proxy baptisms, he explained that the "record itself had legal standing in the next life and therefore had to be accurately presented and preserved." Leonard, *Nauvoo: A Place of Peace*, 238. It would appear that in early Salt Lake City the difficulty of gathering and keeping accurate records put a temporary brake on performing baptisms for the dead.
48. Wilford Woodruff, in *Journal of Discourses*, 18:191, 6 April 1876. As Brigham Young said in 1854: "As I have frequently told you [salvation for the dead] is the work of the Millennium. It is the work that has to be performed by the seed of Abraham, the chosen seed, the royal seed, the blessed of the Lord." Brigham Young, in *Journal of Discourses*, 2:138, 3 December 1854.

> They will then open your minds and tell you principles of the resurrection of the dead and how to save your friends. . . . You have got your temples ready: now go forth and be baptized for those good people. . . .
>
> Before this work is finished, a great many of the Elders in Israel in Mt. Zion will become pillars in the temples of God to go no more out and [will] . . . say "Somebody came into the temple last night; we did not know who he was, but . . . He gave us the names of a great many of our forefathers that are not on record, and he gave me my true lineage and the names of my forefathers for hundreds of years back. He said to me . . . take them and write them down, and be baptized and confirmed . . . and receive of the blessings of the eternal priesthood for such and such an individual, as you do for yourselves."[49]

Orson Pratt foresaw yet another solution. "How can all this be done?" he asked.

> By the Urim and Thummim, which the Lord God has ordained to be used in the midst of his holy house, in his Temple. . . . When that instrument is restored to the house of God, to the Temple of the Most High, our ancestry, that is, the ancestry of all the faithful in the Church . . . will be made manifest. Not all at once, but by degrees. Just as fast as we are able to administer for them, so will the Lord God make manifest, by the manifestation of holy angels in his house, and by the Urim and Thummim, those names that are necessary, of our ancient kindred and friends, that they may be traced back to the time when the Priesthood was on the earth in ancient days.[50]

Until such times, baptisms for the dead would be placed on hold.[51]

---

49. Brigham Young, in *Journal of Discourses*, 6:294–95, 15 August 1852.
50. Orson Pratt, in *Journal of Discourses*, 16:261–62, 7 October 1873.
51. There were other scattered and isolated references during these years to baptisms for the dead, such as the following injunctions given to Addison Pratt before his return to the islands of the South Pacific to resume his earlier missionary endeavors there: "When you get to [the] Islands build a tabernacle for baptizing for the dead and for the endowments for the Aaronic P[riesthood]." But so far as is yet known, no such ordinances were ever performed there. General Church Minutes, 8 April 1849, CR 100 318, box 2, folder 10.

93	Sons and daughters (deceased)
75	Brothers and sisters
63	Grandchildren
79	Nieces and nephews
38	Sons- and daughters-in-law
21	Brothers- and sisters-in-law
44	Cousins
4	Grandparents
19	Great-grandchildren
52	Friends
12	Parents and stepparents

Notes:
- Far more descendants than parents/grandparents or great-grandparents (likely had died young)
- 10% were friends; 90% family
- None more than four generations back

Figure 4: Nature of Relationships for Early Utah Territory Proxy Temple Work

However, this ordinance, like an old wind cone catching a sudden breeze, gradually revived after the ending of the Civil War with Wilford Woodruff leading the charge. On 14 June 1867 he was baptized by George Q. Cannon and confirmed by President Brigham Young for his father, Aphek Woodruff, who had died six years before. Immediately afterward his wife, Phebe Carter Woodruff, was baptized by George Q. Cannon for Wilford's stepmother, Azubah Hart Woodruff, who had died in 1851, and confirmed by Brigham Young. Ten more such ordinances were performed in June, all in the Endowment House. During 1867 ninety-two baptisms for the dead were conducted. The corresponding number for 1868 was 432.[52]

A close examination of the 524 deceased persons for whom baptisms

---

52. Endowment House Baptism for the Dead Record Books. Book A, 1–12; see also the *Wilford Woodruff's Journals*, 6:348, 14 June 1867. For those baptisms for the dead performed at Winter Quarters, see the Journal of Elijah F. Sheets, 24 January and 6 April 1847; Trustees Minutes, 21 November 1847, Brigham Young Papers and *Wilford Woodruff's Journals*, 3:356, 4 April 1848. One cannot state with authority that there were not more, perhaps many more, such baptisms performed during these years. However, the lack of available records prohibits such a conclusion. The fact is, systematic recording of proxy baptisms did not resume after Nauvoo until 1867 and

were performed in 1867 and 1868 reveals something of the nature of the practice. The great majority of these proxies were older folk, like the Woodruffs, who were baptized for deceased sons and daughters, brothers and sisters, grandchildren, and nieces and nephews. It was more descendants and less ancestors, more the immediate generation than the more distant past (see Figure 4).

Fifty-two out of 524, or 10 percent were for "friends," and not family members. Such figures would indicate that the revival of baptisms for the dead was a "family-driven" initiative, not a Church-wide decree, and that the memory of the living—in these cases for immediate families and close friends—served as substitutes for records.[53]

All this changed dramatically, however, beginning in June 1869 when 582 baptisms were performed in the Endowment House, more than all of 1867 and 1868 combined. The year of 1869 saw a grand total of slightly over 5,500 such ordinances in what was clearly a turning point for work for the dead. After 1869, the numbers of baptisms for the dead performed annually in the Endowment House grew exponentially, reaching almost 20,000 in 1874 (see Figure 5).

What accounts for the renewal of this practice in the desert? As already alluded to, the ending of the Civil War in 1865 brought a collective sigh of relief to a war-torn nation and to a Latter-day Saint community wondering just what the future might hold. Talk of a return to Missouri was receding with the growing realization that the future of the Church lay in the West, not the East. And although it is true that the Saints remained virtually neutral during the war, it is possible that one response to its terrible death toll could have been an increased commitment to baptisms for the dead.

A second consideration was the coming of the railroad. At least in

---

when it did, clerks in the Church Historian's office could find only a handful of such ordinances having been recorded. Very few private journals in this period reference the ordinance.

53. There is no evidence of the existence of a library or archive within the Endowment House of those baptized in the Endowment House.

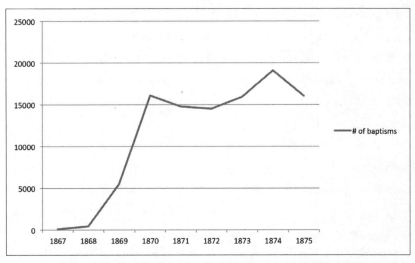

Figure 5: Baptisms Performed in the Endowment House, 1867–1875

partial response to the coming of the iron horse was the organization of the Young Men's and Young Women's Retrenchment Societies on a Church-wide basis to protect and shield the youth from the evil "Gentile" influences of the East now coming down the track in the form of new fashions, forms of entertainment, educational philosophies, illicit behaviors, and a trainload of other "worldly" influences. So, too, did Brigham Young revitalize a moribund Relief Society on a Church-wide basis to provide a greater role and voice for female Latter-day Saints in anticipation of the coming cultural, intellectual, and religious tensions that the railroad was bound to foster. And might not temple work be part of the equation of preparation and defense? Whatever the reasons, the first real spike in the numbers of baptisms for the dead came in June 1869, just a month after the 10 May completion of the transcontinental railroad at Promontory Point some 100 miles away from Temple Square.

A third possible factor may have been the so-called Godbeite apostasy of the late 1860s and 1870s. An intellectual dissenting movement led by William S. Godbe that flowered in 1869, "Godbeism" was a movement of liberal-minded dissenters such as T. B. H. Stenhouse, George Watt

(Brigham Young's personal secretary), E. L. T. Harrison, Edward Tullidge, and Godbe himself who devalued the Book of Mormon and the Doctrine and Covenants, rejected belief in a personal deity, the Resurrection, and the Atonement of Christ, and opposed the economic policies and overall leadership of Brigham Young. Forming their own church with former apostle Amasa Lyman at the head, the Godbeite movement later went on to found the *Salt Lake Tribune*.[54]

Central to the Godbeite movement was its belief in Spiritualism and communication with the dead through séances, so-called "automatic writings" or written communications with the deceased, ectoplasms, and all the paraphernalia of the paranormal. Spiritualism had erupted with the Fox sisters in Rochester, New York, not far from Palmyra, back in 1848 and had mushroomed in popularity in the wake of so many untimely deaths brought on by the Civil War. With its outreach to the spirits of the dead, Spiritualism brought closure to many whose sons, brothers, and fathers had died, often in lonely agony and pain, far away from home and loved ones who could only reach out in forlorn despair and emotional emptiness. Arthur Conan Doyle, creator of Sherlock Holmes, would later do much to popularize this pseudoreligion during and immediately after World War I.[55]

Since at least 1853 and the laying of the cornerstone of the Salt Lake Temple, Church authorities had been well aware of this phenomenon, regarding it essentially as a counterfeit movement with its insidious parallels to temple ordinances. Warned Parley P. Pratt, the Saints must learn to discriminate "between the lawful and the unlawful mediums or channels of communication—between the holy and impure, the truths and falsehoods thus communicated."[56]

---

54. For the most comprehensive study of the Godbeite movement, see Ronald W. Walker's highly readable *Wayward Saints: The Godbeites and Brigham Young* (Urbana: University of Illinois Press, 1998).
55. Arthur Conan Doyle, *The History of Spiritualism* (New York: G. H. Doran Company, 1926).
56. Parley P. Pratt, in *Journal of Discourses*, 2:45, 6 April 1853; see also Michael W. Homer, "Spiritualism and Mormonism: Some Thoughts on Similarities and Differences," *Dialogue: A*

Without denying the possibility of communing with the dead, authorities increasingly warned against "the doings of the Spirit Rappers" and that such manifestations were a tool of the devil. Declared Brigham Young in 1870, "Take all who are called spiritualists and see if they can produce the order that is in the midst of this people. Here are system, order, organization, law, rule and facts. Now see if they can produce any of these features. They cannot. Why? Because their system is from beneath, while ours is perfect and is from above; one is from God, the other is from the devil, that is all the difference."[57] The main point of divergence was that Spiritualism aimed at communion with the dead; whereas temple work sought redemption for the dead. One was yearningly inquisitive; the other satisfyingly redemptive and based upon scripture. Under no circumstances were the two to be equated.

Was the reinstitution of baptisms for the dead in the late 1860s in some way an effort to blunt this Spiritualist movement? The connection is admittedly tenuous; however, well-known Latter-day Saint scholar T. Edgar Lyon certainly thought so. In a biography of his ancestor, John Lyon, he wrote, "Beginning in 1867 and continuing through 1869, Lyon and his family conducted a spiritual campaign to baptize their dead ancestors. This may have served as a counter to the Godbeites, who argued that the Church had become too materialistic and had departed from its earlier spiritual manifestations."[58]

A fourth factor was the increased number of genealogical records, and more to the point, the greater availability of more accurate ancestral records than ever before. The rise of state historical/genealogical societies in the United States is of relatively recent vintage and parallels the growth of the nation. While British, French, and other European "antiquaries" can trace their beginnings to the 1600s and early 1700s, their American

---

Journal of Mormon Thought 21, no. 1 (Spring 1994): 171–91.
57. Brigham Young, in *Journal of Discourses*, 13:266, 6 October 1870; see also Homer, "Spiritualism and Mormonism," 181.
58. T. Edgar Lyon Jr., *John Lyon: The Life of a Pioneer Poet* (Provo, Utah: Religious Studies Center, Brigham Young University, 1989), 174.

counterparts came later, most after the birth of the Republic. One reason for this delay was the colonial American disdain for European aristocratic tendencies, some even considering it bad taste to speak of ancestors; however, that attitude gradually changed over time giving rise to new historical societies. For instance, the American Philosophical Society in Worcester, Massachusetts, began in 1743, the American Academy of Arts and Sciences in 1780, and the most famous of all American historical societies—the Massachusetts Historical Society—in 1790. Many others soon followed as shown in Figure 6 with their numbers multiplying in direct relationship to the country's westward expansion.

The Rise of American Historical/Genealogical Societies[59]

Institution	Year Organized
Massachusetts Historical Society	1790
New York Historical Society	1804
American Antiquarian Society	1812
Rhode Island State Historical Society	1822
New Hampshire	1823
Pennsylvania	1824
Connecticut	1825
Indiana	1830
Ohio	1831
Virginia	1831
American Historical Society	1835
Louisiana	1836
Vermont	1838
Georgia	1839
Maryland	1844
New England Historic Genealogical Society	1844
Tennessee	1849
Wisconsin	1849
Minnesota	1849
Missouri	1849

Figure 6: The Rise of Genealogical Societies in the United States

---

59. Julian P. Boyd, "State and Local Historical Societies in the United States," *The American Historical Review* 40, no. 1 (October 1934): 10–25.

Thus, by the mid-1800s, at least twenty-five agencies had been established, about a third of them in New England. A score of societies were organized between 1850 and 1860 and a comparable number in the following decade. The *Deseret Evening News* noted this trend in 1875 when it reported, "The rapidly growing interest in genealogy and family history is shown in the fact that 359 genealogical works have appeared in the United States since 1860."[60] With the stimulus of the centennial observations, more societies were founded in the 1870s than in the previous two decades and at least a hundred more before the turn of the century.[61]

The coming of the railroad and before that, of the telegraph, proved a mixed blessing. With them came the many negatives of increased immorality, crime, access to undesirable fashion and dress, and easier access to outside views and philosophies. Yet on the other hand, it provided access to more accurate information that rapidly became a godsend to genealogical research. The railroad greatly expedited mail deliveries throughout the land and facilitated genealogical research as never before. As one woman noted, "All the good brethren and sisters have been doing their best to get out their relations and friends, and I know many of them who have sent over to England and have spent large sums of money in tracing their pedigrees and genealogies, in order to find out the right names and to be baptized as proxies for the dead who owned those names. I have been baptized for a good many of my own relations, and I mean to be baptized for scores more."[62] In much the same way that twenty-first-century genealogical research has enormously benefitted from the arrival of the computer age, so it began to stir to the sound of the rails, a harbinger of much better things to come. In observing this trend, Brigham Young remarked in 1872, "We are now baptizing for the dead, and we are sealing for the

---

60. *Deseret Evening News*, 5 November 1875.
61. Boyd, "State and Local Historical Societies," 24; see also *Handbook of American Historical Societies* (1926). Proselyting missionaries were also asked to gather as much genealogical information as possible from family members and descendants.
62. Fanny Stenhouse, *Tell It All: The Story of a Life's Experience in Mormonism* (Hartford, Connecticut: A. D. Worthington and Co. Publishing, 1875), 490–91.

dead . . . the history of whom we are now getting from our friends in the east. The Lord is stirring up the hearts of many there, and there is a perfect mania with some to trace their genealogies and to get up printed records of their ancestors."[63]

CONCLUSION

To all these considerations and possible explanations for the revival of baptisms for the dead must one more be added—not a circumstance at all, but a person. By 1867 Wilford Woodruff had served as an apostle for twenty-nine years. When he first heard of this doctrinal practice from Joseph Smith, he said it was like a "shaft of light from the throne of God" and "opened a field wide as eternity" to his mind.[64] He had already baptized a few people for their deceased relations at Winter Quarters. He did so again in Salt Lake City in 1853.[65] He also played a key role in preforming hundreds, if not thousands, of ordinances in that venerable "temple pro tem"—the Endowment House. In fact, he was the first to be proxy baptized when the ordinance resumed in the Endowment House in 1867.[66] And it would be Wilford Woodruff as the first temple president in Latter-day Saint history that would play such a pivotal role in the St. George Temple, as we are about to see.

---

63. Brigham Young, in *Journal of Discourses*, 15:138, 24 August 1872.
64. Wilford Woodruff, in Salt Lake Stake Conference, as published in the *Deseret Weekly*, 25 December 1897, 34.
65. Endowment House Baptism for the Dead Record Book, Book A, 1–12, CR 334 8.
66. The definitive biography of Wilford Woodruff remains Thomas G. Alexander, *"Things in Heaven and on Earth": The Life and Times of Wilford Woodruff*. For a well-researched new study, see Jennifer Ann Mackley, *Wilford Woodruff's Witness of the Development of Temple Doctrine* (Seattle: High Desert Publishing, 2014).

Chapter 7

"What Is Gold or Silver in Comparison to the Redemption of Our Dead?"

THE ST. GEORGE TEMPLE, 1870–1877

What is gold or silver in comparison to the redemption of our dead? Nothing. . . . By this labor in redeeming our dead by proxy much can be accomplished. Our dead can be redeemed. This principle has given me great joy unspeakable at the thought that I can live on the earth to behold my numerous friends redeemed who are in the spirit world. This principle says to us in loud language that the Lord is good and gracious, and his mercies endureth forever.[1]

So wrote Wilford Woodruff. After so many years without a temple in the West, the dedication of the St. George Temple in January 1877 will forever stand as a tribute to the faith and sacrifice of the Saints and a culminating moment in the doctrinal development of the Restoration. It was there that ordinances beyond baptism for the dead were first performed, a critical step forward that would forever change the nature of temple worship and attendance within The Church of Jesus Christ of Latter-day Saints. And Wilford Woodruff, the first temple president in Latter-day Saint history, caught the vision and meaning of such ordinances in ways perhaps no one else did.

---

1. *Wilford Woodruff's Journals*, 7:332–34, 1 March 1877.

"AND THUS BE REWARDED IN DIXIE"

With the Civil War over and an immediate return to Missouri no longer (if ever) an option, and with the transcontinental railroad now very much a reality, Brigham Young moved forward with temple building. At a meeting held 31 January 1871 in the home of resident apostle and president of the Southern Mission, Erastus Snow, President Young asked the local leaders in attendance "what they thought of building a temple in St. George." The response was hardly surprising: "The bare mention of such a blessing from the Lord was greeted with: 'Glory Hallelujah' from Pres. Erastus Snow and all present appeared to share the joy. The brethren unanimously voted in favor of the measure."[2]

A few months later, on 15 April 1871, several other locals first heard the news at a meeting of the St. George School of the Prophets. "A letter was read from Br. Brigham," reads Charles Walker's account, stating that the time had come that the Saints could build a temple to the Most High in St. George. "A thrill of joy seemed to pass over the Assembly of Elders present, at the announcement. It is to be built of stone plastered inside and out. The length 196', width 142', and 80' high, two stories with a large hall on each story with room on each side, and a baptismal font in the basement. Br. Brigham and George A. Smith will be down next October to commence the work and give directions concerning its erection."[3]

But of all places, why St. George? It certainly was not the center of the Great Basin Kingdom and in 1870 was but a tiny community in a windswept desert 301 miles south of Church headquarters. A former resident described it as follows:

---

2. James Bleak Diary, 21 January 1871. James G. Bleak Collection, MSS 1691. Perry Special Collections, HBLL, BYU.
3. Walker, *Diary*, 329, 15 April 1871. The actual dimensions of the finished temple were 141 feet 8 inches long, 93 feet 4 inches wide, and 135 feet high to the top of the weather vane. On 16 October 1878 lightning destroyed the original squatlike dome and tower, which were later replaced with a higher, more majestic-looking tower.

> *Here we have a fine view of the rocks and sands and barren desolation of sterile Dixie of southern Utah and a more forbidding aspect man never saw. . . . This place when contrasted with the bustle and business of Salt Lake seems very dull. A person can walk up and down this town for hours and scarce see a man—no business, no railroad nor locomotive whistle, nor express wagon, nor auctions, nor saloon, music, no theatres or circus or dances—all still and peace. In fact, it seems more like the city of the dead than the living.*[4]

Certainly one reason was as a reward to the faith and perseverance of those gritty, selfless men and women who had sacrificed so much to settle the hard, arid country of southern Utah and northern Arizona where summer temperatures came more out of hell than from heaven. Brigham admitted:

> *This is a desert country, but it is a splendid place to rear the Saints. I regret to hear of any wishing to leave; these, however, are but few. . . . We want to build a Temple here and we can do this. You may take the people of St. George, or you may take the little settlements of Washington, Harrisburg, and Leeds and I will say that the people of St. George, or the people of these little settlements . . . are better able to build the contemplated Temple in St. George than the whole Church could build the Temple in Kirtland, or than the whole Church could build the Temple in Nauvoo. I was there. I knew the circumstances of the Church at the building of the Temple at Kirtland and at Nauvoo. And I know the circumstances of the people in St. George and in these settlements named.*[5]

As John Taylor put it, "It was found that our Temple in Salt Lake City would take such a long time to build, it was thought best to erect one down here. Why? Because there was a people living here who were more worthy

---
4. Walker, *Diary,* 1, 351–52, 5–6 October 1872.
5. Bleak, Diary, 3–5 November 1871; see also James G. Bleak, "Annals of the Southern Utah Mission, Book B," 1:175–80, MS 22894, Church History Library.

The St. George Temple under construction, circa 1875.

The St. George Temple under construction, circa 1876.

than any others. Who were more worthy of the blessings of a Temple than those who had displayed the self-abnegation exhibited by the pioneers of the south?"[6] Upon hearing the news, one local poet put it this way, "Now boys pray don't get weary, there's plenty of work ahead. God says build ye a temple through Brigham Young, our head. In which we can go forth soon and baptize for our dead, And thus be rewarded in Dixie."[7]

There were other equally compelling reasons for the red sands of Dixie. Brigham Young, who had previously established a winter home in St. George, loved the climate and the people there. Yet more to the point, he had reluctantly concluded that for a multitude of reasons—a faulty initial foundation, the Utah War, a host of problems transporting granite stones, his own "go-slow" attitude in case the Church should ever decide to move back to Missouri—he would not live to see the completion of the Salt Lake Temple. And with the rising din over plural marriage and the inevitable squeeze by a federal government determined to stomp out the practice, even if it meant the destruction of Latter-day Saint society and its belief systems, St. George would also provide an "asylum," Zion's fortress, and a place of quiet refuge from the encircling storm. Indeed, many of those who had already moved to St. George to work on the temple were from polygamous households. Furthermore, it was hundreds of miles closer to the Lamanite missions in southern Utah and Arizona.

"UPON THE PRINCIPLES OF THE UNITED ORDER"

Contrasted with the seemingly interminable delays in building the Salt Lake Temple, construction of the St. George Temple progressed much more rapidly. Groundbreaking occurred on 9 November 1871, with Brigham Young turning the first shovelful of earth and George A. Smith offering the

---
6. Taylor, in *Journal of Discourses*, 23:14, 9 November 1881; see also Janice Force DeMille, *The St. George Temple: First 100 Years* (Hurricane, Utah: Homestead Publishers, 1977), 5.
7. Walker, *Diary*, 1:339, 29 December 1871. Sung to the tune "Marching to Georgia."

dedicatory prayer.[8] Truman O. Angell once again served as temple architect with Miles Romney general superintendent of construction.

Excavation work proved difficult since workers had to pick the dirt loose and load it into wagons by hand. Because of subterranean moisture, a drainage system was required before a solid foundation of black volcanic rock could be put into place. Eventually, on 10 March 1873, masons laid the cornerstone for the foundation. Robert Gardner was responsible for obtaining and shipping one million board feet of lumber needed for the temple, most of which had to be hauled by ox teams some eighty miles over a new road "begun under the direction of the United Order" from northern Arizona. The last stones were laid on the walls in early March 1875 in preparation for the roof timbers. Meanwhile the baptismal font and oxen made in Salt Lake City were transported to St. George in the summer of 1875. With construction work virtually completed by the summer of 1876, landscaping began in November.

George Q. Cannon, upon first seeing the temple in late 1876, described it in glowing terms:

> We were all eager to get a glimpse of the temple as we were crossing the hills, and when we saw it, it stood out in bold relief and in marked contrast with the black and red hills which surround the little valley in which St. George stands. The temple is pure white, and is a massive, unique building. It excited peculiar emotions in all the party to witness once more a temple erected to the Most High God.[9]

Cannon had more to say after visiting the interior of the temple.

> The font looks very elegant; probably there is no such font in existence. It is cast iron and everything connected with it, even the oxen upon which it stands, and is painted very beautifully. The font is being bronzed. From the basement we ascended into the grand hall;

---
8. General Church Minutes, 9 November 1871, CR 100 318, box 3, folder 57.
9. George Q. Cannon Journals, 9 November 1876.

and here . . . my emotions almost overpowered me. I felt as though I [did not want] to talk but to yield to the sweet impressions of the occasion. The hall is beautifully proportioned and the workmanship is very superior. I never saw better plastering in any country or any building. The stands are very elegant, and I felt as though I trod on holy ground.[10]

The catalyst for completing the temple as quickly as possible was not only Brigham Young's determination to finish it in his lifetime but also his desire to reestablish the United Order among the Saints and with it, a return to living the law of consecration. At its core, the law of consecration preached caring for the poor and fostering unity among the people and took issue with the inequities of laissez-faire capitalism and rampant individualism. The accumulation of wealth for its own sake was never to be the goal; rather, it was to be the building of the Kingdom of God upon the earth and serving others selflessly.

Operating very much like a religiously motivated community cooperative, the intent of the United Order, or what was referred to as the "stepping stone to the Order of Enoch," was both economic and spiritual. Announced in conference in 1874 during construction of the St. George Temple, it aimed at maintaining "one common interest" or spirt of unity among the Saints, eradicating the poor among them, while also thwarting Gentile trade and businesses. It required of each person in the community to contribute his or her property to the Order in return for equivalent capital stock. Members also pledged all of their time, labor, energy, and ability to make their local chapter of the Order successful. All such property became subject to the direction of a local elected Board of Management. Furthermore, members pledged to encourage home manufacturers, cease importing, and to deal only with other members of the Order.[11]

While the period of depression which followed the Panic of 1873

---

10. George Q. Cannon Journals, 10 November 1876.
11. Arrington, *Great Basin Kingdom*, 328.

SALT LAKE CITY, AUGUST, 1874.

To the Bishop and the Board

of the United Order in your Ward:

It is very desirable that work on the Temple being built at St. George, be prosecuted to completion by the 1st of April next, if possible; therefore we solicit you to learn who, in your ward, you can fit up to start for St. George on or about the 12th of October next, and send with them such portions of their families as they may wish to assist in household labors until about the 1st of April next, also groceries, flour, beans, peas, dried apples, salt, and pork and bacon if they wish, sufficient to last the same period of time; also such tools as each one expects to use in his labor. Beef, dried peaches, raisins and vegetables it is expected can be supplied by the brethren in the southern settlements.

The teams taking the laborers and their effects south will directly return, except such as may be needed there, which will probably be but few.

The laborers needed are stone-cutters, stone-masons, their tenders, joiners, carpenters, quarrymen, lumbermen, and common laborers.

The same winter clothing will be requisite in St. George as is needed for comfort in our more northern settlements, and thick soled or wooden-bottomed boots and shoes to prevent colds and rheumatism from the damp mineral soil of that region.

It is expected you will use due diligence in obtaining the desired information and furnishing it to us in season for having the needed number all ready to start at the time specified.

All labor and furnishings, as above called for, are designed to be a free donation.

Your brethren in the Gospel,

BRIGHAM YOUNG,
GEORGE A. SMITH,
DANIEL H. WELLS.

"We had built the temple in the United Order."

offered leaders "precisely the opportunity they had desired" to experiment with their economic institutions,[12] the United Order was as much a spiritual renewal—a mini-reformation—and recommitment as it was an economic order. Designed to prepare a modern Zion "for the return of the City of Enoch at Christ's Second Coming," it anticipated a people one in heart and mind, with no rich or poor among them. As Brigham Young put it: "We ha[ve] commenced to build Temples, which was a very necessary work and which was centering the feelings of the people for a still further union of effort."[13]

It was not enough simply to participate in this "Order of Enoch," as it was sometimes called. As evidence of its religious underpinnings, one had to be baptized into it. For instance, on 11 July 1875, "Fifty persons took the covenant" in Order[ville] City, Utah Territory, "and were baptized and a very good spirit prevailed."[14] Many others were baptized into the United Order in the above-mentioned baptismal font that was shipped to St. George from Salt Lake City as a gift from Brigham Young.[15] There is even record of baptisms by proxy for the dead into the Order.[16] Such baptisms reconfirmed "all former washings and anointings and ordinations," clearly foreshadowing its place in future temple worship.[17] As stake

---

12. Arrington, *Great Basin Kingdom*, 323.
13. Brigham Young, Salt Lake Stake General Minutes, 11 August 1877, LR 104 11.
14. Allen Frost Reminiscences and Journals, MS 1914, Church History Library. "I was the fiftieth person baptized," he recorded in the margins of an entry for 11 July 1875. Reminiscences of Allen Frost, 86. The wording for the United Order baptismal ordinance was as follows: "_____ (name of person being baptized), having authority of Jesus Christ, I baptize you for the remission of sins, and the renewal of your covenants, with a promise that you will observe the rules of the United Order in the name of the Father, Son, and Holy Ghost." Logan Temple Letterpress Copybook, CR 308 5, folder 2, 157, Church History Library.
15. This font was dedicated on 11 August 1875. It would appear that these early baptisms into the United Order occurred within the not-yet completed St. George Temple. DeMille, *The St. George Temple*, 41. Kent Huff states that the first use of the term "United Order" occurred on 6 April 1874. Kent W. Huff, "Brigham Young's United Order," (unpublished manuscript, Provo, Utah, 1994), 110.
16. Journal of James G. Bleak, 26 November 1878, MS 12047. Some bishops throughout the Territory were baptized into the United Order as early as July 1875. Huff, "Brigham Young's United Order," 100.
17. Sevier Utah Stake Miscellaneous Minutes, 101, 1 July 1875, LR 8243 11, Church History Library; and St. George Utah Stake Melchizedek Priesthood Minutes and Records, 26 January 1878, LR 7836 13, Church History Library.

president Joseph A. Young of the Sevier Stake interpreted it, the United Order "was but a stepping stone to that which would be given."[18]

Many onlookers saw the building of the temple as an expression of the United Order and certainly in fulfillment of its ideals and objectives, and viewed their many financial sacrifices in living it as essential to building the St. George Temple. "We had built the Temple in the United Order," is how one participant described it.[19] And again from Brigham Young: "This temple in St. George is being built upon the principle of the United Order; and when we cease our selfishness, and our whole interest is for the building up of the Kingdom of God on the earth, we can then build Temples, and do anything we want to, with united voice and hands."[20] Certainly Church leaders saw the building of temples as a standing invitation to the membership to contribute tithes and offerings in a more faithful and sustained way, that their construction would in the short run cost a great deal of money, but in the long run would bless the whole Church. As Franklin D. Richards said in 1881: "Tithing is one of the principles that we have got to conform to in order to enter into the Temples of the Lord."[21]

And while it is true that the Order as an economic experiment eventually failed and faded away (John Taylor ended it in May 1882), it nevertheless did promote thrift, created employment, and assured better, faster development of resources. Again from Arrington: "The United Order . . . helped to keep Utah economically independent of the East longer and more completely than would otherwise have been the case."[22] And spiritually, many managed to live by the precepts of "the great experiment."[23]

---

18. Joseph A. Young, Priesthood Meeting, Sevier Utah Stake Miscellaneous Minutes, 5 September 1874.
19. Marius Ensign, St. George Utah Stake Melchizedek Priesthood Minutes and Records, 26 January 1878.
20. Brigham Young in St. George, 10 January 1875, in Bleak, "Annals of the Southern Utah Mission."
21. F. D. Richards, Sevier Utah Stake Historical Record, 4:121, 26 November 1881, LR 8243 11, Church History Library.
22. Arrington, *Great Basin Kingdom*, 338. For more on the United Order, see also Leonard J. Arrington, Feramorz Y. Fox, and Dean L. May, *Building the City of God: Community and Cooperation among the Mormons* (Salt Lake City: Deseret Book Company, 1976), ch. 6–14.
23. Sevier Utah Stake Miscellaneous Minutes, 1875, 42.

Its central spiritual emphasis—obedience to the law of consecration—lived on inside the walls of the temple where it found permanent expression in temple covenants. Said Brigham Young: "Several attempts had been made to work in the United Order, and almost as many failures were the result. In consequence of tradition and the weakness of our human nature, we could not bring our feelings to obey this Holy requirement. The spirit had prompted [me] to see if the brethren would do anything by way of an approach to it, and hence we had commenced to build a Temple, which was a very necessary work and which was centering the feelings of the people for a still further union of effect."[24]

"WHY HAS THIS SUBJECT RESTED UPON ME MORE THAN OTHER MEN?"

No one was likely more excited about completing the St. George Temple than Wilford Woodruff and, in preparation for the event, he had busied himself in family history work throughout the summer and fall of 1876. "Glory, hallelujah," he confided in his journal for June 20, "for in spite of the Devil through the blessing of God I have had the privilege this day of going into the Endowment House and with my family have been baptized for 949 of my dead relatives. I felt to rejoice that after forty-three years labor in the Church . . . that I had the privilege of going into a baptismal font with my eldest brother, Azmon Woodruff, and my children to redeem our dead."[25]

Since his conversion in 1833, Woodruff had viewed his membership as incomplete without the companionship of family and friends. In July

---

24. Brigham Young, Salt Lake Stake Priesthood Meeting, 11 August 1877, Salt Lake Stake General Minutes (1876–1880), 2:45. "What was the United Order?" asked Brigham Young's son, Apostle Brigham Young Jr., in April 1877. "It was the order of heaven, the system which prevailed among the heavenly hosts, as we should find when we get to where God and His Christ dwelt. . . . The progress of the members of this Church who will not receive and carry out the principles of the United Order is at an end; and this Temple [Saint George] will be a means to test the faithfulness and purity of the Latter-day Saints." Bleak, "Annals of the Southern Utah Mission,"102, 8 April 1877.
25. *Wilford Woodruff's Journal*, 7:277, 20 June 1876.

1838 he returned as a missionary to his beloved Connecticut, teaching and converting members of his immediate family. There he baptized his father, his stepmother, his uncle, and several others. As he left Nauvoo, he recorded the following: "A peculiar charm was thrown around my soul as I left the threshold of my father's house, having the confidence that if I never see my father in the flesh again I shall meet him in the first resurrection. I had a desire in my heart that all the ordinances of the fullness of the gospel might also be administered unto father and mother Carter that they may sleep in peace."[26] He harbored a special interest in his mother, who had died when he was but an infant. While in Nauvoo he was baptized in her behalf, as well as for two of his brothers, both sets of grandparents, and many other deceased kin.[27]

Wilford Woodruff—first temple president, St. George Temple.

Woodruff was well aware that he possessed this interest in family history and temple work to a far greater degree than most others did. "I have had this spirit upon me since I first entered this Church," he once confided in his journal. Driven to record his feelings and the events of his life in most minute detail, Woodruff knew this compulsion extended to family history and temple work as well. As he wrote in his journal in 1875:

> *This was the gift of God to me and the question has often rested [upon] me, "Why are these things so? Why has this subject rested upon me more than other men?" . . . For I seem a marked victim for the devil from the day I was born. . . . [T]he devil knew if I got into the*

---

26. *Wilford Woodruff's Journal*, 2:430–31, 23 July 1844; see also 1:264, 1 July 1838.
27. *Wilford Woodruff's Journal*, 2:177, 29 May 1842.

> *Church . . . I would write the History . . . and leave on record the doings, works and teachings of the prophets and Apostles, Elders and Saints in the latter days, and that I would attend to the ordinances of the House of God for my father's household and friends, both for the living and the dead.*[28]

"I believe it will take all the ordinances of the gospel of Christ to save one soul as much as another," he said on another occasion. "Those who have died without the gospel will have to receive the gospel in the spirit world from those who preach to the Spirits in Prison and those who dwell in the flesh will have to attend to all the ordinances of the gospel for and in their behalf by proxy and it will take 1,000 years . . . before the work will be finished attending to all the ordinances for all the dead who have died without the gospel."[29]

A man of recurring dreams and numerous visions and who had been prone to so many life-threatening accidents, Woodruff believed he had been spared for this very moment.[30] With the death of his longtime counselor Heber C. Kimball in June 1868, Brigham Young came to rely more and more on the inspiration, loyalty, and inherent spirituality of the man from Connecticut. It was he who had taken a lead in the administering of temple ordinances of every kind in the Endowment House, sealing over 5,600 couples, performing more than 6,000 endowments, and baptizing for the dead hundreds of family members and friends. Thus Brigham Young's appointment of Wilford Woodruff to be the president of the St. George Temple hardly came as a surprise.

Unfortunately, the same protection from fatal accidents did not extend to his twenty-year-old son, Brigham Woodruff, who drowned in the Bear River while duck shooting on 16 June 1877, and whose body floated downriver seventy miles before being recovered. The news was a

---

28. *Wilford Woodruff's Journal*, 7:55, 20 January 1875.
29. *Wilford Woodruff's Journal*, 6:390, 15 January 1868.
30. Mackley, *Wilford Woodruff's Witness*, 396–97.

devastating blow to the family and a test of faith all around. "My son Brigham has lost his life apparently for a trifle," Woodruff mournfully confided in his journal. "We cannot always comprehend the ways of Providence. There is a mystery hanging over this affair to me. . . . He had received his endowments. . . . I have thought that as I was doing so much for the dead here in the Temple in St. George, that it might be necessary to have one in the family in the spirit world."[31] It was an emotional wound from which Wilford Woodruff never fully recovered and underscored in his heart and soul the possible interconnections, intercommunications, and emotional renderings and ties between the living and the dead.

"A PERFECT SET OF ENDOWMENTS"

Construction work now fully completed, the St. George Temple was dedicated 1 January 1877 on what Wilford Woodruff called "a very important day to the Church and Kingdom of God on the Earth."[32] Over two thousand people crowded so tightly into the temple that none could bow their knee. At 12:30, after the choir had sung "The Spirit of God like a Fire Is Burning," President Woodruff stood on the upper step of the font and offered the dedicatory prayer. Among other things he dedicated the temple block, the land, the water tank, the foundation, the inner and outer walls, all the windows, stairways, all the doors, the baptismal font and its boiler, engine and pipes leading to the font, the twelve oxen, the many rooms in the temple, and much more. He then called upon heaven for a special blessing upon President Brigham Young who, suffering severely from rheumatism, had to be carried in a chair by three men from one room to another. "He has been with thy people through all their afflictions and persecutions and led them to these mountains of Israel and guided and directed the settlements of thy saints and all the affairs of Zion

---

31. *Wilford Woodruff's Journal*, 7:355, 16 June 1877. Within a month of Brigham Woodruff's death, his father had five single women sealed to him. *Journal*, 7:358, 8 July 1877. Emily Jane, one of those sealed to Brigham, died 8 May 1878.
32. This dedication was for those portions of the temple already completed and should not be confused with the more public, more formal dedication that occurred four months later on 6 April 1877.

as inspired by the power of God in this the last dispensation and fullness of times. . . . Lay thy hand upon thy servant Brigham unto the renewal of his body and the healing of his infirmities and the lengthening out of his days and years." And while prayers for blessings were the order of the day, Woodruff also called upon heaven to chastise and punish the nation for its "sins, wickedness, and abominations" in shedding the blood of the "Prophets and Saints which cry unto God day and night for vengeance" and for its innumerable other crimes and disorders.[33]

Elder Erastus Snow then dedicated the main room over the font, and Brigham Young Jr. the sealing room, at which time President Young rose from his chair and in great pain and difficulty walked into the lower stand and made the following closing remarks, which constituted a history of temple building up until that time. "I cannot consent in my feelings to retire from this house without exercising my strength . . . in speaking to this people," he began.

> *We reared up a temple in Kirtland but we had no basement in it nor a font or preparations to give Endowments for the living or the dead. . . . Joseph located the site for the Temple in Jackson Co. Mo. and . . . also laid the cornerstone for a Temple in Far West Caldwell County Mo. But these temple[s] were not built. We built one in Nauvoo. . . . It is true we left Brethren there with instructions to finish it and they got it nearly completed before it was burned but the Saints did not enjoy it. . . . This house was built here in this place purposely where it is warm and pleasant in the winter time and comfortable to work also for the Lamanites. . . . What do you suppose the fathers would say if they could speak from the dead? Would they not say we "have lain here thousands of years here in this prison house waiting for this dispensation to come. Here we are bound and fettered in the association of those who are filthy. . . ." When I think upon this subject I want the tongues of seven thunders to wake up the people.*

---

33. *Wilford Woodruff's Journal*, 7:303–8, 1 January 1877.

Jan 7. 1877

E E E E This is a very important day to the Church and Kingdom of God on the Earth. President Brigham Young, The Apostles Wilford Woodruff, Erastus Snow, Brigham Young Jr with some two thousand Saints assembled within the walls of the Temple of our God, built in St George, for the purpose of Dedicating certain Portions of it unto God that we might be prepared to Commence giving Endowments, and Blessings and sealing unto the Saints. At 30 Minutes past 12 oclok Elder W. Woodruff stood on the upper step of the font and Called the attention of the people and said we are this day blessed with a privilege that but few since the days of Adam have Even Enjoyed, but few of the sons of Adam have Even had the privilege of Entering into a Temple built by the Commandment of God in which to administer in ordinances both for the living and the dead. We have now assembled to dedicate portions of this Temple unto God, and I have a request to make of all the saints who are present and to suppose all who are profess to be Saints for none others should be have. I realize that this assembly Cannot bow the knee in their Crowded Condition but you Can bow your heads and your hearts unto God and this I want you to do this day and those who offer up Prayers in the dedication of this Temple I want their words repeated in secret by this assembly before the Lord that our prayers may ascend into the Ears of the Lord of Sabaoth that they may be answered upon our heads. The saints do not prize as they should the blessings they Enjoy, as it Cloths of this room wh[?] The following Hymn was sung The spirit of God like a fire is burning Then Erastus Snow announced that Elder Wilford Woodruff would Offer the dedication Prayer

Wilford Woodruff's Journal, *entry for 7 January 1877.*

Can the Fathers be saved without us? No. Can we be saved without them? No. And if we do not wake up and cease to long after the things of this earth we will find that we as individuals will go down to Hell although the Lord will preserve a people unto himself.[34]

Baptisms for the dead began on 9 January 1877 when Wilford Woodruff "went into the font and baptized Suzie Amelia Young Dunford, a daughter of Brigham Young, for and in behalf of her friend, Mary Sheppard (an English girl). Brother Brigham, lame as he was, by the aid of his crutch and stick ascended the steps up to the font and witnessed the first Baptism. I stood near the font, and watched them baptize and could not refrain from shedding tears of joy on beholding the commencement of so great a work."[35] Elder Woodruff then baptized and confirmed the first 141 persons, President Young laying on hands at the same time. John L. Smith baptized the next 83 persons making 224 for the day. The floodgates now opened, by year's end, 30,384 baptisms for the dead had been performed in the new temple, almost three times the known number in the Nauvoo Temple. Over the next three years, the corresponding figure would mushroom to almost 100,000.

Two days later, on 11 January, "We gave endowments for 63 for the living and 10 for the dead," Woodruff happily recorded.[36] The very first deceased person to be so endowed was the same Mary Shepherd (or Sheppard), born in Denmark in 1835 and whose baptism for the dead had been performed just two days earlier. Of the remaining nine, six were of deceased females and three for deceased males.

---

34. *Wilford Woodruff's Journal*, 7:317–18, 1 January 1877. At the conclusion of his remarks and for emphasis, Brigham Young pounded the podium with his hickory cane filled with knots with such force that three of the knots were buried into the wood and remained there for a generation. *Journal*, 7:320.
35. Walker, *Diary*, 569, 9 January 1877. Woodruff was also in attendance in the Nauvoo Temple when the font was first used for baptisms for the dead. *Wilford Woodruff's Journal*, 2:138–39, 21 November 1841.
36. *Wilford Woodruff's Journal*, 7:321, 11 January 1877.

"THE REDEMPTION OF OUR DEAD"

Seasoned Nauvoo Temple ordinance and Salt Lake City endowment worker, Alonzo H. Raleigh, wrote reverently of the occasion:

> *Endowments commenced in the [St. George] Temple and for the first time Endowments for the dead in this dispensation. 72 persons received their Endowments. I took the lead in the washing and anointing and instructions in the same, washed, anointed and clothed the first person, and took the general lead of the same, all through, by promptings by direction of President Brigham Young through Elder Woodruff, we were late getting through. It was the most responsible and complicated day's work I [have] ever done, as most of the workmen were new in the labor and the prompting devolved almost entirely on me for nearly all the parts.*[37]

By the end of January, 112 endowments for the dead had been performed (66 female and 46 male) and by year's end, 13,160 (7,910 females and 5,250 males)[38]—one-fourth the total number witnessed in the Endowment House over its thirty-four years of operation.[39] Included in this number were Don Carlos Smith, Alvin Smith, and Joseph Smith Sr.[40] It was, as George A. Smith once put it, "the beginning of an immense work"[41] with Wilford Woodruff referring to the new system as "a perfect form of endowments."[42]

What followed in the days and weeks thereafter was nothing less than a schooling in matters of the temple. Part of these necessary adjustments unquestionably pertained to the logistics of handling so many patrons going through the temple at one time. "At work in the endowments," Raleigh again confided, "136 persons were passed through. The house was tolerably crowded, though we got through in good season, having two vails to

---

37. Alonzo Hazelton Raleigh Diary "B," 1861–1887, 11 January 1877, Church History Library.
38. Saint George Temple Endowments: Dead: Male and Female Index and Record book, CR 343 6, Church History Library.
39. St. George Temple Records, 330–42, CR 343 57, Church History Library.
40. St. George Temple Endowments: Dead: Male and Female Index and Record Book, 94, 97.
41. St. George Utah Melchizedek Priesthood Minutes, 25 December 1874.
42. *Wilford Woodruff's Journal*, 7:340, 21 March 1877; see also Journal History, 21 March 1877.

The St. George Temple completed.

work at which doubles the capacity of the House in that respect, a thing not practiced before as far as we have any knowledge."[43] A careful student of temple worship, having served for years in the Council House and the Endowment House as a lead worker, Raleigh knew of the continuity of the endowment through the years. "I have endeavored to fully understand the principle as it has been revealed, having worked in them over 25 years and the last half of that time constantly, when there was any endowments given, which no other person has in this generation."[44]

After several weeks of such work, Brigham Young instructed Woodruff and others to write out the revised ceremony "from beginning to end"

---

43. Raleigh Diary, 210, 15 February 1877. Raleigh himself had brought down from Salt Lake City this particular veil which Daniel H. Wells had entrusted to him especially for this occasion. Raleigh Diary, 206, 29 November 1876. A third veil was soon added, which allowed for faster flow through.
44. Raleigh Diary, 210, 16 February 1877.

for consistency and accuracy in all future applications. Recalled Wilford Woodruff:

> *President Brigham Young requested me to take charge of the Temple, which I did. He also requested me to write all the ordinances of the Church, from the first baptism and confirmation through every ordinance of the Church. Geo. Q. Cannon assisted some in this writing, and when I had finished it to the satisfaction of the President, he said to me, "Now you have before you an ensample to carry on the endowments in all the temples until the coming of the Son of Man." . . . I parted with Brigham Young for the last time in the flesh at 9:30 am on April 16, 1877 when he started for Salt Lake City. . . . When I left St. George I placed the Presidency of the Temple in the hands of John Daniel Thompson McAllister who was to preside over it in my absence.*[45]

On February 12, Alonzo Raleigh recorded that he was "engaged all day and evening with President Woodruff, John D. T. Mcallister [Woodruff's first counselor] and [L. John] Nuttall under the direction of President B. Young in reorganizing parts of the endowment"—a likely reference to needed adjustments for accommodating large companies of patrons.[46]

Finally, by the first day of spring, the first winter temple semester was complete. Wrote a triumphant Wilford Woodruff, "President Brigham Young has been laboring all winter to get up a perfect form of endowments, as far as possible. They having been perfected, I read them to the

---

45. Wilford Woodruff signed statement, 26 March 1883, entitled "History of the St. George Temple. Its Cost and Dedication and the Labor Therein," in Letter File of David H. Cannon, Wilford Woodruff Letterpress Copybook. Of this wrote Wilford Woodruff: "Brigham Young Jr. and myself wrote out a part of the ceremony of the endowment." *Wilford Woodruff's Journal*, 7:322, 15 January 1877. Daily drafts were submitted for Brigham Young's review and approval. The important objective was to ensure accuracy, with the work being very much a team effort. Brigham Young also called on others to assist him in finalizing the lecture given at the veil. For instance, George Q. Cannon wrote as follows, just two days after endowments began in the temple: "In the evening President Young desired me to go through and correct the lecture which is delivered to those receiving their endowments, at the vail." Journals of George Q. Cannon, 13 April 1877.
46. Raleigh Diary, 12 February 1877.

company today."⁴⁷ Said an equally jubilant Brigham Young just days later, "The Lord had accepted this Temple and the labors of the Saints. A great joy and rejoicing had been manifested in the Spirit World on account of the labors performed by the Saints for the Dead."⁴⁸ Concluded Alonzo Raleigh, "I realize it to be by far the best winter's work that I have ever done."⁴⁹ As a tribute to all those who had worked so long and hard in building the St. George Temple, the annual general conference of the Church was held in April 1877 within the temple itself, during which the entire building was formally dedicated.⁵⁰

It was also in St. George that temple apparel began to change. On 1 February 1877 Wilford Woodruff and Lucy Bigelow Young, one of Brigham's wives, became the first temple ordinance workers to dress entirely in white. "I dressed in pure white doe skin [a soft cloth fabric] . . . from head to foot . . . white pants vest and coat the first example in any temple of the Lord in this last dispensation. Sister Lucy B. Young also dressed in white" an obvious representation of the purity of temple worship, thereby setting a standard of dress for later generations to follow.⁵¹

It is important to note that the endowment for the dead was the critical ordinance so long promised but not yet delivered to the Saints. While the Kirtland Temple was a place of preparatory washings and anointings, and the Nauvoo Temple one of baptisms for the dead and endowments and sealings for the living, it was in the St. George Temple where endowments for

---

47. Journal History, 21 March 1877. From all available evidence, the wording and presentation of the St. George Temple endowment ceremony replicated in large measure that first given in the Nauvoo Temple years before. Blaine M. Yorgason, in his fine study of the St. George Temple, infers that the dramatic or theatrical presentation of the endowment ceremony performed there was in all essentials similar to that given in the Nauvoo Temple. Blaine M. Yorgason, Richard A. Schmutz, and Douglas D. Alder, *All That Was Promised: The St. George Temple and the Unfolding of the Restoration* (Salt Lake City: Deseret Book Company, 2014), 256–57, 282–83.
48. Walker, *Diary*, 584, 7 April 1877.
49. Raleigh Diary, 213, 31 March 1877.
50. Many of those who came from Salt Lake City, including the General Authorities, took advantage of this special temple conference to remain in St. George for a few days to perform endowments for the dead for their own ancestry.
51. *Wilford Woodruff's Journal*, 7:325, 1 February 1877. See also Journal History, 1 February 1877. President Young was sick at the time.

the dead commenced. If baptism for the dead was the justifying ordinance by which the dead could be redeemed and enter into the celestial kingdom, then the endowment on their behalf was the sanctifying ordinance of exaltation for the highest degree of the celestial kingdom. If the dead waiting in the spirit world could now receive their endowments, it therefore meant that such dead were worthy of receiving the priesthood. And if deceased ancestors could receive the priesthood, then families could be reunited.

With this expanded vision of family temple work a critical innovation in St. George was that of sealing deceased children to their deceased parents. Prior to St. George, work for the dead was primarily individualistic in nature. Baptisms for the dead did not seal family members together. Even sealing deceased married couples together did not include sealing children to their parents. What began in St. George was *family-centered* temple work wherein deceased couples could receive their endowments, be sealed one to another, and then have their deceased children sealed to them in a reconstruction of family units and (later) intergenerational linkages as far back as the records allowed. Of the first 106 endowments for the dead performed, 35 were for deceased children, nieces, and nephews, 23 for deceased spouses, brothers, and sisters, 13 for deceased grandchildren, 25 for deceased friends, and only one for a deceased parent. The number of sealings of deceased children to their parents grew exponentially from virtually zero in 1877 to over 60,000 before the end of the century.[52]

When referring to his own father who had died and was buried back in Quincy, Illinois, Brigham Young said:

> *My father died before the endowments were given. None of his children have been sealed to him. If you recollect, you that were in Nauvoo, we were very much hurried in the little time we spent there after the Temple was built. . . . Our time, therefore, was short, and we had no time to attend to this. . . . Some brethren here are anxious*

---

52. Report, 31 December 1898, Church Historian's Letterpress Copybooks (1842–1992), CR 100 39, Church History Library.

to know whether they can receive endowments for their [deceased] sons or for their daughters. No, they cannot until we have a Temple. . . . A man can be baptized for a son who died before hearing the Gospel . . . but no one can receive endowments for another, until a Temple is prepared. . . . We administer just so far as the law permits us to do.[53]

This emphasis on redeeming the dead through sealing past families together caught the imagination of the Saints as perhaps no other element of temple work could or did. And in this dawning of modern temple ordinances, temple work even went beyond family kinships; indeed, there was also much interest in doing work for deceased friends. Wrote one patron: "At night getting a recommend for my wife, Abigail, to go through the Temple for her mother and friends."[54] Later on, Charles Walker "went through the temple for a friend of Brother Folsom. This is the first time I have been through the endowments for the Dead, Reuben Clark was the one I went through for. I felt happy and blessed."[55] Early temple workers were quick to complete work for beloved friends as well as family names, especially if such departed friends were seen as being likely sympathetic to the message of the restored gospel.

Nor was it just friends and associates. Well known in Church history is Wilford Woodruff's vision in August 1877 of scores of famous seventeenth- and eighteenth-century men and women, including the signers of the Declaration of Independence and most of the deceased presidents of the United States, as well as famous writers, scientists, discoverers, and religious leaders from both sides of the Atlantic. Woodruff and McAllister worked together all day on 21 August baptizing in behalf of 121 of these famous luminaries. Wrote Woodruff, "I felt thankful that we had the privilege and the power to administer for the worthy dead, especially for the

---

53. Brigham Young, in *Journal of Discourses*, 16:187–88, 4 September 1873.
54. Walker, *Diary*, 573, 29 January 1877.
55. Walker, *Diary*, 578, 21 March 1877. Walker and others performed such temple work often for friends before performing it for family members.

signers of the Declaration of Independence, that inasmuch as they had laid the foundation of our Government that we could do as much for them as they had done for us."[56]

Baptisms for the dead had been performed for most of these deceased figures previously, for some several times. What makes this experience unique is that they were now to receive their endowment. Of this vital new advancement in temple work, Woodruff later recorded:

> *Two weeks before I left St. George, the spirits of the dead gathered around me, wanting to know why we did not redeem them. Said they, "You have had the use of the Endowment House for a number of years, and yet nothing has ever been done for us. We laid the foundation of the governments you now enjoy, and we never apostatized from it, but we remained true to it, and were faithful to God." These were the signers of the Declaration of Independence, and they waited on me for two days and two nights. I thought it very singular, that notwithstanding so much work had been done, and yet nothing had been done for them. The thought never entered my heart, from the fact, I suppose, that heretofore our minds were reaching after our immediate friends and relatives.*[57]

Immediately after Lucy Bigelow Young had been baptized for Martha Washington and seventy other "eminent" women of the world, Woodruff "called upon all the Brethren and Sisters who were present to assist in getting endowments for those that we had been baptized for"—a work that transpired over the next three days.[58]

---

56. *Wilford Woodruff's Journal*, 7:369, 21 August 1877. One likely reason for why this vision has never been canonized is that it was a personal experience of Wilford Woodruff and not one given to him as the President of the Church. Furthermore, he was not always consistent in how he described the event. Sometimes he said it was while meditating upon such things; other times, he implied that it was a dream vision.
57. Wilford Woodruff, in *Journal of Discourses*, 19:229, 17 September 1877.
58. *Wilford Woodruff's Journal*, 7:369, 21–24 August 1877. Tom Alexander states that by inaugurating temple work for deceased people he did not know, Woodruff was opening a "new path in vicarious work for the dead." Thomas G. Alexander, "An Apostle in Exile: Wilford Woodruff and the St. George Connection," Juanita Brooks Lecture Series (1994), 16.

Another significant adaptation was not just the allowance for, but the encouragement of, non-family members doing another family's proxy work. This was not a particularly new concept, but it was introduced in St. George on a much grander scale than before. To illustrate, on Woodruff's seventieth birthday, several sisters joined him at the temple for the purpose of proxy endowments for several women, "some of whom had been sealed to him in past years"—a special kind of birthday gift. Woodruff wrote:

> *A few days ago I went into the sealing room where I often go to pray, and while there I went before the Lord with this subject resting upon my mind. . . . And while I prayed the Spirit of the Lord rested upon me and conveyed the following testimony to me: Let my servant Wilford call upon the [sisters] in Zion and let them enter into my Holy Temple . . . and there let them receive their . . . endowments for and [in] behalf of the wives who are dead and have been sealed to my servant, Wilford, or those who are to be sealed to him, and this shall be acceptable unto me saith the Lord.*[59]

Previously, with either baptisms or endowments, generally only family members would stand in as proxy for family names; now others were being encouraged to participate as if they were family members. Furthermore, because the time involved in a single endowment could then take several hours, proxy work by others for family names greatly accelerated the process for a particular family. "This was merely a key to me," Woodruff said. "Light burst upon my understanding. I saw an Effectual door open to me for the redemption of my dead. And when I saw this I felt like shouting Glory Hallalulah to God and the Lamb." That night, he recorded in his journal that his seventieth birthday had been one of revelation and inspiration and "among the most wonderful events of the last dispensation. . . . This door which is open for the redemption of the dead in this manner

---

59. *Wilford Woodruff's Journal*, 7:331, 1 March 1877.

will accomplish great and important results.... By this labor in redeeming our dead by proxy much can be accomplished."⁶⁰

"NO ONE CAN STEAL OUR LABORS"

Whereas before one received his or her own endowment once and for all, now the faithful would be called upon to return to the temple *over and over again* to perform that ordinance vicariously for departed loved ones and friends. Thus regular temple attendance would soon become the order of the day, *a standing invitation* to the entire membership to return to the temple often. This expanded vision of temple work soon became a labor of love and for many "a joy unspeakable."⁶¹ Said Karl G. Maeser, founding principal of Brigham Young Academy: "The life-giving power of Temples is apparent to the Saints.... The redemption of our dead and the living depends upon the erection of Temples."⁶² Henry Eyring, a counselor in the St. George Stake presidency, "spoke of the building of temples and the ordinances attended to therein, that we [were] the first who could enjoy the privileges of entering into a temple and officiating therein."⁶³ Addison Everett spoke in a meeting about the work he was doing "for his old friends and neighbors" some of whom he claimed, "had appeared to him in his dreams" and "he was delighted to work for them."⁶⁴ "In laboring for our dead relatives and friends, no one can steal our labors," said William Smith of St. George.⁶⁵ William Perkins may have summarized it best: "The work of redeeming the dead is the greatest work ever done upon the earth."⁶⁶

---

60. *Wilford Woodruff's Journal*, 7:332–33, 1 March 1877. Confirming this point, Woodruff recorded six years later that "through the Blessings of God [I] have been Enabled in connexion with my family, of being baptized for about 3,000 of my dead relatives and also through the assistance of friend[s] I have been Enabled to get endowments in the Temple of St. George for about 2,500 of my relatives." *Wilford Woodruff's Journal*, 8:156, 1 March 1883.
61. *Wilford Woodruff's Journal*, 7: 333, 1 March 1877.
62. Provo Utah Central Stake General Minutes, 1849–1977, 29 April 1877, LR 9629 11, part 3.
63. St. George Utah Stake Melchizedek Priesthood Minutes and Records, 25 August 1877.
64. St. George Utah Stake Melchizedek Priesthood Minutes and Records, 315, 29 June 1878.
65. St. George Utah Stake Melchizedek Priesthood Minutes and Records, 310, 25 May 1878.
66. St. George Utah Stake Melchizedek Priesthood Minutes and Records, 267, 25 August 1877.

Women especially found new meaning for themselves in temple worship. "We cannot go out to preach," said Elizabeth Morse in a St. George Relief Society meeting in April 1878, "but we can go to the temple to redeem the dead."[67] Lucy B. Young was called by her husband to serve not only as an ordinance worker but as the temple's first matron, though that title was not then applied. "Her heart was full in the prospect of being received by [her dead] with open arms, as all would be by those who could not do the work for themselves. She desired to live to redeem hundreds of her dead."[68] Said Sister O. C. Nelson in Manti, "It has strengthened me so much to go into the Temple that I cannot tell how much I feel to encourage my sisters to go there. Many days have I been there I have felt that I could raise my voice and praise God."[69]

In an age prior to women serving full-time Church missions, temple work became a well-attended outlet of newfound devotion, a form of "missionary labor" among Latter-day Saint women.[70] Seventy-nine female ordinance workers were called in St. George between 1877 and 1890 with a female president over such.[71] Margaret Mustard spoke in one Relief Society meeting of how thankful she was "to have been brought to St. George where a temple of the Lord has been erected, and to have been made a partaker in its blessings."[72] Added a Sister Durham of Parowan, "When I came here to work in the temple I felt my weakness, I was afraid I could not learn what I came here for, but the Lord has blest me, and I am doing better than I thought."[73] And declared Minerva W. Snow, plural

---

67. St. George Utah Stake Relief Society Minutes and Records, 1868–1973, 4 April 1878, LR 7836 14.
68. St. George Utah Stake Relief Society Minutes and Records, 5 July 1877. When the Manti and Logan temples were dedicated, Lucy Young trained female ordinance workers at both places. Yorgason, *All That Was Promised*, 281.
69. Manti South Ward Relief Society Minutes and Records, 1882–1973, 98, 19 September 1888, LR 5252 14.
70. St. George Relief Society Minutes and Records, 6 March 1879.
71. St. George Temple Female Ordinance Workers, circa 1917, CR 343 3.
72. St. George Relief Society Minutes and Records, 6 July 1883, LR 7836 14.
73. St. George Relief Society Minutes and Records, 2 October 1884.

St. George Temple wagon and female temple workers, St. George, Utah, circa 1880s.

wife of Elder Erastus Snow, "I believe that having the Temple has wrought great changes in this people."[74]

One other important reason why women and men began flocking to the temple was for baptisms for health. Since the very early days of the Restoration when missionaries healed the sick, members had sought blessings for health and strength. Anointing the sick with oil had occurred in both the Kirtland and Nauvoo Temples and many members, like Naaman of old, had been baptized seven times for health in the Mississippi River, the Nauvoo Temple, and along the Mormon trail. Not a few sick children under the age of eight were likewise so baptized. Most members associated its potency, as a ritual, to the temple. As historians Jonathan Stapley and Kristine Wright have well shown, for many years "baptisms for healing was the most common living temple ordinance" in Utah Territory.[75] Thus many came to the temple not merely to do work for the living and the dead but also for the restoration of their health.[76] Temples set apart special

---

74. St. George Relief Society Minutes and Records, 1 February 1883.
75. Stapley and Wright, "They Shall Be Made Whole," 95.
76. This was particularly the case with the Manti Temple for reasons not entirely clear. "My labors of late have been in the Manti Temple," A. H. Lund once reported, "and there I have seen many cases of healing." *Deseret News*, 12 October 1889.

days just for the healing of the sick and many temple workers, male and female, administered to the sick as part of their duties. As one such worker noted, "We who have worked in the Temple have seen the sick healed."[77] This practice continued for almost another fifty years when in 1922 the First Presidency discontinued it (at the same time rebaptisms were discontinued in the Church), likely to keep the focus on salvific ordinances within the temple and because of advances in medical treatments.

For all the above reasons, temple worship became a newfound recurring experience, a constant invitation for covenant renewal, redemption of the dead and family sealing, recovery of health, and changing personal behavior—a place to return to repeatedly. "The dead are upon our minds day and night," said John D. T. McAllister, first counselor in the St. George Temple presidency. "The brethren and sisters up north will be coming down by hundreds."[78] Later he corrected himself: "they would come by thousands."[79]

Commenting on this newfound enthusiasm for and dedication to temple work, John Taylor referred to it as a "movement" among the people and the leadership. "Why did President Young feel so?" he asked. "Because the spirit of God rested upon him, prompting him to move in this direction. Why did the brethren of these several quorums so readily respond to the call? Because the same spirit rested upon them . . . and the saints generally are all interested in this movement, [and have] evinced the same desire to accomplish this work of Temple building, as the saints of foreign lands do to gather to Zion."[80]

"OUR CHILDREN HAVE NOT BEEN TRADITIONATED"

And come by the thousands they did—from near and far! Indeed, the construction of the temple greatly strengthened the call to gather to

---

77. Sister Lowry, Manti South Ward Relief Society Minutes, 12 October 1889.
78. J. D. T. McAllister, St. George Melchizedek Priesthood Minutes and Records, 26 May 1877.
79. J. D. T. McAllister, St. George Melchizedek Priesthood Minutes and Records, 4:78, 26 February 1881.
80. From a discourse by John Taylor in the Ogden Tabernacle, transcribed 21 October 1877. *Deseret News*, 17 April 1878.

"THE REDEMPTION OF OUR DEAD"

Zion from across the country and around the world. Furthering the augmented role of temple participation was the calling of scores of male and female temple workers. In the first year of operations of the St. George Temple, 46 male and 63 female general laborers put in a total of 7,141 volunteer shifts. Wilford Woodruff attended 84 days; his first counselor, John D. T. McAllister, attended 248 days. In addition, women contributed 674 cleaning days in 1878 with men serving as night watchmen and Sunday guards.[81]

O. H. Berg was one of the very first temple workers called from Provo in early 1877 to travel the 260 miles south to work in the new temple. "It is a miracle to erect such a House in the midst of a desert," he observed, "and by a people poor and driven into a wilderness."[82] David John, also of Provo, was another such worker. Serving a temple mission in 1882, he was baptized for several hundred of his deceased ancestors and performed hundreds of endowments for the dead for both his own ancestors and hundreds of others. "I have learned that there were given no endowments for the dead in Kirtland or Nauvoo," he recorded with some surprise. "They only baptized for the dead, and gave endowments for the living."[83] And speaking of the eighty-nine dead persons he "had been through the temple for," Jehu Cox proclaimed, "This was the greatest work he had ever done."[84] Agness McQuarrie testified in a Relief Society meeting "that at first it was a great trial to her to come to this place, but now thought that it was one of the best places on the earth to make saints."[85] Some even wished that they would "like to die in the temple."[86]

With the Saints beginning to flock to the temple in ever-greater numbers came the augmented sense of their being "Saviors on Mount Zion"

---

81. St. George Temple Record Book, 1877–1899, CR 343 57.
82. O. H. Berg, Provo Utah Central Stake General Minutes, 20 March 1877.
83. David John Diaries, 1:353, 26–27 June and 12 September 1882, MSS 21, Perry Special Collections, HBLL, BYU.
84. St. George Utah Stake Minutes of Melchizedek Priesthood Meetings, 23 May 1878, LR 7836 13, vol. 3.
85. Agness McQuarrie, St. George Relief Society Minutes and Records, 6 July 1883, LR 7836 14.
86. Lucy B. Young, St. George Relief Society Minutes and Records, 1 December 1881, LR 7836 14.

for generations past. "We more or less hold the keys for our dead," said Franklin D. Richards while speaking at a stake conference in Richfield. "There [have] been baptized for the dead more than 100,000 in the St. George Temple. Men and women cannot receive their exaltation until they are sealed together. How can we become Saviors unless we save somebody[?] We can become Saviors by being baptized and receiving endowments for our dead. . . . Our children have not been traditionated and we should teach them the principles of the Gospel."[87]

A corollary to these newfound temple blessings and opportunities was a developing sense of urgency, bordering on guilt, that some leaders increasingly laid upon the membership for not participating. Said one local leader, "Our friends will ask us when we go behind the veil why we did not relieve them from bondage and if we have neglected to do so we shall feel very sorry."[88] And from Franklin D. Richards, "How sad it will seem, if we are taken away and are met at the other side by our relations, who ask, 'Have you done this work for us?' And we say, 'No.' But if we can meet them and say, 'Yes, We have done the work for you' how joyful will that consciousness be to us."[89] This sense of members' failing in their responsibility to save the dead developed gradually and in direct proportion to the growing expectation for the Saints to participate in savings ordinances for the dead, particularly endowments for the dead.

Commensurate with the joy many felt in their newfound temple service was a counterbalancing unease that there was so much to do with such little time to do it. Good or bad, positive or negative, it was all part of a growing temple sensibility. If the catechisms of the aforementioned Mormon Reformation had affected a new level of commitment without

---

87. Franklin D. Richards, Sevier Stake Conference, Sevier Stake Historical Record, 1880–1883, 26 November 1881, LR 8243 11.
88. Eldon J. Pierce, Sevier Stake Historical Record, 4:27–28, 3 November 1884, LR 8243 11.
89. Franklin D. Richards, Manti Temple Historical Record, 1888–1999, 20, 21 May 1888, CR 348 21.

the temple, so now did the bishops' and stake presidents' temple recommend interviews.[90]

What impact increased temple attendance had on personal behavior is impossible to gauge, but certainly such worthiness questions came more often and more regularly than ever before. Though sometimes given leniently "as from a feeling of sympathy" or as encouragement for many to get to the temple for their first time, the widespread use of temple recommend interviews imposed a growing sense of personal accountability, obedience, faithfulness, and integrity. And the payment of tithing was a vital part of such interviews. "It is absolutely necessary to require payment of tithing and donations," one stake president instructed his bishops.[91] And one's failure to pay tithing would not only disqualify temple attendance but would also contribute to the collective sense of persecution among the Saints generally. "We may expect our enemies to continue to persecute us and pass laws against this people, unless we pay our tithing."[92] With the press of business so great upon the First Presidency, starting in 1891 it was deemed no longer necessary for the President of the Church to cosign temple recommends.[93]

Temple attendance also influenced fashion choices and moral behavior.[94] "Do not come to the temple with the fashion of the world on you,"

---

90. Up until late 1891, temple recommends had to be endorsed by the President of the Church. After this time the signature of local bishops and stake presidents was sufficient. James R. Clark, ed., *Messages of the First Presidency* 3:228; see also Devery Scott Anderson, ed., *The Development of Latter-day Saint Temple Worship, 1845–2000: A Documentary History* (Salt Lake City: Smith-Pettit Foundation, 2011), 50–54.
91. Franklin Spencer, 20 September 1879, Sevier Stake Historical Record B, 1879–1885, 3:25. Said John Taylor in 1877, "Those desiring to receive the benefit of these ordinances must obtain a recommend from the bishop of the ward or settlement in which they reside, or in the absence of the bishop, the recommend may be signed by the president of the stake. . . . No person will be eligible to receive these blessings except they have been rebaptized." Anderson, *Development of Latter-day Saint Temple Worship*, 43.
92. Franklin Spencer, Sevier Stake Historical Record, 4:230, 27 Aug 1882, LR 8243 11.
93. First Presidency Letter, 6 November 1891. This decision applied to almost all ordinances in the House of the Lord. Clark, *Messages of the First Presidency* 3:228.
94. George Teasdale, Sevier Stake Historical Record, 3:213–14, 2 December 1882, LR 8243 11.

said John D. T. McAllister in a St. George Relief Society meeting.[95] Even in matters of dress and sexual conduct, temples played an ever greater role than before. Sexual relations between married partners were discouraged for at least a week before attending.[96] And by the late 1880s, adherence to the Word of Wisdom—abstaining from tobacco, liquor, hot drinks—was becoming part of such temple recommend interviews.[97] The point is that increased temple attendance likely influenced behavior among thousands of believing patrons anxious to do their part in redeeming the dead. An increased emphasis on the law of tithing, the Word of Wisdom, personal purity, and other expressions of obedience, sacrifice, and worthiness played out upon the everyday lives of thousands of men and women. "We are thankful that a deeply earnest, devout spirit characterizes the administrations of the brethren and sisters who assist in the Temple," said Woodruff, "and the same spirit evidently rests upon those who are administered to."[98] Recurring temple attendance would now accomplish what the Mormon Reformation had set out to do some twenty years before.[99]

---

95. John D. T. McAllister, St. George Stake Relief Society Meeting Minutes, 6 December 1877, LR 7836 14.
96. "A woman should not go for a week after her menses were upon her; a man should not have intercourse with his wife for several days; but should be clean in body and exercised in spirit previous thereto. His clothing should be changed once or twice before going there." Brigham Young, Brigham Young Letterpress Copybook, 29:320.
97. Anderson, *Development of Latter-day Saint Temple Worship*, 83. The following instructions were issued for those interested in coming to the newly completed St. George Temple: "Those who wish to receive endowments for themselves or friends, should be provided with oil or means to purchase it. The sisters should be provided with 2 or 3 white shirts, and the brethren have their garments to button from the back clear round and up the front, and shirts made to reach down to the knees or a little below or one may be pieced to the length for the occasion. Before the Brethren and Sisters go into the Temple to receive their endowments they must wash all over perfectly clean. Men and women should have no sexual intercourse for a week or more previous to their going into the Temple to receive their endowments." Letter of Instructions to all Church Bishops, 13 January 1877, signed by Brigham Young, John W. Young, Wilford Woodruff, Erastus Snow, and Brigham Young Jr., Richfield Utah Stake General Minutes, 1872–1977, 185, LR 8243 11, Church History Library.
98. Wilford Woodruff to Brigham Young, Brigham Young Letterpress Copybook, June 2 1877.
99. Said Brigham Young in 1856, "A great many people want their endowment; but I never wish to give another man or woman their endowments, until they have reformed from whatever they may have done amiss. I had as soon give the devil his endowment, as to confer it upon some men and women who profess to be Latter Day Saints; I want them to reform first." Journal History, 9 November 1856.

As Wilford Woodruff explained: "We would like to see the names of every man, woman, and child in the Church recorded in the Archives of the Temple as having contributed something towards its erection and completion."[100] Horace S. Eldridge of Provo related to the sacrifices of the Saints back in Nauvoo erecting the temple there, despite "their sickness and poverty" and spoke of "the reluctance we would have, or experience, on entering the Temple of the Lord if we had not committed to the same."[101] The goal was to create a spirit of sacrifice and a pervasive temple mind-set among the people.

"TO TURN THE HEARTS OF THE FATHERS TO THE CHILDREN"

These many changes and advances to temple work in St. George received strong scriptural validation and doctrinal support with the canonization of several past temple-centered revelations and their incorporation into the 1876 edition of the Doctrine and Covenants, an action which occurred just less than one year before the dedication of the St. George Temple.[102] These included section 2 (Moroni's reading of Malachi 4:5–6 and of turning the hearts of the fathers and of the children one to another); section 13 on John the Baptist's restoration of the Aaronic Priesthood; section 109 on the dedication of the Kirtland Temple and section 110 and its account of the return of Moses, Elias, and Elijah in 1836 in the Kirtland Temple; sections 121–123 being the Liberty Jail revelations; and section 132 on celestial marriage. Prior to 1876 these revelations and visions were known among the membership but had not been particularly stressed or emphasized.

The canonization of these remarkable sections—so rich in temple history and doctrine—was nothing less than a reclamation of past revelation,

---

100. Wilford Woodruff, 20 October 1887, published as "An Address from President Woodruff in Relation to the Manti Temple" in the *Deseret News*, 26 October 1887.
101. Provo Utah Central Stake General Minutes, 11 March 1879.
102. The Church of Jesus Christ of Latter-day Saints accepts the Holy Bible, the Book of Mormon, the Doctrine and Covenants, and the Pearl of Great Price all as books of holy scripture, thus setting the faith very much apart from other Christian religions.

a heightened reverence for and rediscovery of the word of the Lord that had come a half-century before. They became the touchstone of temple-related discourse and provided the necessary intellectual, doctrinal, and scriptural justification and framework for those new temple ordinances now to be enjoined. Such action established a precedent for the 1976 canonization of section 138 a century later—Joseph F. Smith's vision of the dead—that he had received fifty-eight years before, a clear example of how the history and development of temple work has been a process of accumulating revelation, practice, and adaptation, "line upon line, here a little, there a little."[103]

Though not alone, Orson Pratt may well have been among the first to publicly sermonize, in August 1859, on the importance of the vision of Moses, Elias, and Elijah and to emphasize its place in modern scripture.

> *The strangers who have attended our meetings, have oftentimes heard from this stand, that the dispensation in which we live was intended to benefit, not only the generation living, but also past generations that have lain in their graves for ages. You have heard this often hinted at, but perhaps no one since you have attended our meeting[s] has taken up the subject to any great length, but merely a few words thrown out and there it was left, . . . however, [it] was said to give you an understanding that we believe God will have something to do with the generations of the dead, that the children that are living here on the earth would be required to feel after their fathers that are in their graves.*[104]

Then again in 1872 he spoke of Elijah's return.[105] Orson Pratt clearly

---

103. It would be incorrect, however, to conclude that the doctrine of the gospel being taught to deceased spirits in prison was not taught in these years. For instance, Elder Erastus Snow said in 1887 that after his death, Joseph Smith "went and preached [the gospel] to the spirits who are in prison. And so have all the elders of Israel who have lived righteous lives, magnified their callings and ministered in their priesthood to the living, after death, being organized, I believe, as the church here and set to work in their missionary labors in the spirit world, to carry the gospel to their fathers whose spirits were in prison." *Salt Lake Herald*, 9 October 1887. One of the significant contributions of Joseph F. Smith's 1918 vision of the dead was to show that Christ Himself did not go to the deceased spirits in prison but that He "organized" His forces to do so.
104. Journal History, 28 August 1859.
105. Orson Pratt, in *Journal of Discourses*, 15:44–53, 7 April 1872.

The city of St. George, Utah, with temple in background, circa 1890.

championed this doctrine more than any of his colleagues, which may explain why it was he that headed up the committee to canonize these revelations in 1876.

Particularly well known is the sacred place section 110 now holds in the pantheon of Restoration scripture. It tells of the return of Moses, Elias, and Elijah to Joseph Smith and Oliver Cowdery in the Kirtland Temple in April 1836 and their restoration of specific keys, prophetic commissions, and temple-related covenants and administrations. Elijah declared, "Behold, the time has fully come, which was spoken of by the mouth of Malachi—testifying that he [Elijah] should be sent, before the great and dreadful day of the Lord come—to turn the hearts of the fathers to the children, and the children to the fathers, lest the whole earth be smitten with a curse" (D&C 110:14–15). With this declaration came the understanding of the place for temple ordinances for and in behalf of the dead who live on hereafter in a paradise/spirit world existence. There they await the opportunity to be taught the fullness of the gospel of Christ, though such saving ordinances as baptism would yet have to be performed for them by proxy by living mortals in a sacred temple.

Though referred to in modern discourse as the scriptural cornerstone of temple work, prior to 1876 this revelation, as discussed in an earlier chapter, was not overly emphasized. Joseph Smith seldom, if ever, directly referenced it in any of his later sermons. And relatively infrequently did Brigham Young or his counselors do so for most of his presidency.[106] In fact, it was not even published until November 1852 in the *Deseret News* by direction of Willard Richards. What led to its canonization in 1876 is not yet entirely clear, but Orson Pratt, a member of the original Quorum of the Twelve formed in 1835, was the driving force in its preservation and eventual canonization.[107]

After 1876, references to these early Kirtland visions became more frequent. Speaking of them, John Taylor said in Salt Lake City in October 1877:

> *Why a desire to build Temples? What for? That we may administer therein in these ordinances in which we are so greatly interested. You heard through Brother Woodruff how many more administrations there had been for the dead than for the living. This is because Elijah had been here and has delivered the keys that turn the hearts of the children to the fathers and we are beginning to feel after them. Hence we are building a temple here, one in Sanpete, another in Cache Valley, and we have one already built in Saint George. . . . Do we devote our labor and our means? Yes, we do; and it is this spirit*

---

106. Brigham Young, speaking in 1852, did refer to the Lord sending "the keys of Elijah the Prophet" but shied away on this and most other occasions from discussing the actual return of Elijah to the Kirtland Temple. *Journal of Discourses*, 6:283–98, 15 August 1852.

107. Trever R. Anderson, "Doctrine and Covenants Section 110: From Vision to Canonization" (master's thesis, Brigham Young University, 2010), 12–13, 54–55. As Anderson notes, at Brigham Young's death in August 1877, Pratt was in England overseeing the printing of the Book of Mormon on new electrotype plates. With the consent of John Taylor, then president of the Quorum of the Twelve, Pratt printed the Doctrine and Covenants using the same latest technology. Taylor recommended the inclusion of cross references and explanatory notes and during their communication agreed to include several new sections heretofore not incorporated. This new 1876 edition was finally ratified by conference vote in October 1876. In all, 26 sections were added: 2, 13, 77, 85, 87, 108–111, 113–118, 120–123, 125–126, 129–132, and 136.

which rests upon us that is prompting us to do it, and it will not rest until these things are done.[108]

One month later, James L. Hart, a local Church leader from Bear Lake said: "An angel came to the earth with the everlasting Gospel." And Elijah "had also come and revealed the doctrine of the baptism for the dead, and that the hearts of the fathers should be turned to the children, and vice versa [and] for that reason temples had been built and others were in course of erection. Although it was a stumbling block to the world, yet such had been revealed."[109]

Many years later, B. H. Roberts summarized the impact this long-neglected vision/revelation was beginning to have upon his fellow believers this way:

> *While the Gospel is preached in the spirit world, it appears from all that can be learned upon the subject that all the outward ordinances, [such] as baptisms, confirmations, ordinations, anointings, sealings, etc. must be performed vicariously . . . for those who accept the gospel in the world of spirits. This is the work that children may do for their progenitors, and upon learning this, the hearts of the children are turned to their fathers; and the fathers in the spirit world, learning that they are dependent upon the actions of the posterity for the performance of the ordinances of salvation, their hearts are turned to the children; and thus the work that was predicted should be performed by Elijah.*[110]

CONCLUSION

It is hard to overemphasize the importance of what happened for the first time in the St. George Temple beginning in January 1877. With the

---

108. Journal History, 12 December 1877.
109. James L. Hart, Logan Utah Cache Stake General Minutes, 2:48, 20 January 1878, LR 1280 11, Church History Library.
110. B. H. Roberts, *The Gospel: An Exposition of its First Principles* (Salt Lake City: Deseret News, 1888, 1913), 253.

introduction of endowments for the dead for both deceased friends and family ancestors, members began returning to the temple on a much more regular basis than before. Such increased temple attendance forged a renewal of their own temple covenants and instilled a heightened sense of family history, temple consciousness, and personal worthiness upon the many who frequented the temple, both men and women. And with the St. George Temple now in operation, with the work of redemption for the dead proceeding at a scale never before seen, and with doctrinal underpinnings now more fully in place, additional temples would soon be constructed even as the storm clouds of opposition were gathering as never before.

Chapter 8

"They Are Aiming a Blow at the Sealing Ordinances"

TEMPLES, FEDERAL MARSHALS, AND PLURAL MARRIAGE, 1877–1888

We are bordering on the Millennium. . . . It is our duty to build these temples. It is our duty to enter into them and redeem our dead. Joseph Smith is preaching to the spirits in prison; so are all the Elders who have died in the faith. There are millions of them there, and they must have the Gospel offered to them. . . . We have one of these temples finished, and we are doing a great work in that temple. A hundred and sixty-two thousand persons have been baptized, and nearly seventy thousand endowments have been given in that temple. We have only just begun this work. We want the Logan temple finished, as also the temple at Manti, that the people may go forth and redeem their dead.[1]

As Wilford Woodruff mentioned above in remarks he gave in 1882, two new temples would be constructed in the wake of the work now being done in St. George: the Logan and the Manti temples. But they would be built at a very steep price. Dark clouds were rushing the horizon, a perfect storm in fact, between a people bound and determined to hold on to their unique religious convictions, and a federal government implacable in its resolve to end once and for all the practice of plural marriage.

---

1. Wilford Woodruff, in *Journal of Discourses* 23:326–32, 10 December 1882.

"ON A STONE QUARRY HILL"—THE MANTI TEMPLE

The ink had scarcely dried on the newly transcribed ceremony of endowments for the dead at St. George when President Brigham Young announced the creation of several new stakes in Utah Territory and the temple plot dedication for the construction of two other temples—one in Sanpete County and the other in Cache County. Leaving St. George on 16 April 1877 for his home in Salt Lake City, an ailing but determined Brigham Young stopped off at Manti, Sanpete County, home to a large number of Scandinavian emigrants, to dedicate the temple site "on a stone quarry hill" previously selected.[2]

The Manti Temple began as a prophecy made by President Young in Ephraim in December 1873: "Before two years we will commence a Temple in San Pete County."[3] Four years later he dedicated the site on 25 April 1877 and appointed William H. Folsom superintendent of construction, who soon afterward became chief architect, replacing Joseph A. Young, who had passed away. As in St. George, "The rules of the United Order . . . were read and adopted for renewal of our covenants wherein all former washings and anointings were renewed."[4]

Remembered Daniel H. Wells, first president of the Manti Temple, of the groundbreaking ceremony: "I was present. . . . Little did I think then, and doubtless such a thought was foreign to all who were present on that occasion, that before these corner stones should be laid he [Brigham Young] would be [gone]; but so it is . . . that the work commenced by

---

2. Journal History, 16 April 1877. Brigham Young died 29 August 1877. The site for the Manti Temple had actually been located in the summer of 1875 with Joseph A. Young as original architect. "It was resolved" at a council meeting in Ephraim "that the pure in heart should build that temple." As with the Salt Lake Temple, Brigham Young identified where the Manti Temple was to be built. Abraham H. Cannon Diaries, 24 August 1890, MSS 62, Perry Special Collections, HBLL, BYU.
3. Brigham Young, Manti Temple Historical Record, 1:14, December 1873. Reference was also made in June 1875 to the same effect.
4. Brigham Young, Sevier Stake Miscellaneous Minutes, 1:101, 1 July 1875. Tradition has it that Brigham Young chose the site because the Angel Moroni had once dedicated it for such a building. Orson F. Whitney, *Life of Heber C. Kimball*, 436. However, few, if any, contemporary records corroborate such an assertion.

"THEY ARE AIMING A BLOW AT THE SEALING ORDINANCES"

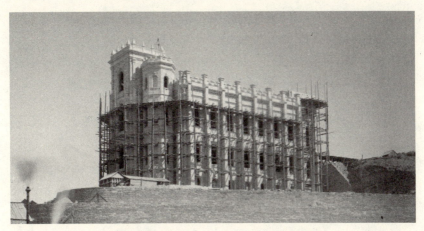

Manti Temple under construction, circa 1882.

the Prophet Joseph, he building upon the foundation thereof, still continues, and that it will continue henceforth and forever, the priesthood being without beginning of days and end of years."[5]

Situated at the point of a hill, the temple was literally built upon a rock—the Manti Stone Quarry—just northeast of the town of Manti and in large measure consisted of stone found at the site, cut and shaped for the temple itself. It took a great deal of time and effort to blast into the rock hill just to prepare a level surface for the foundation of the temple to be laid. One hundred and thirty men were working on the site in 1877/78, many working either as tithe laborers or volunteers to pay back indebtedness to the Perpetual Emigration Fund. With the site now levelled, the cornerstones were laid on 3 August 1878. Built of a buff-colored white limestone taken from nearby quarries, the completed structure measures 171 feet in length, 95 feet in width, and 79 feet high, with walls three and a half feet thick at the base. A tower at the east rises 179 feet high and the tower at the west is ten feet lower. Perhaps the most unique feature of the temple is its two circular stairways, located in the western towers, with their black walnut railings and which wind upward 151 steps. Having no central support,

---

5. Journal History, 14 November 1877.

the stairways represent a magnificent pioneer construction and find little parallel anywhere else in the nation. Under construction five years longer than anticipated because of the needed rock blasting and "tightness for means," the Manti Temple was finally dedicated in May 1888.[6]

"THE WORK IS STEADILY INCREASING" —THE LOGAN TEMPLE

Sensing the need to bring the temple nearer to the people in northern Utah and southern Idaho, President Young, though still unwell, also travelled to Logan, Cache County, where on 17 May 1877 he and others selected "a piece of table land immediately east of the city" overlooking the valley where he challenged the local Saints to build the proposed temple in five years.[7] Ever since the town of Logan had been settled in 1859, area residents had longed for a temple. Years before, Wilford Woodruff, in characteristic visionary language, had prophesied of "a glorious temple [being] built . . . upon the Logan Bench and while you stand in the tower of that Temple and your eyes survey this glorious valley filled with cities and village[s] occupied [with] tens of thousands of the Latter day Saints you will then call to mind this visitation."[8] The first official announcement that a temple would be built came on 6 October 1876 at the general conference of the Church at which time slightly over 10,000 people were

---

6. President Canute Peterson of the San Pete Stake, Sevier Stake Historical Record, 3:316, 23 May 1885. For worthy studies of the Manti Temple, see Victor J. Rasmussen, *The Manti Temple* (Provo, Utah: Community Press, 1988); Barbara Lee Hargis, "A Folk History of the Manti Temple: A Study of the Folklore and Traditions Connected with the Settlement of Manti, Utah, and the Building of the Temple" (master's thesis, Brigham Young University, 1968); Thomas Weston Welch, "Early Mormon Woodworking at Its Best: A Study of the Craftmanship in the First Temples of Utah" (master's thesis, Brigham Young University, 1983); and Glen R. Stubbs, "History of the Manti Temple" (master's thesis, Brigham Young University, 1960).
7. Brigham Young to Alfales Young, 12 October 1876, Brigham Young Letterpress Copybook. It may have been that Wilford Woodruff had even earlier, in 1863, prophesied of a future temple in Logan. "The day will come when your fathers and others have passed away, you will have the privilege of going into the towers of a glorious Temple, which will be built unto the name of the most High upon the Logan Bench east of us." Autobiography and Diary of Mary Ann Weston Maughan, 1817–1898, Digital History Collections, Utah State Merrill-Cazier University Libraries, Utah State University, Logan, Utah.
8. *Wilford Woodruff's Journal*, 22 August 1863. See reference to it in 8:246–48, 8 May 1884.

living in Cache Valley, many of whom were already making cash contributions to the St. George and Salt Lake temples.

Called to serve as first president of the Logan Temple was Marriner W. Merrill with Charles Ora Card appointed superintendent of construction and Truman O. Angell Jr. as architect. On 18 May 1877—at precisely 12 o'clock noon—the site was dedicated and groundbreaking occurred at the southeast corner. Orson Pratt offered the dedicatory prayer.[9] In his remarks that same day, Brigham Young said, "We have dedicated this spot of ground upon which we expect to erect a temple in which to administer the ordinances of the House of God. Into this house, when it is completed, we expect to enter to enjoy the blessings of the Priesthood and receive our anointings, our endowments and our sealings; and the brethren will be sealed to brethren to continue the links and make perfect the chain from ourselves to Father Adam."[10]

The first contract to be let out followed just days later on 29 May for the construction of a road through the canyon to allow for lumber and stone to be more easily transported to the temple site. The cornerstones were laid under the direction of John Taylor, president of the Quorum of the Twelve, on 19 September 1877, less than a month after the death of Brigham Young, with construction beginning very shortly thereafter. President Moses Thatcher of the Cache Stake in Logan reported that within a short time of the announcement of a proposed Logan Temple, the Cache Valley Stake contributed $22,213 towards its construction; from Bear Lake $7,428, and from Box Elder $4,275. By the end of 1877, the corresponding total figure of temple donations was $46,212.[11]

---

9. Journal History, 18 May 1877. A compelling reason to build a temple in northern Utah was to minimize the anxious waiting time and cost of young engaged couples who wanted to be sealed in either the Endowment House or in St. George. Brigham Young felt that engaged couples travelling alone posed unique challenges.
10. James E. Talmage, *House of the Lord*, 199. The first three presidents of the Manti Temple were Daniel H. Wells (1888–1891), Anton H. Lund (1891–1893), and John D. T. McAllister (1893–1906).
11. Moses Thatcher, Logan Utah Cache Stake General Minutes, 2:20, 3–4 November 1877, CR 1280 11; Moses Thatcher, Logan Utah Cache Stake General Minutes, 2:53, January 1878.

As in St. George and Manti, the Logan Temple was to be built upon the principles laid down in the United Order. It would also be accompanied by the construction of a nearby tabernacle. During construction, Charles W. Penrose spoke of the place of temples and families in a way seldom heard before. He referred to how temple work would foster unity among families. The labor spent in building the temple, he emphasized, was "all important to seek to pleasure union among our families," "as families [were] the foundation of a kingdom, and inasmuch as we pursue this course the reach of God, and his blessings would rest upon us, and the Saints behind the veil would operate with us, and accelerate the word of God."[12] This reference to temples and families inextricably connected is important as it foreshadowed a changing perspective, with the future emphasis on families and temple work in a way not heard previously. Elder Charles C. Rich alluded to the "many blessings bestowed upon us as a people since our settlement in these valleys; nowhere [had] he observed the same blessing bestowed upon any people."[13]

By the end of the year 1877, the walls of the foundation were raised to the level of the ground, and by the end of 1879 the north and south walls were up some fifty feet. In December of 1879, Orson Pratt contrasted the good spirit of sacrifice and devotion prevalent in building the temple to the rampant immoralities and intoxications so characteristic of building the railroads in the West.[14] As workers labored faithfully on the temple, "home missionaries" scoured the nearby valleys and communities to continue gathering donations for the temple.

Completed in just seven years, the dimensions of the five-story Logan Temple were 171 feet long, 95 feet wide, and 86 feet high at the square, with an octagonal tower at each corner one hundred feet high, with a large square tower at each end. The rock used in the building, brought

---

12. Charles W. Penrose, Logan Utah Cache Stake General Minutes, 2:99–100, 3 August 1878.
13. Charles C. Rich, Logan Utah Cache Stake General Minutes, 2:57, January/February 1878.
14. Orson Pratt, Logan Utah Cache Stake General Minutes, 2:41, 23 December 1877.

"THEY ARE AIMING A BLOW AT THE SEALING ORDINANCES"

The Logan Temple, circa 1884.

from nearby quarries, is a very hard limestone. The lumber, mainly red and white pine, came from the nearby Logan Canyon.[15]

President John Taylor, Young's successor, dedicated the Logan Temple on 17 May 1884, four years before the completion of the Manti Temple. During the balance of that year, 21,343 baptisms for the dead were performed in the Logan Temple with another 34,682 in 1885. The corresponding number of endowments for the dead for those first two years of operation stood at 10,022 and 16,709 respectively,[16] in praise of which temple president Marriner W. Merrill said, "The work is steadily increasing as the Saints are becoming acquainted with the nature of the work before them."[17]

Not to be outdone, Abraham O. Smoot, president of the Utah Stake, long-time mayor of Provo, wealthy benefactor and ardent defender of Brigham Young Academy, looked forward to the day when a temple would

---

15. Two workers died during construction of the temple, buried in an avalanche while working in the canyons. For more on the building of the Logan Temple, see Nolan Porter Olsen, *Logan Temple: The First 100 Years* (Logan, Utah: privately published, 1978).
16. Logan Temple Ordinance Statistics, Daily Register of Ordinance Work, Book A, Commencing 21st May 1884 Ending 31st December 1894," CR 308 19, Church History Library.
17. M. W. Merrill to William Budge, Logan Temple Letterpress Copybook, 5 June 1884, no. 10, 1884–1908, box 3, folder 4, CR 308 5, Church History Library.

be built in Utah County. "We are just beginning to have our eyes opened to the importance of this work. I look forward to the time when other temples will be completed throughout the valleys of these mountains," including one, he predicted, "on the beautiful plains north of this city [Provo]."[18] At one point Brigham Young, while visiting Provo in 1873, had spoken of the "propriety of building a temple in this [Utah] county."[19] In the meantime, Provo settled for building a much-beloved tabernacle and Smoot advised the people "to not cease their exertions to build Temples, and the Tabernacle as such works had a great influence and power in weakening the efforts of the enemy."[20]

Abraham Owen Smoot (1815–1895).

These new temples cemented in the minds of many how important temple work was becoming. "A gentleman who lately passed through San Pete County informed us *[the Deseret News]* that he never saw so great a unanimity of sentiment and action among any people, upon the accomplishment of any subject, as is being manifested in that locality in the matter of the Manti Temple. We understand a similar feeling and determination prevail in the northern part of the territory in relation to the

---

18. Abraham O. Smoot, Provo Utah Central Stake General Minutes, 31 May 1884, LR 9629 11. Smoot's prophecy came true with the dedication of the Provo Utah Temple on 9 February 1972 by President Joseph Fielding Smith who was eight years old at the time of Smoot's prediction.
19. Journal History, 1 June 1873.
20. Abraham O. Smoot, Provo Utah Central Stake General Minutes, 4 November 1882. The Provo Tabernacle served Utah County for over a hundred years until destroyed by fire in December 2010. It was replaced by the beautiful Provo City Center Temple, which was dedicated on 20 March 2016. See Susan Easton Black, Glenn Rawson, and Dennis Lyman, *The Story of the Provo City Center Temple, Commemorative Edition* (American Fork: Covenant Communications, 2015).

"THEY ARE AIMING A BLOW AT THE SEALING ORDINANCES"

Temple at Logan."[21] This temple-building fever captured the hearts and imaginations as well as the sacrifices of thousands. It was a case of the temples catching up to the people, i.e., that they were now being built closer to where the people were living throughout the Territory—an essential factor in explaining the growth of temple consciousness among the Latter-day Saints.

"WHERE WOULD WE BE WITHOUT A TEMPLE"

Local Church records show that, while hundreds of workers dedicated their time and labor to the building of these new temples, several thousand others gave of their money and means. And as with the building of the Nauvoo Temple, each new temple kept its own Book of the Law of the Lord in which the names of those who made contributions of time, money, and means were faithfully recorded. For instance, masons, quarry men, freighters, and carpenters came from Fayette, Salina, Richfield, Glenwood, Monroe, Annabella, Prattville, and from scores of other wards and communities to work on the Manti Temple in answer to the call for specifically trained laborers, often for weeks or even months at a time of donated labor, and with tools they themselves usually furnished.[22] In return, the members of the various United Orders and wards supplied the workers with the necessary grains, vegetables, and other needed commodities.

Church headquarters levied each stake in the four newly drawn temple districts with a "large appropriation" or assessment "debt" to be paid in cash or by contributions in kind. Each adult within each stake was asked to donate fifty cents monthly, and this at a time when bread cost four cents a loaf and a common laborer's wages in New York were ninety cents a day.[23] As seen in Figure 7, the kinds of donations were long and varied,

---

21. *Deseret News*, 20 June 1877.
22. Sevier Stake Historical Record, 2:75, 7 November 1874.
23. Sevier Stake Historical Record, 4:52, 26 February 1881; also 4:237, 24 September 1882. For wages, see the [San Francisco] *Daily Evening Bulletin*, 9 February 1878, no. 106. Solicitations were made for funds throughout each district, as per the following: "This is to certify that Bishops George Farn[s]worth and Elder Cyrus H. Wheelock are duly appointed to travel in the Manti Temple District to preach the Gospel and receive donations and receipt for the same in behalf of

> St. George Temple Donations, 1870s–1900
>
> Potatoes, mutton, "home goods," oats, leather, flour, cabbage, dried apples, molasses, coffee, butter, pottery ware, onions, quilts, tobacco, pork, shoes, peas, socks, hay, cheese, apples, cucumbers, honey, chickens, peaches, wine, melons, flannel, barley, wheat, soap, eggs, salt, tallow, eggs, yarn, corn, guarding hours, carrots, fish, brooms, blacksmithing services, beef, preserves, grapes, days of labor.

Figure 7: St. George Temple Donations in Kind.

with everything from potatoes, cabbage, and dried apples, to quilts, coffee, tobacco, and blacksmithing services.[24] Apostle Lorenzo Snow even advised the sisters to devote the proceeds of the sale of their "Sunday eggs" to the construction effort.[25] Sister Nancy Clark of Farmington, Utah, "produced, prepared, reeled, and put in condition for the loom, the silk for the first dress piece of that material ever manufactured in Utah." The fabric was silver gray and cost forty-five dollars.[26] Because of these sacrifices, a widespread and deepening sense of temple building grasped the Saints, to the point that A. K. Thurber, counselor in the Sevier Stake presidency, could say: "With all our institutions and commandments we have received, where would we be without a temple wherein we can receive blessings in behalf of our dead."[27]

In fact, the emphasis on and payment of tithing increased in direct proportion to the rising consciousness of temple worship. Said Franklin Spencer at an 1882 Sevier Stake conference: "There is no man worthy of

---

the Manti Temple, and we cheerfully recommend them to the Presidents of Stakes, Bishops of the several wards, and all the Saints." W. H. Folsom to "Whom It May Concern," Manti Temple Letterpress Copybook, 1(5 December 1877–24 June 1885), 5 November 1880. The request for a fifty cent per day donation was something of an admission that tithing contributions alone were not covering all the costs. "If the full tithing of the people was paid there would be no need of any further calls upon the people of a financial character." A. O. Smoot, Provo Utah Central Stake General Minutes, 4 March 1882.

24. St. George Temple Donation Records, 1873–1901, CR 343 1, Church History Library.
25. St. George Stake General Minutes, 1 June 1885.
26. Mary Eliza Crosby Waddington Journal and Reminiscences, 1840–1889, MS 20159, Church History Library.
27. A. K. Thurber, Sevier Stake Historical Record, 4:240, 8 October 1882.

"THEY ARE AIMING A BLOW AT THE SEALING ORDINANCES"

going into the Temple of the Lord to receive him a wife unless he pays his tithing. . . . We may expect our enemies to continue to persecute us and pass laws against this people, unless we pay our tithing. We need not expect the Lord to help us unless we carry out his law."[28]

Figure 8 is a representation of how pervasive financial contributions became. These figures, taken from the records of the Utah Central Stake, which stake was some distance removed from any one of the temples, show the number of "temple donors" as of August 1877 as compared to tithe payers. In this then-typical stake, with a membership of over 11,500, there were 2,685 families. Of these, 2,122 were tithe payers (79 percent) and 1,362 were also temple donors (almost 50 percent). If such figures hold for the other stakes, half the families of the Church were donating at least some amount of cash to temple building projects in addition to their tithing donations. Such sacrifices illustrate the widespread growth in temple sacrifice and awareness among the Latter-day Saints in the 1870s and 1880s.

Ward	Families	Baptisms	Marriages	Tithe Payers	Temple Donors	Total Members
Provo 1st	135	41	2	159	126	543
Provo 2nd	81	4	—	78	55	323
Provo 3rd	85	17	2	53	37	328
Provo 4th	147	66	2	125	40	662
Provo 5th	34	7	—	15	30	144
Springville	318	18	—	234	214	1,152
Spanish Fork	346	56	1	315	65	1,473
Salem	85	6	1	43	31	416
Payson	357	40	5	243	212	1,701
Spring Lake	20	2	—	20	20	90
Santaquin	125	36	—	110	102	494
Cedar Valley	87	47	—	57	85	388
Lehi	224	24	4	181	64	851
Alpine	49	2	—	55	30	262

---

28. Franklin Spencer, Sevier Stake Historical Record, 4:230, 27 August 1882.

Ward	Families	Baptisms	Marriages	Tithe Payers	Temple Donors	Total Members
Amer. Fork	244	56	2	157	35	1,221
Goshen	74	—	—	65	48	245
Pl. Grove	264	74	5	212	168	1,210
TOTALS	**2,685**	**496**	**24**	**2,122**	**1,362**	**11,513**

Figure 8: August 1877 Statistical Report of the Utah Central Stake of Zion (Utah County)

Precisely what percentage of the total costs of temple construction was met by these private donations of the Saints is not known; however, it was substantial. By the middle of 1881, over half a million dollars had been donated with much more to come.[29]

"WE ARE NOT GOING TO DESERT THE KINGDOM OF GOD"

As we have seen, a host of reasons—the canonization of revelation, the dramatic increase in baptisms for the dead, the introduction of endowments for the dead, the building of four new temples—pointed to a new era in temple worship and devotion. There would never again be a retreat from the paramount place temples were coming to occupy in Latter-day Saint doctrine, thought, and practice. Many, young and old, longed to serve in the temple as they had never done before, including Thomas Bullock, well remembered as the chief clerk of the vanguard company of Saints to the Valley but now in his declining years. "I do not want to die," he wrote, "until I have been baptized for or seen attended to, the ordinances to set free 4 or 5000 souls, altho' it may take me five years to do it, then I can welcome death to pass me through the door to Joseph, Hyrum, Willard, and all my old friends holding the Priesthood: then I will have my jubilee, and realize the meaning of Joseph's words, something that will do me good, something that will prove a comfort to me in my old age."[30]

---

29. *Wilford Woodruff's Journal*, 8:23, 4 April 1881.
30. Thomas Bullock to Edward Hunter, Thomas Bullock Collection 1830–1939, 9 August 1881, MS 27307, Church History Library. Bullock died four years later, in 1885.

"THEY ARE AIMING A BLOW AT THE SEALING ORDINANCES"

However, this rise in temple consciousness came in direct relation to the increasing intensity of government-sponsored raids against plural marriage throughout the Territory. Inasmuch as President Wilford Woodruff would one day place the painful dilemma facing the Latter-day Saints as fundamentally a choice between saving the temples or continuing to live plural marriage, we must here pause and take more than a mere cursory look at the "principle" of plural marriage. More to the point, we must explore why the enduring commitment to it.

It may prove challenging to the modern Latter-day Saint reader to comprehend fully the commitment of the nineteenth-century Church to this practice. Since the Manifesto of 1890 (see the following chapter) the practice has been discontinued by the same spirit of revelation that originated it and is now subject to Church discipline and excommunication. As President Gordon B. Hinckley said in general conference in 1998: "More than a century ago God clearly revealed unto His prophet Wilford Woodruff that the practice of plural marriage should be discontinued, which means that it is now against the law of God. Even in countries where civil or religious law allows polygamy, the Church teaches that marriage must be monogamous and does not accept into its membership those practicing plural marriage."[31] What was right in one time, place, and circumstance may very well not be acceptable in another. Nevertheless, the allegiance to this principle evidenced the faith of the Saints to follow counsel and to obey their leaders. In the end, what they finally sacrificed to preserve the temples manifests unparalleled devotion to the rising cause of redemption for the dead on a scale never before witnessed.

In the face of mounting political pressure, jolting Supreme Court decisions, and recurring opposition, the Saints held firm. Just as the federal government was expanding civil rights to former black slaves in the wake of the Civil War, it was also taking careful aim at punishing the Confederate South. Coming within a vote of impeaching President

---

31. Gordon B. Hinckley, "What Are People Asking about Us?" *Ensign*, November 1998, 71.

Andrew Johnson for his perceived defense of Southern rights and privileges, Congress passed one punitive law after another upon the South, imposing military rule throughout the region, disenfranchising former Confederate soldiers, barring them from holding federal office and serving on juries, and imposing "carpetbagger" governors and other federal officers on Southern states. To recoin Lincoln's phrase, it was almost "with malice towards some, and charity for few." The "wave the bloody shirt" election of Ulysses S. Grant in 1868, former leading general of the Union forces during the Civil War, solidified in the minds of many a country more bent on punishing the South than on reconciling. And for those who had "eyes to see and ears to hear," once slavery had been abolished and the South fittingly punished, Congress would inevitably turn its attention to that other "twin relic of barbarism" in the West.[32]

The government of the United States had made it abundantly clear for several years that the Territory of Utah would never become part of the Union so long as the Church continued its practice of polygamy, which had been officially announced in conference in 1852. Johnston's Army of 1857 had also been an expression of government insistence against plural marriage and had not the Civil War intervened, the matter would likely have come to a head much sooner than it did. Both Democratic and Republican administrations recognized the nation's abhorrence of the practice as an affront to traditional family values and, perhaps more important, the positive political dividends to themselves for attacking it.

The first fire bell in the night rang in 1862 when Congress passed the Morrill Anti-Bigamy Act. This three-pronged act levied penalties against anyone practicing bigamy or plural marriage, annulled the Utah territorial legislature's incorporation of the Church, and limited the value of real estate the Church could acquire or hold to $50,000. Any piece of real estate worth more than that figure could be confiscated by the government.

---

32. John A. Wills, "The Twin Relics of Barbarism," *Historical Society of Southern California, Los Angeles*, 1, no. 5 (1890), 40–44.

"THEY ARE AIMING A BLOW AT THE SEALING ORDINANCES"

Although aimed at plural marriage, the Morrill Act also took aim at what many believed was an "unrepublican," imperialistic corporate ecclesiastical structure exercising excessive economic power in the West. However, Lincoln chose not to enforce it believing that it was better to court the support of the Latter-day Saints during the Civil War than to make enemies of them. This hands-off attitude won him the respect of many in Utah Territory who genuinely mourned his assassination in 1865.[33]

Soon after his election, President Grant launched a judicial crusade against the Latter-day Saints with the appointment of Chief Justice James B. McKean, a New York lawyer long associated with Republican party opposition to polygamy. Zealously accepting his assignment to root out polygamy by strictly enforcing the law, McKean pursued a most ambitious strategy. This included allowing US marshals to impanel juries thereby preventing local members from jury duty, a practice many in government felt was a source of local power. McKean also aimed at multiplying convictions and prison sentences, and granting citizenship to new arrivals only if they pledged to abide by the Anti-Bigamy Law of 1862. He even went so far as to deny American citizenship to those who had taken plural wives before the Morrill law was passed. Removed from office after a turbulent four-year tenure, McKean proved a thorn in the Church's side.

Things only intensified in the 1870s as Washington continued to tighten its grip. In 1874, Congress passed the Poland bill, which placed the judiciary firmly in federal hands. It did so by providing federal courts a monopoly over both criminal and most civil cases and by curtailing the jurisdiction of territorial probate courts that had existed on the local level since 1849 and which had generally been presided over by local officials, mostly bishops. This bill also changed the process for choosing jurors, opening the door for easier prosecution of polygamy in the federal courts

---

33. Mary Jane Woodger, "Abraham Lincoln and the Mormons," in *Civil War Saints*, 76–77.

of Utah while likewise making provision for any cases of polygamy or bigamy to be appealed to the United States Supreme Court.[34]

That same year England-born George Reynolds, an avowed polygamist and private secretary to Brigham Young, allowed himself to be arrested in something of a test case to settle the question of the constitutionality of the Morrill Anti-Bigamy Act. Voluntarily giving evidence against himself, Reynolds was found guilty of bigamy but his conviction was overturned on a technicality by the Utah Territorial Supreme Court. In October 1875 he was indicted a second time for violating the Morrill Act, with the trial resulting in another guilty verdict. He was subsequently sentenced to two years' hard labor and a $500 fine. When the territorial supreme court this time upheld the conviction, the Church appealed to the United States Supreme Court which, to the stunning surprise and alarm of Church leaders, eventually upheld the lower court's decision in January 1879, thereby affirming the constitutionality of the Anti-Bigamy Act on the narrow grounds that the First Amendment protected only religious belief, not conduct.

Although the Supreme Court's ruling came as a severe blow, its immediate impact was limited. The louder the opposition from women's groups, Protestant ministries, and a phalanx of eastern politicians, the more firmly did the Saints cling to their faith. Believing that freedom of religion was a constitutional right and that as per the First Amendment "Congress shall make no law respecting an establishment of religion, or prohibiting the free exercise thereof," the Latter-day Saints, in acts of rare defiance to law, exercised a degree of civil disobedience in "render[ing] unto Caesar the things that are Caesar's and unto God the things that are God's." President John Taylor, Brigham Young's successor, and a fierce defender of the practice of plural marriage to the day he died, made his stance abundantly clear when in 1879 he said the following:

---

34. Edwin Brown Firmage and Richard Collin Mangrum, *Zion in the Courts: A Legal History of the Church of Jesus Christ of Latter-day Saints, 1830–1900* (Urbana and Chicago: University of Illinois Press, 1988), 148–49.

"THEY ARE AIMING A BLOW AT THE SEALING ORDINANCES"

George Quayle Cannon (center, seated) serving time in the Sugarhouse Prison, circa 1888.

We acknowledge our children, we acknowledge our wives, we have no mistresses. We had no prostitution until it was introduced by monogamy, and I am told that these other diabolical deeds are following in its train. The courts have protected these people in their wicked practices. We repudiate all such things, and hence I consider that a system that will enable a man to carry out his professions, and that will enable him to acknowledge his wife or wives and acknowledge and provide for his children and wives, is much more honorable than that principle which violates its married relations, and, whilst hypocritically professing to be true to its pledges, recklessly violates the same and tramples upon every principle of honor.[35]

Congress then passed yet another punitive law—the Edmunds Act of 1882—designed to "put teeth" into the 1862 Morrill law. Signed into

---

35. *The Supreme Court Decision in the Reynolds Case: Interview between President John Taylor and O. J. Hollister,* reported by G. F. Gibbs (Salt Lake City, n.p., 1879), 4, 7, as cited in Allen and Leonard, *The Story of the Latter-day Saints* (1992), 399–400.

law by President Chester A. Arthur on 22 March, this act dramatically simplified and expedited the prosecution of polygamy. It defined polygamy as a crime, abolished the need to prove polygamous marriages by creating a new and much easier way to prosecute the offense called "unlawful cohabitation," and provided punishment for polygamy with fines of up to $500 and five years in prison and for unlawful cohabitation with fines of up to $300 and six months imprisonment. No longer would one have to prove polygamy; just the appearance of it could lead to arrest for cohabitation. It also disenfranchised and barred from public office anyone guilty of living in polygamy or unlawful cohabitation, and forbade any polygamist or "co-hab" from jury service. This harsh new law also established a "Utah Commission" of five men to help enforce provisions of the new act and to oversee future elections. In short order the Commission disenfranchised 12,000–14,000 Latter-day Saints and disqualified them from voting without benefit of trial.[36]

John Taylor (1808–1887).

The Edmunds Act ushered in that ugly period known as "the Raid Era," a veritable crusade in which marshals combed both city and countryside by day and by night, often in disguise as census takers or peddlers, in order to "catch" the unwary, to force wives to testify against their husbands, even to force children to speak against their parents. Birthday parties and family gatherings often turned into inquisitions, ten- and twenty-dollar bounties were offered for certain men captured, and a spirit of fear and

---

36. Firmage and Mangrum, *Zion in the Courts*, 160–67. Three years later, in 1885, the Idaho Territorial Legislature passed a law containing the notorious "Idaho Test Oath," which disenfranchised practically all members of the Church, whether or not polygamists, by requiring them either to swear they did not believe in or belong to a church that believed in plural marriage, or to lose their voting rights. This law was upheld by the United States Supreme Court in February 1890.

"THEY ARE AIMING A BLOW AT THE SEALING ORDINANCES"

suspicion spread everywhere. Almost any contact between a man and his supposed spouse was viewed as cohabitation or at least the presumption of cohabitation.

In response, families devised secret identification codes and practices to alert others of advancing marshals and associated spies and informers. Many men went into hiding in barns and fields, byways and forests, or fled to various other hiding places. Often their wives and families were left in the most destitute circumstances. Some families even devised mirror reflection signs to alert neighboring towns of prowling marshals. Wilford Woodruff, to avoid detection, went into the wilderness of Arizona's San Francisco Mountains for months at a time. When infrequently back in St. George, he even slept in an upper room of the St. George Temple to avoid detection.[37] When his wife, Phebe, died in 1885, to avoid detection he sadly watched through the window as the hearse and funeral cortege carried his wife's remains to the cemetery.

The Edmunds Act led several families to seek refuge beyond the borders of the United States where parts of their families could be relocated without breaking the law. The movement into Mexico first began from the Arizona settlements in February 1885. Under the direction of Edward A. Noble, many moved into the state of Chihuahua, eventually settling in beautiful Colonia Juárez. President John Taylor, who had been converted in eastern Canada so many years before, felt that members might also be better treated north of the border than in the United States. Hence he called Charles O. Card, president of the Cache Valley Stake, to lead a group of hardy pioneers to southern Alberta where in 1887 they located a settlement on Lee's Creek, a tributary of St. Mary's River. The remarkable success of that pioneering effort and the growth of the Church in western Canada led to the Cardston Temple eventually being dedicated there in 1923.

---

37. It is true that some sought refuge and safety in the temples during the height of the Raid Era. However, no marshals ever gained entrance into any one of them, so far as is known. Rumors that have persisted for years that giant Nephite warriors posted guard at the entrance to the Logan and other temples are the stuff of mythology and are without factual historical corroboration.

Yet defiantly, Church membership and leaders stood firm. Anna Ivins of St. George said in meeting that "She did not fear the Commissioners nor the Edmunds Bill! For they could only do what the Lord wanted them to do."[38] "The whole United States Government [is] united at war against us," Woodruff recorded at the end of 1885. "The Edmunds Bill take[s] away all the civil, political and religious rights of the Latter-day Saints and nothing but the God of Heaven can save us. But the God of Heaven will save his people and protect his Church, Zion and Kingdom and fight the battles of his Saints and destroy our enemies. . . . The hour of God's judgment has come. Let our Nation prepare for that which awaits her."[39]

This judicial witch hunt, what many called a "reign of terror," was painfully successful and led to the arrest and imprisonment of over 1,300 otherwise law-abiding co-habs, plus several women for contempt of court for refusing to answer questions relative to their marital status. Many of those arrested, faithful as they were to practicing plural marriage, were Church leaders at the local levels. Because of overcrowding conditions in Sugar Creek prison in Salt Lake City, some were sent to prison in far-away Detroit, Michigan. George Q. Cannon and some other General Authorities "served time" also. Even President Taylor, a man without a home but a prophet still among his people, went into hiding, moving from house to house and from friend to friend for much of the last two and a half years of his life. Such disappointments and disruptions led to his declining health and in large measure resulted in his death in a Kaysville hiding place just fifteen miles north of Salt Lake City on 25 July 1887.

"WE SHOULD NOT GIVE IT UP"

Convinced that their conflict with America was a "war" to defend their faith and a sure sign of the impending apocalypse, the faithful stoutly defended plural marriage. As one local leader put it: "We have signaled the

---

38. Anna Ivins, St. George Utah Stake Relief Society Minutes and Records, 7 September 1882.
39. *Wilford Woodruff's Journal*, 8:351, 31 December 1885.

flag of our enemy and we should prepare for action."[40] While the percentage of new plural marriages declined significantly in the 1880s relative to the percentages in the 1850s, historian Kathryn Daynes has well argued that "decline, however dramatic, is not demise" and that while the percentage of Latter-day Saints practicing plural marriage may have gradually decreased in the 1870s and 1880s, the actual numbers of those practicing it definitely increased. Furthermore, the belief in the divine origin of plural marriage "united Mormons in a way that transcended differences in practice and set them apart from other Americans." Daynes asserts that while the relative decline of new plural marriages made accepting the Manifesto easier for younger generations, "the institution was still vigorous during the raids in the 1880s and took a long time to die even after the Manifesto."[41] Historian Jan Shipps claims that the Saints identified themselves as a people set apart and "were willing to defend to the last possible moment the practice of polygamy" to maintain that difference.[42]

And St. George was undoubtedly the community most committed to living the principle. Lowell C. Bennion has argued that because so many faithful Saints had been called to settle there starting in 1861, they were especially obedient to the call to marry plurally. Close to 30 percent of St. George husbands had more than one wife, and in 1870, when the St. George Temple was announced, 45 percent of all residents in St. George and surrounding towns and villages lived in plural marriage households (as parents, children, etc.). That figure held fairly firm throughout the decade.[43] Kathryn Daynes also shows that the building of the temple itself increased to some extent "in-migration" of polygamous marriages. "The relationship between the temple and prevalence of polygyny was direct

---

40. Franklin Spencer, Sevier Stake Historical Record, 4:205, 28 May 1882.
41. Kathryn M. Daynes, *More Wives than One: Transformation of the Mormon Marriage System, 1840–1910* (Urbana: University of Illinois: Press, 2001), 174; see also 102 and 105.
42. Jan Shipps, *Mormonism: The Story of a New Religious Tradition* (Chicago and Urbana: University of Illinois Press, 1987), 125.
43. Lowell C. Bennion, "Mapping the Extent of Plural Marriage in St. George, 1861–1880," *BYU Studies* 51, no. 4 (Winter 2012): 27–45. Bleak put the figure as high as 50 percent. Bennion, "Plural Marriage in St. George," 29.

and significant" but not "dramatic."[44] It is not possible, from available temple records, to show what percentage of temple sealings were of the plural marriage variety, since one's marriage status was generally not recorded, but from 1877 to 1888 a good many likely were.[45]

Despite the relative statistical decline in new plural marriages in the 1870s and 1880s, and perhaps because of it, private journals and local Church records are peppered with spirited defenses of the practice. "It is the duty of every Elder in Israel to take to himself wives, and raise up a righteous family," Erastus Snow said in St. George in 1882, "and shame on the man that does not do it. If I have a son that will go back on my testimony in relation to plural marriage, I will cast him off from my family and disown him. I advise the Elders of Israel to take wives, I mean plural wives . . . and all men who fight it will sink."[46] Angus M. Cannon, president of the Salt Lake Stake, said in regards to the principle, "Of course there were extenuating circumstances, but we were not called upon to make exceptions" and that those who "would break through the traditions of their fathers and receive this principle would become the rulers in the midst of Israel." [47]

While it is true that a majority of the Saints did not live in plural marriage, and not all were asked to practice or were expected to live plural marriage, the numbers who did so are nevertheless impressive. "Probably half" of those living in Utah Territory in 1857 "experienced life in a polygamous family" in one way or another as a husband, wife, or child. By 1870, that figure had fallen to "25 to 30 percent" of the population with the percentage decreasing annually.[48] Two-thirds of polygamous men had

---

44. "Both economic and religious reasons reinforced St. George's commitment to the Church and its leaders, which in turn strengthened their commitment to plural marriage." Kathryn M. Daynes, "Striving to Live the Principle in Utah's First Temple City," *BYU Studies* 51, no. 4 (Winter 2012): 75 and 80. Daynes also shows that the prevalence of plural marriage in Manti was also high, though not at the same levels as St. George. Daynes, "Striving to Live the Principle," 70.
45. The number of new plural marriages in St. George actually increased from 1877 to 1880. Daynes, "Striving to Live the Principle," 73–75.
46. David John Diaries, 1:396, 27 October 1882.
47. Angus M. Cannon, Salt Lake Stake General Minutes, 28 December 1881.
48. "Plural Marriage and Families in Early Utah," Gospel Topic Essays, 2014, https://www.lds.org/topics/plural-marriage-and-families-in-early-utah?lang=eng (accessed 4 October 2018).

only two wives at a time. Because of the nearly equal sex ratio, plural marriage could never have been practiced by everyone. Indeed, one of the only reasons it continued was the tradition of older men marrying younger women of the next generation.[49]

Polygamy, as practiced by the Saints, was not bigamy where one spouse does not know of the other(s) but was authorized marriages and most often required the permission of the first wife. Permission of the President of the Church was necessary for the performance of such plural marriages although in some cases, the President of the Church asked or assigned men to take plural wives. Women were free to choose their spouses and divorce was surprisingly more lenient and more freely granted than some might have assumed. The per capita inequality of wealth diminished as economically disadvantaged women married into more financially stable households. Ethnic intermarriages also increased as so many new converts migrating to Zion came from Scandinavia. Plural marriage also led to the birth of a much larger number of children overall in the Territory than what would have been if this principle had not been in place.[50] And sociologists and historians generally agree that such marriages were based "more on religious belief than on romantic love." While there were abuses of the practice, it certainly was a call to sacrifice and unselfishness and required the total allegiance of those who lived it, women and men.

"A PART AND PORTION OF OUR FAITH"

So why this unbending commitment to plural marriage, to what some referred to as "the capstone" of their faith? While it bears repeating that monogamy was ever the "prevalent marriage form in Utah," even in

---

49. Daynes, "Striving to Live the Principle," 71.
50. "Plural Marriage and Families in Early Utah." For further study on the topic of plural marriage among the Saints between 1852 and 1890, see Laurel Thatcher Ulrich, *A House Full of Females: Plural Marriage and Women's Rights in Early Mormonism: 1835–1870* (New York: Alfred A. Knopf, 2017); Kathryn M. Daynes, *More Wives than One*; Thomas G. Alexander, *Mormonism in Transition: A History of the Latter-day Saints, 1890–1930*. (Urbana: University of Illinois Press, 1986); and Jessie L. Embry, *Mormon Polygamous Families: Life in the Principle* (Salt Lake City: Greg Kofford Books, 2008).

communities like St. George where the rate of plural marriages was higher than anywhere else,[51] it was nevertheless clear that a faithful member, and certainly anyone holding responsible positions within the Church, was expected to uphold the principle. And this expectation only increased in light of rising persecution. As George Q. Cannon said: plural marriage "was a law obligatory upon all; and that while some men may receive the celestial glory who had only one wife and who had no wife at all even, still there must be a willingness on the part of all to receive and put in practice that doctrine and law."[52]

First of all, it was essentially a matter of covenant, indissolubly interwoven in the minds of many with their hopes of eternal salvation. Those who had entered into plural marriage had done so in what they firmly believed was within the bonds of marriage. "Did not every man and woman covenant that all they had was on the altar? Let us try to save ourselves. He that does the will of his Father has power."[53] Thus there was a marital duty and a covenant responsibility to fulfill.

Second, many rooted the practice in the very early history of the Church and with Joseph Smith himself. Joseph F. Smith, later sixth President of the Church and nephew of the founding prophet, insisted that Joseph Smith had revealed it as early as 1831 and had taken several wives in Nauvoo, though his wife, Emma, had sometimes objected. The essential doctrine was "the eternity of the marriage covenant and it included a plurality of wives" and that "all who become heirs of God and joint heirs of Christ must obey this law or they cannot enter in the fullness."[54] Abraham O. Smoot testified "in plain and simple language that Joseph Smith did teach them the doctrine of plurality of wives, and that he was the first man that taught them the same and advocated it in their

---

51. Daynes, "Striving to Live the Principle," 73.
52. George Q. Cannon Journals, 13 August 1879.
53. Henry Mitchell, St. George Utah Melchizedek Priesthood Minutes and Records, 28 July 1877.
54. Joseph F. Smith, 4 March 1883. See also remarks by Joseph F. Smith, General Minutes of the Provo Utah Central Stake, 27 February 1881, LR 9629 11.

"THEY ARE AIMING A BLOW AT THE SEALING ORDINANCES"

Living the principle of eternal marriage.
Left to right: Sarah Russen Kirkham (1857–1929), George Kirkham (1852–1923), Mary Russen Kirkham (1855–1942); the Russen women were sisters.

hearing."[55] And from Wilford Woodruff: "If the Prophet Joseph had refused the revelation on Celestial marriage, the Church would have stopped there."[56] Thus their history demanded it of them.

Third, the faithful viewed celestial marriage as a command of God, essentially one given "to raise up seed." Orson Pratt's famous August 1852 sermon explaining and defending the practice had made clear that it was "a part and portion" of the faith, that it was the means of fulfilling the Lord's charge to Adam and Eve "to multiply and replenish the earth." Furthermore, it was part of the Abrahamic Covenant, and that through

---

55. Abraham O. Smoot, General Minutes of Provo Utah Central Stake, 26–27 February 1881, LR 9629 11 Part 2. Bishop Dennison L. Harris of Monroe recalled how as a boy he had heard Joseph Smith "declare earnestly and in tears" that God had "revealed to him the principle of Celestial marriage, and said that he and his people must accept this principle or be damned: his enemies threatened to kill him if he did." Dennison L. Harris, Sevier Stake Historical Record, 3:19, 23 August 1879.
56. Wilford Woodruff, General Minutes of Provo Utah Central Stake, 1 August 1875, LR 9629 11.

"a plurality of wives" a "numerous and faithful posterity can be raised up." And since the world was giving in to immorality, prostitution, and corruption, "among the Saints is the most likely place for those [noble, pre-existent] spirits to take their tabernacles."[57] Even before Elder Orson Pratt's 1852 public announcement, many were teaching the need to obey it. "Beware of opposing the Principle," warned one local stake leader to a priesthood gathering in Manti in 1851. "A curse would follow those who would oppose that principle," he said, and then went on to show "the effect of opposing any principle which God has revealed."[58]

Furthermore, some taught it as a requirement for entrance into the highest degree of the celestial kingdom. "Some people have supposed that the doctrine of plural marriage was a sort of superfluity," said Joseph F. Smith in Salt Lake City in 1878, "or non-essential to the salvation or exaltation of mankind. In other words, some of the Saints have said, and believed, that a man with one wife, sealed to him by the authority of the Priesthood for time and eternity, will receive an exaltation as great and glorious, if he is faithful, as he possibly could with more than one. I want here to enter my solemn protest against this idea, for I know it is false."[59]

Certainly it had been emphasized as a commandment during the Mormon Reformation of 1856 when the number of new plural marriages reached an all-time high in relation to the population.[60] Zina B. Young, speaking in Logan, "bore testimony to the truth of the Gospel and knew that polygamy was true and that an angel with a drawn sword appeared to

---

57. Orson Pratt, in *Journal of Discourses*, 1:53–66, 29 August 1852, as recorded by G. D. Watt. In a later sermon given in 1859, Pratt returned to much the same theme. Ironically no other book of scripture, he said, so condemns the practice as does the Book of Mormon. "But even that sacred book makes an exception in substance as follows—'Except I the Lord command my people.'" Orson Pratt, in *Journal of Discourses*, 6:351, 24 July 1859.
58. President Isaac Morley, Manti Ward General Minutes, 17–18, 19 January 1851, LR 5253 11.
59. Joseph F. Smith, *Deseret Evening News*, 7 July 1878; see also "History of the Church" 63:2498.
60. In an 1857 letter to George A. Smith, Wilford Woodruff reported as follows: "We have had a great reformation this winter; some of the fruits are . . . all have been baptized from the Presidency down; all are trying to pay their tithing and nearly all are trying to get wives, until there is hardly a girl 14 years old in Utah, but what is married, or just going to be. President Young has hardly time to eat, drink, or sleep, in consequence of marrying the people and attending to the endowments." Journal History 2, 1 April 1857.

"THEY ARE AIMING A BLOW AT THE SEALING ORDINANCES"

Joseph and commanded him to enter into it. [She] alluded to the fact that many of the sisters jeered at this doctrine, [but] if they knew what they were doing, they would not do so."[61] Hannah Romney, speaking in a St. George Relief Society meeting, referred to the "stir" then being made in the courts. "Said all who had ever had the Spirit of God should know that it is a command from God and where practiced in righteousness would bring comfort and happiness to those who embraced it."[62] It was, as many phrased it, "the path of our duty"[63] and "we should not give it up."[64]

Furthermore, many viewed polygamy as a divinely sanctioned means of their spiritual refinement, a sacred test of their allegiance to the kingdom of God no matter whence or where the opposition. "The hand of God is in the crusade that has been instituted against us," said Wilford Woodruff. "In fact we have not had persecution enough to make us sufficiently humble and to unite us as we should be."[65] And from another, "It is my firm opinion, that the Lord will not permit our oppressors to go beyond what is essential to purify his people, and bring us into line to magnify our callings in the Priesthood, and to bear off the kingdom victorious before all men."[66] And no matter the challenges, their duty and responsibility was to live it, despite every cost.

Others saw it as evidence of their being the chosen generation of God, a peculiar people with a special, albeit unpopular, commission. Said David John, "the Latter-day Saints are the favored ones of the Lord and therefore despised and contended against by the adversary of all good and his emissaries."[67] And for some others it was a matter of pride in doing what some even in their own midst criticized, a necessary passport to Church leadership and the one proven way to preserve their religious legacy. "Many of

---

61. Zina B. Young, Logan Utah Cache Stake Minutes, 2:67, 10 January 1878.
62. Hannah H. Romney, St. George Relief Society Minutes and Records, 6 February 1879.
63. President Daniel D. McArthur, St. George Utah Stake General Minutes, 16, 15 November 1885, LR 7836 11.
64. President W. H. Segmiller, Sevier Stake Historical Record, 4:73, 8 May 1881.
65. Wilford Woodruff, St. George Utah Stake General Minutes, 16, 14 June 1885.
66. David John Diaries, 1:494, 7 May 1885.
67. David John, Provo Utah Central Stake General Minutes, 1 September 1882.

our leaders are passing away," said Bishop John H. Smith at Provo in May 1877. "Are the young Elders preparing themselves for positions of trust and honor? Some are seeking to hide their parentage from the world—ashamed of being polygamous children. That is not my position. I am truly proud of it."[68] Apostle Brigham Young Jr. had little patience for those Latter-day Saints who ducked their responsibility, chose not to take plural wives and let their fellow members take the brunt for doing so. "We are passing through an ordeal," he said. "Some of the brethren say . . . 'Well, it is a pretty good thing, is it not . . . that I did not take another wife?' If I were to tell what I feel, I would say that this Kingdom would never have been established if it had not been for the polygamists. There never would have been a temple built; and if any man who is a monogamist receives a blessing in the Temple of God, he receives it because polygamists bless him there."[69]

Others were of the conviction that their obedience to this law would save and sanctify not only themselves but also the very nation opposed to them and be the means of preserving the Constitution. W. H. Segmiller spoke on the "destiny" of this people and that "no weapon formed against Zion would prosper. We should adhere steadfastly to this principle notwithstanding the opposition of Congress—that the time would come when Deseret would step forth and save the Constitution."[70] And from A. K. Thurber of the Sevier Stake: "We will plead and contend, for our rights as citizens until we [as] Latter-day Saints step forward and save the Constitution."[71] Thus adherence to the principle was for many both a spiritual refinement personally and an urgent responsibility politically.

And for a few it was one of the last signs of the times leading up to the

---

68. John A. Smith, Provo Utah Central Stake General Minutes, 6 May 1877.
69. Brigham Young Jr., Manti Temple dedication, Manti Temple Historical Record 1888–1899, 2:63, 17 May 1888.
70. W. H. Segmiller, Sevier Utah Stake Historical Record 1880–1883, 192, 23 February 1879, LR 8243 11. Sevier Stake President A. K. Thurber, responding to news of passage of the Edmunds Act in 1882 said likewise, "We are members of the kingdom of God and we will eventually rule and govern all the nations of the earth. . . . We will plead and contend for our rights as citizens until the Saints step forward and save the Constitution." A. K. Thurber, Sevier Stake Historical Record, 4:179, 19 March 1882, LR 8243 11.
71. A. K. Thurber, Sevier Stake Historical Record 1880–1883, 4:179, 19 March 1882.

inevitable apocalypse as spoken of in the book of Revelation and in various sections of the Doctrine and Covenants. Whether he viewed 1890 as fulfillment of an earlier prophecy of Joseph Smith that if he were to live to be eighty-five he might see Christ's Second Coming (D&C 130), one local leader said: "The signs that [were] to be given before the Second Coming of the Saviour [are] transpiring every day and his coming is not far distant."[72] And from David John: "When the Saints will keep the commandments of God . . . he will cause wonders to be performed in the midst of Zion, even unto deliverance from her foes, and confusion and destruction will overtake the wicked. . . . The waste places of Zion will be rebuilt and Christ will come and dwell among his people."[73] Thus, adherence to plural marriage would ensure, and might even hasten, the inevitable end day, and the ushering in of the Millennium depended in large measure upon the obedience of God's chosen people living this principle.[74]

Finally, the line between maintaining plural marriage and protecting the expanded role of temple ordinances became increasingly thin, especially after the passage of the Edmunds Act of 1882. The spirited defense of one was applied to the defense of the other in such a manner that the consciousness of the place of temples rose in direct correlation to the intensity of opposition arrayed against plural marriage. Said one local stake leader: "They are aiming a blow at the sealing ordinances of the Lord's House."[75] And from George Q. Cannon: "This labor of building Temples would arouse the active hostility and the vengeance of the wicked; . . . that the construction of Temples would evoke the deadly hatred of the wicked, and the adversary would do all in his power to destroy the people engaged

---

72. Franklin Spencer, Sevier Stake Historical Record 1880–1883, 4:276, 21 January 1883. See also entry for 28 May 1882. For more on the feeling of an impending apocalypse and a divine judgment on the land, see Alexander, *Things in Heaven and Earth*, 237–38.
73. David John Diaries, 7 May 1885.
74. Some believed the revelation given to the Prophet Joseph Smith in 1843 (Section 130) meant that the Second Coming might well come in 1890. "If thou livest until thou art eighty-five years old, thou shalt see the face of the Son of Man; therefore let this suffice, and trouble me no more on this matter" (D&C 130:15). A careful perusal of local records does show a slight uptick in references by some as to the Second Coming in 1890 but it was not a widespread conviction or teaching.
75. Franklin Spencer, Sevier Stake Historical Record 3:168, 23 May 1882.

in this work."[76] President Franklin Spencer of the Sevier Stake said: "The great and final conflict is upon us between Christ and anti-Christ. . . . We must sanctify this land that we may keep the statutes and judgments. We are doing a marvelous work in the building of these Temples. How are we going to keep the enemy out of those temples if not by sanctifying the land by the payment of our tithes and offerings?"[77] And from A. O. Smoot, president of the Provo Utah Central Stake: "The cause of this uprising against us is because we are building temples, paying a little better tithing and are becoming more united and the Devil knows these things."[78] In an epistle of 1886, the First Presidency issued this culminating statement: "Notwithstanding the violent and unabating opposition which is arrayed against us, the work of ministering in the ordinances of the Lord's House continues. . . . It must not surprise us if the rage of the arch-enemy of mankind increases and his emissaries grow more relentless and cruel, more brutal and inhuman in their efforts to stay this work as the number of temples increases and the thousands of Israel go in thereto to minister the ordinances of salvation for their ancestors and departed friends."[79]

CONCLUSION

Soon after the dedication of the St. George Temple, Brigham Young carried the vision of temple building to Manti and Logan. At great sacrifice, the Church and its membership went to building these additional

---

76. George Q. Cannon, Manti Temple Historical Record, 2:56, 17 May 1888.
77. Franklin Spencer, Sevier Stake Historical Record, 3:168, 23 May 1882.
78. Abraham O. Smoot, Provo Utah Central Stake General Minutes, 15 January 1882.
79. An Epistle of the First Presidency, Semi-Annual Conference, Coalville, Utah, October 1886, https://lib.byu.edu/collections/mormon-publications-19th-20th-centuries/.This is not to suggest that all plural marriages were performed in the temples or in the Endowment House. There were some instances when such marriages were performed by General Authorities in the local communities they were visiting, in local homes and meetinghouses. For instance, Elder John Taylor while visiting Logan in 1877 "referred to the subject of marriage; and as a matter of local interest intimated that proper arrangements would be made so that this ordinance might be performed at home, instead of having to go to St. George." John Taylor, Logan Utah Cache Stake Minutes, 2:223, 3–4 November 1877. Plural marriages were usually done by application to the President of the Church, after being recommended by the proper local officer(s).

"THEY ARE AIMING A BLOW AT THE SEALING ORDINANCES"

temples with an unremitting sense of sacrifice and dedication. The "movement" of temple work was taking hold as never before and President Young lived to see the day.

Simultaneous to this "movement," however, was an ever increasing pressure by the United States government to bring the Church to its knees over the matter of plural marriage. Congress passed law after law beginning with the Morrill Anti-Bigamy Act of 1862 and continuing on into the 1880s against the principle. Yet for a battery of historical and doctrinal reasons, the Saints flintlike continued as resolute as before. While never more than a minority practiced plural marriage, the expectation to do so remained firm and their reputation as a polygamous society had spread far and wide. Committed to the defense of its temple-building mission, as well as to the "principle" no matter what the cost, it was clear that The Church of Jesus Christ of Latter-day Saints was on a collision course with the government of the United States and with the rest of the nation, the outcome of which now bears the most careful scrutiny.

Chapter 9

"Which Is the Wisest Course?"

THE ROAD TO RECONCILIATION, 1888–1890

The question is this: Which is the wisest course for the Latter-day Saints to pursue: to continue to attempt to practice plural marriage, with the laws of the nation against it and the opposition of sixty millions of people, and at the cost of the confiscation of all the Temples, and the stopping of all the ordinances therein, both for the living and the dead, and the imprisonment of the First Presidency and Twelve . . . or, after doing and suffering what we have through our adherence to this principle to cease the practice and submit to the law, and through doing so leave the Prophets, Apostles and fathers at home so that they can instruct the people and attend to the duties of the Church, and also leave the Temples in the hands of the Saints, so that they can attend to the ordinances of the Gospel, both for the living and the dead?[1]

So explained Wilford Woodruff as President of the Church shortly after he had issued the Manifesto in 1890 designed to signal the end of plural marriage. Few, if any, then alive had a fuller understanding of temple work since Kirtland or a richer appreciation of temple doctrine and ordinances. And as we have seen, he had been a witness to, if not the prime instigator and participant in, many of these important changes, especially those since 1877. At the same time, Woodruff had long been a stalwart

---

1. "Excerpts from Three Addresses by President Wilford Woodruff Regarding the Manifesto" following the Manifesto (Official Declaration 1—D&C), as given by Wilford Woodruff, Logan Utah Cache Stake Conference, 1 November 1891, reported in *Deseret Weekly*, 14 November 1891.

advocate of the "principle" of plural marriage, which by the 1880s had become the great point of controversy with the rest of the nation. Through inspiration and a deepening understanding of revealed scripture, he saw his way to a resolution of what seemed to be an impossible dilemma. Thus no one was better equipped to proclaim the Manifesto and then convince the membership of the Church that in the final analysis, temple work had so flowered and grown in meaning that it would now preempt plural marriage. It was a rocky road that came at an enormous price but a necessary transition nonetheless, instigated by one who knew full well the costs and ramifications of his actions.

The dedicatory services of the Manti Temple in May 1888 rivaled in Pentecostal fervor and display those of the Kirtland Temple fifty-two years before.[2] Private dedication services ran from 17 to 19 May, largely to deter arrests of Church leaders, and the more public services followed from 21 to 23 May. If the many contemporary accounts are to be believed, this was a glorious time of prophecies, healings, visions, and of hearing heavenly strains of music. Several who attended heard heavenly voices and an angelic choir "in some other part of the temple." Some said they saw "a bright halo of light" hovering over many of the speakers while a few said they witnessed the spirits of Joseph Smith, Brigham Young, John Taylor, and Jedediah H. Grant surrounding apostle John W. Taylor as he spoke.[3] Others saw shafts of sunbeam envelope speaker after speaker until, as one observer put it, "great and rich blessings . . . were poured out upon us here, and that full free flow of the Spirit of God has been with us ever since."[4] John D. T.

---

2. This was especially true of the private dedicatory services for Church leaders presided over by Wilford Woodruff a few days earlier on 17–19 May 1888. For reasons of expediency, Woodruff did not attend the more heavily attended, public dedicatory services that immediately followed 21–23 May.
3. George Q. Cannon indicated that there was no time when heavenly manifestations would be "more likely to be given" than at the dedication of a temple. St. George Stake General Minutes, vol. 17, 27 May 1888; Journal History, 10, 2 July 1888.
4. M. F. Farnsworth to George Teasdale, Manti Temple Letterpress Copybooks, 2:30–33, 2 July 1888. For corroborative accounts see Journal History, 24 May and 2 July 1888. See also Wilford Woodruff to Bro. and Sis. Atkin, Wilford Woodruff Letters, 11 June 1888, MS 5264, Church History Library.

Manti Temple completed, 1888.

McAllister remarked as follows: "Many heavenly manifestations were given at the dedication," he said, comparing the Pentecostal displays at the dedication of the Kirtland Temple with what was now happening at the Manti Temple. "Heavenly singing was heard by some, and others saw heavenly sights."[5] News of such things spread far and fast among the Saints.

These special services and solemn assemblies, held within the walls of the temple, were off limits to the general public and offered a respite from the unrelenting gaze of federal marshals, apostates, and other enemies and antagonists. And leaders took full advantage of the opportunity to speak freely and openly of the acute difficulties The Church of Jesus Christ of Latter-day Saints was then facing. Said George Q. Cannon, First Counselor in the First Presidency:

> *The United States are only performing their part to help fulfil the destiny that God has predicted concerning us, and that awaits us. Those*

---

5. John D. McAllister, St. George Utah Stake Minutes, vol. 17, 16 June 1888.

schemes of spoilation in which we are engaged are only part of the great programme that was announced thousands of years ago by the prophets of God. . . . It is almost appalling to see the success of their efforts; every time they put their hands forth to take anything it seems as though the power of resistance, on our part melts away, and we have no opportunity, apparently, of defending ourselves, and we ask ourselves, perhaps with fear and trembling, where will this end? What will result?

He then answered his own query:

It seemed to be an hour of darkness with us. It seemed as though we were left almost to ourselves, and God has hidden his face from us, because of the success of our enemies. But this is not so. God is as near to us today as he ever was, and nearer. The heavens are opened to our cries. He knows our hearts and the feelings that animate us. He is aware of our condition; His angels are aware of us, and they encircle us and will be around us to shield us against the attacks of the wicked.[6]

Eighty-one-year-old Wilford Woodruff, as President of the Church, then arose and declared the following:

The question has been asked: "Are the Twelve Apostles going to desert the celestial law of God?" I say, no, never; neither in this world nor the world to come. What Bro. Cannon has said is true. It is the law of God. It is the fullness of the everlasting Gospel. This Kingdom and government cannot be perfected without that law. That law gives the children of God the highest exaltation and glory on the face of the earth and in the heavens. No man can obtain a fullness without that law. Are we going to deny that law? We are not. Our brethren need not be afraid that President Woodruff and the Apostles are going to deny the faith, or any part of it. We are not, nor I don't think we ever shall.[7]

---

6. George Q. Cannon, Manti Temple Dedication, Manti Temple Historical Record, 2:56–58, 17 May 1888.
7. Wilford Woodruff, Manti Temple Dedication, Manti Temple Historical Record, 61–62, 17 May 1888. One of the last things President Woodruff did during the dedication was to consecrate on

And yet, within two and a half years of this fervent declaration, President Woodruff would find himself issuing his famous "Manifesto," signaling the intention to stop the practice of patriarchal marriage throughout the Church. What happened in so short a time to bring about so monumental a change? What realization did he come to? And did he see himself betraying a trust or conceding a commission?[8]

"THERE HAVE BEEN CONCESSIONS MADE"

Public protests and private declarations notwithstanding, Church authorities had been giving long and careful thought throughout the 1880s about the meaning and future of plural marriage and how it might be made more acceptable to both the "Gentile" populations and to the growing number of Latter-day Saints unwilling or unable to embrace it. Both the future well-being of teh ChurchEvidence has already shown that as significant as plural marriage was, the majority of the membership had not, and would not, embrace it. For instance, one young mother, just after the birth of a son, wrote the following ditty:

> *The Lord has blessed us with another son*
> *Which is the seventh I have Bord*
> *May he be the father of many lives*
> *But not the husband of many wives.* [9]

As historian B. H. Roberts observed, there was "a certain restiveness" manifested among many in the Church and "murmurings and

---

the temple altar the seer stone which Joseph Smith had used for receiving some of his revelations. *Wilford Woodruff's Journal*, 8:499–500, 17–18 May 1888.
8. Reliable standard sources for this period are Thomas G. Alexander, *Things in Heaven and Earth*; Thomas G. Alexander, *Mormonism in Transition*; B. H. Roberts, *A Comprehensive History of the Church of Jesus Christ of Latter-day Saints*; James B. Allen and Glen M. Leonard, *The Story of the Latter-day Saints*; Leonard J. Arrington, *Great Basin Kingdom*; Gustive O. Larson, *The "Americanization" of Utah for Statehood* (San Marino, California; The Huntington Library, 1971); Richard D. Poll, "The Americanization of Utah," *Utah Historical Quarterly* 44 (Winter 1976); Kenneth W. Godfrey, "The Coming of the Manifesto," *Dialogue: A Journal of Mormon Thought* 5 (Autumn 1970); and Davis Bitton, *George Q. Cannon*.
9. Journal of Willard Richards, Willard Richards Papers 1821–1854, 10 February 1847, MS 1490, Church History Library.

complainings" about how difficult living the law of plural marriage had become.[10] In March 1882 the First Presidency and the Quorum of the Twelve had "considered it wisdom" for a legally married man to live with only one wife under the same roof. Two years later, discussions centered on broadening the meaning of polygamy to include being married to two or three women consecutively after their deaths, a definition not supported. George Q. Cannon offered a somewhat liberal opinion that "there would be men in the Celestial kingdom that had but one wife and some who had no wife and some who had several wives would not get there at all."[11] Statements by Charles Penrose and George F. Richards during 1887/88 and prepared under the direction of Joseph F. Smith had already begun to move the Church in the direction of making plural marriage optional rather than mandatory.[12] And in 1888, the Twelve instructed missionaries and local leaders not to preach plural marriage publicly. Furthermore, within days of its dedication, Woodruff directed that no "plural sealings" be done in the Manti Temple. "We don't intend to give our enemies a chance to raid the temple," he said. "If they come, they must take my word for it; if they get in, they will have to break in."[13] George Q. Cannon went so far as to admit that "there have been concessions made. The Spirit of the Lord has led his servants to give counsel in certain directions, that was not expected until quite recently, and they have been led to consent to measures that seem to those who are not acquainted with the operations of the Spirit to be in a wrong direction. But no man who has lived near unto God has walked in darkness in regard to these things."[14]

For all of his visions, sermons, and denunciations of the government,

---

10. B. H. Roberts, *Comprehensive History of the Church*, 6:217.
11. *Wilford Woodruff's Journal*, 8:92, 24 March 1882.
12. Alexander, *Things in Heaven and Earth*, 267.
13. Wilford Woodruff, 28 May 1888, Manti Temple Historical Records 2:41. There is no evidence US marshals ever "broke in" to any temple; however, many Latter-day Saints found temporary refuge by hiding in one or another of the temples. For instance, Wilford Woodruff and J. D. T. McAllister had upper room "apartments" in the St. George Temple.
14. George Q. Cannon, Manti Temple Dedication, Manti Temple Historical Records, 2:56–58, 17 May 1888.

President Woodruff took a "wait and see" attitude, leaving open the door for a possible future revelation and reconciliation of this most troubling issue. Writing in September 1885 he said:

> *I have felt for several years that there was a change coming over Zion and over our nation and the world at large.* . . . *The United States government has sent judges and marshals to Utah to prosecute all the Mormons they can for polygamy and cohabitation with their own wives and they have turned it more into persecution than prosecution until our prisons are crowded with the leading men of the Church* . . . *and the United States Government with the editors and priest[s] are laboring to destroy the Saints of God. We shall see.*[15]

POLITICAL CHECKMATE

Meanwhile, the political pressures brought to bear against the Church intensified, a steady drumbeat of opposition and oppression. In 1887 Congress passed the Edmunds-Tucker Act. This draconian measure officially dissolved The Church of Jesus Christ of Latter-day Saints as a legal corporation and directed the attorney general to institute proceedings to accomplish this end. It also required the Church to forfeit to the government most real estate worth in excess of $50,000; placed control of territorial public education squarely in the hands of federal officials; abolished the Nauvoo Legion; disenfranchised Utah women; and dissolved the Perpetual Emigration Fund.[16] Despite the fasting and prayers of the Saints, their last faint hopes that perhaps the Edmunds-Tucker Act would be invalidated were dashed in May 1890 when the Supreme Court of the United States narrowly ruled (5–4) in favor of the government in upholding the constitutionality of the act. Stunned at the court's decree that the United States government had the right to virtually abolish an organized

---

15. *Wilford Woodruff's Journal*, 8:334, 21 September 1885.
16. On 12 February 1870, Utah's territorial legislature had passed a women's suffrage bill, but the Edmunds-Tucker Act outlawed this right as part of the effort to do away with polygamy.

religion, Wilford Woodruff and the other Church authorities now weighed their few remaining alternatives.

In upholding the constitutionality of the Edmunds-Tucker Act, the Supreme Court ruled that polygamy was "a crime against the laws, and abhorrent to the sentiments and feelings of the civilized world" and that the government had every right to confiscate Church properties so long as they were used for "charitable purposes."[17] The subsequent decision of government receivers to go after the temples was most disconcerting. The St. George, Manti, Logan, and the unfinished Salt Lake temples would now be targeted for escheatment and would fall under public ownership and control, a surrender the Church viewed as untenable.[18] "Lightning has just struck," wrote Woodruff in November 1887. "Marshal [Frank H.] Dyer took possession of our [First Presidency] office today. Locked up all the desks and took the keys."[19]

President Woodruff remembered all too well the forced departure of the Saints from the Kirtland Temple in 1838 and the desecrations and destruction of the Nauvoo Temple in the late 1840s, and he was adamantly opposed to losing such sacred structures ever again. As John Taylor said: "If we were to turn over to-day these buildings to the religious world, they would know no more how to use them legitimately, than a baby would know what to do with algebra; neither would we had not the Lord taught us by revelation from heaven."[20] Nonetheless, although the Church took desperate legal efforts to transfer ownership of several of its properties from

---

17. United States 49th Congress, Session 2 (1887) *Statutes at Large*, 635:24 stat. sec. 13. See also *Great Basin Kingdom*, 375.
18. The act, however, excluded from escheat buildings and grounds "held and occupied exclusively for purposes of the worship of God, or parsonage connected therewith, or burial grounds." *Statutes at Large*, 635 (1887): sec. 13. Also cited in Alexander, *Things in Heaven and Earth*, 253 and 410. In return, the Church rented the properties back, paying $12 per year for the temple block, $2,400 for the tithing office, and $1,200 for the Gardo House, which had long served as home to the President of the Church. *Things in Heaven and Earth*, 253. A later government-appointed receiver made it very clear, however, that he believed the temples were subject to confiscation. *Things in Heaven and Earth*, 266–67.
19. *Wilford Woodruff's Journal*, 8:247, 23 November 1887.
20. *Deseret News*, 17 April 1878, from transcription of a John Taylor discourse, 21 October 1877, in the Ogden Tabernacle.

the trustee-in-trust or Presidency of the Church to private individuals and "temple associations," government seizure was now virtually inevitable.

Undoubtedly other factors were in play. The first was financial. The cost of constructing the temples was substantial. The daily payroll of the St. George, Logan, and Manti temples had been at least $200/day with the Salt Lake Temple figure coming in at $300/day for several years. It is estimated that in sum the St. George Temple had cost $1,000,000; the Logan Temple, $770,000; the Manti Temple, $1,000,000; and the Salt Lake Temple, at least $4,000,000, not counting the costs of building the associated tabernacles in St. George, Manti, Logan, and Salt Lake City.[21] Such heavy expenditures came at a time of severe financial difficulty for the Church, saddled as it was with rapidly rising legal costs incurred in defending itself, in addition to defending numerous individual members charged with unlawful cohabitation under provisions of the Edmunds Act of 1882. While it may well be argued that tithing receipts were bound to increase as the faithful returned over and over again to the temple, such ambitious building projects came during one of the most financially stressful times in Church history. Furthermore, tithing receipts had significantly decreased as members feared that their contributions would be confiscated by a hated federal government.[22] And if the temples were to be confiscated, membership donations would almost certainly decrease dramatically. The truth was that the Church could not afford to continue to fight the United States government in court.

Surely another factor in proclaiming the Manifesto was political, specifically the desire for statehood. Well known was the repeated rejection of all six previous territorial petitions for statehood going back to 1849. The 1890 court ruling reiterated once and for all the cold, checkmate reality that any hope for Utah statehood was a dead issue. As long as plural

---
21. Roberts, *Comprehensive History*, 6:504–5.
22. Tithing receipts declined from an average of more than $500,000 a year in the 1880s to approximately $350,000 per year in 1890. By mid-1898 the Church stood $2.3 million in debt, principally to bankers outside of Utah. Alexander, *Mormonism in Transition*, 5.

marriage persisted with Church support, Utah would continue to be a territory governed by outside appointees invariably critical of the faith. It would once again be taxation without representation, religion without defense, and control without compassion—in other words, more of the same old tired story.

The social costs of interrupting family life through arrest and imprisonment also weighed heavily on almost everyone's mind. Over 1,300 men had been arrested and imprisoned at the Sugarhouse penitentiary (and in Arizona and Michigan jails) for unlawful cohabitation while a few women were also jailed for not testifying against their husbands. A great many families were thrown into poverty because of it. The devastating impact on the family because of the federal raids cannot be underestimated for it virtually destroyed an entire social order and community, leaving little in its wake.

Finally, with various General Authorities serving time in prison or away in hiding for months at a time, the Church was suffering from intermittent leadership, an ecclesiastical government on the run. Conferences were minimized and reduced, with leaders constantly looking over their shoulders at who might be in the audience or on their trail. The Raid confiscated the full attention of Church leadership and drained the once free and happy inspiration of its speakers. Surely the Church could not continue to function much longer effectively with a deflected, hunted, and imprisoned leadership.

Where to turn? In April 1889 and again in September 1890, President Woodruff embarked upon two working vacations to California where he and his counselors met with such business and political leaders as Isaac Trumbo, Alexander Badlam (a nephew of Samuel Brannan of early Latter-day Saint settlement fame in California), C. P Huntington and W. W. Stow of the Southern Pacific Railroad, Henry Bigelow of the *San Francisco Examiner*, Senator Leland Stanford (R–Calif.), Judge M. M. Estee, and other Republican congressional leaders on matters pertaining to a possible political resolution to the impasse. President Woodruff encountered a friendlier attitude than he had noticed in the past, and carried on extensive discussions, if not negotiations. Yet to what extent these influenced him has never been fully determined.[23] Safe to say, he was looking for solutions.

"I'VE HAD THIS SPIRIT UPON ME FOR A LONG TIME"

As important as these several considerations unarguably were, they may not have been the decisive factors in coming to a final decision, at least not in President Woodruff's eyes. His back against the wall, he sought solutions from restored scripture, Church history, his own life's experiences, and through fervent prayer. Certainly under consideration was the twelfth article of faith, which states: "We believe in being subject to kings, presidents, rulers, and magistrates, in obeying, honoring, and sustaining the law." Now that the Edmunds-Tucker Act had been upheld by the Supreme Court as the constitutional law of the land, further legal challenges seemed out of the question. During the dark days of Missouri persecution a half century before, an earlier impasse had been resolved through revelation: "Therefore, I, the Lord, justify you, and your brethren of my church, in befriending that law which is the constitutional law of the land; And as pertaining to law of man, whatsoever is more or less than this, cometh of evil" (D&C 98:6–7). If the "constitutional law" includes that which is upheld by the Supreme Court, the path forward was made clear. "Wherefore, be subject to the powers that be, until he reigns whose right it is to reign, and subdues all enemies under his feet" (D&C 58:22). A later Nauvoo revelation made provision for compromise and concession when required:

> *Verily, verily, I say unto you, that when I give a commandment to any of the sons of men to do a work unto my name, and those sons of men go with all their might and with all they have to perform that work, and cease not their diligence, and their enemies come upon them and hinder them from performing that work, behold, it behooveth me*

---

23. Alexander, *Things in Heaven and Earth*, 249–52.

to require that work no more at the hands of those sons of men, but to accept of their offerings (D&C 124:49, see also 56:4).[24]

Wilford Woodruff was also well aware of prophecy. While addressing a Sanpete Stake conference in 1882, he referred to some of the ancient prophecies "that in none of them had it been stated that the Kingdom of God should be overthrown in this dispensation. The Lord has set his hand to fulfill his promises to Israel."[25] And as the first temple president of the Church, he was well aware of the scores of revelations and scriptures in the Doctrine and Covenants concerning the fundamental importance of temple work, many of which, as discussed previously, had been canonized just a few years before in 1876.[26] He was also pre-millennialist in his thinking in that he and those closest to him were of the expectation that the Millennium was a very impending reality and that the God of Heaven would overrule all for the good of the Saints regardless of what the government may or may not do.

Often wondering why his life had been spared on so many different occasions and why he had outlived John Taylor, a younger man than he was, President Woodruff explained that his decision to stop the "practice" of plural marriage was a divine "commandment" long in the making, a gradual series of inspirations that came in the context of preserving the temples. In 1888 Woodruff said that "ever since there was a probability that the Government would take away our property, and not permit us to own any"—which had first surfaced as a possibility in the Morrill Act of 1862—"I have many times prayed to the Lord, to preserve these temples,

---

24. This passage of scripture in particular was centerpiece to the addresses given at the October 1890 Manifesto conference of the Church. Most of these scriptures were quoted by various speakers during the Manifesto conference.
25. Wilford Woodruff, 19 November 1882, as published in the *Deseret News*, 6 December 1882.
26. From a modern perspective, one wonders why the Manifesto conference did not reference the Book of Mormon passage of scripture that says that if the Lord desires to "raise up seed" through plural marriage, He would command His people (Jacob 2:30). Otherwise, it was unnecessary. Such a reference seems to imply that plural marriage might be best seen as a temporary subset of the higher law of eternal marriage, enjoined and revoked as needed. Perhaps one reason for not doing so was the long-standing defense of plural marriage from across the pulpit for so many decades.

that they should not be defiled by our enemies. I have had a strong testimony many times in my prayers, that the Lord would grant this to his people. . . . If we as a people do our duty, as Latter-day Saints, this will never be granted to our enemies."[27] Thus he had been considering such possible action or a form thereof for almost thirty years. Speaking at the St. George Temple in 1891, David H. Cannon, counselor in the St. George temple presidency, reported that he had heard President Woodruff explain "that if it had not been for the issuance of the Manifesto our Temples would have been taken away from us, and he said that the Lord did not design any such thing."[28]

Woodruff later elaborated upon this point. "I saw exactly what would come to pass if there was not something done," he remarked in a Logan stake conference in November 1891. "I have had this spirit upon me for a long time. But I want to say this: I should have let all the temples go out of our hands, I should have gone to prison myself, and let every other man go there, had not the God of heaven commanded me to do what I did do: and when the hour came that I was commanded to do that, it was clear to me. I went before the Lord, and I wrote what the Lord told me to write."[29]

It would appear that the Manifesto derived from Woodruff's own personal inspiration and was not the work of counselors or committees. "When Pres. Woodruff prepared his manifesto," wrote Abraham H.

---

27. Wilford Woodruff, Manti Temple Dedication, Manti Temple Historical Record, 2:51, 17 May 1888. Knowing that what he had brought forth was of divine origin, Woodruff on another occasion remarked: "In the name of Jesus Christ I say that God has not forsaken the Presidency or the Twelve. He inspired me to issue the manifesto and if He had not done so I should never have taken that course even though all ordinances for the living and dead had ceased, and our temples had fallen into the hands of our enemies." Wilford Woodruff, 2 April 1891, in Abraham H. Cannon, *An Apostle's Record: Journals of Abraham H. Cannon*, ed. Dennis B. Horne (Clearfield, Utah: Gnolaum Books, 2004) 180.
28. St. George Temple Meeting Minutes, 4:158, 3 November 1891.
29. "Excerpts from Three Addresses" following D&C: Official Declaration 1. A good example of how some rank and file members reacted to President Woodruff's explanation of the Manifesto may be seen in the following sister's testimony given after she had listened to him dedicate the Salt Lake Temple. "[She] said President Woodruff had the manifesto many times revealed unto him but kept it back for a long time, saw in a Vision that our Temples, and all our privileges would be taken away from us." E. Casto, Manti South Ward Relief Society Minutes and Records, 2:71, 10 April 1893.

Cannon, "it was without the aid or suggestions of his counselors. He took a clerk and went to a room alone. There under the spirit of inspiration he dictated the declaration he desired to make, and there was only one slight change made therein when it was read to Counselors Cannon and Smith."[30] And in carefully chosen terms, he referred to it almost always not as a revelation but as a "commandment from God."

Although it is absolutely true that the desire for statehood was a critical factor in his deliberations, the more paramount doctrinal question in Woodruff's mind boiled down to choosing between two earnest priorities: either to continue in the principle and practice of plural marriage, or to preserve and promote the sense of temples rising, or in other words, the legacy of the past and the promising future of temple work and with it, a much enlarged vision of redemption for the dead. Thus his question, "Which is the wisest course for the Latter-day Saints to pursue?"

By the end of 1885, President Woodruff had seen to it that 3,188 of his own family ancestors and deceased friends had received their baptisms for the dead, and that 2,518 of the same had received their endowments. Likewise, he had participated at the altar for 1,171 deceased couples.[31] There likely was no one alive more personally involved in work for the redemption of the dead than he was. The prospect of now forfeiting to a secular government what had become so personally precious and important was enormously troubling to him.

And thousands of members, both patrons and workers, were now catching the spirit of temple work as never before. One such individual, Lewis Barney, wrote the following to his granddaughter of his work at the Manti Temple: "I am now in Manti all alone and living in my wagon trying to attend to the ordinances of the gospel for the redemption of the dead that belongs to the Barney family. I and your grandmother had done

---

30. *An Apostle's Record*, 155. George Q. Cannon said that President Woodford presented what he had written to him and George Gibbs and others and desired them to respond. "When we went over it I suggested several emendations, which were adopted." The George Q. Cannon Journal, 1849–1901, 24 September 1890.
31. *Wilford Woodruff's Journal*, 8:354, 31 December 1885.

all we could. . . . I wish that you were here to help me in this great work. This thing rests on my shoulders and mind heavier than anything because our salvation depends on its accomplishment."[32]

The table on the next page, which admittedly covers a few more years beyond the date of the Manifesto, is most revealing.[33] The large number of baptisms for the dead—over 965,000—is six times the numbers performed in the Endowment House and over seventy-five times the number performed in the Nauvoo Temple. If the corresponding figures from the Nauvoo Temple and Endowment House are added, the total number of baptisms for the dead swells to over 1.1 million. This statistic takes on added importance when one recalls that for almost twenty-five years, there were no baptisms for the dead performed. Once reintroduced, there were five times as many baptisms for the dead performed between 1877 and 1898 as in all the years previously. Clearly the temple had become the guardian of baptisms for the dead in statistically significant ways.

Furthermore, the vision of Wilford Woodruff to do such ordinances for family members, friends, and even unknown deceased persons of prominence was unfolding in dramatic fashion. As noted in the chart, the number of endowments for the dead during this period equaled almost thirteen times the number of living endowments performed. In addition to baptisms and endowments for the dead, over 143,000 sealings (marriages) of deceased couples also took place. With each endowment session lasting at least four hours, plus the substantial travel time to and fro, we begin to see the new and increased time commitment to temple attendance. There were now so many more reasons to return to the temple than ever before—specifically, the ordinance of endowment for the dead which was nothing less than a recurring invitation to return to the temple over and over again.

Nor should one underestimate or overlook the impact of ordinance

---

32. Journal of Lewis Barney, 167, Perry Special Collections, HBLL, BYU.
33. Report, 31 December 1898, Church Historian's Letterpress Copybooks (1842–1915), CR 100 39, Church History Library. According to Wilford Woodruff's own account, by the end of 1889, 499,958 baptisms, 209,544 endowments, 22,845 children sealings, and 8,751 adoptions had been performed in all three temples then in operation. *Wilford Woodruff's Journal*, 9:80.

Ordinances in the Four Temples, from the Commencement to December 31, 1898*

	St. George Temple from Jan. 1877		Logan Temple from 1884		Manti Temple from 1888		Salt Lake Temple from 1892		Totals	
	Living	Dead	Living	Dead	Living	Dead	Living	Dead	Living	Dead
Baptisms, First	881	278,060	1,211	291,181	1,225	187,851		208,332	3,317	965,424
Baptisms, Renewals	1,086		3,740		4,452				9,278	
Baptisms, Health	3,204		7,717		13,779		5,340		30,040	
Endowments	6,467	131,654	16,339	143,451	6,489	98,541	9,157	114,805	38,452	488,451
Ordinations	1,241	52,115	304	58,284	316	41,981	104	45,479	1,965	197,859
Marriages/Sealings	3,402	42,164	8,036	37,160	3,230	34,499	3,963	29,277	18,631	143,100
Children to Parents	4,105	6,085	11,045	11,540	7,046	15,706	8,337	27,465	30,533	60,796
Adoptions	517	6,162	168	421	443	6,095	74	700	1,202	13,378
Totals	20,903	516,240	48,560	542,037	36,980	384,673	26,975	426,058	Grand Total: 2,002,426**	
Totals in Each Temple	537,143		590,597		421,653		453,033			

*Report, 31 December 1898, Church Historian's Letterpress Copybooks (1842–1992), CR 100 39, Church History Library. Used with permission. The figures for the St. George Temple are substantiated in the St. George Temple Records Book, 1877–1899, CR 343 57, Church History Library.

** These figures do not include those ordinances performed in either the Salt Lake Council House or the Endowment House. At least 2,200 endowments for the living were performed in the Council House 1851–1854. And in the Endowment House, 134,053 baptisms for the dead, 68,767 marriage sealings of both living and deceased couples, and 54,170 endowments for the living were performed between 1855 and 1889. See "Endowment House Records 1851–1885," Church History Library. See also Tingen, "The Endowment House, 1855–1889."

work for *the living* in all four temples during this twenty-two-year span. There were almost 140,000 living ordinances performed including approximately 3,300 living baptisms, some 30,000 baptisms for health, 40,000 endowments for the living, nearly 20,000 living sealings, 30,000 sealings of living children to their parents, and other ordinances.[34]

Taken in the aggregate, the number of temple ordinances performed for both the living and the dead in all four Utah temples between 1 January 1877 and the end of 1898 totaled over two million, with more than thirteen times as many ordinances performed for the dead than for the living. And this at a time when total membership was less than 300,000. In contemplating these figures, Wilford Woodruff's justification for the Manifesto bears repeating, "so that the dead may be redeemed." "A large number has already been delivered from the prison house in the spirit world by this people, and shall the work go on or stop? This is the question I lay before the Latter-day Saints. You have to judge for yourselves. I want you to answer it for yourselves. I shall not answer it; but I say to you that that is exactly the condition we as a people would have been in had we not taken the course we have" (D&C: Official Declaration 1).

"AND NOW THE DAWN WAS BREAKING" —REACTION TO THE MANIFESTO

President Woodruff presented his Manifesto to the leadership of the Church on 24 September 1890. "In broken and contrite spirit" he

---

34. Looking ahead, after the turn of the century, temple work progressed at an even faster rate of activity. The total number of temple ordinances performed from 1842 to the end of 1929 in all temples of the Church were as follows:

Ordinance	Living	Dead
Baptism	n/a	6,973,367
Endowments	239,022	4,449,670
Ordinations, Elders	3,310	1,822,119
Sealings, Wives to Husband	119,263	640,977
Children sealed	98,899	1,009,038
Adoptions	2,507	14,693
Totals	463,001	14,909,864

Roberts, *A Comprehensive History,* 6:495.

explained that in answer to his prayers, the Lord had revealed that the Church must relinquish the practice, a deliberate choice of words. Elder Marriner W. Merrill, a member of the Twelve Apostles, saw it in much the same way as did the prophet and wrote that it was the only way to "retain the possession of our Temples and continue the ordinance work for the living and the dead, which was considered more important than continuing the practice of plural marriages for the present."[35]

Most other leaders accepted his conclusion but not without serious soul-searching discussion. Certainly this was the case with Woodruff's counselor, Joseph F. Smith.

> *With a face like wax, his hands outstretched, in an intensity of passion that seemed to sweep the assembly, he declared that he had covenanted, at the altar of God's house, in the presence of his Father, to cherish the wives and children whom the Lord had given him. They were more to him than life. They were dearer to him than happiness. . . . But—He dropped his arms. He seemed to shrink in his commanding stature like a man stricken with a paralysis of despair. The tears came to the pained construction of his eyelids. "I have never disobeyed a revelation from God," he said. "I cannot—I dare not—now." He announced—with his head up, though his body swayed—that he would accept and abide by the revelation. When he sank in his chair and covered his face with his hands, there was a gasp of sympathy and relief, as if we had been hearing the pain of a man in agony.*[36]

Later that same day the Manifesto was given out to the press. When questioned, Woodruff clarified the point that it applied not just to

---

35. Marriner W. Merrill, "Notes from the Miscellaneous Record Book, 1886–1906," Record Book 1, 24 September 1890, in *New Mormon Studies CD-ROM: A Comprehensive Resource Library, 2009 Edition.*
36. Frank J. Cannon and Harvey J. O'Higgins, *Under the Prophet in Utah—The National Menace of a Political Priestcraft* (Boston: C. M. Clark Publishing Company, 1911), 102–11, as cited in Bitton, *George Q. Cannon*, 314. See also Larson, *The Americanization of Utah*, 262–63.

members in the United States but throughout the Church.[37] The next day he recorded in his diary as follows:

> *I have arrived at a point in the history of my life as President of the Church . . . where I am under the necessity of praying to the Lord and feeling inspired by his spirit I have issued the following Proclamation: . . . Inasmuch as laws have been enacted by congress forbidding plural marriages, which laws have been pronounced constitutional by the court of last resort, I hereby declare my intention to submit to those laws, and to use my influence with the members of the church over which I preside to have them do likewise. . . . And I now publicly declare that my advice to the Latter-day Saints is to refrain from contracting any marriage forbidden by the law of the land. [Signed] Wilford Woodruff, President of the Church of Jesus Christ Of Latter-day Saints.*[38]

Covenant, history, commandment, refinement, constitution, commitment—for all of this to change in one swooping announcement was more than many could immediately grasp or accept. Responses to the Manifesto announcement at the ensuing October conference varied dramatically from a high state of emotional agitation, bordering on disbelief and reluctance if not resistance, to quiet, faithful acceptance and profound relief. Although the sustaining vote was said to be unanimous, it was in fact carried by a "weak vote."[39] Many simply could not vote to sustain the measure one way or another. Most sat stunned and seeking more, much more, advice and counsel on how to proceed. It was one thing to make declarations; but where were the directions on how to proceed? Even revelation needs explanation. Like a giant ship coursing through turbulent seas, the principle and practice of plural marriage, what Thomas Alexander called the "previous

---

37. Allen and Leonard, *Story of the Latter-day Saints*, 421.
38. *Wilford Woodruff's Journal*, 9:114–16, 25 September 1890, as printed in *Deseret News*, 4 October 1890.
39. Marriner W. Merrill, "Notes from the Miscellaneous Record Book, 1886–1906," Record Book 1, 6 October 1890, in *New Mormon Studies CD-ROM*.

paradigm," could not and would not stop overnight.⁴⁰ It would take time, further directions and persuasions, cajolings and commandments, before finally charting a whole new course in which the Saints could adjust to living in a pluralistic, multidenominational, democratic American society. This may account for the fact that some continued to practice plural marriage long after 1890 and it would take years—and several apostasies, revelations, and a Second Manifesto in 1904—to effect a more perfect stoppage of the practice.⁴¹

Joseph F. Smith (1838–1918).

Responses to the Manifesto among the rank and file membership are a challenge to find. Some were clearly disappointed; others relieved. Many polygamous wives had to make adjustments to their thinking. One such woman, Annie Clark Tanner, who was married to the general superintendent of the Church Sunday School, and who had delivered her second baby alone on the floor while in hiding just a month before the Manifesto was delivered, admitted that upon hearing of the news she felt let down and disappointed. As a "wandering" polygamous wife who had gone to great lengths to hide her identity to protect her husband from arrest, she had long been a committed advocate of plural marriage. But

---

40. Alexander, *Mormonism in Transition*, 14.
41. Allen and Leonard, *Story of the Latter-day Saints*, 443, and Bitton, *George Q. Cannon*, 409. See also Alexander, *Mormonism in Transition*. For a thorough study of post-Manifesto plural marriage, see B. Carmon Hardy, *Solemn Covenant: The Mormon Polygamous Passage* (Urbana and Chicago: The University of Illinois Press, 1992). A "Second Manifesto," issued by President Joseph F. Smith fourteen years later in 1904 during the height of the Reed Smoot hearings in Washington, threatened to excommunicate those who continued to practice plural marriage.

for all her earlier convictions, "a great relief came over her" upon hearing the news, and she compared her "feelings of relief with the experience one has when the first crack of dawn comes after a night of careful vigilance over a sick patient." She went on, "At such a time daylight is never more welcome; and now the dawn was breaking for the Church."[42]

Those who had preached and lived the principle and who, in many instances, had served prison sentences because of it, would likely have felt betrayed had it not come from one so long respected and revered. As one of the Church's finest missionaries and temple builders, Wilford Woodruff had given his all in defense of the kingdom of God for almost sixty years, since his baptism in 1834. His was a trusted prophetic voice, one tutored under Joseph Smith, Brigham Young, and John Taylor. And while a few leaders and members abandoned their faith in resistance to the Manifesto, the vast majority followed their prophet into a new day.

Few were more surprised than the United States marshals and other federal government officials, several of whom were in attendance in the Tabernacle. Sitting as dumbfounded as their Latter-day Saint counterparts,

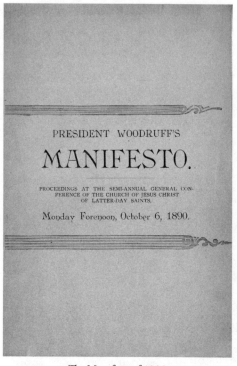

The Manifesto of 1890.

---

42. Paula Kelly Harline, *The Polygamous Wives Writing Club: From the Diaries of Mormon Pioneer Women* (Oxford and New York: Oxford University Press, 2014), 161–62.

they seemed not to know quite how to react. Chief Justice Charles Zane, however, promptly responded affirmatively, believing that President Woodruff was acting in good faith. By 1893 most civil rights were restored, including the right to vote, serve on juries, and to hold office. In due time, Church properties and funds were returned.

Response to the Manifesto from the "outside world" was tentatively positive. While some remained suspicious, others genuinely applauded the Church's action. Jonathan Blanchard, for example, first president of Wheaton College in Illinois and one of America's leading reformers and avid abolitionists, could not withhold from congratulating President Woodruff on his courageous decision. "I have read, with profound interest and gratitude to God, your late Proclamation vs. Polygamy," he wrote. "And if, as I hope, that [it] . . . shall be done away, I see no reason for refusing Utah admission as a state. . . . Your proclamation, and the vote of your General Conference have given me friendly feelings toward the Mormons; and begotten a hope that your Communion may, under God, become, simple and pure, 'The Church of Jesus Christ of Latter day Saints' indeed by relinquishing errors incident to your early history, and the horrors which, as a people you have passed through."[43]

The dilemma of caring for plural marriage families in the post-Manifesto era was a highly complicated matter. The instructions were for a man to live with only one wife and family but to continue to support his other wives and children as well as he possibly could, seldom an easy thing to do. "The Manifesto only refers to future marriages," Woodruff explained, "and does not affect past conditions. I did not, could not, and would not promise that you would desert your wives and children. This you cannot do in honor."[44] The federal government, meanwhile, under President Grover Cleveland offered an amnesty of sorts in 1893,

---

43. Jonathan Blanchard, ex-president of Wheaton College, to Wilford Woodruff, First Presidency (Wilford Woodruff) General Correspondence, 23 October 1890, CR 1 171, Church History Library.
44. *The Apostle's Record: The Journals of Abraham H. Cannon*, 164.

recognizing only one marriage but not requiring a man to divorce his other wives—a silent admission of the need to provide and care for extended families.

Three St. George testimonials conclude this discussion. Charles Smith spoke of how the Manifesto was a "test" of their commitment and of "being able to understand the spirit of the Manifesto, and the words of the authorities in explanations. If we read and endeavor to understand the mind of the Lord we put our trust in the Lord and fear Him who can cast the soul into hell. The Lord has given us a test to see if we would stand up to the covenants, in the holy order."[45] Nephi W. Savage realized the hand of the Lord in it, despite the fact that "some feel weak-kneed on account of this Manifesto." He expressed it "as right to obey a constitutional law or a law which had been so declared by the highest tribunal of the Land, [that] God will not require this at our hands for the time being . . . We must hold fast to the word of God."[46] And finally from Israel Ivins of St. George, "I do not think there is any foolishness talked although some men say it is fogyism [sic]. Things that are transpiring may look strange, but all will come out right, speaking of the Manifesto of Bro. Woodruff. I should like it when I die that the last words I say shall be [;] this is the true work of God."[47]

CONCLUSION

The reasons for President Woodruff's seeming about-face on plural marriage and his resultant Manifesto announcement are complex and varied. They included the straightened financial condition of the Church; the suffering of the Saints in light of ever-tightening government pressure, if not persecution; the long-held, fervent desire for statehood; and the inability of many Saints to live the principle. As important as these factors

---

45. Charles Smith, St. George Melchizedek Priesthood Minutes and Records, 5:510, 26 April 1891.
46. Nephi W. Savage, St. George Melchizedek Priesthood Minutes and Records, 5:486, 27 September 1890.
47. Israel Ivins, St. George Melchizedek Priesthood Minutes and Records, 5:486, 27 September 1890. At that same meeting, Alexander Findlay said: "I believe the gospel is true [even] if we do stop practicing polygamy."

surely were, however, for a goodly number of Saints it was revelation that stopped one practice while enshrining the other, and a growing understanding that what they were preserving was at least as important as what they were giving up. Only in appreciating fully what had to be abandoned does one begin to plumb their allegiance to temple work. It was as though the Latter-day Saint sense of the importance of temple work and of its history and development had finally caught up with its long-standing defense of polygamy, that the expanded mission of redemption for the dead was a vision of such newfound importance that nothing could be allowed to get in its way. Clearly the mission of the Church was progressing in a remarkable way, and the culture and meaning of what it meant to be a Latter-day Saint were destined to change with it. As important as plural marriage had become in the late nineteenth century, temples and temple worship had preceded it and now had overtaken the practice in doctrinal importance. For a variety of economic, demographic, cultural, geographic, and even theological reasons, plural marriage could not be enjoined or expected of all Latter-day Saint populations, male or female, whereas the commission to redeem the dead in all its new temple-centered particulars and family-saving ordinances was a paramount, permanent expectation of all. Parallel to the commission to evangelize the world, temple worship was the other great continuum in Latter-day Saint history and an undergirding definition of what the gospel of the Restoration had ever been since Moroni's "glad tidings from Cumorah." And President Woodruff would live to see one of the finest moments in Latter-day Saint temple worship.

Chapter 10

"Run This Chain Through as Far as You Can Get It"

THE SALT LAKE TEMPLE AND NEW ADVANCEMENTS IN TEMPLE WORK, 1890–1898

We want the Latter-day Saints from this time to trace their genealogies as far as they can, and be sealed to their parents, and run this chain through as far as you can get it. . . . This is the will of the Lord to his people, and I think when you come to reflect upon it you will find it to be true.[1]

  The completion of the Salt Lake Temple, after forty years of construction, surely is one of the most important moments in Church history. Its construction, symbolism, architecture, and interior are worthy of discussion as the "Grand Temple" of the Restoration. Yet the story of temples in the nineteenth century did not end with its completion. Wilford Woodruff, as fourth President of the Church, proclaimed yet another revelation equally as important as the Manifesto when in 1894 he ended the law of adoption in favor of members being sealed in the temples to their own ancestry. This momentous move led to the organization of the Utah Genealogical Society in 1894, which in years to come would become the largest genealogical society in the world with over five and a half billion records. With the practice of plural marriage now in recession, Utah was admitted to the Union two years later in 1896. Finally, in 1898, President Woodruff would pass away leaving a temple legacy never to be forgotten.

---

1. Wilford Woodruff, *Deseret Evening News*, 14 April 1894.

"RUN THIS CHAIN THROUGH AS FAR AS YOU CAN GET IT"

"IT WILL HAVE SIX TOWERS"
—THE SALT LAKE TEMPLE

Forty years in the building since Brigham Young had identified a plot of ground near City Creek, and at an eventual cost of more than $4,000,000, the Salt Lake Temple lagged far behind the others in being completed. Albeit inspiring, the building of the Salt Lake Temple is a frustrating story of one interruption after another. There were times when many wondered if the Millennium would come beforehand.

As to its final appearance, Brigham Young gave a hint at what design he had in mind for the temple at the cornerstone laying in 1853. He said,

> *I scarcely ever say much about revelations, or visions, but suffice it to say, five years ago last July I was here, and saw in spirit the Temple not ten feet from where we have laid the corner-stones. I have not inquired what kind of Temple we should build. Why? Because it was represented before me. I have never looked upon that ground, but the vision of it was there. Wait until it is done. I will say, however, that it will have six towers, instead of one.*[2]

Brigham Young appointed his long-time friend, Truman O. Angell, as Church architect in 1850 with Daniel H. Wells selected as a "Committee of One" to supervise construction in his capacity as superintendent of Church Public Works.

But it was Angell who, more than anyone else, was responsible for fleshing out the full architectural design.[3] An 1833 convert from Providence, Rhode Island, who had worked as a joiner on the Kirtland Temple, he served as Church architect from 1850 to 1861 and again from 1867 until his death

---

2. Brigham Young, in *Journal of Discourses*, 1:133. Wilford Woodruff also had a dream vision many years before of what the final temple should look like. In it he saw a fine-looking temple built of granite stones. Every time someone mentioned building it of adobe, brick, or some other material, he would say to himself, "No, you will never do it," perhaps because of his dream. Woodruff, *Journal of Discourses*, 21:299–300.
3. Wallace Alan Raynor, "History of the Construction of the Salt Lake Temple" (master's thesis, Brigham Young University, 1961), 21.

in 1887.[4] In 1855/56 Angell travelled on a special architectural mission to Great Britain and France to study construction and building designs such as the British Houses of Parliament, the National Gallery, Nelson's Monument on Trafalgar Square, and perhaps most especially, St. Paul's Cathedral.

From 1853 to 1855 work slowly progressed on laying a sixteen-foot-thick base foundation consisting of 7,478 tons of 101,000 cubic feet of hard rock. The original red butte sandstone walls were a few feet high when Johnston's Army arrived in the city in 1858, at which point Brigham Young ordered the walls be torn down and the foundation covered with dirt so that it looked "nothing more than a plowed field."[5] The impending invasion of the army, however, proved something of a blessing in disguise for when work recommenced in 1860, large cracks were noted on the sandstone foundation walls, necessitating their removal.

In the meantime, large outcrops of granite deposits, in reality syenite (a crystalline, igneous rock), had been discovered up Little Cottonwood Canyon nineteen miles southeast of the city with the resulting decision to follow Woodruff's dream and build the temple of solid granite. As with building the Kirtland Temple years earlier, the stonework proved the most daunting. Quarrying began in 1860 with further quarrying work moving near Alta in 1870. Moving large granite stones by cranes and winches, wagons and log rollings, proved a formidable challenge, and daily taxed the expert supervision of James C. Livingston, who was in charge of the quarries for thirty-three years. It took four days to move stones from the quarry to the building site, which led to the contemplation of building a canal, a part of which was built. However, the completion of the railroad in 1869 and the building of a spur line up the canyon in 1873 allowed for much easier transportation of mammoth stones of granite, some as big as a house in size and each weighing hundreds of tons.

---

4. William H. Folsom replaced Angell as chief architect from 1861 to 1867 and then later served as Angell's assistant.
5. Brigham Young to John M. Bernhisel, Brigham Young Letterbooks, no. 4, 6 May 1858, as cited in Raynor, "Construction of the Salt Lake Temple," 37.

"RUN THIS CHAIN THROUGH AS FAR AS YOU CAN GET IT"

Quarrying granite rocks in Little Cottonwood Canyon for the Salt Lake Temple.

Preparing stones for the Salt Lake Temple.

Although hewing out and transporting the giant stones from the canyon was truly a remarkable feat, cutting them precisely to size was even more challenging. Every hewn stone was lettered, numbered, and billed to its proper place, as per the architect's unfolding design, and careful stonecutting work was the tallest order of every day. Subsequently, not until 1867 did the temple walls rise above the ground. Eleven years later, right after Brigham Young's death, the walls stood 40 feet high; by 1879, 45 feet; by 1883, 85 feet; and by 1889, 160 feet.

During the 1860s, from 90 to 150 men were working daily on the temple, either contributing tithing labor or as wage earners at up to three dollars a day. After 1876, over 200 men were working daily on site, what James Talmage described as "the one great work-shop of the intermountain commonwealth" and certainly the largest single project undertaken by the Trustee-in-Trust of the Church, working through the Public Works.[6] To the unending frustrations of Church architects and engineers, however, there were never enough skilled craftsmen and expert stonecutters available to work at the temple block. Many were away building railroads or colonizing new cities. And, unfortunately, four workers were killed while working on the temple.

Nor was there ever enough money. With the decisions to build the three other temples, resources were spread extremely thin, despite the hundreds of thousands of dollars raised through special monthly donations from the Saints. And as previously noted, the legal costs in defending the interests of the Church were substantial. Nor did the leadership of the Church ever feel that enough members were paying their tithing. As George Q. Cannon complained, "If this people would pay one-tenth of their tithing this temple [Salt Lake] could be pushed forward to completion very speedily. As a people we have been very negligent in paying our tithing."[7]

The passage of the Edmunds-Tucker Act ground all work to a halt until the question of legal ownership was resolved; however, once the temple title was relinquished by the US government in 1888, work recommenced. With the demolition of the Endowment House in 1889, final

---

6. Talmage, *House of the Lord*, 126–28.
7. George Q. Cannon, in *Journal of Discourses*, 14:122–29, 8 April 1871.

The Salt Lake Temple under construction.

construction moved into high gear but always in keeping with Angell's original plan. Angell himself died in 1887.[8]

The Salt Lake Temple is symmetrical in design, the eastern half being a duplicate of the western half, only slightly taller, and the northern half a repeat of the southern. The three towers on each end, east and west, with their spires and finials, are duplicates of each other. The walls, eight feet thick at the base, taper in thickness to six feet as they ascend upwards. All windows, both arched and oval, above the basement are framed with oolite and recede three feet from the face of the walls to the window sash. The temple's dimensions are 186 feet 6 inches long, 118 feet 6 inches wide, and 167 feet 6 inches high at the square, and it covers 21,850 square feet. The center tower on the west end stands 204 feet but its eastern counterpart, representing the greater priesthood, is 6 feet higher, excluding the angel Moroni statue which stands another 12 feet 5½ inches high.

The symbolism employed throughout what is still referred to as the "Grand Temple," extending from towers to doorknobs, is rich and deliberate and references much of the doctrines and ordinances associated with it. The building faces east, toward Nauvoo, Kirtland, and Jackson County, Missouri. The three eastern towers represent the First Presidency of the Melchizedek Priesthood; those on the west, the Presiding Bishopric of the Aaronic Priesthood. There are thirty-four earth stones or globes situated twenty-eight inches above ground level, each weighing more than three tons; fifty moon stones higher up, each one representing the moon in one of its four quarters; and fifty sun stones near the level of the roof, each cut to represent the body of the sun with a serrated edge of fifty-two points illustrative of the sun's rays for every week of the year. There are also 104 five-pointed star stones found all over the building and another 184 stones depicting the planet Saturn with its rings. Just below the capstones on the two principal buttresses of the eastern towers are the two cloud stones,

---

8. Said Daniel H. Wells at the funeral of Truman O. Angell, "Brother Angell needs no monument at his grave, for as long as the Salt Lake Temple stands, that is monument enough for him." Wendell J. Ashton, *Theirs is the Kingdom* (Salt Lake City: Bookcraft Co., 1945), 125.

each weighing 3,000 pounds, representing the billowing clouds through which rays of light are shining, clearly a symbol of revelation and inspiration. The west center tower's principal façade depicts the constellation Ursa Major (the Big Dipper) with its two pointer stars in line with the North Star, meaning that those who lose their way may find it again by aid of the priesthood.[9] The doorways at the four principal entries, each 16 feet high and 8½ feet wide, encase 12-foot-high oak doors. The finely crafted doorknobs on each door feature a beehive representing "Deseret" and bear the inscription "Holiness to the Lord." On each side of the doorways flanking the center tower is a canopied niche in the granite, large enough to receive a statue of heroic proportions.[10]

Inscribed above the molded windows in the center tower of both the east and west ends are the words: "I am Alpha and Omega" (Revelation 1:8), a figurative reminder of both time and eternity. Below these inscriptions are clasped hands representing brotherhood and fellowship. Above the upper windows in stone is depicted the "All-Seeing Eye" of the Great Jehovah. The principal inscription stone on the east center tower, completed just one day before the dedication, bears the following words:

Holiness to the Lord
THE HOUSE OF THE LORD
Built by the Church of Jesus Christ of Latter-day Saints
Commenced April 6, 1853
Completed April 6, 1893

The spherical capstone was laid on 6 April 1892 in front of an audience of over 40,000 people. Eager onlookers crowded housetops and windows of nearby buildings. Fathers held their children on their shoulders so that they might glimpse the sight. Just before the hour of noon

---

9. Raynor, "Construction of the Salt Lake Temple," 153–78; see also James E. Talmage, *House of the Lord*, 162–64.
10. Talmage, *House of the Lord*, 166. For several years, the niches at the east end of the temple were occupied by statues of Joseph and Hyrum Smith, which were later moved elsewhere on Temple Square.

approached, chief architect Don Carlos Young shouted from the top of the temple, "The capstone is now ready to be laid." On cue, President Woodruff stepped to the platform and said: "Attention all ye house of Israel, and all ye nations of the earth! We will now lay the top stone to the Temple of our God, the foundation of which was laid by the Prophet, Seer, and Revelator, Brigham Young."[11] He then touched an electric button which lowered the capstone into place. Elder Lorenzo Snow, president of the Quorum of the Twelve and soon to be first president of the Salt Lake Temple, gave the sacred shout: "Hosanna! Hosanna! Hosanna! To God and the Lamb! Amen! Amen! And Amen!" This was thrice given, with the waving of handkerchiefs and expressions of joy from the assembled crowd. A moment later the assembled thousands led by the choir burst into singing "The Spirit of God like a Fire Is Burning," the temple anthem written by W. W. Phelps and sung for the first time at the dedication of the Kirtland Temple fifty-six years before. It must have seemed to those few in the audience who remembered that long ago day in 1836 that it all had come full circle, temple work that is, from near the shores of Lake Erie, to the banks of the Mississippi, and now to the borders of the Great Salt Lake. Later that day, the capstone was surmounted by the great statue of the angel Moroni, made of copper heavily gilded in gold.[12] This marked the first time the angel Moroni statue ever graced a temple, setting a precedent still used today, where possible.

Still, the temple remained incomplete. Although its exterior lay finished, much of the interior remained in a "state of chaos and confusion," to borrow Talmage's phrase.[13] Thus on this day of dedication, Elder

---

11. *Deseret Evening News*, 6 April 1892.
12. Sculpted by Utah-born Cyrus E. Dallin (who was not a member of the Church) and made in Salem, Ohio, the angel Moroni statue was made of twenty-four-gauge hammered copper, heavily gilded with gold leaf. Representing the angel of the Restoration (Revelation 14:6), the statue is anchored by a twenty-seven-foot rod that extends downward into the eastern tower in a unique suspension system design (Raynor, "Construction of the Salt Lake Temple," 178.) Several of the early drawings had represented the angel in a flying position in both east and west towers consistent with the angel on the Nauvoo Temple (Raynor, 188).
13. Talmage, *House of the Lord*, 138.

"RUN THIS CHAIN THROUGH AS FAR AS YOU CAN GET IT"

The angel Moroni atop the Salt Lake Temple.

Francis M. Lyman proposed that out of deference to Wilford Woodruff's wishes to live to see the temple completed in one year's time, the assembly pledge themselves individually and collectively to do everything in their power to raise money and assistance to purchase the necessary furnishings, complete the interior woodwork, install the mural paintings, and provide the many wonderful decorations so characteristic of the Salt Lake Temple—all in time for the following April.

Mechanics and millworkers, plasterers and painters, engineers and electricians, and a wide variety of other skilled laborers worked around the clock installing everything from crown moldings to tapestries, chandeliers to plumbing and heating features. An annex on the north side as an office and reception center also had to be built. In the basement, three feet below the floor level, baptismal room workers installed an elliptical-shaped baptismal font twenty-one feet in diameter on the backs of twelve life-sized, cast-iron oxen with bronzed bodies and silvered horns. In line with the upward movement from room to room that had characterized the Endowment House, from the garden room, one may ascend the thirty-five-step grand stairway with its massive balustrade, made of cherry wood, to the upper corridor running forty feet north and south, and from there to the world room depicting a fallen world and Adam and Eve's expulsion from the Garden of Eden. From the northwest corner of this room is a large doorway leading into another, equally large apartment featuring the terrestrial world (also called the lecture room), with its veil of the temple leading to the magnificent celestial room, the grandest of all rooms with its mirrors and canvas scenes representing the presence of God. Nearby are sealing rooms, one for the living and one for the dead, each with altars and chairs, where husbands and wives, parents and children, are sealed together for time and eternity. In between them and designed in "splendid simplicity" is the sacred Holy of Holies, eighteen feet in diameter, reserved for special prayers and ordinances of exaltation.

Near the landing of the granite stairway in the southeast tower on the third floor is the Dome Room, at the center of which is a large dome, fifty-one feet in circumference, and the ceiling of the Holy of Holies already described. West of the Dome Room and still on the third floor are various council rooms for the Quorum of the Twelve, the Seventy, the Elders, the First Presidency and High Council. A very large auditorium or main assembly room occupies virtually all of the fourth floor, with pulpits raised on a terraced platform at each end, the east representing the Melchizedek and the west the Aaronic Priesthood, with seats of reversible construction, allowing for attendees to face either direction—all as in the Kirtland Temple.[14] Each of the main endowment rooms features highly impressive mural paintings designed to add to and capture the changing meanings

---

14. Talmage, *House of the Lord*, 181–200.

and faces of the endowment.[15] The next floor has an elevator landing at the west and a cross-corridor connecting the two corner towers at both the east and west ends of the temple. Four granite stairways in each of the four corner towers lead from basement to roof, each step of solid granite.

Many doubted the possibility of completing the interior of the temple in just one year. Nevertheless, thanks to the intrepid efforts of hundreds of workers acting under the direction of architect Joseph Don Carlos and "the assiduous labors, faith and persistency and watchfulness of bishop John R. Winder," the interior of the Salt Lake Temple was indeed completed in 364 days, allowing the temple to be dedicated while President Woodruff was still alive on 6 April 1893.[16] Twenty-three different dedicatory services lasted from that day until 18 May, with some 75,000 people attending. During that time, the First Presidency invited several hundred "outsiders" or nonmembers to visit the temple who were surprised and delighted at the richness and beauty displayed in the workmanship. As he had done with the Manti Temple, President Woodruff offered the dedicatory prayer.[17]

As a special invitation and inducement for as many Latter-day Saints to attend the temple as possible, President Woodruff, in the same spirit of John Taylor during the 1880 Jubilee celebrations, announced a revelation "telling him to let every person into this Temple who had been in this church and were not cut off." He went on to say, "Our brothers, who've been off the track, would receive recommends to go there."[18] His

---

15. Rachel Cope, "John B. Fairbanks: The Man behind the Canvas" (master's thesis, Brigham Young University, 2003).
16. Journal History, 6 April 1893.
17. Marion D. Hanks, "Salt Lake Temple," in *Encyclopedia of Mormonism*, 3:1252–54. Anthony W. Ivins said that the spirit and power of God was never in this dispensation poured out in stronger degree than at the dedication meeting of the Salt Lake Temple. "The day has come," he said, "when Zion is to be favored . . . that Satan would from that Dedication time be more limited in power than [he] had ever been." Anthony W. Ivins, St. George Utah Stake Minutes, vol. 18, 7 May 1893.
18. Helen Mar Kimball Whitney, *A Widow's Tale*, 6:538, 1 April 1893. See also excerpts of Wilford Woodruff's Address, Journal History, 2, 5 April 1893.

Salt Lake dedication services, 9 April 1893.

announcement was a tender mercy to the membership of the Church and brought many back into the circle of temple worship.

How compelling this invitation may have been is not known but what is clear is that so many people began attending the Salt Lake Temple that attendance at the other three temples temporarily fell off. As James Bleak said in St. George: "The Salt Lake Temple was pretty well patronized [since those in and around Salt Lake City no longer needed to travel to faraway temples], but in the Logan and Manti Temple districts, the work has fallen off considerably."[19] It would take time for attendance at the other temples to catch up to their earlier statistics.

"LET EVERY MAN BE ADOPTED TO HIS FATHER"

The Salt Lake Temple may have been fully completed in 1893 but the doctrines of temple work were still developing. In April 1894 President Woodruff proclaimed a highly influential revelation ending the law of adoption. Overshadowed since by the Manifesto, this statement is of no less importance to temple work. Explaining that none of the previous

---

19. James G. Bleak, St. George Temple Meeting Minutes, 7:91, 20 November 1895.

"RUN THIS CHAIN THROUGH AS FAR AS YOU CAN GET IT"

Presidents of the Church had received "all the revelations that belong to this work," Woodruff said that "there will be no end to this work until it is perfected." He then announced the following major change in policy:

> *When I went before the Lord to know who I should be adopted to, the Spirit of God said to me, "Have you not a father, who begot you?" "Yes, I have." "Then, why not honor him? Why not be adopted to him?" "Yes," says I, "that is right." I was adopted to my father, and should have had my father sealed to his father, and so on back; and the duty that I want every man who presides over a Temple to see performed from this day henceforth and forever, unless the Lord Almighty commands otherwise, is, let every man be adopted to his father. When a man receives the endowment, adopt him to his father; not Wilford Woodruff, not to any other man outside the lineage of his father. That is the will of God to this people... We want the Latter-day Saints from this time to trace their genealogies as far as they can, and be sealed to their parents, and run this chain through as far as you can get it.... This is the will of the Lord to his people, and I think when you come to reflect upon it you will find it to be true.... It is right, for children to be sealed to their parents, and they to their parents just as far back as we can possibly obtain the records.... [And when all completed] the last obtainable member [should be] sealed to the Prophet Joseph, who stands at the head of this dispensation.[20]*

Like the Manifesto, this revelation was long in coming. As discussed in an earlier chapter, spiritually adopting members (and occasionally prominent deceased nonmembers whose baptisms had been performed) to living and deceased Church leaders, most notably living and former General Authorities of the Church, was a practice that had remained popular for many years, even after the introduction of endowments for the dead in 1877. Several thousand such ordinances were performed in the

---

20. *Deseret Evening News*, 14 April 1894; see also Clark, *Messages of the First Presidency*, 3:252–60. Though never canonized as doctrine in the Doctrine and Covenants, Woodruff clearly and often testified that this statement came as a revelation from God.

St. George, Manti, and Logan temples. Many longed to be sealed to those beloved missionary leaders who had converted them. The practice grew increasingly antiquated as more and more families chose to be sealed to their ancestors, but it nevertheless remained attractive to more than a few, like a trusted backup plan.

The lynchpin to the practice of adoption had always been the sealing to priesthood authority. However, since endowments for the dead incorporated provision for the teaching of the gospel to the dead in the spirit world, and with it the conditional bestowal of priesthood authority and office to past generations of family ancestors, and also led to sealings or marriages for the dead, the long-standing practice of spiritual adoptions no longer held the doctrinal urgency it had forty years previous. Whereas there had been over 488,000 endowments for the dead performed in the temples between 1877 and the close of the century, only 15,000 adoptions had been performed during that same time period—for both living and dead (see charts in previous chapter). Temple work was thus becoming significantly more family-centered than before and much more personalized. Wilford Woodruff's 1894 revelation ending the practice of spiritual adoptions owed everything to the beginning of endowments for the dead in 1877 and certainly foreshadowed Joseph F. Smith's vision of the dead (D&C 138) announced twenty-four years later.

It may be that the Manifesto aimed at ending plural marriage also led to the termination of the law of adoption, or vice versa. If the law of adoption can be likened to the vertical spinal column to the body politic of Church membership, and plural marriage the horizontal extensions thereto—like the branches of a tree—once the column or trunk was no longer necessary, the appendages accordingly fell away. Therefore the ending of one may have influenced the termination of the other. Certainly the statements ending both practices came from the same man and at nearly the same time. With men and their many sealed wives no longer being sealed (adopted) to other men, the practice of plural marriage lost the center pole that had held it in place. And just as Woodruff had long contemplated the Manifesto, he had done the same in regard to the law of adoption. In his revelation on the matter, he made clear that from now on men and women were to be sealed to their own parents and ancestors who were being taught the gospel in the spirit world. With a fuller doctrinal understanding now in place that deceased ancestors were receiving the priesthood through endowments for the dead in holy temples, living descendants could now safely be sealed to their own priesthood-bearing ancestors. One can hardly overemphasize the enormous impact this directive has had on modern family history work and on Church temple attendance, for surely it marked a paradigm shift in temple consciousness.[21]

With the ending of the law of adoption in favor of family intergenerational sealings of deceased ancestors, it should therefore come as no surprise that President Wilford Woodruff founded the Genealogical Society of Utah later that same year (1894) with Elder Franklin D. Richards, Church Historian, serving as first president from 1894 to 1899. He also urged the Saints to trace and submit their own family lineages for temple work.[22] Discussions concerning the establishment of such a society had been circulating among the highest levels for years, but it was not until Duncan McAllister, previously associated with the Latter-day Saints' Genealogical Bureau, petitioned the Church on this issue in early 1893 that things really began to move.[23] Soon afterward the Society, originally located in the old Historian's Office at 58 East South Temple in Salt Lake City, was organized. Work promptly began on constructing shelves for a beginning library, one destined to become the largest of its kind in the world.[24]

---

21. Like plural marriage, the law of adoption did not end overnight. Records show that this ordinance was occasionally permitted as late as 1955.
22. James B. Allen, Jessie L. Embry, Kahlile B. Mehr, *Hearts Turned to the Fathers: A History of the Genealogical Society of Utah, 1894–1994* (Provo, Utah: BYU Studies, 1995), 40–46; see also Gordon I. Irving, "The Law of Adoption," and Richard E. Bennett, "Line upon Line, Precept upon Precept," 62–64.
23. Allen et al., *Hearts Turned to the Fathers*, 44–45.
24. Renamed FamilySearch, the Society as of 2007 housed hundreds of thousands of books and 2.4 million rolls of microfilm containing some two billion names. Now digitized, it has more than

The original Utah Genealogical Society.

This gradually developing policy change of being sealed to one's own ancestry rather than to prominent ecclesiastical leaders gave rise to a keener sense of the dead and of a sharpened belief that they, in their present sphere of existence, were likewise reaching out across a great gulf to the living. John Taylor, expounding on Wilford Woodruff's vision of the Founding Fathers and other prominent men and women of the past, put it this way:

> *You have perhaps heard him testify of visits that he has had from the spirit world, the spirits of men who once lived on the earth, desiring him to officiate for them in temple ordinances. This feeling is planted in the hearts of the people; and the Priesthood in the heavens are watching over us; they are ministering spirits sent forth to minister*

---

five billion names from around the world and 4,745 family search centers. It is today the premier genealogical society in the world.

to those who shall be heirs of salvation, says the Apostle; and if we were not the recipients of their ministrations and watchful care, we should be in a poor condition. They are operating in the heavens, and we are on the earth; they cannot be made perfect, neither we without them; it requires the combined and united efforts of both parties, directed by God Himself to consummate the work we are engaged in.[25]

Despite what temple these ordinances were being performed in, the anecdotal evidence of the spirits of the dead communicating with their living descendants in very literal ways is archivally well documented. In 1870 at the Endowment House, there were several reports of such happenings. "We are performing a great work here for the dead," Robert Bell of Richmond reported, "and they seem to appreciate it for in many instances they have appeared and requested their living friends to do their work for them. Only a short time ago a little girl lately from England the only one of her family . . . went to the endowment House to be baptized for her grandmother but being young and a little nervous she was afraid to go into the water until her grandmother who died in England appeared and asked her how long she would keep her waiting and in suspense."[26] Many years later, James G. Bleak of the St. George Temple told of an experience one of his fellow temple workers had sometime before. "One day three women stood before him and one of them said, 'Here are three of your aunts, why do you not do something for them.' When he went home this man inquired of his sister, and he found that those three names had been left off the list. Here you see how the dead are feeling out for help from those who are on the earth. The Lord will honor those who come here and labor for their dead."[27] Many temple presidents, workers, and patrons attested to similar experiences.

John D. T. McAllister, second president of the St. George Temple and

---

25. John Taylor, in *Journal of Discourses*, 19:159, 14 November 1877.
26. Robert Bell to his father and mother, Robert Bell Correspondence, 29 June 1870, MS 5903, Church History Library.
27. Bleak, St. George Temple Minutes, 7:91, 20 November 1895.

later president of the Manti Temple, added the following: "I used to sleep here in my turn with others in the N. E. corner of [the] old dining room. The corner was screened in and I slept alone for a while. That was before my family came here to St. George. While sleeping in the room I thought the room was full of dead people and they seemed to say to me, 'Here we have been waiting for 10 years.'"[28]

John David Thompson McAllister (1827–1910).

Many other temple workers and visitors to the temple, especially in the late 1880s and 1890s, spoke of sensing the presence of the dead in companies within the temple, of having to stay awake during the endowment lest the deceased person for whom they were officiating not be endowed, and of reciting the necessary wording precisely at the risk of jeopardizing the opportunity for the deceased person. Fellow temple presidency member, David H. Cannon, instructed temple workers in much the same vein when he "enjoined upon those going [through] for the dead to be very particular. It is a new company of the dead, that is endowed each day; they are endowed but once. Therefore how careful we should be."[29]

Correspondingly, the rising responsibility placed upon the membership of the Church to seek after the salvation of their own ancestral families gave rise to a heightened sense of belonging to them, of seeking their welfare, even allowing for the possibility of communication one

---

28. McAllister, St. George Temple Minutes, 7:343–44, 3 September 1896.
29. David H. Cannon, 6 November 1894, St. George Temple Minutes, 6:233. Again from James Bleak: "Let us give strict attention. Those who personate the dead, let them do so correctly. There are waiting souls, now in this room, who are anxiously waiting to have this performed for them." Bleak, 16 November 1894, St. George Temple Minutes, 6:239. Occasional appearances of the dead are also recorded.

with another. Not to be equated with Spiritualism, as discussed earlier, this temple-centered pursuit was not a seeking after the dead but rather a quest for their redemption. It led to a lively belief in the need for generations past and present to care one for another in profoundly spiritual and emotional ways.

Mention should also be made of two other Church practices that were changed during this period. The first was that of changing the monthly fast day from the first Thursday in each month to that of the first Sunday. This was in recognition of changing work patterns among the Saints who were moving in large numbers from rural to urban centers and were now working during the week and generally having Sundays off. Having a midweek fast day was no longer practical. A second change was the termination of the ordinance of rebaptisms for the living. Long performed as a way of reconsecration and rededication, now that temples were in full operation the need for such a renewal was superseded and replaced by other forms of covenant renewal, including the sacrament and the endowment.[30] Likewise, the ritual of baptisms for health was discontinued in 1922.

STATEHOOD

With the issuance of the Manifesto, the political atmosphere changed and a new era of cooperation between church and state ensued. While disagreements still remained, both Saints and "Gentiles" sought reconciliation and greater mutual understanding. Husbands were not required to reject their plural families or children but rather to live with only one of their families. In January 1893 President Benjamin Harrison issued an amnesty to all those who had been in compliance with the law since 1890 and he was followed by President Grover Cleveland who issued a more general amnesty. At the same time, the former Church political party—the People's Party—and the more anti-LDS party—the Liberal Party—were both disbanded and the Church led an effort to align membership along

---

30. Roberts, *Comprehensive History of the Church*, 6:348–49; Allen and Leonard, *Story of the Latter-day Saints*, 425–26.

traditional Democratic or Republican lines. By 1896, most if not all titles to properties escheated to the government were restored to the Church.

In late 1895, a political convention assembled in Salt Lake City to draw up the first constitution of the proposed state of Utah. Declaring that plural marriage would be "forever prohibited" in the state of Utah, and with support from within and outside the Church, the pathway was now clear for statehood, which proclamation was signed into law by President Grover Cleveland and proclaimed on 4 January 1896. On that day, the Territory of Utah, after a near half-century of petitioning, became the forty-fifth state of the Union amidst tremendous local celebrations and festivities. Heber M. Wells, a faithful Latter-day Saint, served as Utah's first elected governor.

"I WAS ALMOST COVERED UP WITH FLOWERS" —WOODRUFF'S FINAL YEARS

On 1 March 1897, President Woodruff celebrated his ninetieth birthday with a throng of 12,000 who came to the Tabernacle to mark this special occasion. "I was almost covered up with flowers and roses," he recalled. "At the close of the services myself and wife, Emma, took seats upon elevated chairs and shook hands with the congregation as they passed us. . . . Of course our arms ached when we got through, but it was a great day. All the papers published our speeches and likenesses. It is very remarkable how my life has been preserved through so many years, considering what I have passed through in my day and generation."[31]

The year 1897 also marked the jubilee anniversary of the arrival of the pioneers into the Salt Lake Valley and was marked by wide-scale celebrations, parades, the coinage of gold medals, and the dedication of the Brigham Young and Pioneer monuments at the head of Main Street in Salt Lake City. President Woodruff, though feeble and in declining health, participated in the festivities and recalled clearly the day he and Brigham

---

31. *Wilford Woodruff's Journal,* 9:449, 1 March 1897.

"RUN THIS CHAIN THROUGH AS FAR AS YOU CAN GET IT"

Young had entered the Valley fifty years before and the moment they marked the site for the Salt Lake Temple. In almost begrudging praise of the pioneers, Judge Charles C. Goodwin, longtime editor of the *Salt Lake Tribune* and a robust critic of the Church, wrote: "They wore out their lives in toil. They suffered without plaint. From nothing they created a glorified state. Honor and reverence and glory everlasting be theirs."[32]

In 1898 President Woodruff's health rapidly deteriorated, despite every effort of his longtime private secretary, L. John Nuttall. Asthma had troubled him for a long time. Occasional visits to the West Coast had brought temporary relief but no real lasting benefit. That summer he traveled again to San Francisco seeking comfort but died there early in the morning of 2 September 1898 in the home of Isaac Trumbo. Years before, Woodruff had directed in a memo "Concerning My Death and Burial" that the color black not be used in his coffin [or] the vehicle that would take his body to the grave, that his family and friends not "wear any badge of mourning for me at my funeral or afterwards." And "If the laws and customs of the spirit world will permit, I should wish to attend my funeral myself, but I shall be governed by the counsel I receive in the spirit world."[33]

His remains were brought back to Salt Lake City by a special train, tendered free by the Rio Grande Western Railroad. Thousands of men and women from all walks of life and representing both defenders and critics of the Church attended his funeral held in the Tabernacle. From compilations recorded in his own journal, he had traveled during his lifetime over 172,000 miles, attended 7,655 meetings, preached 3,562 times, organized 51 branches of the Church, converted hundreds if not thousands of new members, and performed countless thousands of ordinances for both the living and the dead. His handwritten journals to this day constitute an

---

32. Roberts, *Comprehensive History of the Church*, 6:350.
33. Wilford Woodruff Letterpress Copybook, 25.

Funeral of President Wilford Woodruff, September 1898.

original documentary, a historical treasure which continues to prove invaluable to an accurate study of Mormon history.

Unquestionably Wilford Woodruff played an enormously important role in the history of the Church. He was one of its most successful missionaries. He brought the Church into the modern era with the Manifesto ending the practice of plural marriage without betraying the convictions and revelations of his predecessors and without surrendering the soul and mission of the Church. Principled and courageous with deep spiritual commitments, he nonetheless came to know the value of compromise and of being reasonable. Such a stance laid the groundwork for Utah's admission into the Union. A prolific reader of history and a student of the scriptures, he was the founder of modern temple work in that he supervised the completion of several new temples, promoted endowments for the dead, ended the law of adoption and replaced it with family history and the sealing of living generations to past ancestral associations. He was a kind, good man, a loyal husband and father, whose life was spared over and over again.

CONCLUSION

The changes wrought by President Wilford Woodruff in the last seven years of his life have had a profound impact upon the doctrines, practices, and history of The Church of Jesus Christ of Latter-day Saints. The ending of the practice of plural marriage with the Manifesto of 1890, the beginning of endowments for the dead and the sealings of past generations in marriage, the reconstruction of family ties and units, the ending of emphasis on the law of adoption, and the establishment of the Utah Genealogical Society and with it the strong emphasis on family history, have changed much of what it means to be a member of the Church. At the same time, however, President Woodruff preserved the central place of temple work and recognized, through his expanded vision of redemption of both the living and the dead how truly important temple worship had become. His vision left an indelible imprint upon an expanding Restoration.

Epilogue
"The Present Is Only a Beginning"

This work has come a long way in its study of the rise of temples and of temple consciousness among the Latter-day Saints from 1830 to the end of the nineteenth century. Our road has wound its way from Jackson County, Missouri, to Kirtland, Ohio, and to Nauvoo, Illinois, and from there across the great American Plains to the valleys of the Rocky Mountains—a remarkable journey of faith tested in times of severe affliction and recurring persecution. Clearly this work has focused far less on the architecture, construction, and symbolism of Latter-day Saint temples and much more on the history, doctrines, and meaning of temples and their increasing hold on the minds and hearts of believers. Likewise it has given place for the spirit of sacrifice and consecration that has characterized the devotion of the Saints in their ever-growing allegiance to temple worship.

And as was said in the beginning, the birthday cake of temple worship did not suddenly arrive all ready for the party. Rather, the story of Latter-day Saint temples and temple worship in the nineteenth century featured one critical new development after another, one sacrifice upon another, and one revelation leading to yet another. Under the direction of a succession of prophets, culminating in the remarkable expansion of ordinances for the dead at St. George, the preservation and expansion of temple work as signaled by President Woodruff in his Manifesto of 1890, and the eventual termination of the law of adoption, a growing sense of the importance of temples among the Saints transitioned into a new and sacred place of prominence.

From four active temples in 1900 to over 200 either announced, in renovation, or in use today, temple building has escalated at an unprecedented pace. The Church now relies on teams of architects, and the styles of the temples vary depending on the country and culture, and even local codes and restrictions. Temples that used to be built with funds raised primarily by local congregations are now built with aggregate Church funds. The advancement from handwritten four-generation sheets to cloud-based apps has empowered members to participate in temple work from start to finish, from nearly any place in the world. Even the temple presentation has changed significantly. Film began to be used in the 1970s, with significant changes made over time. Other parts of the temple worship have also seen transitions, some for convenience, others to embrace cultural sensitivities. Temple clothing too has improved, as new fabrics and styles have been developed and instituted. Yet, with all these advances and innovations, the fundamentals of temple work have remained remarkably consistent.

As important as these changes and developments have been, everything so far can be described as but prologue to what has been happening recently within the Church—foundational might be an even better term. Revelation by its very nature implies change in policies, procedures, and understandings. Such changes in the past presage the possibility, if not the likelihood, of continual revelations in the future and with them adaptations and dynamic new developments in temple work and understanding.

We give the final word to Wilford Woodruff:

> *This is a preparation necessary for the second advent of the Savior; and when we shall have built the temples now contemplated, we will then begin to see the necessity of building others, for in proportion to the diligence of our labors in this direction, will we*

comprehend the extent of the work to be done, and the present is only a beginning. When the Savior comes, a thousand years will be devoted to this work of redemption; and temples will appear all over this land of Joseph—North and South America—and also in Europe and elsewhere; and all the descendants of Shem, Ham, and Japheth, who receive not the gospel in the flesh, must be officiated for in the Temples of God, before the Savior can present the kingdom to the Father, saying, "It is finished."[1]

---

1. Wilford Woodruff, *Journal of Discourses,* 19:229–30, 16 September 1977.

Primary Sources

Angell, Truman O. Autobiography. Typescript. MSS 937. L. Tom Perry Special Collections, Harold B. Lee Library, Brigham Young University. Also transcribed online at Book of Abraham Project. http://www.boap.org/LDS/Early-Saints/TAngell.html.
Barney, Lewis. Life Sketch. Nauvoo Lands and Records Office, Nauvoo, Illinois.
Bell, Robert. Correspondence. MS 5903. Church History Library, Salt Lake City.
Bigler, Henry W. Autobiographies. Typescript. L. Tom Perry Special Collections, Harold B. Lee Library, Brigham Young University.
Bleak, James G. Annals of the Southern Utah Mission, circa 1905. MS 22894. Church History Library, Salt Lake City.
———. Collection. L. Tom Perry Special Collections, Harold B. Lee Library, Brigham Young University.
———. Diary. In James G. Bleak Collection, MSS 1691. L. Tom Perry Special Collections, Harold B. Lee Library, Brigham Young University.
Book of Abraham Project. "Journals, Diaries, Biographies, Autobiographies and Letters of Some Early Mormons and Others Who Knew Joseph Smith, Jr. and/or His Contemporaries." Transcripts. http://www.boap.org/LDS/Early-Saints (accessed 4 October 2018).
Bradshaw, Gilbert. "The Council House as a House for Sacred Ordinances in the Early Church." Unpublished undergraduate research paper, in possession of the author.
Bullock, Thomas. Collection, 1830–1939. MS 27307. Church History Library, Salt Lake City.
———. Journals, 1843–1849. Microfilm. MS 2737, box 65. Church History Library, Salt Lake City.
Burket, George. Journal, 1835 September to 1836 May. Transcript. MS 10340. Church History Library, Salt Lake City.
Cannon, Abraham H. Diaries. MSS 62. L. Tom Perry Special Collections, Harold B. Lee Library, Brigham Young University.
Cannon, George Q. Journal of George Q. Cannon. https://www.churchhistorianspress.org/george-q-cannon?lang=eng. Online only.
Carter, Eliza Ann to James C. Snow, 22 Jul. 1837, unpublished. In Reid N. Moon, "Jane Austen Meets the Wild West: Letter from a Young Woman in Kirtland,"

313

PRIMARY SOURCES

Meridian Magazine, 25 April 2017. http://ldsmag.com/jane-austen-meets-the-wild-west-letter-from-a-young-woman-in-kirtland/ (accessed 3 October 2018).

Church Historian's Letterpress Copybooks, 1842–1915. CR 100 39. Church Historian's Office, Church History Library, Salt Lake City.

Church Historian's Office Journal. CR 100 1. Church History Library, Salt Lake City.

Draper, William. "Biographical Sketch of the Life and Travels and Birth and Parentage of William Draper who was the son of William Draper and Lydia Lathrop [Luthdrop] Draper." Typescript. L. Tom Perry Special Collections, Harold B. Lee Library, Brigham Young University.

Duncan, Chapman. Autobiography. Typescript. L. Tom Perry Special Collections, Harold B. Lee Library, Brigham Young University.

Endowment and Sealings, Book A. Microfilm. Family History Library, Salt Lake City.

"Endowment House Baptism for the Dead Record Books, Book A." Microfilm. Family History Library, Salt Lake City.

"Endowment House [Council House] Records 1851–1855." Microfilm. Family History Library, Harold B. Library, Brigham Young University.

Fielding, Joseph. Journal, 1843 December–1859 March. MS 1567. Church History Library, Salt Lake City.

First Presidency (Wilford Woodruff) General Correspondence, 1887–1898. CR 1 171. Church History Library, Salt Lake City.

Frost, Allen. *The Diary of Allen Frost*, 1838–1901, 2 vols. 1949. L. Tom Perry Special Collections, Harold B. Lee Library, Brigham Young University.

———. Reminiscences and Journals. MS 1914. Church History Library, Salt Lake City.

Fullmer, John S. Letterbook, 1836–1881. MS 117. Church History Library, Salt Lake City.

General Church Minutes 1839–1877. CR 100 318. Church History Library, Salt Lake City.

Hancock, Levi. Journal. Typescript. L. Tom Perry Special Collections, Harold B. Lee Library, Brigham Young University.

Hascall, Irene Ursulia. Hascall Family Letters. MS 22096. Church History Library, Salt Lake City.

"History of the Church, 1839–ca.1882." Also called "History of Brigham Young." CR 100 102. Church Historian's Office, Church History Library, Salt Lake City.

Holbrook, Caroline Frances Angell Davis. A Sketch of the Life and Experiences of Caroline Frances Angell Davis Holbrook. Holbrook Family Organization Website, accessible through Book of Abraham Project. http://www.boap.org/LDS/Early-Saints/CAngell.html (accessed 26 September 2016).

Hovey, Joseph G. Papers, 1845–1856, circa 1933. MS 1576. Church History Library, Salt Lake City.

Jacob, Norton. The Life of Norton Jacob. Typescript. L. Tom Perry Special Collections, Harold B. Lee Library, Brigham Young University.

John, David. Diaries. MSS 21. L. Tom Perry Special Collections, Harold B. Lee Library, Brigham Young University.

Johnson, Joel Hills. "A Journal or Sketch of the Life of Joel Hills Johnson." MS 8237, item 67. Church History Library, Salt Lake City.

Journal History of The Church of Jesus Christ of Latter-day Saints, 1896–2001 July. CR 100 137. Church History Library, Salt Lake City.

PRIMARY SOURCES

Kimball, Heber C. Autobiography and Journals, 1837–1845. Typescript. MS 2737, box 7. Church History Library, Salt Lake City.

———. Journals. MSS 6142. L. Tom Perry Special Collections, Harold B. Lee Library, Brigham Young University.

Kimball, J. Golden. Diaries, 1885–1932. Photocopy of holograph. Special Collections, J. Willard Marriott Library, University of Utah.

Kirtland High Council Minutes. MS 3432. Church History Library, Salt Lake City.

Lee, John D. Agatha M. P. Henrie Family Papers. MS 25741. Church History Library, Salt Lake City.

"Legal, Business, and Financial Records." Online only. *The Joseph Smith Papers*, 2018. http://www.josephsmithpapers.org/the-papers/legal-business-and-financial-records (accessed 2 October 2018).

Logan Temple Letterpress Copybook, 1877–1908. CR 308 5. Church History Library, Salt Lake City.

Logan Temple Ordinance Statistics, Daily Register of Ordinance Work, "Book A, Commencing 21st May 1884 Ending 31st December 1894." CR 308 19. Church History Library, Salt Lake City.

Logan Utah Cache Stake General Minutes, 1860–1978. LR 1280 11. Church History Library, Salt Lake City.

Lyman, Amasa M. Journals, 1832–1877. MS 2737, boxes 67–68. Church History Library, Salt Lake City.

Manti North Ward Relief Society Minutes and Records, 1883–1973. LR 5251 14. Church History Library, Salt Lake City.

Manti South Ward Relief Society Minutes and Records, 1882–1973. LR 5252 14. Church History Library, Salt Lake City.

Manti Temple Historical Record, 1888–1999. CR 348 21. Church History Library, Salt Lake City.

Manti Temple Letterpress Copybooks, 1877–1959. Vol. 2. CR 348 5. Church History Library, Salt Lake City.

Manti Ward General Minutes, 1850–1862, 1877. LR 5253 11. Church History Library, Salt Lake City.

Manti Ward Relief Society Minutes and Records, 1871–1877. LR 5253 14. Church History Library, Salt Lake City.

Maughan, Mary Ann Weston. Autobiography and Diary, 1817–1898. Digital History Collections, Utah State Merrill-Cazier University Libraries, Utah State University, Logan, Utah. http://digital.lib.usu.edu/cdm/ref/collection/Diaries/id/17056 (accessed 1 December 2018).

McArthur, Daniel D. Autobiography. Typescript. MSS 476. Manuscript Collection, L. Tom Perry Special Collections, Harold B. Lee Library, Brigham Young University.

Meeks, Priddy. Autobiography and Journal. Online at Book of Abraham Project. https://www.boap.ord/LDS/Early-Saints/PMeeks.html.

Merrill, Marriner W. "Notes from the Miscellaneous Record Book, 1886–1906." Notes from Record Book 1, 1890 compiled by George D. Smith. *New Mormon Studies CD–Rom: A Comprehensive Resource Library 2009 Edition*. Salt Lake City: Signature Books, 2009.

Nauvoo Baptisms for the Dead, Book A. Microfilm. Family History Library, Salt Lake City.

PRIMARY SOURCES

Nauvoo Temple Sealings and Adoptions of the Living and Index, Book A. Microfilm. Family History Library, Salt Lake City.

Nuttall, John. "Diary of John L. Nuttall." In L. John Nuttall Papers, 1854–1903. MS 1269. Church History Library, Salt Lake City.

Phelps, William W. Papers. MSS 810. L. Tom Perry Special Collections, Harold B. Lee Library, Brigham Young University.

Pratt, Parley P. Correspondence, 1842–1855. MS 897. Church History Library, Salt Lake City.

Pre-Endowment House Ordinances 1847–1854. Microfilm. Family History Library, Salt Lake City.

Provo Utah Central Stake General Minutes, 1849–1977. LR 9629 11. Church History Library, Salt Lake City.

Provo Utah Central Stake Manuscript History and Historical Reports, 1849–1977. LR 9629 2. Church History Library, Salt Lake City.

Raleigh, Alonzo H. Diary, 1861 February–1886 February. MS 6172. Church History Library, Salt Lake City.

———. Journal, 1853 September–1861 February. MS 13912. Church History Library, Salt Lake City.

Richards, Franklin D. Journal. In Richards Family Collection, 1837–1961. MS 1215. Church History Library, Salt Lake City.

Richards, Willard. Journal. Willard Richards Papers. MS 1490. Church History Library, Salt Lake City.

Richfield Utah Stake [Sevier Stake] General Minutes, 1872–1977. LR 8243 11. Church History Library, Salt Lake City.

Richfield Ward General Minutes, 1876–1904. LR 8762 11. Church History Library, Salt Lake City.

Salt Lake Stake General Minutes: 1869–1977. LR 604 11. Church History Library, Salt Lake City.

Salt Lake Stake Manuscript History and Historical Reports, 1847–1849. 4 vols. Microfilm. LR 604 2. Church History Library, Salt Lake City.

Scott, James Allen. Journal. MS 1398. Church History Library, Salt Lake City.

Sevier Utah Stake [Richfield Stake] Historical Record, 1880–1883. Volumes 1–4. LR 8243 11. Church History Library, Salt Lake City.

Sheets, Elijah F. and Margaret H. Journals, 1845 August–1904 July. MS 1314. Church History Library, Salt Lake City.

Shurtliff, Luman A. Biographical Sketch of the Life of Luman Andros Shurtliff, 1807–1864. Typescript. MSS SC 88. L. Tom Perry Special Collections, Harold B. Lee Library, Brigham Young University.

Smith, George A. Papers. MS 1322. Church History Library, Salt Lake City.

Smith, Joseph F., comp. "Sealings and Adoptions, 1846–1857." Microfilm. Special Collections, Family History Library, Salt Lake City.

Staines, William C. Diary, 1857 September–1859 February. MS 2453. Church History Library, Salt Lake City.

St. George Temple Donation Records, 1873–1901. CR 343 1. Church History Library, Salt Lake City.

St. George Temple Endowments: Dead. Male and Female Index and Record Book. CR 343 6. Church History Library, Salt Lake City.

PRIMARY SOURCES

St. George Temple Female Ordinance Workers, circa 1917. CR 343 3. Church History Library, Salt Lake City.

St. George Temple Meeting Minutes: 1885 November 5–1888 February 14. 9 vols. CR 343 44. Church History Library, Salt Lake City.

St. George Temple Records, 1877–1899. CR 343 57. Church History Library, Salt Lake City.

St. George Utah Stake General Minutes, 1864–1977. LR 7836 11. Church History Library, Salt Lake City.

St. George Utah Stake Melchizedek Priesthood Minutes and Records, 1863–1973. LR 7836 13. Church History Library, Salt Lake City.

St. George Utah Stake Relief Society Minutes and Records, 1868–1973. LR 7836 14. Church History Library, Salt Lake City.

Strang, James J. James Jesse Strang Collection. Yale Collection of Western Americana, Beinecke Rare Book and Manuscript Library, Yale University.

Strang, James J. to Emma Smith, 22 February 1846. Typewritten copy of original manuscript. L. Tom Perry Special Collections, Harold B. Lee Library, Brigham Young University.

Taylor, John. Collection 1829–1894. MS 1346. Church History Library, Salt Lake City.

Tingen, James Dwight. "The Endowment House, 1855–1889." Unpublished research paper, 1974. L. Tom Perry Special Collections, Harold B. Lee Library, Brigham Young University.

Turley, Richard E., ed. *Selected Collections from the Archives of The Church of Jesus Christ of Latter-day Saints.* 2 vols. 78 DVDs. Provo, UT: Brigham Young University Press, 2002.

Waddington, Mary Eliza Crosby. Journal and Reminiscences, 1840–1889. MS 20159. Church History Library, Salt Lake City.

Whitney, Horace K. Journals, 1843; 1846–1847. MS 1616, box 9. Church History Library, Salt Lake City.

Woodruff, Wilford. Journals and Papers, 1828–1898. MS 1352. Church History Library, Salt Lake City.

———. Letterpress Copybook. MS 23181. Church History Library, Salt Lake City.

———. Letters, 1885–1894. MS 5264. Church History Library, Salt Lake City.

Young, Brigham. Brigham Young Letterpress Copybook Transcriptions, 1974–1978. MS 2736. Transcribed by Edyth Jenkins Romney. Church History Library, Salt Lake City.

———. Office files, 1832–1878. CR 1234 1. Church History Library, Salt Lake City.

———. Papers. 1857–1877. MS 16924. Church History Library, Salt Lake City.

Secondary Sources

Alexander, Thomas G. "An Apostle in Exile: Wilford Woodruff and the St. George Connection." Juanita Brooks Lecture Series, St. George, UT, 1994.
———. *Mormonism in Transition: A History of the Latter-day Saints, 1890–1930*. Urbana: University of Illinois Press, 1986.
———. "The Odyssey of a Latter-day Prophet: Wilford Woodruff and the Manifesto of 1890." In *In the Whirlpool: The Pre-Manifesto Letters of President Wilford Woodruff to the William Atkin Family, 1885–1890*, edited by Reid L. Neilson. Norman, OK: Arthur H. Clark Company, 2011.
———. *"Things in Heaven and on Earth": The Life and Times of Wilford Woodruff, A Mormon Prophet*. Salt Lake City: Signature Books, 1993.
Alford, Kenneth L, ed. *Civil War Saints*. Provo, UT: Religious Studies Center, Brigham Young University; Salt Lake City: Deseret Book Company, 2012.
Alford, Kenneth L., and Richard E. Bennett, eds. *An Eye of Faith: Essays Written in Honor of Richard O. Cowan*. Provo, UT: Religious Studies Center, Brigham Young University; Salt Lake City: Deseret Book Company, 2015.
Allen, James B. "Emergence of a Fundamental: The Expanding Role of Joseph Smith's First Vision in Mormon Religious Thought." In *Exploring the First Vision*, edited by Samuel Alonzo Dodge and Steven C. Harper, 227–66. Provo, UT: Religious Studies Center, Brigham Young University, 2012.
———. "One Man's Nauvoo: William Clayton's Experience in Mormon Illinois." *Journal of Mormon History* 6 (1979): 37–59.
Allen, James B., and Glen M. Leonard. *The Story of the Latter-day Saints*. Salt Lake City: Deseret Book Company, 1976.
———. *The Story of the Latter-day Saints*. 2nd ed., revised. Salt Lake City: Deseret Book Company, 1992.
Allen, James B., Jessie L. Embry, and Kahlile B. Mehr. *Hearts Turned to the Fathers: A History of the Genealogical Society of Utah, 1894–1994*. Provo, UT: BYU Studies, 1995.
Anderson, Devery S., ed. *The Development of Latter-day Saint Temple Worship, 1846–2000: A Documentary History*. Salt Lake City: Smith-Pettit Foundation, 2011.

SECONDARY SOURCES

Anderson, Devery S., and Gary James Bergera, eds. *The Nauvoo Endowment Companies, 1845–1846: A Documentary History.* Salt Lake City: Signature Books, 2005.
Anderson, Karl Ricks. *Joseph Smith's Kirtland: Eyewitness Accounts.* Salt Lake City: Deseret Book Company, 1989.
Anderson, Trever R. "Doctrine and Covenants Section 110: From Vision to Canonization." Master's thesis, Brigham Young University, 2010.
Andrew, Laurel B. *The Early Temples of the Mormons: The Architecture of the Millennial Kingdom in the American West.* Albany, NY: State University of New York Press, 1978.
Angell, Truman O. "His Journal." In *Our Pioneer Heritage.* Vol. 10 (1967) of 20 volumes, compiled by Kate B. Carter, 195–213. Salt Lake City: Daughters of Utah Pioneers, 1958–1977.
Arrington, Leonard J. *Brigham Young: American Moses.* New York: Alfred A. Knopf, 1985.
———. "Church Leaders in Liberty Jail." *BYU Studies* 13, no. 1 (Winter 1973): 20–26.
———. *Great Basin Kingdom: An Economic History of the Latter-day Saints, 1830–1900.* Cambridge, MA: Harvard University Press, 1958.
———. "Oliver Cowdery's Kirtland, Ohio, 'Sketch Book.'" *BYU Studies* 12, no. 4 (Winter 1972): 1–15.
Arrington, Leonard J., Feramorz Y. Fox, and Dean L. May. *Building the City of God: Community and Cooperation among the Mormons.* Salt Lake City: Deseret Book Company, 1976.
Ashton, Wendell J. *Theirs Is the Kingdom.* Salt Lake City: Bookcraft, 1945.
Ashurst-McGee, Mark, David W. Grua, Elizabeth Kuehn, Alexander L. Baugh, and Brenden W. Rensink, eds. *Documents, Volume 6: February 1838–August 1839.* Vol. 6 of the Documents series of *The Joseph Smith Papers,* edited by Ronald K. Esplin, Matthew J. Grow, and Matthew C. Godfrey. Salt Lake City: Church Historian's Press, 2017.
Backman, Milton V. Jr. *The Heavens Resound: A History of the Latter-day Saints in Ohio 1830–1838.* Salt Lake City: Deseret Book Company, 1983, 2002.
———. "Truman Coe's 1836 Description of Mormonism." *BYU Studies* 17, no. 3 (Spring 1977): 1–9.
Backman, Milton V. Jr., and Robert L. Millet. "Heavenly Manifestations in the Kirtland Temple: D&C 109, 110, 137." In *Studies in Scripture Volume 1: The Doctrine and Covenants,* edited by Robert L. Millet and Kent P. Jackson, 417–31. Salt Lake City: Deseret Book Company, 1989.
Bagley, Will. *Blood of the Prophets: Brigham Young and the Massacre at Mountain Meadows.* Norman, OK: University of Oklahoma Press, 2002.
Barney, Lewis. *One Side by Himself: The Life and Times of Lewis Barney, 1808–1894.* Logan, UT: Utah State University Press, 2001.
Baugh, Alexander. "For Their Salvation Is Necessary and Essential to Our Salvation: Joseph Smith and the Practice of Baptism and Confirmation for the Dead." In *An Eye of Faith: Essays Written in Honor of Richard O. Cowan,* edited by Kenneth L. Alford and Richard E. Bennett, 113–38. Provo, UT: Religious Studies Center, Brigham Young University; Salt Lake City: Deseret Book Company, 2015.
———. "'For This Ordinance Belongeth to My House:' The Practice of Baptism for the Dead Outside the Nauvoo Temple." *Mormon Historical Studies* 3, no 1 (Spring 2002): 47–58.
———. "The History and Doctrine of the Adam-ondi-Ahman Revelation (D&C 116)." In *Foundations of the Restoration: Fulfillment of the Covenant Purposes,* edited by

SECONDARY SOURCES

Craig Ostler, Michael MacKay, and Barbara Morgan Gardner, 157–88. Provo, UT: Religious Studies Center, Brigham Young University; Salt Lake City: Deseret Book Company, 2016.

Beecher, Maureen Ursenbach, and Davis Bitton, eds. *New Views of Mormon History: Essays in Honor of Leonard J. Arrington*. Salt Lake City: University of Utah Press, 1987.

Bennett, Richard E. "'Dadda, I Wish We Were out of This Country': The Nauvoo Poor Camps in Iowa, Fall 1846." In *The Iowa Mormon Trail: Legacy of Faith and Courage*, edited by Susan Easton Black and William G. Hartley, 155–70. Orem, UT: Helix Publishing, 1997.

———. "'Has the Lord Turned Bankrupt?' The Attempted Sale of the Nauvoo Temple, 1846–1850." *Journal of the Illinois State Historical Society* 95, no. 3 (Autumn 2002): 235–263.

———. *The Journey West: The Mormon Pioneer Journals of Horace K. Whitney with Insights by Helen Mar Kimball Whitney*. Provo, UT: Religious Studies Center, Brigham Young University; Salt Lake City: Deseret Book Company, 2018.

———. "Lamanism, Lymanism and Cornfields." *Journal of Mormon History*, 13, no. 1 (1986–1987): 45–59.

———. "'Line upon Line, Precept upon Precept': Reflections on the 1877 Commencement of the Performance of Endowments and Sealings for the Dead." *BYU Studies* 44, no. 3 (Summer 2005): 38–77.

———. *Mormons at the Missouri: Winter Quarters, 1846–1852*. Norman, OK: University of Oklahoma Press, 1987, 2004.

———. "'My Idea Is to Go Right through Right Side up with Care': The Exodus as Reformation." Paper presented at the Leonard J. Arrington Mormon History Lecture Series No. 3. Logan, UT: Special Collections and Archives, Merrill Library, Utah State University, 6 November 1997.

———. "'The Upper Room': The Nature and Development of Latter-day Saint Temple Work, 1846–1855. *Journal of Mormon History* 41, no. 2 (April 2015): 1–34.

———. *We'll Find the Place: The Mormon Exodus, 1846–1848*. Norman, OK: University of Oklahoma Press, 1997, 2009.

———. "'Which Is the Wisest Course?' The Transformation in Mormon Temple Consciousness, 1870–1898." *BYU Studies* 52, no. 2 (Spring 2013): 5–43.

Bennett, Richard E., Susan Easton Black, and Donald Q. Cannon. *The Nauvoo Legion in Illinois: A History of the Mormon Militia 1841–1846*. Norman, OK: Arthur H. Clark Company, 2010.

Bennion, Lowell C. "Mapping the Extent of Plural Marriage in St. George, 1861–1880." *BYU Studies* 51, no. 4 (Fall 2012): 27–45.

Bishop, M. Guy. "'What Has Become of Our Fathers?' Baptism for the Dead at Nauvoo." *Dialogue: A Journal of Mormon Thought* 23, no. 2 (Spring 1990): 85–97.

Bitton, Davis. *George Q. Cannon: A Biography*. Salt Lake City: Deseret Book Company, 1999.

Black, Susan Easton. *Annotated Record of Baptisms for the Dead, 1840-1845: Nauvoo, Hancock County, Illinois*. Provo, UT: Center for Family History and Genealogy, Brigham Young University, 2002.

———. "How Large Was the Population of Nauvoo?" *BYU Studies* 35, no. 2 (Spring 1995): 91–94.

———. *Who's Who in the Doctrine & Covenants*. Salt Lake City: Bookcraft, 1997.

SECONDARY SOURCES

Black, Susan Easton, and Richard E. Bennett, eds. *A City of Refuge: Quincy, Illinois*. Salt Lake City: Millennial Press, 2000.

Black, Susan Easton, and William G. Hartley, eds. *The Iowa Mormon Trail: Legacy of Faith and Courage*. Orem, UT: Helix Publishing, 1997.

Black, Susan Easton, Glenn Rawson, and Dennis Lyman. *The Story of the Provo City Center Temple, Commemorative Edition*. American Fork, UT: Covenant Communications, 2015.

Blumell, Lincoln H., Matthew J. Grey, and Andrew H. Hedges, eds. "'The Word of the Lord in the Original': Joseph Smith's Study of Hebrew in Kirtland." In *Approaching Antiquity: Joseph Smith and the Ancient World*. Provo, UT: Religious Studies Center, Brigham Young University; Salt Lake City: Deseret Book Company, 2015.

Blythe, Christopher J. "'The Highest Class of Adulterers and Whoremongers': Plural Marriage, the Church of Jesus Christ (Cutlerite) and the Construction of Memory." *Dialogue: A Journal of Mormon Thought* 46, no. 2 (Summer 2013): 1–39.

———. "'Nearly All the Factions': The Polygamous Passages of William Smith, Lyman Wight, and Alpheus Cutler." In *The Persistence of Polygamy: From Joseph Smith's Martyrdom to the First Manifesto, 1844–1890*, edited by Newell G. Bringhurst and Craig L. Foster. Independence, MO: John Whitmer Books, 2013.

———. "The Upper Room Work: Esotericism in the Church of Jesus Christ (Cutlerite), 1853–1912." *Journal of Mormon History* 40, no. 3 (Summer 2003).

Boyd, Julian P. "State and Local Historical Societies in the United States." *The American Historical Review* 40, no. 1 (October 1934): 10–25.

Brooks, Juanita. *The Mountain Meadows Massacre*. Norman, OK: University of Oklahoma Press, 1950.

Brown, Lisle G. *Nauvoo Sealings, Adoptions, and Anointings: A Comprehensive Register of Persons Receiving LDS Temple Ordinances 1841–1846*. Salt Lake City: Smith-Pettit Foundation (distributed by Signature Books), 2006.

———. "The Sacred Departments for Temple Work in Nauvoo: The Assembly Room and the Council Chamber." *BYU Studies* 19, no. 3 (Fall 1979): 361–74.

———. "'Temple Pro Tempore': The Salt Lake City Endowment House." *Journal of Mormon History* 34, no. 4 (Fall 2008): 1–68.

Brown, Matthew B. *Exploring the Connection between Mormons and Masons*. American Fork, UT: Covenant Communications, 2009.

Brown, Samuel Morris. *In Heaven as It Is on Earth: Joseph Smith and the Early Mormon Conquest of Death*. Oxford and New York: Oxford University Press, 2012.

Buerger, David J. *The Mysteries of Godliness: A History of Mormon Temple Work*. San Francisco: Smith Research Associates, 1994.

Bushman, Richard Lyman. *Joseph Smith: Rough Stone Rolling*. New York: Alfred A. Knopf, 2005.

Campbell, Craig S. *Images of the New Jerusalem: Latter-day Saint Faction Interpretations of Independence, Missouri*. Knoxville, TN: University of Tennessee Press, 2004.

Cannon, Abraham H. *An Apostle's Record: The Journals of Abraham H. Cannon*. Edited by Dennis B. Horne. Clearfield, UT: Gnolaum Books, 2004.

Cannon, Donald Q., and Lyndon W. Cook, eds. *Far West Record: Minutes of The Church of Jesus Christ of Latter-day Saints, 1830–1844*. Salt Lake City: Deseret Book Company, 1983.

Cannon, Frank J., and Harvey J. O'Higgins. *Under the Prophet in Utah: The National Menace of a Political Priestcraft*. Boston: C. M. Clark Publishing Company, 1911.

SECONDARY SOURCES

Carter, Kate B., comp. *Our Pioneer Heritage.* 20 vols. Salt Lake City: Daughters of the Utah Pioneers, 1958–1977.

Clark, James R., comp. *Messages of the First Presidency of The Church of Jesus Christ of Latter-day Saints, 1833–1964.* 6 vols. Salt Lake City: Bookcraft, 1965.

Clayton, William. "Come, Come Ye Saints." In *Hymns,* no. 30. Salt Lake City: Church of Jesus Christ of Latter-day Saints, 1985.

———. *An Intimate Chronicle: The Journals of William Clayton.* Edited by George D. Smith. Salt Lake City: Signature Books, 1991.

———. *William Clayton's Journal: A Daily Record of the Journey of the Original Company of "Mormon" Pioneers from Nauvoo, Illinois to the Valley of the Great Salt Lake.* Published by the Clayton family. Salt Lake City: The Deseret News, 1921.

Cincinnati Journal and Western Luminary, 14 April 1836–19 October 1837.

Collier, Fred C., and William S. Harwell, eds. *Kirtland Council Minute Book.* Salt Lake City: Collier's Publishing, 1996.

Colvin, Don F. "The Fate of the Temple," in *Nauvoo Temple: A Story of Faith.* Provo, UT: Religious Studies Center, 2002: 253–87.

Compton, Todd. *In Sacred Loneliness: The Plural Wives of Joseph Smith.* Salt Lake City: Signature Press, 1997.

Compton, Todd, and Charles M. Hatch, eds. *A Widow's Tale: 1884–1896, Diary of Helen Mar Whitney.* Vol. 6 of *Life Writings of Frontier Women.* Edited by Maureen Ursenbach Beecher. Logan, UT: Utah State University Press, 2003.

Conference Reports of The Church of Jesus Christ of Latter-day Saints. Salt Lake City, *Deseret News,* October 1907.

Cook, Lyndon W., and Milton V. Backman Jr., eds. *Kirtland Elders' Quorum Record, 1836–1841.* Provo, UT: Grandin Book Co. 1985.

Cope, Rachel. "John B. Fairbanks: The Man behind the Canvas." Master's thesis, Brigham Young University, 2003.

Corrill, John. *A Brief History of the Church of Jesus Christ of Latter Day Saints, 1839.* St. Louis: Printed for the author, 1839.

Cowan, Richard O. "The House of the Lord in Kirtland: A 'Preliminary' Temple." In *Regional Studies in Latter-day Saint Church History: Ohio,* edited by Milton V. Backman Jr. Provo, UT: Department of Church History and Doctrine, Brigham Young University, 1990.

———. *Temple Building Ancient and Modern.* Provo, UT: Brigham Young University Press, 1971.

Curtis, Kirk M. "History of the St. George Temple." Master's thesis, Brigham Young University, 1964.

Davidson, Karen Lynn, David J. Whittaker, Mark Ashurst-McGee, and Richard L. Jensen, eds, *Histories, Vol. 1: Joseph Smith Histories, 1932–1844.* Vol. 1 of the Histories series of *The Joseph Smith Papers,* edited by Dean C. Jessee, Ronald K. Esplin, and Richard Lyman Bushman. Salt Lake City: The Church Historian's Press, 2012.

Davidson, Karen Lynn, Richard L. Jensen, and David J. Whittaker, eds., *Histories, Vol. 2: Assigned Histories, 1831–1847.* Vol. 2 of the Histories series of *The Joseph Smith Papers,* edited by Dean C. Jessee, Ronald K. Esplin, and Richard Lyman Bushman. Salt Lake City: The Church Historian's Press, 2012.

Davis, Richard Hyatt. Biography of Elijah Funk Sheets. Photcopy of typescript. MS 9874. 1987. Church History Library, Salt Lake City.

SECONDARY SOURCES

Daynes, Kathryn M. *More Wives than One: Transformation of the Mormon Marriage System, 1840–1910*. Urbana, IL: University of Illinois Press, 2001.

———. "Striving to Live the Principle in Utah's First Temple City: A Snapshot of Polygamy in St. George, Utah, in June 1880." *BYU Studies* 51, no. 4, (Winter 2012): 69–95.

DeMille, Janice Force. *The St. George Temple: First 100 Years*. Hurricane, UT: Homestead Publishers, 1977.

De Pillis, Mario Stephen. "The Development of Mormon Communitarianism, 1826–1846." PhD diss., Yale University, 1960.

Derr, Jill Mulvay. *Women of Covenant: The Story of Relief Society*. Salt Lake City: Deseret Book Company, 1992.

Derr, Jill Mulvay, Carol Cornwall Madsen, Kate Holbrook, and Matthew J. Grow, eds. *The First Fifty Years of Relief Society—Key Documents in Latter-day Saint Women's History*. Salt Lake City: The Church Historian's Press, 2016.

Deseret News. Salt Lake City. 1850–

Deseret Weekly. Salt Lake City. 1888–1898.

Doyle, Arthur Conan. *The History of Spiritualism*. New York: G. H. Doran Company, 1926.

Ehat, Andrew F. "Joseph Smith's Introduction of Temple Ordinances and the 1844 Mormon Succession Question." Master's thesis, Brigham Young University, 1982.

Ehat, Andrew F. and Lyndon W. Cook, eds. *The Words of Joseph Smith*. Provo, UT: Grandin Book Company, 1991.

Elders' Journal of The Church of Jesus Christ of Latter-day Saints. Kirtland, Ohio, Oct.–Nov. 1837; Far West, Missouri, July–Aug. 1838.

Embry, Jessie L. *Mormon Polygamous Families: Life in the Principle*. Salt Lake City: Greg Kofford Books, 2008.

Ensign of Liberty, of the Church of Christ, 1847–1849, edited by William E. McLellin. Prepared by the Smith-Petit Foundation and Signature Books online at https://archive.org/details/EnsignOfLiberty18471849.

Erikson, Keith A., and Lloyd D. Newell. "The Conversion of Artemus Millet and His Call to Kirtland," *BYU Studies* 41, no. 2 (2002): 77–115.

Esplin, Ronald K. "The Emergence of Brigham Young and the Twelve to Mormon Leadership, 1830–1841." PhD diss., Brigham Young University, 1981. Also available as "The Emergence of Brigham Young and the Twelve to Mormon Leadership, 1830–1841," *Dissertations in Latter-day Saint History*. Provo, UT: Joseph Fielding Smith Institute for Latter-day Saint History; BYU Studies, 2006.

Faulring, Scott H., Kent P. Jackson, and Robert J. Matthews, eds. *Joseph Smith's New Translation of the Bible: Original Manuscripts*. Provo, UT: Religious Studies Center, Brigham Young University, 2004.

Fielding, Joseph. "'They Might Have Known That He Was Not a Fallen Prophet:' The Nauvoo Journal of Joseph Fielding," edited by Andrew F. Ehat. *BYU Studies* 19, no. 2 (Winter 1979): 133–66.

Fields, Clarence L. "History of the Kirtland Temple." Master's thesis, Brigham Young University, 1963.

Firmage, Edwin Brown, and Richard Collin Mangrum. *Zion in the Courts: A Legal History of the Church of Jesus Christ of Latter-day Saints, 1830–1900*. Urbana and Chicago: University of Illinois Press, 1988.

Foote, Kenneth E. *Shadowed Ground: America's Landscapes of Violence and Tragedy*. Austin, TX: University of Texas Press, 1997.

SECONDARY SOURCES

Garr, Arnold K., and C. V. Johnson, eds. *Regional Studies in Latter-day Saint Church History: Missouri.* Provo, UT: Dept. of Church History and Doctrine, Brigham Young University, 1994.

Garrett, H. Dean. "Seven Letters from Liberty." In *Regional Studies in Latter-day Saint Church History: Missouri,* edited by Arnold K. Garr and C. V. Johnson, 189–200. Provo, UT: Dept. of Church History and Doctrine, Brigham Young University, 1994.

Gee, John. *Introduction to the Book of Abraham.* Provo, UT: Religious Studies Center, Brigham Young University; Salt Lake City: Deseret Book Company, 2017.

Givens, George W. *In Old Nauvoo: Everyday Life in the City of Joseph.* Salt Lake City: Deseret Book Company, 1990.

Godfrey, Kenneth W. "The Coming of the Manifesto." *Dialogue: A Journal of Mormon Thought* 5, no. 3 (Autumn 1970): 11–25.

———. "The Importance of the Temple in Understanding the Latter-day Saint Nauvoo Experience: Then and Now." Paper presented at the Leonard J. Arrington Mormon History Lecture Series No. 6. Annual Lecture, Logan, UT, 25 October 2000. Paper 5. https://digitalcommons.usu.edu/arrington_lecture/5.

Godfrey, Kenneth W., Audrey M. Godfrey, and Jill Mulvay Derr. *Women's Voices: An Untold History of the Latter-Day-Saints 1830–1900.* Salt Lake City: Deseret Book Company, 1982.

Godfrey, Matthew C., Spencer W. McBride, Alex D. Smith, and Christopher James Blythe, eds. *Documents, Volume 7: September–January 1841.* Vol. 7 of the Documents series of *The Joseph Smith Papers,* edited by Ronald K. Esplin, Matthew J. Grow, and Matthew C. Godfrey. Salt Lake City: Church Historian's Press, 2018.

Grey, Matthew J., Lincoln H. Blumell, and Andrew H. Hedges, eds. "'The Word of the Lord in the Original.' Joseph Smith's Study of Hebrew in Kirtland." *Approaching Antiquity: Joseph Smith and the Ancient World.* Provo, UT: Religious Studies Center, Brigham Young University; Salt Lake City: Deseret Book, 2015.

Grow, Matthew J., and R. Eric Smith, eds. *The Council of Fifty: What the Records Reveal About Mormon History.* Provo, UT: Religious Studies Center, Brigham Young University; Salt Lake City: Deseret Book Company, 2017.

Grow, Matthew J., Ronald K. Esplin, Mark Ashurst-McGee, Gerrit J. Dirkmaat, and Jeffrey D. Mahas, eds. *Council of Fifty, Minutes, March 1844–January 1846.* First volume of the Administrative Records series of *The Joseph Smith Papers,* edited by Ronald K. Esplin, Matthew J. Grow, and Matthew C. Godfrey. Salt Lake City: Church Historian's Press, 2016.

Hales Brian. *Joseph Smith's Polygamy.* 3 volumes. Salt Lake City: Greg Kofford Books, 2013.

Hales, Laura H., ed. *A Reason for Faith: Navigating LDS Doctrine and Church History.* Salt Lake City: Deseret Book Company, 2016.

Handbook of American Historical Societies. Hartford, CT: A. D. Worthington and Co. Publishing, 1926.

Hardy, B. Carmon. *Solemn Covenant: The Mormon Polygamous Passage.* Urbana and Chicago: The University of Illinois Press, 1992.

Hargis, Barbara Lee. "A Folk History of the Manti Temple: A Study of the Folklore and Traditions Connected with the Settlement of Manti, Utah, and the Building of the Temple." Master's thesis, Brigham Young University, 1968.

Harline, Paula Kelly. *The Polygamous Wives Writing Club: From the Diaries of Mormon Pioneer Women.* Oxford and New York: Oxford University Press, 2014.

Harper, Steven C. "Freemasonry and the Latter-day Saint Temple Endowment Ceremony."

SECONDARY SOURCES

In *A Reason for Faith: Navigating LDS Doctrine and Church History*, edited by Laura H. Hales, chapter 12. Salt Lake City: Deseret Book Company, 2016.

———. "Pentecost Continued: A Contemporaneous Account of the Kirtland Temple Dedication." *BYU Studies* 42, no. 2 (Spring 2003): 5–22.

Hauglid, Brian M. *A Textual History of the Book of Abraham: Manuscripts and Editions.* Vol. 5 of *Studies in the Book of Abraham*. Provo, UT: Maxwell Institute, Brigham Young University, 2010.

Hedges, Andrew H., Alex D. Smith, and Richard Lloyd Anderson, eds. *Journals, Volume 2: December 1841–April 1843*. Vol. 2 of the Journals series of *The Joseph Smith Papers*, edited by Dean C. Jessee, Ronald K. Esplin, and Richard Lyman Bushman. Salt Lake City: Church Historian's Press, 2011.

Hedges, Andrew H., Alex D. Smith, and Brent M. Rogers, eds. *Journals, Volume 3: May 1843–June 1844*. Vol. 3 of the Journals series of *The Joseph Smith Papers*, edited by Ronald K. Esplin and Matthew J. Grow. Salt Lake City: Church Historian's Press, 2015.

Hill, Marvin S., C. Keith Rooker, and Larry T. Wimmer. *The Kirtland Economy Revisited: A Market Critique of Sectarian Economics.* Provo, UT: Brigham Young University Press, 1977.

Hinckley, Gordon B. "What Are People Asking about Us?" *Ensign*, November 1998, 70–72.

Homer, Michael W. *Joseph's Temples: The Dynamic Relationship between Freemasonry and Mormonism.* Salt Lake City: University of Utah Press, 2014.

———. "Spiritualism and Mormonism: Some Thoughts on Similarities and Differences." *Dialogue: A Journal of Mormon Thought* 27, no. 1 (Spring 1994): 171–91.

Howlett, David J. *Kirtland Temple: The Biography of a Shared Mormon Sacred Space.* Urbana, IL: University of Illinois Press, 2014.

Huff, Kent W. *Brigham Young's United Order: A Contextual Interpretation.* Provo, UT: By the author, distributed by Theological Thinktank, 1994.

Hughes, William E. "A Profile of the Missionaries of The Church of Jesus Christ of Latter-day Saints, 1849–1900," Master's thesis, Brigham Young University, 1986.

Irving, Gordon. "The Law of Adoption: One Phase of the Development of the Mormon Concept of Salvation, 1830–1980." *BYU Studies* 14, no. 3 (Summer 1974): 291–314.

Ivie, Evan, and Douglas C. Heiner. "Deaths in Early Nauvoo, Illinois, 1839–1846, and in Winter Quarters, Nebraska, 1846–1848." In *Religious Educator* 10, no. 3 (2009): 163–74.

Jacob, Margaret. *The Origins of Freemasonry: Facts and Fictions.* Philadelphia: University of Pennsylvania Press, 2006.

Jensen, Richard L. "Transplanted to Zion: The Impact of British and Latter-day Saint Immigration upon Nauvoo." *BYU Studies* 31, no. 4 (Winter 1991):76–87.

Jensen, Robin Scott, and Brian M. Hauglid, eds. *Revelations and Translations, Volume 4: Book of Abraham and Related Manuscripts.* Vol. 4 of the Revelations and Translations series of *The Joseph Smith Papers*, edited by Dean C. Jessee, Ronald K. Esplin, and Richard Lyman Bushman. Salt Lake City: Church Historian's Press, 2018.

Jensen, Robin Scott, Richard E. Turley Jr., and Riley M. Lorimer, eds. *Revelations and Translations, Volume 2: Published Revelations.* Vol. 2 of the Revelations and Translations series of *The Joseph Smith Papers*, edited by Dean C. Jessee, Ronald K. Esplin, and Richard Lyman Bushman. Salt Lake City: Church Historian's Press, 2011.

SECONDARY SOURCES

Jessee, Dean C. "The Kirtland Diary of Wilford Woodruff." *BYU Studies* 12, no. 4 (Spring 1972): 1–26.

———. *The Personal Writings of Joseph Smith*. Salt Lake City: Deseret Book Company, 1984.

———. "'Walls, Grates, and Screeking Iron Doors': The Prison Experience of Mormon Leaders in Missouri, 1838–1839." In *New Views of Mormon History: Essays in Honor of Leonard J. Arrington,* edited by Maureen Ursenbach Beecher and Davis Bitton, 19–42. Salt Lake City: University of Utah Press, 1987.

Jessee, Dean C., Ronald K. Esplin, and Richard Lyman Bushman, eds. *The Joseph Smith Papers*. 18 vols. Salt Lake City: Church Historian's Press, 2008–.

Jessee, Dean C., Mark Ashurst McGee, and Richard L. Jensen, eds. *Journals, Volume 1: 1832-1839*. Vol. 1 of the Journals series of *The Joseph Smith Papers,* edited by Dean C. Jessee, Ronald K. Esplin, and Richard Lyman Bushman. Salt Lake City: Church Historian's Press, 2011.

Johnson, Melvin C. *Polygamy on the Padernales: Lyman Wight's Mormon Villages in Antebellum Texas, 1845–1858*. Logan, UT: Utah State University Press, 2006.

Jorgensen, Danny L., and Andrew Leary. "Anointed Queens and Priestesses: Alpheus Cutler's Plural Wives." *The John Whitmer Historical Association Journal* 38, no. 1 (Spring/Summer 2018): 55–79.

The Joseph Smith Papers. http://josephsmithpapers.org/.

Journal of Discourses. 26 vols. Liverpool: F. D. Richards, 1855–1886.

Juvenile Instructor, Salt Lake City, 1866–1929.

Kelly, Charles, ed. *Journals of John D. Lee, 1846–47 and 1859*. Salt Lake City: privately printed for Rolla Bishop Watt by Western Printing Company, 1938. Located in Church History Library, Salt Lake City.

Kimball, Heber C. *On the Potter's Wheel, The Diaries of Heber C. Kimball*. Edited by Stanley B. Kimball. Urbana, IL: The University of Illinois Press, 1981.

Kimball, Stanley B. ed. *On the Potter's Wheel, The Diaries of Heber C. Kimball*. Urbana, IL: The University of Illinois Press, 1981.

Kinkead, Joyce. "A Schoolmarm All My Life: Personal Narratives from Frontier Utah: A Biographical Sketch of Martha Spence Haywood 1811–73." In *New Mormon Studies CD-ROM: A Comprehensive Resource Library 2009 Edition,* compiled by George D. Smith. Salt Lake City: Signature Books, 2009.

Largey, Dennis, ed. *Doctrine and Covenants Reference Companion*. Salt Lake City: Deseret Book Company, 2012.

Larson, Gustive O. *The "Americanization" of Utah for Statehood*. San Marino, CA: The Huntington Library, 1971.

Latter Day Saints' Messenger and Advocate. Kirtland, OH. 1834–1837.

Latter-day Saints' Millennial Star. Liverpool. Manchester, England. 1840–1970.

Launius, Roger D. *Joseph Smith III: Pragmatic Prophet*. Urbana, IL: University of Illinois Press, 1988.

———. *The Kirtland Temple: An Historical Narrative*. Independence, MO: Herald Publishing House, 1986.

Lee, John D. *Journals of John D. Lee, 1846–47 and 1859,* edited by Charles Kelly. Salt Lake City: privately printed for Rolla Bishop Watt by Western Printing Company, 1938. Located in Church History Library, Salt Lake City.

Leonard, Glen M. *Nauvoo: A Place of Peace, A People of Promise*. Provo, UT: Brigham Young University Press; Salt Lake City: Deseret Book Company, 2002.

SECONDARY SOURCES

Loving, Kim R. "Ownership of the Kirtland Temple: Legends, Lies and Misunderstandings." *Journal of Mormon History* 30, no. 2 (Spring 2004): 1–80.

Ludlow, Daniel H., ed. *Encyclopedia of Mormonism: The History, Scripture, Doctrine, and Procedure of the Church of Jesus Christ of Latter Day Saints*. 5 vols. New York: Macmillan Publishing Company, 1992.

Lyman, Edward Leo. *Political Deliverance: The Mormon Quest for Utah Statehood*. Urbana and Chicago: University of Illinois Press, 1986.

Lyon, T. Edgar Jr. *John Lyon: The Life of a Pioneer Poet*. Provo, UT: Religious Studies Center, Brigham Young University, 1989.

MacKinnon, William P. "Epilogue to the Utah War: Impact and Legacy." *Journal of Mormon History* 29, no. 3 (Fall 2003): 186–248.

———"Into the Fray: Sam Houston's Utah War." *Journal of Mormon History* 39, no. 3 (Summer 2013): 198–243.

Mackley, Jennifer Ann. *Wilford Woodruff's Witness of the Development of Temple Doctrine*. Seattle: High Desert Publishing, 2014.

Marquardt, H. Michael. *The Joseph Smith Egyptian Papers: A History*. Cullman, AL: Printing Service, 1981.

Marshall, W. G. *Through America: Or Nine Months in the United States*. London: Sampson, Low, Marston, Searle & Irvington, 1881.

"Masonry." Church History Topics. The Church of Jesus Christ of Latter-day Saints. https://www.lds.org/study/history/topics/masonry?lang=eng (accessed 1 December 2018).

Matthews, Robert J. *A Plainer Translation: Joseph Smith's Translation of the Bible: A History and Commentary*. Provo, UT: Brigham Young University Press, 1975.

McConkie, Bruce R. *Mormon Doctrine*. 2nd ed. Salt Lake City: Bookcraft, 1966.

McDermott, John Francis. *The Lost Panoramas of the Mississippi*. Chicago: University of Chicago Press, 1958.

McNulty, W. Kirk. *Freemasonry: Symbols, Secrets, Significance*. London: Thames and Hudson, Ltd., 2006.

Millet, Robert L., and Kent P. Jackson, eds. *Studies in Scripture Volume 1: The Doctrine and Covenants*. Salt Lake City: Deseret Book Company, 1989.

Muhlestein, Kerry, and Megan Hansen. "'The Work of Translating': The Book of Abraham's Translation Chronology." In *Let Us Reason Together: Essays in Honor of the Life's Work of Robert L. Millet*, edited by J. Spencer Fluhman and Brent L. Top. Provo, UT: Religious Studies Center, Brigham Young University; Salt Lake City: Deseret Book Company, 2016.

Neilson, Reid L., and Nathan N. Waite, eds. *Settling the Valley, Proclaiming the Gospel. The General Epistles of the Mormon First Presidency*. New York City: Oxford University Press, 2017.

Newell, Linda King, and Valeen Tippetts Avery. *Mormon Enigma: Emma Hale Smith*. Garden City, New York: Doubleday and Company, 1984.

Nibley, Hugh. "The Meaning of the Kirtland Egyptian Papers." *BYU Studies* 11, no. 4 (Summer 1971): 350–99.

Oaks, Dallin H. "Joseph, The Man and the Prophet," *Ensign*, May 1996, 71–73.

Ogden, D. Kelly. "The Kirtland Hebrew School (1835–36)." In *Regional Studies in Latter-day Saint Church History: Ohio*, edited by Milton R. Backman Jr., 63–87. Provo, UT: Department of Church History and Doctrine, Brigham Young University, 1990.

Ohio Observer. Hudson, Ohio, 1840–1855.

SECONDARY SOURCES

Olsen, Nolan Porter. *Logan Temple: The First 100 Years.* Privately published, 1978.

Orton, Chad M. "This Shall Be Our Covenant: Brigham Young and D&C 136." *Religious Educator* 19, no. 2 (2018): 119–51.

Ostler, Craig, Michael MacKay, and Barbara Morgan Gardner, eds. *Foundations of the Restoration: Fulfillment of the Covenant Purposes.* Provo: Religious Studies Center, Brigham Young University; Salt Lake City: Deseret Book Company, 2016.

Packer, Boyd K. *The Holy Temple.* Salt Lake City: Bookcraft, 1980.

Parkin, Max H. "Conflict at Kirtland: A Study of the Nature and Causes of Internal and External Conflict of the Mormons in Ohio between 1830 and 1838." Master's thesis, Brigham Young University, 1966.

———. "Joseph Smith and the United Firm: The Growth and Decline of the Church's First Master Plan of Business and Finance, Ohio and Missouri, 1832–1834." *BYU Studies* 46, no. 3 (Summer 2007): 5–62.

Paulsen, David L., Roger D. Cook, and Brock M. Mason. "Theological Underpinnings of Baptism for the Dead." *BYU Studies* 35, no. 3 (Fall 2016): 101–16.

Perego, Ugo A., Natalie M. Myers, and Scott R. Woodward. "Reconstructing the Y-Chromosome of Joseph Smith: Genealogical Application." *Journal of Mormon History* 31, no. 3 (Summer 2005): 70–88.

Peterson, Paul H. "The Mormon Reformation." Provo, UT: Joseph Fielding Smith Institute for Latter-day Saint History, Brigham Young University, 2002.

Phelps, Leah Y. "Letters of Faith from Kirtland." *Improvement Era* 45, no. 8 (August 1942): 529.

"Plural Marriage and Families in Early Utah." Gospel Topics. The Church of Jesus Christ of Latter-day Saints. October 2014. https://www.lds.org/topics/plural-marriage-and-families-in-early-utah?lang=eng (accessed 4 October 2018).

"Plural Marriage in Kirtland and Nauvoo." Gospel Topics. The Church of Jesus Christ of Latter-day Saints. October 2014. https://www.lds.org/topics/plural-marriage-in-kirtland-and-nauvoo?lang=eng (accessed 1 December 2018).

Poll, Richard D. "The Americanization of Utah." *Utah Historical Quarterly*, 44 (Winter 1976): 76–93.

Porter, Larry C. "Alvin Smith: Reminder of the Fairness of God." *Ensign,* September 1978, 65–67.

Pratt, Parley P. *The Autobiography of Parley Parker Pratt.* Salt Lake City: Deseret Book Company, 1980.

Prince, Carl E. "The Great 'Riot Year': Jacksonian Democracy and Patterns of Violence in 1834." *Journal of the Early Republic,* 5 (1985): 1–19.

Quinn, D. Michael. "Latter-day Saint Prayer Circles." *BYU Studies* 19, no. 1 (Winter 1979): 79–105.

———. "The Mormon Succession Crisis of 1844." *BYU Studies* 16, no. 2 (1976): 187–233.

———. "The Practice of Rebaptism at Nauvoo." *BYU Studies* 18, no. 2 (Spring 1978): 226–32.

Rasmassen, Victor J. *The Manti Temple.* Provo, UT: Community Press, 1988.

Raynor, Wallace Alan. "History of the Construction of the Salt Lake Temple." Master's thesis, Brigham Young University, 1961.

The Return 1–3, Davis City, Iowa, 1888–1890.

Roberts, B. H. *A Comprehensive History of The Church of Jesus Christ of Latter-day Saints, Century One.* 6 vols. Provo, UT: Brigham Young University Press, 1965.

SECONDARY SOURCES

———. *The Gospel: An Exposition of its First Principles*. Salt Lake City: Deseret News, 1913.

Robinson, Ebenezer, 1832–1843. In *The Return*, 1–3. Davis City, Iowa, 1888–1890.

Robison, Elwin C. *The First Mormon Temple: Design, Construction, and Historic Context of the Kirtland Temple*. Provo, UT: Brigham Young University Press, 1997.

Rogers, Brent M, Elizabeth A. Kuehn, Christian K. Heimburger, Max H Parkin, Alexander L. Baugh, and Steven C. Harper, eds. *Documents, Volume 5: October 1835–January 1838*. Vol. 5 of the Documents series of *The Joseph Smith Papers*, edited by Ronald K. Esplin, Matthew J. Grow, and Matthew C. Godfrey. Salt Lake City: Church Historian's Press, 2017.

Romig, Ronald E. *Eighth Witness: The Biography of John Whitmer*. Independence, MO: John Whitmer Books, 2014.

Rowley, Dennis. "The Mormon Experience in the Wisconsin Pineries, 1841–1845." *BYU Studies* 32, no. 1 (Winter 1992): 119–48.

Scherer, Mark A. *The Journey of a People: The Era of Reorganization, 1844 to 1946*. Independence, MO: Community of Christ Seminary Press, 2013.

———. *The Journey of a People: The Era of Restoration, 1820 to 1844*. Independence, MO: Herald House Publishing, 2013.

———. *The Journey of a People: The Era of Worldwide Community, 1946 to 2015*. Independence, MO: Community of Christ Seminary Press, 2016.

Shipps, Jan. *Mormonism: The Story of a New Religious Tradition*. Chicago and Urbana: University of Illinois Press, 1987.

———. "The Principle Revoked: Mormon Reactions to Wilford Woodruff's 1890 Manifesto." In *In the Whirlpool: The Pre-Manifesto Letters of President Wilford Woodruff to the William Atkin Family, 1885–1890*, edited by Reid L. Neilson, 113–24. Norman, Oklahoma: Arthur H. Clark Company, 2011.

Smith, Andrew F. *The Saintly Scoundrel: The Life and Times of Dr. John Cook Bennett*. Urbana and Chicago: University of Illinois Press, 1997.

Smith, George D. *Nauvoo Polygamy: "But We Called It Celestial Marriage."* Salt Lake City: Signature Books, 2008.

———, comp. *New Mormon Studies CD-ROM: A Comprehensive Resource Library 2009 Edition*. Salt Lake City: Signature Books, 2009.

Smith, Joseph F. *Gospel Doctrine*. 12th ed. Salt Lake City: Deseret Book Company, 1961.

Smith, Joseph Jr. *History of The Church of Jesus Christ of Latter-day Saints*. 7 vols. Edited by B. H. Roberts. 2nd ed., rev. Salt Lake City: Deseret Book Company, 1961.

———. "History, 1838–1856, volume C-1 [2 November 1838–31 July 1842]." Online only. *The Joseph Smith Papers*. http://www.josephsmithpapers.org/paper-summary/history-1838-1856-volume-c-1-2-november-1838-31-july-1842/261 (accessed 20 September 2018).

———. "History, 1838–1856, volume E-1 [1 July 1843–30 April 1844]." Online only. *The Joseph Smith Papers*. https://www.josephsmithpapers.org/paper-summary/history-1838-1856-volume-e-1-1-july-1843-30-april-1844/294 (accessed 28 November 2018).

———*The Words of Joseph Smith*. Edited by Andrew F. Ehat and Lyndon W. Cook. Provo, UT: Grandin Book Company, 1991.

Smith, Lucy Mack. *Lucy's Book: A Critical Edition of Lucy Mack Smith's Family Memoir*. Edited by Lavina Fielding Anderson. Salt Lake City: Signature Books, 2001.

———*The Revised and Enhanced History of Joseph Smith by His Mother*. Edited by Scot

SECONDARY SOURCES

Facer Proctor and Maurine Jensen Proctor. Salt Lake City: Deseret Book Company, 1996.
Snow, Eliza R., comp. *Biography and Family History of Lorenzo Snow*. Salt Lake City: Deseret News, 1884.
Staines, William C. "Reminiscences of William C. Staines." *Contributor* 12 (November 1890–October 1891): 196–99.
Staker, Mark Lyman. *Hearken, O Ye People: The Historical Setting of Joseph Smith's Ohio Revelations*. Salt Lake City: Greg Kofford Books, 2009.
Stapley, Jonathan A. "Adoptive Sealing Ritual in Mormonism." *Journal of Mormon History* 37, no. 2 (Summer 2011): 53–118.
———. *The Power of Godliness: Mormon Liturgy and Cosmology*. New York: Oxford University Press, 2018.
Stapley, Jonathan A., and Kristine L. Wright. "'They Shall be Made Whole': A History of Baptism for Health." *Journal of Mormon History* 34, no. 4 (Fall 2008): 69–112.
Stavish, Mark. *Freemasonry: Rituals, Symbols and History of the Secret Society*. Woodbury, MN: Llewellyn Publications, 2007.
Stenhouse, Fanny. *Tell It All: The Story of a Life's Experience in Mormonism*. Hartford, CT: A. D. Worthington and Company Publishing, 1875.
Stout, Hosea. *On the Mormon Frontier: The Diary of Hosea Stout*. Edited by Juanita Brooks. 2 vols. Salt Lake City: University of Utah Press, 2009.
Stubbs, Glen R. "History of the Manti Temple." Master's thesis, Brigham Young University, 1960.
Talmage, James E. *The House of the Lord: A Study of Holy Sanctuaries Ancient and Modern*. Salt Lake City: The Church of Jesus Christ of Latter-day Saints, 1912.
Taylor, John. *John Taylor's Nauvoo Journal*. Edited by Dean C. Jessee. Provo, UT: Grandin Book Company, 1996.
Times and Seasons. Commerce/Nauvoo, IL. November 1839–February 1846.
Tobler, Ryan G. "'Saviors on Mount Zion': Mormon Sacramentalism, Mortality, and the Baptism for the Dead." *Journal of Mormon History* 39, no. 4 (2013): 182–238.
Trumbower, Jeffrey A. *Rescue for the Dead: The Posthumous Salvation of Non-Christians in Early Christianity*. New York: Oxford University Press, 2001.
Tullidge, Edward W. *The Women of Mormondom*. New York City: Tullidge and Crandall, 1877.
Turner, Rodney. "Jesus Christ and the Command to Repent (D&C 18 and 19)." In *Studies in Scripture: Volume One, The Doctrine and Covenants*, edited by Robert L. Millet and Kent P. Jackson, 100–108. Salt Lake City: Deseret Book Company, 1989.
Tvedtnes, John A. "Baptism for the Dead in Early Christianity." In *The Temple in Time and Eternity*, edited by Donald W. Parry and Stephen D. Ricks, 43–54. Provo, UT: The Foundation for Ancient Research and Mormon Studies, Brigham Young University, 1999.
Ulrich, Laurel Thatcher. *A House Full of Females: Plural Marriage and Women's Rights in Early Mormonism: 1835–1870*. New York: Alfred A. Knopf, 2017.
Underwood, Grant. *The Millenarian World of Early Mormonism*. Urbana, IL: University of Illinois Press, 1993.
United States Senate. Proceedings Before the Committee on Privileges and Elections of the United States Senate in the Matter of the Protests Against the Right of Hon. Reed Smoot, A Senator from the State of Utah, to Hold His Seat. 4 vols. Washington: Government Printing Office, 1904–1906.

SECONDARY SOURCES

Van Orden, Bruce A., ed. "Writing to Zion: The William W. Phelps Kirtland Letters (1835–1836)." *BYU Studies* 33, no. 3 (Fall 1993): 543–91.

Walden, Barbara, and Lachlan Mackay. *House of the Lord: The Story of the Kirtland Temple.* Independence, MO: John Whitmer Historical Association, 2008.

Walker, Charles Lowell. *The Diary of Charles Lowell Walker.* Edited by A. Karl Larson and Katharine Miles Larson. Logan, UT: Utah State University Press, 1980.

Walker, Ronald W. *Wayward Saints: The Godbeites and Brigham Young.* Urbana: University of Illinois Press, 1998.

Walker, Ronald W., Richard E. Turley Jr., and Glen M. Leonard. *Massacre at Mountain Meadows: An American Tragedy.* Oxford: Oxford University Press, 2008.

Welch, Thomas Weston. "Early Mormon Woodworking at Its Best: A Study of the Craftmanship in the First Temples of Utah." Master's thesis, Brigham Young University, 1983.

Wells, Quentin Thomas. *Defender: The Life of Daniel H. Wells.* Logan, UT: Utah State University Press, 2016.

Whitney, Helen Mar Kimball. "Life Incidents," *Woman's Exponent*, 9–10 (1880–1882).

———. "Scenes and Incidents in Nauvoo," *Woman's Exponent*, 11 (1882–1883).

———. *A Widow's Tale: 1884–1896 Diary of Helen Mar Kimball Whitney.* Edited by Todd M. Compton and Charles M. Hatch. Vol. 6 of *Life Writings of Frontier Women*, edited by Maureen Ursenbach Beecher. Logan, UT: Utah State University Press, 2003.

———. *A Woman's View: Helen Mar Whitney's Reminiscences of Early Church History.* Edited by Jeni Broberg Holzapfel and Richard Neitzel Holzapfel. Salt Lake City: Bookcraft, 1997.

Whitney, Horace K., and Helen Mar Kimball Whitney. *The Journey West: The Mormon Pioneer Journals of Horace K. Whitney with Insights by Helen Mar Kimball Whitney.* Edited by Richard E. Bennett. Provo, UT: Religious Studies Center, Brigham Young University; Salt Lake City: Deseret Book Company, 2018.

Whitney, Orson F. *History of Utah.* 4 vols. Salt Lake City: George Q. Cannon and Sons, Publishers, 1893.

———. *Life of Heber C. Kimball.* Salt Lake City: Stevens and Wallace, Inc., 1945.

Wills, John A. "The Twin Relics of Barbarism." *Historical Society of Southern California* 1, no. 5 (1890): 40–44.

Woman's Exponent. Salt Lake City. 1872–1914.

Woodruff, Wilford. *Leaves from My Journal: A Journey of Faith.* Sandy, UT: Leatherwood Press, 2005. First published Salt Lake City: Juvenile Instructor Office, 1882.

———. *Wilford Woodruff's Journal, 1833–1898.* Typescript. 9 vols. Edited by Scott G. Kenney. Midvale, UT: Signature Books, 1983.

Yorgason, Blaine M., Richard A. Schmutz, and Douglas D. Alder. *All That Was Promised: The St. George Temple and the Unfolding of the Restoration.* Salt Lake City: Deseret Book Company, 2014.

Young Women's Journal, Salt Lake City, 1889–1929.

Index

Abrahamic Covenant, 39, 255–56
Academies, Church-sponsored, 179–80
Adam-ondi-Ahman, Missouri, 50
Adams, James, 79, 83
Adams, John Quincy, 51
Adoption, law of, 88, 125–33, 286, 298–305
Alexander, Thomas, 280–81
Alger, Fanny, 90
Ancestral records, 181–82, 188–91
Anderson, Karl Ricks, 18n15
Angell, Solomon, 147
Angell, Truman O., 19, 92, 143, 147, 166–67, 197, 235, 287–88, 292
Apostasy, 42–45, 128, 181, 186–87
Apostolic keys, 161–63
Arrington, Leonard, 16, 52, 179–80, 201

Babbitt, Almon W., 61, 101–3
Backman, Milton V. Jr., 25–26, 39n68
Banvard, John, 95
Baptism: into LDS Church, 85; rebaptism, 140–41, 167–68n7, 173, 305; in United Order, 200; for health, 219–20, 305
Baptisms for the dead: revelations concerning, 54–60, 62; performance of, 60–63; in Nauvoo Temple, 63–65; significance of, 73–74; and doctrine of eternal marriage, 86; at Winter Quarters, 125; and law of adoption, 126; in Endowment House, 170; reinstitution of, 180–91; in St. George Temple, 208; following Manifesto, 276–78
Barney, Lewis, 111, 275–76
Beaman, Louisa, 90
Bell, Robert, 303
Benjamin, Asher, 21n19
Bennett, John C., 68, 82–83n16, 91
Bennion, Lowell C., 251
Benson, E. T., 153
Berg, O. H., 221
Bible, 29n45. *See also* Joseph Smith Translation
Bidamon, Lewis, 90
Blanchard, Jonathan, 283
Bleak, James, 298, 303–4
Blessings, given by women, 133–34
Boggs, Lilburn W., 75
Book of Abraham, 30–31, 32, 77
Book of Mormon, 4
Book of Moses, 4
Book of the Law of the Lord, 71, 239
Brewster, James Colin, 45
Broderick, Thomas E., 146
Brown, Benjamin, 29n43
Brown, Samuel, 58
Brunson, Seymour, 60
Buchanan, James, 174–75
Buell, Prescindia, 52
Bullock, Thomas, 126, 152, 242

333

INDEX

Bump, Jacob, 14–15, 19
Burket, George, 40n72
Burr, Francis, 141n8
Burton, Alma, 76
Bushman, Richard, 46

Cabet, Etienne, 110
Cahoon, Reynolds, 14, 65, 81
Camp Floyd, 175
Camp of the Saints, 46
Canada, 249–50
Cannon, Abraham H., 274–75
Cannon, Angus M., 252
Cannon, David H., 153n42, 274, 304
Cannon, George Q.: on restoration of temple ordinances, 162n60; on Endowment House, 169–70; on continuing revelation, 171–72; on St. George Temple, 197–98; on plural marriage, 254, 259–60, 267–68; on heavenly manifestations, 263n3; and discontinuation of plural marriage, 264–65; on Manifesto, 275n30; on tithing, 290
Card, Charles Ora, 235, 249
Carter, Eliza Ann, 43
Carter, Jared, 14
Celestial kingdom: sealings to, 26n35; vision of, 37–38, 58; and plural marriage, 256
Celestial marriage, 39n68, 55, 83–92, 225, 255. *See also* Sealings
Channing, William Ellery, 51
Children: and Kirtland Temple dedication, 36–37; salvation of, 38; sealing of, to parents, 87–88, 171n20; sealing of deceased, to parents, 213–14
Church of Christ, 45
Church property, government seizure of, 269–71, 274
Civil law, subjection to, 272
Civil War, 165–66, 175–78, 185, 243–44
Clark, Nancy, 240
Clark, Reuben, 214
Clayton, William, 91, 92–93, 139
Cleveland, Grover, 305, 306
Clothing: temple, 212; temple attendance's influence on, 223–24

Coe, Truman, 15
Community of Christ (Reorganized Church of Jesus Christ of Latter Day Saints), 2–3, 45, 94n44, 108n81
Confederate South, 243–44
Consecration, 6, 16–17, 198–202
Contributions, for temple construction, 71, 223, 235, 236, 239–42
Corrill, John, 23–24, 25n31, 40
Council House, 142–51, 152, 163, 166, 180
Cowan, Richard O., 22–23n23, 88
Cowdery, Oliver, 3–4, 26, 33, 44
Cox, Jehu, 221
Crosby, Taylor, 146
Cumming, Alfred, 174
Cutler, Alpheus, 65, 88n22, 107–8
Cutler, Lois, 88n22

Dallin, Cyrus E., 294n12
Danites, 68
Daynes, Kathryn, 251–52
Dead: salvation of, 37–38, 54–63, 89; endowment for, 77, 125, 300; marriages for, 88–89. *See also* Baptisms for the dead; Spirit world
Degrees of glory, 37–38, 57, 58, 84
Dixon, Christopher, 103n69
Donations, for temple construction, 71, 223, 235, 236, 239–42
Draper, William, 33–34
Dunford, Suzie Amelia Young, 208
Durham, Sister, 218

Edmunds Act (1882), 247–50, 268–69, 272
Egyptian alphabet / Papers, 30
Eldridge, Horace S., 225
Elias, 39, 226–29
Elijah, 39–40, 159–60, 226–29
Endowment House, 165, 166–74, 180–81, 185, 186
Endowments: in Kirtland, 21–23; preliminaries, 23–24; preparation for, 24–25; events of, 26–27; origin of Kirtland Temple, 29–32; purpose of Kirtland Temple, 32–33; in Nauvoo, 76–83, 95–99; for dead, 77, 125, 300;

INDEX

recording of ordinance, 98n57; in Salt Lake Council House, 145–51; sealings done before, 153n42; performed in Endowment House, 167, 169–70; proxy, in St. George Temple, 208–10, 212–13, 214–15; adjustments made to, 210–12
Eternal marriage, 39n68, 55, 83–92, 225, 255. *See also* Sealings
Everett, Addison, 217
Exaltation, 84, 86
Eyring, Henry, 217

Family history work, 181–82, 188–91, 202–5
Farnsworth, George, 239–40n23
Far West, Missouri, 48, 49–50
Fast day, 305
Feet, washing, 26–27
Fielding, Joseph, 83n17
Fielding, Mary, 41
Folsom, William H., 232
Ford, Thomas, 75, 91n37
Founding Fathers, proxy work done for, 214–15, 302–3
Frost, Allen, 200n14
Fullmer, John S., 101–2

Gardner, Robert, 197
Garrett, H. Dean, 52
Gathering of Israel, keys of, 39
Gathering of Saints, 4–5, 69, 142
Genealogical societies, 188–90, 286, 301–2
Genealogy, 181–82, 188–91, 202–5
Gilbert, Elizabeth, 108
Godbe, William S., 186–87
Godbeism, 186–87
Goodwin, Charles C., 307
Grant, Ulysses S., 245
Great Britain, migration of Saints from, 69
Grundy, Isaac, 123

Hamilton, George, 103
Hammond, Francis A., 146
Hammond, Mary Jane Dilworth, 146

Hancock, Levi, 17
Harris, Dennison L., 255n55
Harris, Martin, 45
Harrison, Benjamin, 305
Hart, James L., 229
Hascall, Irene, 114–15
Health, baptisms for, 219–20, 305
Hebrew School, 31–32
Hendricks, Elizabeth, 123
Heywood, Joseph L., 101–2
Hierro, Sabino, 141n8
Higbee, Elias, 65, 72
High schools, Church-sponsored, 179–80
Hinckley, Gordon B., 243
Historical societies, 188–90. *See also* Genealogical societies
Holy Ghost, 86–87
Hovey, Joseph, 68
Howland, Henry, 155
Howlett, David, 20n18
Huntington, Prescindia Lathrop, 35, 36–37
Hutchinson, Margaret, 123
Hyde, Orson, 99, 100

Icarians, 110
Idaho Test Oath, 248n36
Independence, Missouri, Temple Lot, 4–5
Industrial Revolution, 178–79
Iowa crossing, 117–19
Israel, gathering of, 39
Ivins, Anna, 250
Ivins, Anthony W., 297n17
Ivins, Israel, 284

Jackson County, Missouri, possible return to, 175–77
Jacob, Norton, 97
Jacques, Vienna, 16, 60
James, 162n59
John, David, 221, 257, 259
Johnson, Andrew, 243–44
Johnson, Benjamin F., 15
Johnson, Joel Hills, 18
Johnston's Army, 244, 288
John the Baptist, 55–56
Jones, William, 73n66

335

INDEX

Joseph Smith Translation, 4, 6–7, 30–31, 60. *See also* Book of Abraham
Justice, and salvation of dead, 57n16

Kane, Thomas L., 175
Kimball, Heber C., 19, 25, 79, 80, 129, 176n35
Kimball, Prescinda Huntington Buel, 149
Kimball, Vilate, 61, 62, 133–34
King Follet discourse, 89
Kirtland, Ohio: as Church epicenter, 5–6; consecration in, 16–17; population of, 17; apostasy in, 42–45; Saints leave, 45–46; baptisms for the dead performed in, 61
Kirtland Camp, 46
Kirtland Safety Society Bank, 42–44
Kirtland Temple: Wilford Woodruff's first time seeing, 11; construction of, 12–21; design of, 19–21; dedication of, 33–37; visions received in, 37–40, 227; spiritual manifestations following dedication of, 40–42; following Saints' departure from Kirtland, 44–45; efforts to sell, 101–8; Brigham Young on, 158. *See also* Endowments

Lamanites, mission to, 6
Law, subjection to, 272
Law, William, 79, 91
Law, Wilson, 91
Lee, John D., 126–27
Leonard, Glenn, 71
Lewis, Tarleton, 141n8
Liberty Jail, 51–52
Lincoln, Abraham, 165–66, 244, 245
Livingston, James C., 288
Logan Temple, 231, 234–39, 260, 270
Lyman, Amasa, 147, 187
Lyman, Francis M., 295
Lyon, John, 188
Lyon, T. Edgar, 188

Mace, Wandle, 66
Mackinnon, William, 174
Maeser, Karl G., 217

Manifesto (1890), 262–63, 266, 271, 274–84
Manti Temple, 231, 232–34, 239, 260, 263–64, 267, 270
Marks, William, 79, 91, 94n44
Masonry, 82–83
Matthews, Robert J., 29n45
McAllister, Duncan, 301
McAllister, John D.T., 220, 223–24, 263–64, 304
McArthur, Daniel D., 88n24
McBride, Reuben, 147
McConkie, Bruce R., 39n68
McKean, James B., 245
McLellin, William E., 45, 103n69
McQuarrie, Agness, 221
Meeks, Priddy, 101
Melchizedek Priesthood, 23–24
Mercy, and salvation of dead, 57n16
Merrill, Marriner W., 235, 237, 279
Mexico, 249
Millennium, 129, 130n41, 182n48, 273
Miller, Eleazer, 147
Miller, George, 72, 79, 88n22
Millet, Robert L., 39n68
Millet, Artemus, 14–15, 21
Missionary work, 39, 142, 146
Missouri: challenges in, 49–52; failure to establish Zion in, 50–51; possible return to Jackson County, 175–77. *See also* Adam-ondi-Ahman, Missouri; Far West, Missouri
Morality, 223–24
Morley, Isaac, 152
"Mormon Rebellion," 165, 174–75, 288
Mormon Reformation, 173, 224, 256
Moroni, 3, 159–61, 232n4
Moroni statue, 294n12
Morrill Anti-Bigamy Act (1862), 244–45, 246–47, 274
Morse, Elizabeth, 218
Moses, 38–39, 226–29
Mountain Meadows Massacre, 175
Murdock, Sarah Zufelt, 146
Mustard, Margaret, 218

Nat Turner Rebellion (1831), 51
Nauvoo, Illinois: deaths in, 59–60;

INDEX

advantages of, over Kirtland, 68–72; growth of, 69; economy of, 70–71; endowment in, 76–83; and doctrine of eternal marriage, 83–92; and "Second Comforter" ordinance, 92–93; Saints driven from, 100–101, 108–10, 113–15; preparations to leave, 101–8, 116; Brigham Young on, 112; disincorporation of, 113; timing of departure from, 116–17

Nauvoo Agricultural and Manufacturing Association, 70–71

Nauvoo Covenant, 115

Nauvoo House, 72, 73

Nauvoo Legion, 68–69

Nauvoo Lodge, 82

Nauvoo Masonic Hall, 82

Nauvoo Temple: Wilford Woodruff on, 47; legacy of, 54–55, 110–11; baptisms performed in, 63–65; construction of, 65–73; historical context of, 75–76; Relief Society's role in history of, 81; completion of, 93–94; design of, 94–95; endowment in, 95–99; women workers in, 97–98; dedication of, 99–100; efforts to sell, 101–8; vandalism of, 109–10; and preparations to leave Nauvoo, 116; Brigham Young on, 158–59

Nelson, O. C., 218

New and everlasting covenant, 83–92. *See also* Celestial marriage

Neyman, Cyrus Livingston, 60

Neyman, Jane, 60

Noble, Edward A., 249

Nuttall, John L., 79n9, 307

Oaks, Dallin H., 44n78

Oath of Vengeance, 115–16n6

"Olive Leaf" revelation, 7–8

Packer, Boyd K., 22–23n23

Papyrus scrolls, 30

Partridge, Edward, 6, 25n26

Penrose, Charles W., 236, 267

Perkins, William, 217

Persecution: and construction of Kirtland Temple, 17–18; in Nauvoo, 108–10, 113–15

Peter, 162n59

Phelps, W. W., 27, 38, 148

Play, William N., 66

Plural marriage: in Nauvoo, 89–92; and sealings performed in Salt Lake Valley, 155–56; discontinuation of, 243, 262–65, 274–79; government attack on, 243, 244–50, 261, 268–71, 274; commitment to, 243, 250–60; impact of, 253; performance of, 260n79; opposition to, 266–68; factors influencing discontinuation of, 268–72, 284–85; and statehood, 271, 283, 305–6; reactions to discontinuation of, 279–84

Poland bill (1874), 245–46

Poor Camps, 109

Poverty, of early Saints, 15

Pratt, Addison, 146, 183n51

Pratt, Ann Agatha Walker, 146

Pratt, Orson, 29n44, 44, 136, 183, 226–28

Pratt, Parley P.: converts Sidney Rigdon, 6; on revelations concerning temple work for dead, 7; on endowment, 28–29; on Joseph Smith's sermon, 42; apostasy of, 44; on eternal marriage, 87; on scurvy, 120; on apostolic keys, 162; on lack of ancestral records, 181; on communication with spirit world, 187; on Logan Temple, 236; on plural marriage, 255

Pratt, Phoebe Eldred Soper, 146

Priesthood: restoration of, 38–40; and interpretation of temple doctrines, 159–63

Primary, 179

Prince, Carl, 51

Prominent men and women, proxy work done for, 214–15, 302–3

Provo Tabernacle, 238

Provo Temple, 238

Proxy marriages, 88–89

Purcell, john, 103

Purity, 223–24

337

INDEX

Quincy, Illinois, 54, 61
Quorum of the anointed, 80

Raleigh, Alonzo H., 209–10, 211, 212
Rebaptism, 140–41, 167–68n7, 173, 305
Red Brick Store, 77, 78–79, 87
Relief Society, 78, 80–82, 179, 186
Reorganized Church of Jesus Christ of Latter Day Saints (Community of Christ), 2–3, 45, 94n44, 108, 108n81
Resurrection, 85–86
Revelation(s): looking forward to temple construction, 6–8; concerning temple work in Nauvoo, 52–54; on baptism for the dead, 55–60, 62; on Nauvoo House, 72; concerning marriage, 84; given to Brigham Young, 122–23; canonization of, 225–29
Reynolds, George, 246–47
Rich, Charles C., 236
Rich, Harriet Sargent, 147
Richards, Franklin D., 100, 201, 222, 301
Richards, George F., 267
Richards, Hepzibah, 45–46
Richards, Willard, 79, 152
Rigdon, Sidney, 6, 34, 43, 64, 80n11, 91
Roberts, B. H., 229, 267
Robison, Edwin C., 15n5
Rockwood, Albert P., 148
Rogers, Aurelia Spencer, 179
Romney, Hannah, 257
Romney, Miles, 197

Salt Lake City Tabernacle, 177
Salt Lake Temple: plan for, 140; Brigham Young on, 150–51; laying of cornerstones of, 156–59; completion of, 163, 286; Brigham Young's contributions to, 163–64; construction of, 173, 176, 178, 288–92; and "Mormon Rebellion," 175, 288; baptismal font in, 180; cost of, 270; architectural design of, 287, 292–93; symbolism employed in, 292–93; laying of capstone of, 293–94; interior of, 294–97; dedication of, 297–98
Salt Lake Valley, 136–37; Brigham Young on temple construction in, 1; Saints travel to, 137–39; settlement of, 139–42; rebaptisms in, 140–41; immigration to, 142, 148; Council House in, 142–51; sealings performed in, 151–56; evacuation of, 165, 175; jubilee anniversary of arrival in, 306–7
Savage, Nephi W., 284
School of the Elders, 31
School of the Prophets, 24, 31, 179, 193
Scurvy, 120
Sealing keys, restoration of, 39–40
Sealings: and law of adoption, 88, 125–33, 286, 298–305; performed at Winter Quarters, 123–25; performed in Salt Lake Valley, 151–56; performed in Endowment House, 167; of deceased families, 213–14; and commitment to plural marriage, 259–60. *See also* Celestial marriage
Sealing up, 26n35
"Second Comforter" ordinance, 92–93
Second Coming, 259
Segmiller, W. H., 258
Seixas, Joshua, 31
Sharp, Thomas C., 109
Sheets, Elijah, 123
Shepherd, Mary, 208
Shipps, Jan, 251
Shurtliff, Luman, 67–68
Slavery, 50–51
Smith, Alvin, 37–38, 58–59
Smith, Charles, 284
Smith, Don Carlos, 59
Smith, Emma: and apostasy in Kirtland, 44; proxy baptism performed by, 63; receives endowments, 80; sealing of, 86; and plural marriage, 90, 254; James J. Strang's letter to, 106–7
Smith, George A., 27n39, 37, 104n71, 153–54, 209
Smith, Hyrum, 12, 14, 63, 79, 82, 90, 115–16n6
Smith, John, 152
Smith, John H., 257–58
Smith, John L., 208
Smith, John R., 95
Smith, Joseph: instruction of, 3–4; and construction of Kirtland Temple,

INDEX

12, 13–14, 18–19; and endowment, 21–22, 28, 33; on preparation for endowment, 25; and Hebrew School, 31–32; and Kirtland Temple dedication, 34–35; and visions received in Kirtland Temple, 37–40; speaks in Kirtland Temple, 42; and apostasy in Kirtland, 42–45; moves to Far West, 48; on Adam-ondi-Ahman, 50; confinement of, in Liberty Jail, 51–52; revelations on temple work given to, 52–54; on Quincy, Illinois, 54; and revelation on baptism for the dead, 55–60, 62; and construction of Nauvoo Temple, 65–66, 67, 72–73; on gathering of Saints, 69; on Nauvoo, 70; as trustee-in-trust of Church, 71; and Nauvoo endowment, 77–80; establishes Relief Society, 80–81; Masonry and, 82; sealing of, 86; on Holy Ghost, 86–87; sealings performed by, 87; on salvation of dead, 89; on sealing ordinance, 89; and plural marriage, 89–91, 254–55; and "Second Comforter" ordinance, 92; on Saints' acceptance of temple ordinances, 93; successor to, 94, 104–8; martyrdom of, 115–16n6, 122; and law of adoption, 131; Moroni's appearances to, 159–61; and apostolic keys, 161–62; and missionary labors in spirit world, 226n103. *See also* Joseph Smith Translation

Smith, Joseph F., 150, 162n59, 173–74, 226, 254, 256, 279–80
Smith, Joseph Sr., 59
Smith, Lucy Mack, 18, 21n20, 60n26, 63
Smith, William, 217
Smoot, Abraham O., 237–38, 254–55
Snow, Eliza R., 20n18, 35, 118, 149, 157–58
Snow, Erastus, 153, 226n103, 252
Snow, Lorenzo, 240, 294
Snow, Minerva W., 218–19
Spencer, Franklin, 240–41, 260
Spiritualism, 187–88
Spirit world, 56–57, 226n103, 302–4
Sprague, Samuel S., 147, 148

Staines, William C., 104n72, 145, 148
Staker, Mark, 23
Stapley, Jonathan, 219
Statehood, 271, 283, 305–6
St. George Temple: significance of, 192, 229–30; reason for location of, 193–96; construction of, 196–98; and United Order, 198–202; dedication of, 205–8; proxy work done in, 208–10, 212–13, 214–15; and adjustments made to endowment, 210–12; and change in temple clothing, 212; and sealing of deceased children to deceased parents, 213–14; and proxy work done by non-family members, 216–17; and regular temple attendance, 217–19; and baptisms for health, 219–20; attendance at, 220–21; and urgency in temple work, 221–23; and impact of increased temple attendance, 223–24; donations for, 240; and plural marriage, 251–52; cost of, 270
Strang, James J., 104–7

Talmage, James E., 57, 290
Tanner, Annie Clark, 282
Tanner, John, 16
Taylor, John: on temple work, 2, 220; on tithing and temple work, 64; on sale of Kirtland and Nauvoo Temples, 103n69, 104; on Council House, 143; on temple ordinances given outside temple, 153n37; on construction of St. George Temple, 194–96; on temple recommends, 223; and vision of Moses, Elias, and Elijah, 228–29; and printing of Doctrine and Covenants, 228n107; and Logan Temple, 235, 237; on plural marriage, 246–47, 260n79; calls pioneers to Canada, 249; goes into hiding, 250; on spiritual manifestations, 302–3
Technological advances, 178–79
Telegraph, 190
"Temple, The" (Snow), 157–58
Temple attendance: influence of increased, 223–24; following completion of Salt Lake Temple, 298

INDEX

Temple clothing, 212
Temple consciousness, rise in, 240–43
Temple quorum, 80
Temple recommends, 64, 154, 223
Temple work: evolution of, 2–3, 311; before organization of Church, 3–4; as obsession of early Saints, 46, 47; revelations concerning, 52–54; additions to, in Nauvoo, 55; records for, 62; done outside temples, 152–53, 172; doctrinal and historical justification for, 159–63; done by non-family members, 216–17; regular, 217–19; urgency in, 221–23; Saints' commitment to, 243–44; and discontinuation of plural marriage, 262–63; following Manifesto, 276–79
Thatcher, Moses, 235
Thompson, Mercy R., 98
Thurber, A. K., 240, 258
Time, sealings for, 155
Tithing, 64, 71, 149n32, 154, 173, 201, 223, 240–41, 270, 290
Tobler, Ryan G., 65
Transcontinental railroad, 178, 185–86, 190–91
Tucker, Hilary, 103
Turner, Rodney, 57n16

United Firm, 13
United Order, 198–200, 232, 239
Urim and Thummim, 183
U.S. government: attack on plural marriage, 243, 244–50, 261, 268–71, 274; and discontinuation of plural marriage, 262–63, 264–65
Utah Genealogical Society, 286, 301–2
Utah statehood, 271, 283, 305–6
Utah Territory. *See* Salt Lake Valley

Vision(s): of Celestial kingdom, 37–38, 58; received in Kirtland Temple, 37–40, 227; given to Wilford Woodruff, 214–15, 287, 302–3; given to Joseph F. Smith, 226; of Moses, Elias, and Elijah, 226–29; of Salt Lake Temple, 287

Walker, Charles, 170, 193, 214
Weeks, William, 66
Wells, Daniel H., 65, 143, 147, 173–74, 232–33, 287, 292n8
Wells, Heber M., 306
Westward migration: decision to undertake, 114–15; challenges during, 117–19; deaths during, 120; and law of adoption, 132–33; of vanguard company, 137–39
Wheelock, Cyrus H., 239–40n23
Whitmer, David, 27
Whitmer, John, 23, 27
Whitney, Elizabeth Ann, 87–88, 147, 149
Whitney, Helen Mar Kimball, 46, 118
Whitney, Newel K., 13, 81–82, 87–88, 129
Wight, Lyman, 50, 72, 107
Williams, Frederick G., 13, 14n3, 44
Winder, John R., 297
Winter Quarters: establishment of, 118–19; sickness and death at, 120; ordinances performed at, 121–25; adoption sealings at, 125–33; women's role at, 133–34
Winter Quarters Nebraska Temple, 125n28
Women: contributions of, to Kirtland Temple construction, 19, 21n20; and Kirtland Temple endowment, 27n39; contributions of, to Nauvoo Temple construction, 67; receive endowments, 80; and Nauvoo Relief Society, 80–82; as Nauvoo Temple workers, 97–98; render service at Winter Quarters, 133–34; as Council House officiators, 148–49; proxy work done by, 216; and regular temple attendance, 217–18
Wood, Ann Leigh, 153
Wood, John, 153
Woodruff, Aphek, 147, 184
Woodruff, Azmon, 202
Woodruff, Azubah Hart, 184
Woodruff, Brigham, 204–5
Woodruff, Phebe Carter, 184, 249
Woodruff, Wilford: on first seeing Kirtland Temple, 11; on endowment, 27–28; on Nauvoo Temple, 47, 65, 75; on

INDEX

Nauvoo Temple baptismal font, 63–64; and dedication of Nauvoo Temple, 99–100; on arrival in Salt Lake Valley, 139n4; on confirmation and sealing of Apostles, 141; as Council House officiator, 148; on ordinances performed in Endowment House, 167n6; considers return to Jackson County, 177; on Salt Lake City Tabernacle, 177; on lack of ancestral records, 182; and reinstitution of baptism for the dead, 183–84, 191; interest of, in family history work, 202–5; and proxy work in St. George Temple, 208; and adjustments made to endowment, 210–12; and change in temple clothing, 212; proxy work performed by, 214–15; visions of, 214–15, 287, 302–3; and proxy work done by non-family members, 216–17; on worthiness for temple attendance, 224; on contributions to St. George Temple, 225; on temple work and construction, 231; prophesies concerning Logan Temple, 234; and discontinuation of plural marriage, 243, 262–63, 265–66, 274–75, 280, 282–83, 284; and government attack on plural marriage, 249, 250; on plural marriage, 255, 256n60, 257; on government seizure of Church assets, 269–70; searches for solution to plural marriage problem, 271–79; temple work performed by, 275–76; on genealogy and temple work, 286; and laying of Salt Lake Temple capstone, 294; and dedication of Salt Lake Temple, 297–98; and end of adoption sealings, 298–301; and Utah Genealogical Society, 301; final years of, 306–7; death of, 307; legacy of, 307–9; on temple construction, 311–12

Woolsey, James, 127
Woolsey, Sevina, 127
"Word and Will of the Lord," 122–23
Word of Wisdom, 224
Worthiness, 154, 223, 240–41
Wright, Kristine, 219

Young, Brigham: on temple construction in Salt Lake City, 1; and construction of Kirtland Temple, 18–19, 21; on endowment, 22, 26–27, 76, 77, 98n57; and sale of church properties, 45; on baptism for the dead, 62n32, 182n48; and Nauvoo endowment, 79; sealings performed by, 87, 88, 123–24, 152; on plural marriage, 91; and "Second Comforter" ordinance, 92; assumes leadership of Church, 94; and completion of Nauvoo Temple, 94; on events in Nauvoo Temple, 97n54; on activity in Nauvoo Temple, 98–99; as considerate toward Saints, 112; on Nauvoo, 112; decides to go west, 114–15; threats against, 116–17; on travel delays, 117; on persistence of Saints, 120–21; and temple blessings at Winter Quarters, 121–23; and law of adoption, 125, 127–29, 131n42, 131–32, 133; on temple work in Millennium, 129, 130n41; travels west with vanguard company, 137–39; marks Salt Lake Temple lot, 140; institutes rebaptism of living, 140–41; expansion of missionary work under, 142; and construction of Council House, 142–43; on Council House endowments, 147, 149, 150; on Salt Lake Temple, 150–51, 287; on tithing and temple work, 154; and construction of Salt Lake Temple, 157, 158–59, 173; on temple doctrines, 160; on priesthood and temple work, 161–62; contributions of, to Latter-day Saint history, 163–64; on temple and Endowment House, 166, 167; on Endowment House, 171; on children sealed to parents, 171n20; on temple ordinances given outside temple, 172; considers return to Jackson County, 175–76; organizes Young Women's Retrenchment Society, 179; and baptismal font in Salt Lake Temple, 180; on revelation concerning family history, 182–83; on Spiritualism,

341

INDEX

188; on increase in family history work, 191; and construction of St. George Temple, 193, 194, 196, 201; on temples and consecration, 200; on United Order, 202; and St. George Temple dedication, 205–8; and adjustments made to endowment, 210–12; on sealing of families, 213–14; on worthiness for temple attendance, 224n99; and Manti Temple, 232–33; and Logan Temple, 234, 235; on future temple in Provo, 238

Young, Brigham Jr., 202n24, 258

Young, Don Carlos, 294, 297

Young, Joseph, 99, 173

Young, Joseph A., 200–201

Young, Lorenzo, 104

Young, Lucy Bigelow, 212, 215, 218

Young, Zina B., 256–57

Young Men's Retrenchment Society, 179, 185–86

Young Women's Retrenchment Society, 179, 185–86

Zane, Charles, 283

Zion: gathering to, 4–5; failure to establish, in Missouri, 50–51; Orson Pratt on, 136

Zion's Camp, 17, 18n14